INDONESIANS AND THEIR ARAB WORLD

INDONESIANS AND THEIR ARAB WORLD

Guided Mobility among Labor Migrants and Mecca Pilgrims

Mirjam Lücking

SOUTHEAST ASIA PROGRAM PUBLICATIONS

AN IMPRINT OF CORNELL UNIVERSITY PRESS ITHACA AND LONDON

First published 2020 by Cornell University Press

Library of Congress Cataloging-in-Publication Data

Names: Lücking, Mirjam, 1986– author.
Title: Indonesians and their Arab world : guided mobility among labor migrants and Mecca pilgrims / Mirjam Lücking.
Description: Ithaca [New York] : Southeast Asia Program Publications, an imprint of Cornell University Press, 2020. | Includes bibliographical references and index.
Identifiers: LCCN 2020012022 (print) | LCCN 2020012023 (ebook) | ISBN 9781501753114 (hardcover) | ISBN 9781501753121 (paperback) | ISBN 9781501753138 (epub) | ISBN 9781501753145 (pdf)
Subjects: LCSH: Islam—Indonesia—21st century. | Muslims—Indonesia—Social conditions—21st century. | Islam and culture—Indonesia. | Indonesians—Arab countries. | Muslim pilgrims and pilgrimages—Indonesia.
Classification: LCC BP63.I5 L854 2020 (print) | LCC BP63.I5 (ebook) | DDC 297.09598—dc23
LC record available at https://lccn.loc.gov/2020012022
LC ebook record available at https://lccn.loc.gov/2020012023

For Nuki, Ubed, and Mala
in appreciation of dialogic guidance and joint mobility

Contents

Acknowledgments

In writing about guided mobility, I realize how much my own mobility in this project has been guided. I am grateful to all those who guided my physical and intellectual steps and thereby enabled movement and understanding in the first place.

The protagonists of this book are labor migrants and Mecca pilgrims, and their relatives, neighbors, friends, and guides, in Madura and Central Java. I wish to express my deep gratitude to all those who participated in my research and who mostly remain anonymous here. I especially thank my research partners, Nuki Mayasari, Khotim Ubaidillah (Ubed), and Kamalatul Khorriyah (Mala).

My first steps into a part of Indonesia's diverse Islamic culture took place in 2008, when Nuki and I conducted a small research project in Islamic boarding schools (*pesantren*) in Yogyakarta. Throughout the last decade our paths crossed in and beyond research in Indonesia and Germany, and I am grateful to the many joint research experiences and post–field trip discussions that we continue to share.

Ubed guided my way into Madurese society—even when he was not physically there. Our first explorative motorcycle trip in Pamekasan and Sampang was truly eye opening, and what started with the joint spatial mobility developed into intense intellectual mobility and exchange. Beyond the immense support in practical and intellectual research questions, Ubed contributed to this book through useful comments on an earlier version of the manuscript and through his photographs.

Mala, who is not an anthropologist but an agricultural engineer by training, spontaneously engaged in my research activities with a natural talent for ethnographic research. I am thankful for our joint research activities during Ramadan 2014 in Pamekasan and for the generous hospitality offered by her and her family.

Regarding my physical mobility, several institutions enabled me to travel, research, and write. The German Federal Ministry of Education and Research funded a research project from which this book emerged, as part of the Freiburg Southeast Asian Studies Program "Grounding Area Studies in Social Practice," under grant number 01UC1307. The research in Indonesia was approved by the Indonesian Ministry for Research and Technology (Kementerian Riset dan Teknologi) under permit number 028/SIP/FRP/SM/I/2014 and upon invitation by Gadjah Mada University Yogyakarta. At a later stage of the project, the following grants and fellowships provided time and intellectual freedom for work on this book: The STAY!-grant of the Freiburg University Foundation (Neue Universitätsstiftung); a postdoctoral fellowship at the Hebrew University of Jerusalem and with the Center for the Study of Conversion at Ben Gurion University of the Negev, funded by the Israeli Science Foundation under grant number 12/1754; and an ongoing postdoctoral fellowship at the Martin Buber Society of Fellows at the Hebrew University of Jerusalem, which is supported by the German Federal Ministry of Education and Research.

During the research period, the University of Freiburg offered an inspiring academic home, and I cordially thank all members of the Freiburg Southeast Asian Studies Program and the Department of Social and Cultural Anthropology. Special thanks go to Judith Schlehe for her constructive critiques and encouraging supervision and for her efforts to create the Freiburg-Yogyakarta tandem research projects, which established invaluable long-term contacts in Indonesia and inspired me to apply approaches for cooperative research. Jürgen Rüland, who headed the Freiburg Southeast Asian Studies Program, tirelessly supports early career researchers, and I thank him for his valuable advice and for the multifarious Southeast Asia related activities in Freiburg. Moreover, I thank Gregor Dobler for his comprehensive feedback on an earlier version of the manuscript.

Several colleagues in Freiburg inspired my work: Anna Fünfgeld and Stefan Rother enriched my views through the perspective of political science, my colleagues Melanie Nertz, Ita Yulianto, Evamaria Sandkühler, Sita Hidayah, Paritosha Kobbe, and Imam Ardhianto gave me useful feedback on my writing and insights from their own studies on Indonesia; Margarete Brüll, Stefan Seitz, Andreas Volz, Heike Drotbohm, Ingo Rohrer, Anna Meiser, Eric Haanstad, Saskia Walther, Martin Büdel, and Moritz Heck broadened my anthropological horizon and contributed to a good working atmosphere at the department.

My earlier studies at the Department for Islamic Studies at the University of Freiburg and study visits to Syria and Morocco enabled me to get a glimpse of the diversity of the Arab world, which was a trigger for the questioning of claims of an Arabization in Indonesian Islamic traditions. I thank my Arabic teacher, Mohamed Megahed, who was one of the first to introduce me to the richness of Arabic language and culture, and Valerie Köbele, with whom I shared many travels.

Beyond academia, I was greatly supported by friends in Freiburg: Emad Al-Bawab, Anita Bertolami, Hannes Bürkel, Kyle Egerer, Shiva Grings, Alexander Ell, Mareike Krebs, and Jule Westerheide read extracts from the book, discussed my ideas, and refreshed my thoughts. Nadja Bürger helped me significantly with bibliographic challenges and Larissa Mogk encouraged some crucial restructuring of the text. The Freiburg Lindy Hoppers kept me moving and inspired my theory about guiding and following when away from my desk.

My stays in Indonesia fundamentally benefited from the institutional affiliation with Gadjah Mada University (UGM), and I sincerely thank Pak Pujo Semedi, then dean of the faculty of Cultural Studies, and all members of UGM's Department of Anthropology for their support. At Universitas Islam Negeri Sunan Kalijaga in Yogakarta I thank Inayah Rohmaniyah and Muhammad Wildan as well as Tracy Wright Webster, who was affiliated with UIN at the time of research. Furthermore, my work was significantly inspired by the Madura experts Wisma Nugraha Christianto, Abdur Rozaki, Mutmainna Munir, Iskandar Dzulkarnain, and contact with the sociology department of Universitas Trunojoyo Madura.

The friendship, company, and care of Rarasari Emprit, Febri Gahas, Tiyas Gahas, Ibu Gatot, Farha Habsyi, Ibu Heru and her family, Mbak Lani, Ibu Lassi, and Mbak Wiwik boosted my research and enriched my daily research life: *mator sakalangkong* and *matur nuwun*! A warm *terima kasih* goes to Selma, Claudia and Matthias Börner, Nina Gaiser, and Sita Hidayah, who moved like me between Germany and Indonesia and bridged the different worlds while researching.

In the context of cooperation with the School of Culture, History, and Language of the Australian National University, which was financially supported by the DAAD-Go8 program, Ariel Heryanto, Evi Eliyanah, Meghan Downes, and Maria Myutel offered insightful viewpoints from cultural studies, and I thank them for our continuous exchange.

While working on the first drafts of this book manuscript, I greatly benefited from conversations with and feedback from Martin Slama, Agus Suwignyo, Achmad Munjid, Yeri Wirawan, Ray Yen, Olivia Killias, Claudia Derichs, Greg Fealy, Hew Wai Weng, Kathryn Robinson, Nicola Piper, Marjo Buijtelaar, Manja Stephan-Emmrich, Viola Thimm, and Amanda tho Seeth.

Alec Crutchley read the text of this book in its various stages, and I thank him for his diligent language checks. For drawing the maps and patiently adjusting them, I thank Imam Ardhianto. And for letting me use his stunning photograph of an Isra' and Mi'raj celebration in Purwokerto as cover image, I thank Ray Yen.

Two anonymous readers for Southeast Asia Program Publications (SEAP) of Cornell University Press provided very valuable critiques of my manuscript, and I wish to extend my thanks for their commitment. I also sincerely thank the editorial team of SEAP, especially Sarah Grossman and Karen Hwa, for giving me good guidance in preparing the manuscript for publication.

Ironically, the completion of this book takes place in the Middle East. While I conducted my research solely in Indonesia and methodologically focused on returnees' representations of the Arab world, my own move to the Middle East made me ever more aware of the fact that representations of cultural Others say much more about those who make them, rather than those who are represented. I thank Ronit Ricci for opening up the opportunity to look at the Malay-Indonesian world from the Middle East and for her pioneering endeavor to establish Indonesian Studies in Jerusalem.

The awareness of sociocultural positionality is also sharpened through Middle Eastern friendships across borders and boundaries, and I thank my friends in Tel Aviv, Jerusalem, Bethlehem, and Ramallah, especially Nitzan Chelouche, Ghassan Hamdan, Annika Ramsaier, Birte Brotkorb, and Ishaq Rajabi. Moreover, on the final steps of completing this book, I am very grateful to Amit Naamani for his cheerful support, company, and patience.

Last but not least, I thank my brothers, Christian and Markus, and my parents, Monika and Günter Lücking, who got used to my mobility and continuously bridge the spatial distances.

Note on Orthography, Transliteration, Translation, and Dates

Foreign-language terms in this book are written in the original spelling (e.g., Dutch, Indonesian, Javanese, Madurese, and others) and given in italics the first time they are used, with the exception of those terms that have become common in English spelling (such as Qur'an, halal, hajj, umrah) and foreign-language names of institutions and persons. Arabic-language terms are transliterated according to the transliteration standard DIN 31635 of the German Standardization Institute (Deutsches Institut für Normung; DIN), for example *ǧāhilīya* (pre-Islamic time of ignorance). Indonesian-language terms that are derived from Arabic, such as *kitab* (book) or *ulama* (Islamic scholar) are written in the common Indonesian spelling.

British English terms in quotations are maintained in original spelling. Transliterations of Arabic and Indonesian terms that differ from the spelling used in this book are equally maintained in original quotes.

All interviews were conducted in Indonesian language and occasionally with translation to Madurese and Javanese. Quotes from interviews are given in English translation. The translations are mine unless indicated otherwise.

Most dates are given according to the Common Era (CE). When referring to dates of the Islamic Calendar this is indicated as AH (Anno Hijria). Information on finances, such as costs for the pilgrimage to Mecca, is based on the amounts and conversion rates from Indonesian rupiah to US dollar at the time of research.

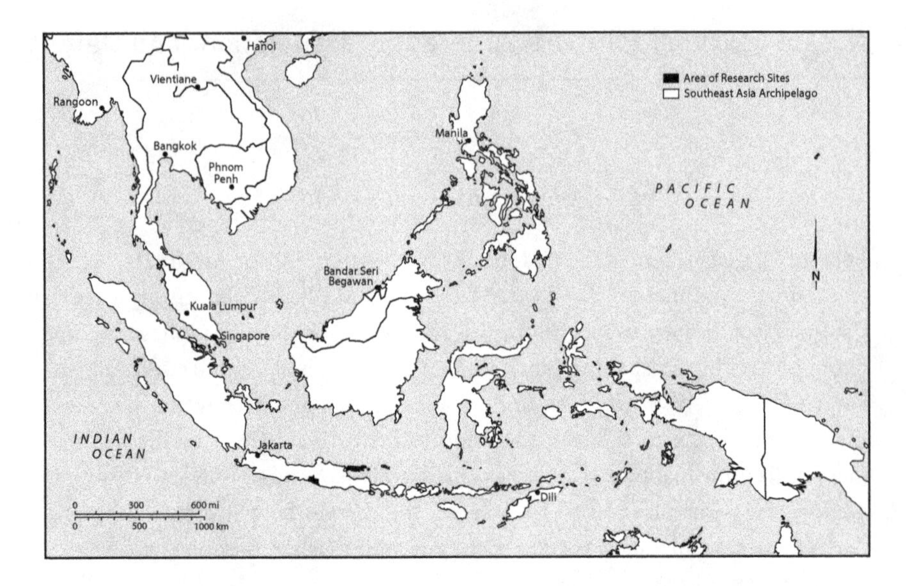

MAP 1. The Indonesian archipelago with Yogyakarta and Madura. Based on a map by Imam Ardhianto from data from Peta Rupa Bumi Indonesia, Badan Informasi Geospasial 2018.

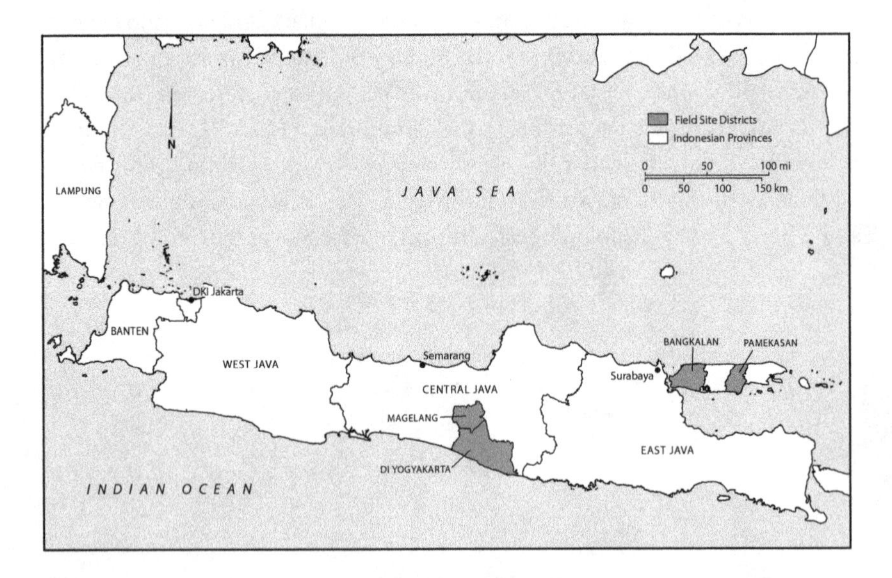

MAP 2. The islands of Java and Madura, indicating the research locations in Central Java in Magelang and Yogyakarta regencies, and in Bangkalan and Pamekasan regencies on Madura island. Based on a map by Imam Ardhianto from data from Peta Rupa Bumi Indonesia, Badan Informasi Geospasial 2018.

Introduction

WHOSE ARAB WORLD IS IT?

Several times during my inquiry into the engagement of Indonesians with the Arab world, I heard a variation on the following joke: Why were there so many prophets in the Middle East and so few in Indonesia? The witty Indonesian punchline was that people in the Middle East needed prophets to teach them how to behave, while Indonesians were already well behaved and good hearted. Many Indonesians also feel that had Mecca, Islam's holiest place, been located in Indonesia, the country would have been flooded with pilgrims who would refuse to leave after discovering its beauty. This kind of commentary lies somewhere between irony and pride, with an element of self-mockery at Indonesia's location at the perceived periphery of the Muslim world while at the same time suggesting that, as the most populous majority Muslim country, a bit more attention could be paid to Indonesia.

However, Indonesians are not only aware of the Arab world as it pertains to Islam. They also relate to Arab countries as destinations for international labor migration. Many women from Indonesia's rural areas emigrate to Saudi Arabia, the United Arab Emirates, Qatar, and Kuwait in search of socioeconomic upward mobility. Their encounter with the Arab world happens in the intimacy of private households where they work and live as domestic workers.

On airplanes from Indonesia to the Middle East, labor migrants and Mecca pilgrims sit next to each other, although in many regions in Indonesia their worlds barely overlap. For Indonesians who accomplish the pilgrimage to Mecca and Medina, the journey to Saudi Arabia is an endeavor of spiritual fulfillment, participation in the global Muslim community, and personal prestige. Labor migration is, by contrast, associated with human rights violations, the ill treatment of migrant women, poverty, exploitation, and social tensions. And yet Indonesians' views on the Arab world are not monolithic and are much more complex than these two contrasting experiences would suggest.

How Indonesians regard the Arab world is relevant because of the increasing Islamic religiosity in private and public life that is considered to be one of the most significant, if not the most significant, social changes in Indonesia since the transition from autocracy to democracy at the close of the millennium. Intensified adherence to religious rules, changing dress codes, and new voices in political Islam have been described as a "conservative turn" (van Bruinessen 2013b). Some radical representatives within this conservative turn demand that Islamic praxis be purified, turning toward Wahhabi interpretations of Islam. Other Indonesian Muslim representatives denounce this as "Arabization" and cleave to indigenous traditions. Strikingly, increasing conservatism goes along with a decline of Islamist influence in formal party politics (Fealy 2019; Buehler 2016, 194; Sidel 2008, 344; van Bruinessen 2013b, 3). Nevertheless, Islamist actors do have influence on public policies; for instance, in the case of sharia regulations, secular parties have given in to Islamists' demands to gain voters and exploit Islamic themes for political and economic purposes (see Buehler 2016). This nourishes a complex web of competing actors, practices, and interpretations, where conservatism appears in many guises (see, among others, Bowen 2015; Buehler 2016; Fealy 2004, 2008, 2019; Hadiz 2016; Künkler and Stepan 2015; Sidel 2008; van Bruinessen 2013a; Wildan 2013). Ordinary people find their own answers to these controversies (cf. Kloos 2017), which indicates their agency and the fact that competition among public actors does not go unchallenged. Labor migrants and pilgrims are among those who seek to make sense of public controversies about what it means to be Muslim, especially in the course of their travels to Arab countries. However, it turns out that their answers do not result from firsthand experiences abroad as much as they do from the ways their mobility is guided. I argue that migrants and pilgrims are not among the bearers of Arab cultural influence. In contrast, their engagement with Arab culture and customs reveals how Indonesians own and localize Arabness and how the local social context determines the outcome of migratory experiences.

By analyzing how labor migrants and Mecca pilgrims represent the Arab world when they return home, I show the ways in which experiences of transnational mobility are related to local sociocultural guidance. Regarding the conservative turn in Indonesia, this contributes to understanding ordinary peoples' responses to controversies about Muslim lifestyles. The ambivalent representations of the Arab world by returning Indonesian migrants and pilgrims call into question the relevance of external influences on Indonesia's Muslim traditions and reveal the impact of inter-Indonesian frictions and regional differences. The juxtaposition of two different groups in society—labor migrants and Mecca pilgrims—and two distinct regions—Central Java and Madura—aims at complementing the above-mentioned studies on Islamic conservatism in Indonesia through perspectives from different regions and different groups of ordinary people, some of whom are considered marginal.

A key tool in understanding the ways in which migrants and pilgrims conceive of and react to the Arab world is the concept of guided mobility. With this concept of guided mobility, I frame how institutional structures, interpersonal relationships, and cultural representations direct various forms of mobility—including spatial and social mobility. The guided mobility framework, which is defined below, helps to explain why and how Indonesians react to the Arab world and to competing offers of guidance: namely, admiring, filtering, or rejecting certain elements. The analytical framework foregrounds the relevance of the local context within transnational mobility in general and within Indonesians' representations of the Arab world in particular.

Their Arab World

To talk about Indonesians and *their* Arab world is to talk about Indonesians' lifeworlds and their ideas of the world (Said 1978).[1] This consideration of the Arab world of Indonesians is not limited to narrative or symbolic representations. Apart from perceptions, images, and representations of "Arab Others," it includes the ownership and experience of "Arabness," which is intrinsically linked to Islamic religiosity. As an example, Arabic language, as the language of the Qur'an, is attributed a holiness that can be accessed by all Muslims regardless of their nationality or ethnicity. Similarly, Muslims from all over the world claim their right to be present at the holy sites in Mecca and Medina.

In Mecca, during the hajj pilgrimage, the fifth pillar of Islamic duties and obligatory for those who are physically, financially, and spiritually capable of performing the ritual, Indonesians realize that they are the largest national group. Many of them return with a sense of pride in having been part of the Indonesian presence in Mecca. I learned from postpilgrimage narratives that Indonesians do not consider their journey to Mecca to be travel to unknown lands. Barbara Metcalf (1990) has argued: "To go to Mecca is to go home" (ibid., 100). The Ka'aba, the house of God, belongs to every Muslim and thus "the journey [to Mecca] moves on the invisible lines which believers create" via daily physical and spiritual orientation toward this center in prayer, sleeping position, and in burial (Metcalf 1990, 100). National borders and confessional conflicts cannot deprive Muslims of their spiritual experiences with the Arab world as a metaphysical concept that features prominently in stories of enlightenment, proximity to God, dream journeys to the holy sites, miracles, and meditation. Obviously, some elements of the Arab world belong to Muslims all over the world. And yet there are many non-Muslim Arabs to whom the Arab world equally belongs. Thus, the Arab world—as an imagined cultural entity and as geographic region—is the exclusive property neither of Arab peoples, nor of Muslims. Moreover, there are Arab minorities outside the geographic area defined as the Arab world, such as the Hadhrami communities in Indonesia (see Abaza 2004; Gilsenan 2003; Mandal 2011, 2012, 2014). This provokes the question of what the so called "Arab world" actually encompasses and why the concept of the Arab world matters at all.

Orientalist representations of the Middle East, such as Glidden's (1972) essay "The Arab World," create an idea of a homogenous Arab world with uniform Arab culture (Said 2003, 48), while in fact it is very diverse.[2] The narrowest definition of the Arab world, commonly referred to as the "standard territorial definition," is derived from the charter of the League of Arab States, with language being the defining feature.[3] Yet this definition is sometimes regarded as problematic because of its exclusion of states that are geographically located in the region and are significantly influenced by Arab culture, as well as peoples in the area who do not identify as Arabs, but as members of a nation or as ethnic minorities (see Frishkopf 2010a, 61; Kronholm 1993, 14).

In the endeavor to show such cultural diversities, challenge hegemonic mappings of the world, and move beyond binary analytical distinctions such as Orient and Occident,[4] I seek in this book to advance the analysis of Orientalizations (Said 1978) as well as Occidentalisms (Carrier 1992; Schlehe 2013b; Schlehe et al. 2013), with a focus on South-South transnational linkages and dynamics of Othering in contexts where the Other constitutes part of the Self.[5] Evidence about the multidirectionality of North-South, South-North, and South-South connections challenges the theoretical conceptualizations in binary oppositions like "the West and the rest" or the Orient and the Occident. As a continuation of Orientalism research, Occidentalism research has examined the multifarious imaginings of what the West encompasses (see Carrier 1992; Coronil 1996). Yet rather than reversing the idea of Orientalism, it is necessary to move beyond dichotomies (Coronil 1996; Schlehe et al. 2013). Schlehe, Nertz, and Yulianto show that in contemporary Indonesia there is "no coherent Occidentalist narrative" (Schlehe et al. 2013, 17) and that Indonesians orient themselves toward various imagined centers, among which, for instance, China as well as the Arab world are significant.

From the point of view of Indonesians, that is, an emic view, the term *Arab world* carries much ambiguity. While I focus on Indonesians' mobility to Arab-speaking countries in the Gulf, my analysis will also show where the emic conceptions generalize Arabness, where they differentiate, and where they go beyond a geographic context like the Arabian Peninsula, as for example regarding Egypt as a center for Islamic education in the Arab world. Speaking about *situated representations* in this context, I analyze the situatedness or embeddedness of such perceptions and representations.

Traveling and Migrating to the Arab World

Next to the intrinsic Arabness of Islamic rituals and traditions all over the world, there is a more recent interest in and engagement with the Arab world in Indonesia, which is evident in the growing number of Indonesians physically moving toward the Middle East for pilgrimage, migration, and education. International tourism is becoming widespread among Indonesians, and the Mecca pilgrimage appears to be one of the most significant reasons for Indonesians' overseas travels.

Every year around 200,000 Indonesians depart for the hajj to Saudi Arabia where they join up to 2.5 million fellow Muslims to perform the pilgrimage rituals on the designated dates of the holy month Dhu al-Hijjah. The number of participants is limited and the official quota is allocated to Indonesia by the Saudi Arabian Ministry of Hajj Affairs, representing approximately one person per million of the Muslim population of Indonesia (Indonesian Ministry of Religious Affairs 2013, 2). Due to increasing wealth, affordable air transportation, and access to mass media, the pilgrimage business is booming (Feener 2004, 204; Quinn 2008, 64; Syarifah 2009). The mass mobility requires a master plan of guidance. Numerous laws, regulations, standard procedures, government agencies, and private intermediaries guide the mobility of pilgrims. The Soekarno-Hatta Airport in Jakarta has opened a hajj terminal due to the immense volume of traffic. Outside the hajj season, this terminal is also used as a labor migrant terminal and the shared airport space is only one of the numerous similarities in the guidance of migrants and pilgrims.

Interest in going on hajj continues to grow, as indicated by the constant increase in hajj registrations and waiting periods of up to twenty years (Indonesian Ministry of Religious Affairs 2016). Due to the long waiting list for the hajj, many Indonesian Muslims resort to undertaking the "minor" or "small pilgrimage," the umrah, which can be done at any time of the year and which is not limited through a quota. The number of documented Indonesian umrah pilgrims grew from approximately 500,000 in 2013 to 1 million in 2014 (Harian Pelita 2014), and ever since the numbers have ranged between 600,000 (Arab News 2019; *Jakarta Post* 2017) and 1.2 million (*Saudi Gazette* 2017, 2018) participants per year. This booming business is part of a general commercialization of religious lifestyles in Indonesia that especially appeal to Indonesia's growing middle classes (see Fealy and White 2008b; Heryanto 2008a, 2011, 2014b; Hew 2012; Hoesterey 2008; Jones 2010; Muzakki 2012; Rudnyckyj 2009, 2010; Sutton 2011; Weintraub 2011b).

Different from the middle-class experiences of pilgrimage and tourism, Indonesian labor migrants—especially female labor migrants—come from rural areas and economically weaker segments of society. The Indonesian government has encouraged labor migration to the Gulf through bilateral agreements with destination countries and systematic recruitment of migrant workers since the 1980s (Ananta and Arifin 2014, 34; Silvey 2004, 247). However, due to numerous reports of violence against domestic workers, the government changed its policies and in 2012 imposed a moratorium on unskilled labor migration to the Gulf. Ever since, the official policies have been inconsistent and differ on the provincial and regional levels. Because of undocumented migration, which increased because of moratoriums, it is hard to determine how many Indonesians currently reside as workers in Arab countries. Estimates range from 300,000 (Ananta and Arifin 2004, 34) to 700,000 (Machmudi 2011, 226) documented migrants and up to 2.1 million undocumented migrants (Machmudi 2011, 226). If these numbers are correct, Saudi Arabia is still the most popular destination for Indonesian labor migrants, followed by Malaysia (Ananta and Arifin 2004).

A third group of Indonesians who move to Arab countries are students who study at the prestigious universities in Cairo (Al-Azhar University) and Mecca (Umm al-Qurrā University). While historically Indonesians' pilgrimages, economic activities, and education in the Middle East were intertwined, today the spheres are more separated even though some students do have part-time jobs to finance their stays and among other things work in the pilgrimage sector. Comprehensive studies on Indonesian students in the Middle East highlight the significance of inter-Indonesian activities, which appear to be more crucial than intellectual exchange with Egyptian or Saudi Muslims (Abaza 1991, 349; Bowen 2003, 39; Laffan 2004, 6; Roff 1970, 73; Schlehe and Nisa 2016).

Indonesians' mobility toward the Arab world is an example of increasing mobility in a globalized world more generally. Ananta and Arifin (2004, 30) describe this as "a new garden for Indonesians—the whole world for them to visit, pursue education and look for job opportunities, and to settle down." The metaphor "garden" appears to encompass the exploration of new opportunities and partaking in "harvesting" the fruits of globalization and increased movement of people, goods, and ideas. The examples at hand show that these forms of mobility, which have existed throughout history, are indeed today accessible to more people. However, they are also highly structured and bureaucratized—or what I call "guided." The metaphorical garden has rather high fences, entrance fees, and strict rules. Even though there is empirical evidence that Indonesians, as well as other peoples around the world, are increasingly mobile, the doors that open up in the course of globalization are not equally open to everyone.

Moreover, the increase of globalized physical movement does not automatically entail economic progress. As an example, a study by the International Organization of Migration (IOM) reveals that in Indonesia, labor migration only contributes to covering basic daily needs, rather than sustainably improving people's living conditions (IOM 2010). In fact, for many people mobility is not so much a free choice or aspiration, but a recurring requirement for maintaining the status quo. These indications demand that a closer look be taken at how spatial mobility is interlinked with social change, how it is experienced by individuals, and what these individuals make of their experiences. Since guidance appears as a common feature in both labor migration and pilgrimage, I take this focus in order to trace the interrelation between physical mobility and social change, including economic as well as cultural-religious changes in Islamic traditions. Guidance emerged as a central aspect from the empirical material and complements ideas in contemporary mobility studies theories.

Guided Mobility

After the "mobilities turn" in social sciences (see Sheller and Urry 2006) and the study of the transformative effects of mobile experiences (see Cresswell 2006; Greenblatt 2010; Ong 1999; Rapport and Dawson 1998; Sheller and Urry 2006), more recent studies have argued that mobility does not always inspire transformation, change, and hybridization, but in many cases is characterized by structural inequalities and stasis (see Cresswell and Merriman 2011b; Hackl et al. 2016; Salazar 2010a, 2011, 2013, 2016a, 2016b; Urry 2007).

Limits of Mobility

Examples of the limits of mobility are the increasing securitization of societies and the hardening of physical borders, such as the US-Mexican border or the EU borders, and the mental boundaries of xenophobia. Among the reasons for the overall limits of mobility are fear and uncertainty (see Bauman 1996, 19; Comaroff and Comaroff 2012, 648).

The limits of different spheres of mobility—spatial, social, and cultural—have recently been more comprehensively discussed in social sciences. This concerns unequal access to a mobile lifestyle (Hackl et al. 2016), the rule of border regimes, and migrants being trapped in transit areas (Hess and Tsianos 2010; Missbach 2015), and the different outcomes of spatial mobility, which itself is not necessarily an aspiration, but can be the result of coercion.

This more recent focus in mobility studies serves as a criticism of the enthusiastic tone of the new mobilities paradigm in which "not stasis but movement was heralded as the new norm" (Hackl et al. 2016, 21) and which followed the euphoria of global mobility at the time of the fall of the Berlin Wall and the end of the Cold War. Disillusionment came with the recent political policies of sealing off "Fortress Europe" while asylum seekers drown in the Mediterranean on Europe's doorstep and the increasing xenophobia arising in the course of the influx of refugees from the Syrian civil war in 2015, which materialized in the popularity of right-wing populist political actors all over Europe. Obviously, control and structuring of movement are more prevalent than free-floating flows or hypermobility (Bougleux 2016, 15–19; Hackl et al. 2016, 22; Hess and Tsianos 2010, 247). Hackl et al. (2016) argue that "the seeming ubiquity of borders and immobilisations underpins the growing acceptance of an order in which only the privileged remain mobile, while others are doomed to a world of limitations and control" (ibid., 20). This leads to the disparate situation in which "highly skilled expatriates, for instance, are somewhat hypermobilised . . . [while] others are stuck in poverty, detained in refugee camps or confined in areas badly connected to industrial zones" (Götz 2016, 10). Many scholars have criticized early mobility studies because of their neglect of global power relations and social hierarchies that structure and stabilize the mobility of a certain group of people while limiting that of others (Hackl et al. 2016, 22). Hackl et al. introduce the concept of "bounded mobilities" as "mobility is always bounded, regulated, mediated, and intrinsically connected to forms of immobility and unequal power relations" (Hackl et al. 2016, 20).

While the concept of "bounded mobilities" presents the structuring of mobilities as restriction and impediment in the European context, I consider the "soft structuring" of mobility, which happens in the mutual exchange between *top-down direction* and *bottom-up demand* for guidance. A crucial aspect of my concept of guided mobility is how people seek orientation and structure. Fruitful contributions to the analysis of less rigid forms of the "boundedness" of mobility are found in "mobility imaginaries" (Salazar 2010a, 64) and the "anxieties of mobility" (Lindquist 2009), which mark the search for guidance and its supply through imaginaries, hopes, dreams, and overall "economies of emotion"

(Lindquist 2009, 150). Thus, in the following, I consider features of guidance as a complementary element to the studies on the limits of mobility.

Circular Mobility in a Multipolar World

Inspired by Salazar's (2010a) differentiation between horizontal mobility (geographic/spatial movement) and vertical mobility (socioeconomic and cultural changes), I propose a threefold differentiation between spatial, social, and cultural mobility. Spatial mobility encompasses physical and geographical movement and occurs through physical processes; social mobility refers to economic and socio-hierarchical movement concerning a person's social status; and cultural mobility means the movement of knowledge, ideas, norms, habits, or as Salazar (2010a, 64) labels it "mobility imaginaries." These three spheres of mobility can be intertwined and overlapping. The analysis of the interrelation of the different spheres of mobility will provide conclusions about the sociocultural effects of spatial mobility.

Regarding the cultural dimension of mobility, a range of anthropological research has shown that globalization involves cultural hybridization and creative local engagements with globally spread cultural elements (Appadurai 1996; Hannerz 1996; Ong 2007; Robertson 1998). Evidence of complex intertwinement between global and local features and "multiple modernities" (Eisenstadt 2000) challenges classic modernization theories in which the West is seen as the main reference point. For Indonesians, for instance, the Arab world may be a reference for "Islamic modernities," while the West is a reference point for democratization and economic advancement. The references to different modernities are "entangled" (Fuchs et al. 2004, 11–16; Randeria 2006, 97–103).

As an example, Comaroff and Comaroff (2012, 15) describe the repercussions of globalization as "southward evolvement," unmasking geographic terms like *North* and *South* as Eurocentric and using them—in a sarcastic manner—as analytical categories that reveal the entanglement of colonization, modernity, Western hegemony, and the economic weakness of the global South. The West is by far not the only reference point in entangled modernities. In the context of global-local intertwinements, South-South connections are often more relevant than orientations toward the so-called West. The historical overview of encounters between Indonesia and the Arab world (chapter 1) gives proof of this. From a non-Western perspective, it's obvious that other reference points, such as the Indian Ocean, used to be much more relevant for historical trade routes between East Africa, the Arabian Peninsula, Persia, the Indian subcontinent, and Southeast Asia.

These contemporary multidirectional orientations are ambivalent. While on the one hand orientation toward the Middle East and Islamic lifestyle features prominently, on the other hand Indonesians "see Arab countries as not only superficially modern but also intolerant, and the West as developed but immoral. In conclusion, there is a widespread hope in Indonesia to combine the advantages of both" (Schlehe et al. 2013, 19). Therefore, my analysis of guidance through situated representations takes the filtering of knowledge and representations into account.

In addition, I depart from the understanding of transnational multicentric contexts in which people refer to several reference points. When I speak of "Indonesians" in this book, I do not mean to fall back into methodological nationalism. On the contrary, I seek to show that the reference points and centers for Indonesians are multifarious. Nation-states might not be the primary reference points for individuals, and they can feel attached to more than one place, creating transnational spaces or *ethnoscapes* (see Appadurai 1996). Inspired by research on transnationalism and transregionalism, I seek to contrast binary categories, which are evident in terms like *international* or *intercultural*, referring to bilateral exchanges, to a consideration of multilaterality and border-crossing social practices.[6] And yet, not everything and everybody is on the move: "Not everything is connected and not everything changes" (Salazar 2010b, 182), which leads back to the insights on the limits of mobility and the need to combine the insights from both directions of study: the multipolarity and the boundedness of mobility.

How Guidance Makes Mobility Meaningful

Thus the concept of guided mobility is grounded in engagement with the theoretical implications of the arguments on "bounded mobilities" (Hackl et al. 2016), the "anxieties of mobility" (Lindquist 2009), and "mobility imaginaries" (Salazar 2010b). Different from cases of "bounded mobilities" that focus on the constraints of mobility, the guided mobility framework indicates that besides confining boundedness, there are forms of structuring, and hence guidance, that mobile actors demand and happily embrace. They experience this guidance not as constraining but as enabling mobility. By foregrounding the sociocultural, interpersonal, and institutional guidance, the conceptual framework allows us to understand how the home context makes transnational mobility meaningful—with all its multidirectionality.

While my observations of mobility between Indonesia and the Middle East confirm that the world has become more mobile for some and distressingly immobile for others, I also argue that generally forms of (im)mobility have become more guided, channeled, and controlled, and that a focus on guidance reveals much about the effects of mobility. The regulation and guidance of moving or of staying put is certainly more prevalent for those who have restricted access to mobility, such as asylum seekers. Yet, apart from this obvious example, there are many contemporary forms of mobility that are increasingly guided. This aspect of guided mobility struck me when I looked at the travels of Indonesian labor migrants and Mecca pilgrims, who appear to experience very different kinds of mobility at first sight, even though their respective mobile experiences are guided in quite similar ways.

While hajj returnees are expected to become spiritually enlightened, morally better persons, and responsible members of society, labor migrants aspire to improve their economic situation and are celebrated as national heroines of foreign remittances. In both cases, societal ideas of morally appropriate behavior and an interlinkage of economic and moral success become a strong normative guidance. The societies' expectations and the unspoken socially accepted and desirable features of self-representation guide migrants and pilgrims in their representations of their journeys and of the Arab world.

The differences and commonalities in the guidance of labor migrants and pilgrims show that it is not mobility per se that drives change, but the ways in which it is guided. The same destination (here Mecca or the Arab world) can result in remarkably different representations and narratives in accordance with guiding factors like the expectations of the home community or popular public discourses. For the Indonesian case, this focus on the guidance of transnational mobility contributes to the understanding of the conservative turn, which is not inspired by outward Arab influence but by local socioeconomic undercurrents that are especially obvious when people cross the physical borders to Arab countries.

Beyond the Indonesian context, the analytical categories of guided mobility and situated representations shall indicate where physical and social movement or change go together and where experiences of spatial mobility support the continuity of familiar values and structures. As Gupta and Ferguson (1992) have argued, in the course of the blurring of physical borders, imagined boundaries become more salient.

Who and What Guides?

In order to define guidance for the context at hand, I will briefly summarize features of guidance that result from studies on guiding, especially tourist guiding. Salazar identifies the activities of guides as ensuring safe conduct, showing the way, interpreting, translating, and explaining. Guides are pathfinders, protectors, companions, bribers, and tutors (Salazar 2010b, 112). This means that guiding requires certain abilities. As an example, guides have to select information and transform it into understandable instructions; they have to consider how their advice becomes applicable. Guides are translators, they have the ability to explain, they act as intermediaries, and satisfy expectations; in the case of tour guides, for example, they represent authentic local culture (Salazar 2010b, 112–16).

Guides often embody the tourists' imaginations of local authenticity (Salazar 2010b, 113; Schlehe 2001, 22). This means that they have to mediate a gap between tourists' expectations and actual experiences (ibid., 79). Because of their skills and interpretative advantage, they have superior knowledge compared to those they guide, but they are also providing services and have to conform to the demands of those guided ones. To satisfy this demand, tour guides draw on guiding narratives that answer peoples' interests and produce "mobility imaginaries" as a "credible illusion of authenticity" (Salazar 2010b, 80). Stereotypes feature prominently in their translations and explanations, as they seem to make the complexity of real life understandable and create the impression of having grasped the culture in a day (ibid., 80). This requires the ability to understand where those that demand guidance want to go or what they want to see and experience. Guidance fulfills these expectations, but it can also initiate them. By making people long for something or hope for something, demand for guidance can be created. In order to guide or lead followers in a preferred direction, the creation of aspirations and needs could obviously be denounced as a form of manipulation.

In Mecca pilgrimages, there is a range of intermediaries who guide the process of pilgrimage, including tour guides for mundane guidance and spiritual leaders who take care of religious guidance. Furthermore, a variety of other guiding persons, from assistants to religious counselors, from medical experts to headmen of travel units, guide Indonesian pilgrims.

Similarly, in labor migration, there are official guides from the government and private agencies, as well as informal recruiters and intermediaries, who play crucial roles, as comprehensively covered by Lindquist (2012). Despite their dubious reputation of being informal or "illegal," these recruiters are quite often respected public figures like teachers and religious leaders, persons who are considered to be knowledgeable and are hired by agencies to recruit within their local community. Trust, credibility, and reliability are considered to be key qualities for these brokers (Lindquist 2012, 74–75). Some of the intermediaries have been labor migrants themselves and are therefore considered able to provide advice from firsthand experience (ibid., 77). Providing guidance and supplying information becomes part of their brokerage. It concerns not only organizational and administrational matters, but also cultural questions and the representation of aspirations related to the potential benefits of labor migration inasmuch as anxieties and fears make guidance eligible. Concerning labor migration to the Gulf, material concerns as well as the prospect of visiting Mecca are among the topics about which people seek reassurance and further information (ibid., 76). Apart from possessing experience and information, the brokers must have influential social networks and must be able to arrange strategic alliances in order to guide effectively (ibid., 81). Thus guidance requires negotiation skills and social competences. Intermediaries who facilitate migrants' emotional needs also sometimes physically guide people and connect them to official institutions, contributing to the creation of a semiofficial and semi-institutionalized "migration infrastructure" (Xiang and Lindquist 2014).

Apart from interpersonal human guides, guidance is institutionalized in the form of norms. Official norms are formulated in guidelines, regulations, rules, and laws, while unwritten norms concern socially acceptable behavior, common procedures, and moral values. Norms and regulations are especially prevalent in administration and bureaucracy, but they also influence the overall functioning of society or what sociologically is referred to as "social structure." However, the structure does not determine actions unchallenged. Through agency and recurring practices, social structure is reproduced, confirmed or blurred.[7] Thus, in a broad understanding of guidance, all forms of social structure could be considered as guiding or shaping human behavior. Widening the idea of guidance even further, physical environment and architecture could also be considered as guiding or structuring lifeworlds.

Yet rather than making the term *guidance* too broad and thereby depriving it of its analytical value, I aim to narrow it. In the analytical framework of guided mobility, I consider interpersonal guidance through social actors, like guides and intermediaries; institutional and legal guidance through laws, regulations, and administrative procedures; and normative guidance through situated representations, including embodied physical representations, like dress codes and uniform and the representations of Others and selves. Guidance is marked by some degree of intentionality and some kind of guiding actor or guiding medium, which differentiates it from a general collective habitus.

Translational Moments

The studies on pilgrimage, migration, and mobility reveal the interplay of structure and agency. In order to understand when, how, and why individuals act in accordance with or deviation from guiding structures, I seek to analyze "translational moments," as moments of adaptation, change, localization, and individual interpretation. With the term *translations*, I do not refer to linguistic translations in the common sense of the term, but to cultural transmissions, transfers, and transformations. In the case of Indonesians' mobility toward the Arab world, these translations are part and parcel of processing experiences of guided mobility and engagement with Arab culture and customs. Translating these experiences means making sense of them in accordance with the return context.

A prominent example of how mobility triggers social change—in the case of Indonesia, for example, changing Islamic traditions—is that of remittances. Financial remittances are considered as enhancing economic development and social remittances like the transmission of norms and values can trigger changes in political, religious, and cultural orientation. To think about translational moments in the context of experiences of guided mobility is to think about the very nature of guidance as explanatory and translational practice. Guidance demands interpretative skills, and therefore I consider that remittances are adjusted to the home context and may even be determined by it through the initiation of certain expectations.

In the course of making movement meaningful, individuals do not only follow various forms of guidance, they also filter between different guiding elements and establish interpretative practices. These interpretative practices entail "mobility capital" (see Salazar 2016a; Jayaram 2016, 20), which means the "resources, knowledge or abilities gained by being mobile" (Salazar 2016a, 285). Gaining interpretative skills, making choices between different offers of guidance, and finding one's own way can transform a guided person into a guiding one. I shall show this for former labor migrants who advance as intermediaries for new labor migrants.

Mobility capital encapsulates capacities to gain various forms of capital that have been defined by Bourdieu (1979). Referring to Marx, Jayaram (2016, 25) argues that mobility capital must be understood as a "process," rather than a "good." Indonesian migrants and pilgrims can gain social, cultural, and economic capital through their mobility. For this transformative act of capitalizing experiences of mobility, an act of interpretation or translation, in the sense of adaptation to the local context, becomes necessary. Eventually the outcome of mobility can be traced in differently transformed values and the way this process is guided.

Interpretative Labor

Further useful thoughts for the analysis of translational moments come from David Graeber (2012). In his essay on the relationship between (structural) violence, bureaucracy, and "interpretative labor," Graeber makes an intriguing argument about the interpretative skills that develop within relationships that are marked by structures of inequality. Inspired by feminist theories, he refers to the example of women in patriarchal systems being occupied with an effort to understand men in order to reach their aims. These theories argue that dependency on men, especially regarding material resources, triggers women's capabilities to analyze and interpret men's behavior. Graeber calls the constant effort of trying to understand and "managing, maintaining, and adjusting the egos," and the "imaginative identification" that this involves, "interpretative labor" (Graeber 2012, 117). This interpretative labor includes the capability to develop empathy for others' perspectives.[8] The superior counterpart in these hierarchical relationships (for instance, an employer of a domestic worker) is often significantly less empathic and knowledgeable. In the endeavor to define a general theory of interpretative labor, Graeber identifies two features in this realm: (1) the process of imaginative identification as a form of knowledge (ibid., 118); and (2) the resultant pattern of sympathetic identification (ibid., 119). Concerning the view of the process of imaginative identification as a form of knowledge, Graeber points out that "within relations of domination, it is generally the subordinates who are effectively relegated [to] the work of understanding how the social relations in question really work" (ibid., 188). As an example, domestic servants often have vast knowledge about their employers' families, observing and analyzing them, trying to figure out how things work, while in contrast employers often don't know anything about their employees (ibid., 188f). This dynamic can also be transferred to the example of Mecca pilgrims, where the guides are those who have to understand their customers in order to meet their expectations of what the Mecca pilgrimage looks like.

The second aspect, sympathetic identification, grasps that imagination and identification, or empathy, tend to bring with them sympathy (ibid., 199). Relating this to the structural inequalities in many working relationships, like domestic work, it means that even though those on the bottom of the social ladder suffer in these working relationships, they also often care about their employers. Therefore, empathy with and thus knowledge or imagination about the Other happens to be unilateral, as Graeber summarizes: "Whether one is dealing with masters and servants, men and women, employers and employees, rich and poor, structural inequality—what I've been calling structural violence—invariably creates highly lopsided structures of the imagination" (ibid., 199).

These thought-provoking ideas inspire the question of the extent to which an interpretative surplus develops in relationships of guidance and what action it triggers. The guides seem to be the ones who have an interpretative skill as they have a broader understanding of the situation. However, sometimes dependency on others hinders people from following their own interests.

As guidance goes in various directions, especially if there are conflicting forms of guidance, those being guided have to choose between competing or contradictory instructions and their own interpretations. This provokes the analysis of translational and interpretative activities from the perspective of those who follow as well as those who guide, juxtaposing interpretations from marginal, peripheral, or subaltern positions with more central and privileged ones. Regarding the element of dependency as a determining matter of who is establishing empathy toward whom, it seems that among Mecca pilgrims and labor migrants there are some overlapping dependencies, like dependency on social relationships in the return context, and differing ones, like dependency on employers in the case of labor migrants, and pilgrimage and travel agents' dependency on the pilgrims—their customers—or the pilgrims' dependency on local religious leaders.

By examining these constellations further among the two different groups and in different regional contexts, I scrutinize whether and under what conditions interpretative labor entails agency and what this means for the characteristics of changes in Islamic traditions in Indonesia.

Defining Guided Mobility

Summing up, mobility is not always marked by flexibility and fluidity. Some forms of mobility are highly regulated, channeled, controlled, and framed. I look at guided mobility as a form of mobility that is less assertive and subject to contestation. The intentional direction of spatial, social, and cultural movements through institutional structures, interpersonal relationships, and situated representations relies on relationships of dependency and on prospects of exploiting various forms of capital from mobile experiences.

Acknowledging the possibility of translational moments like interpretative labor in experiences of mobility implies that guidance, including guidance through situated representations, is not rigid nor static but underpinned by social negotiations. These negotiations include the filtering of various offers of guidance and one's own interpretation and the consideration of the dependencies and prospects of capitalization. For the case of Indonesian migrants and pilgrims, social hierarchies are to some extent negotiable and offers of guidance are made in an environment that is characterized by a pluralization and in some cases a commercialization of guidance.

Based on these theoretical implications, I look at the intersection between experiences of spatial, social, and cultural mobility and the making of situated representations as translational endeavors to make the mobile experiences meaningful and beneficial in the return context. Therefore, the empirical material is presented for the following three themes: (1) patterns of guided mobility in spatial, social, and cultural spheres, scrutinizing different forms of mobility and different forms of guidance in particular (chapters 1 and 2); (2) situated representations, in particular images of Arab Others (chapter 3); and (3) translations and interpretative labor, which inspire deviation from guidance (chapter 4). I estimate the extent to which the experiences and outcomes of mobility are conditioned by social obligations, hegemonic discourses, and obedience to authorities. Here the focus lies on competitive offers of guidance and translations in situated representations.

I provide evidence of the impact of migrants' and pilgrims' mobility to the Arabian Peninsula and their engagement with "Arabness" on Indonesian society. Important to this analysis is the perspective of interpretative labor from "the margins." The seemingly peripheral positions are discussed on a global level (Indonesia as the periphery of the Muslim world) and a local level (lower-class periphery, rural periphery), examining whether perspectives from such positions challenge or affirm hegemonic representations.

The difference between mainstream perceptions and those from peripheral positions becomes evident through the juxtaposition of different groups in society, urban and rural areas and two different Indonesian regions, namely Central Java, known as the center of *Islam Jawa*, and Madura, which is referred to as the "Terrace of Medina" because of its orthodoxy and alleged affinity with the Arab world. In the following section, I introduce these two regions and the methodological approach of the study.

Research Sites and Methodology

It was in August 2011 on a flight from Frankfurt to Jakarta with a layover in Dubai that I first noticed pilgrimage travel groups who were on their way to Saudi Arabia. Their uniformity in dress and travel equipment, as well as the size of their group, caught my attention. People from all walks of life unintentionally come together in the transit areas of the big international hubs, which become areas of nonencounter and coexistence. Frequent travelers know how to move in these "nonplaces" (Augé 1992). They submit to the conventions of international air traffic and airport operating companies, allowing the interior design of airports to guide their steps through shopping and waiting areas. Indonesian pilgrims and labor migrants are easily identifiable because they act differently. They refer to a different guidance, wearing uniform clothing and traveling in groups.

These airport encounters made me aware of the specific guidance of migrants and pilgrims and also of my own situatedness as a Western academic traveler. I chose not to accompany migrants and pilgrims along their various ways but to track their guidance and the outcome of their travels in their homes in Central

Java and Madura. Here they would not be a group member in a uniform travel dress, but an individual returnee. I lived among returnees in different research locations for a total of fourteen months in 2013, 2014, and 2015. My research used an inductive, reflexive, qualitative methodological approach, inspired by the methods of Grounded Theory (see Glaser and Strauss 1967; Corbin and Strauss 1990) such as the constant shifting between analysis and further data generation, reflection and participant observation and interviews that focused on learning about post-travel narratives within the biography of research participants. Recognizing that I am guided by certain social sciences theories and academic education in Western institutions, rather than being strictly inductive, the research process was a dialogue between theory-guidedness and grounded field research.

Coming back to the airport scene, the attraction that Indonesians find in guided package tours and labor migrants' search for guidance triggered the more general question of the relevance of guidance. Obviously, some kind of guidance is inevitable in order to move. The research activities relied on the cooperation and guidance of hosts, research participants, and colleagues. The anthropologists Nuki Mayasari and Khotim Ubaidillah (Ubed), as well as Kamalatul Khoriyah (Mala), supported my research while completing their own studies. Our cooperative research was inspired by the approach of tandem- and team-research created by Judith Schlehe and her colleagues in Freiburg and Yogyakarta (see Schlehe and Hidayah 2014, Schlehe 2013a). In this approach research partners make systematic use of reflections on the different positions of researchers, juxtaposing insider and outsider perspectives. The different research constellations are influenced by the gender, age, social class, nationality, subculture, religion, and ethnicity of researchers. Thus the general data evaluation included reflection on the researchers' impact on the field and certain triggers through the different characteristics.

Just as the researchers' backgrounds shape certain perceptions, migrants' and pilgrims' origins influence their perception of the world. Where a person comes from within Indonesia is also critical to forming their view of the Arab world. Indonesian regions like Aceh, Makassar, or Madura are said to particularly favor of what is labeled as "Arabness," whereas Central Java is a culturally and religiously more heterogeneous region, whose residents often exhibit a distinctive pride in their heritage from Hindu-Buddhist kingdoms and much is made, discursively, of the uniqueness of "Javaneseness." Javanese peoples' claim that other regions are "Arab oriented," must thus also be understood as a Javanese differentiation from these places. Aceh, Makassar, Madura, and to a certain degree, Lombok and West Java are regions in Indonesia that are nicknamed the "Terrace of Mecca" (mainly used for Aceh) or "Terrace of Medina." The island of Madura is a stronghold of Nahdlatul Ulama (NU), Indonesia's largest Muslim organization. The Madurese

NU branches are known to be orthodox, featuring their very own "Arab style," whereas in other regions NU representatives and institutions are famous for propagating Islamic styles that are outspokenly non-Arab—like Islam Jawa—which they promote under the label *Islam Nusantara* (Islam of the Archipelago), emphasizing its plurality, tolerance, and inclusiveness, and its potential to be an international model for the harmonization of Islamic lifestyle, local culture, and liberal democracy. The region of Central Java, with royal courts in Yogyakarta and Surakarta, is considered the center of Islam Jawa, even though Yogyakarta is also home to the headquarters of the NU's rival organization, Muhammadiyah, Indonesia's second largest Islamic organization, representing modernist Islam. This indicates that the differences that I describe in the following exist not only between but also within different regions in Indonesia.

Central Java

In the eyes of many Javanese, Java is the center of the world. Some characters from the Javanese *wayang* shadow puppet play are seen as the ancestors of all world religions (Geertz 1960, 276) and the graves of the Wali Songo (the nine saints who brought Islam to Java), are important destinations for local *ziarah* pilgrimages (Mas'ud 2006; Quinn 2019, 2008; Ubaidillah 2014; Ziemek 1983). The Hindu-Buddhist heritage of Indonesia is valued highly in Central Java and the continuous influence of the nobility in the sultanates of Yogyakarta and Surakarta, who trace their lineage back to the kingdom of Mataram, cultivates local rituals related to the *kejawen* worldview, which is not officially recognized as a religion.[9] The Wali Songo are considered key figures in harmonizing Javaneseness and Islamic identity, as shown by the following account about Sunan Kalijaga, one of the nine saints:

> Myths concerning the construction of the Demak mosque mention Sunan Kalijaga as having fixed the *kiblat* or direction of prayer and by so doing oriented Java towards Mecca and Islam. It is said that after the mosque was constructed it refused to orient itself towards Mecca and spun in circles. Sunan Kalijaga is said to have fixed the direction of the *kiblat* by holding one hand to the center pillar of the mosque and by reaching out with the other and touching the Kabah in Mecca. This myth bends Java towards Mecca and universalist Islam. [Yet] Sunan Kalijaga used the *wayang* and other elements of *Kebudayaan Jawa* as tools for *dakwah*. (Woodward 2011, 180, italics in original)

Thus the Wali Songo personify the ambivalence of the relationship with the Middle East, orienting Indonesia toward Mecca physically and spiritually and at the same time coining a distinctive Islam Jawa. Another important center of Islam Jawa is the royal cemetery in Imogiri in the south of Yogyakarta, sometimes referred to as the Mecca of Java. The cemetery was founded by the most famous sultan of the Mataram kingdom, Sultan Agung (1613–45), who is said to have taken a lump of earth from the Prophet Muhammad's grave in Medina and put it on his future grave site at Imogiri (Schlehe 1998, 56). The royal families of Surakarta and Yogyakarta emphasize their descent from Sultan Agung, and the cemetery in Imogiri remains an important pilgrimage site. The current sultan of Yogyakarta Hamengkubuwono X performed the hajj to Mecca and is seen as being closer to the teachings of normative Islam, attributed to Muhammadiyah. Nevertheless, he maintains annual rituals of local mysticism and offerings, such as offerings to the Queen of the Ocean (see Schlehe 1998). In 2013, he personally issued a *himbauan* (a referral) that advises individuals and institutions not to support labor migration to Saudi Arabia.

Nevertheless, there are large numbers of labor migrants—both in the city of Yogyakarta, which technically is a province of its own with the sultan as its governor, and in the province of Central Java that surrounds Yogyakarta (see maps 1 and 2).[10] In order to provide a comparison between urban and rural areas, the research activities took place in the city of Yogyakarta, in rural areas in Gunung Kidul regency, and on the southern coast of Bantul regency. Moreover, I included the hajj departure center in Surakarta and two villages in Central Java: a village near the Buddhist Borobodur temple and a mountain village in Magelang regency, which I will call Gunungembun[11] throughout this book.[12]

The prevalence of labor migration from Central Java can be indicated by the colloquial practice of calling the mountain village, Gunungembun, by the name *kantong TKW*, which literally means a "female labor migrant pocket," describing the high percentage of female labor migrants in the village.[13] Gunungembun is located on the northern edge of Magelang regency between the cities of Magelang in the south and Salatiga in the north. The relatively chilly and humid climate supports farming activities. However, due to the meagre income from agriculture, many women leave their homes and become migrant workers. Since the 1980s, women from the area have migrated to Saudi Arabia and other Gulf States as well as Malaysia, Hong Kong, Singapore, and more recently, Taiwan and Korea. With seed capital from remittances, new businesses were introduced, among others manual chipboard production.

The women in Gunungembun shared their frustration about not being acknowledged as Mecca returnees, even though many of them had accomplished the hajj during their stay in the Gulf. This differs from the situation in Madura where migrants are also regarded as pilgrims and some pilgrims become migrants.

Madura

The Madurese worldview is notable for the extent to which it forces Westerners to rethink our notions of geography. From the Indonesian perspective, the Middle *East* is of course located to the *west*. For the Madurese, to go west, in Madurese language "ka bère," means to go to Mecca. People from Madura were among the first Indonesians to move west for economic activities, pilgrimage, and religious education, three spheres that are still intertwined in Madura today.

Administratively, the island of Madura is part of the province of East Java (see map 2), yet the people in Madura are ethnically distinct from the Javanese, with different culture, customs, and their own language. As they are located at the edge of historical trade routes and also a maritime society, the Madurese are considered to be particularly adventurous and fond of traveling. The popular saying "Orang Madura berbantal ombak dan berslimut angin" ("The pillow of the Madurese is the waves and their blanket is the wind,") was often used by my Madurese research participants to illustrate restlessness and a strong connection to outward migration. Apart from overseas mobility, the Madurese are known as domestic migrants. The *merantau* narrative, which means circular migration in search of success (Lindquist 2009, 7), is much associated with the Madurese, who are the fourth largest ethnic group in Indonesia and reside on the northern coast of Java, in Kalimantan, and especially in East Java (see Wiyata 2002). Madura is one of the poorest regions in Indonesia and many Madurese leave the infertile island and seek employment elsewhere. More than 16 million Madurese live outside Madura, compared to around 4 million inhabitants living on the densely populated island (Husson 1977, 1995; Nooteboom 2015). Moreover, violent conflicts with the indigenous populations in other areas, for example, the conflict with the Dayak in Kalimantan, result in stereotypes about the Madurese as being particularly prone to violence (see Oesterheld 2017). Besides being considered harsh and violent, the Madurese are said to be invasive and possessive, especially in the sense of occupying public spaces or making use of others' resources: they are, for example, known to control the scrap iron business.[14] Furthermore, they are considered to be particularly brave, proud, and coarse, and many Javanese speak critically of the so-called *carok* tradition, a custom of honor killing and blood revenge. The traditions of bull racing (*kerapan sapi*) and cow breeding, as well as alleged practices of gambling related to them, are much associated with a coarse Madurese masculinity and bandit culture that stands in contrast with Javanese ideas of masculinity, in which the ideal man should be soft, humble, and reserved (see Keeler 1990; Mulder 1997).

Other stereotypes of the Madurese abound: they are also perceived to be particularly pious and the island is considered to be an enclave of orthodox

Islam and a stronghold of the orthodox branch of NU, with numerous *pesantren* (Qur'anic boarding schools) and *kyai* (the schools' leaders and public figures) being the most important point of orientation in Madurese society (Mansurnoor 1990, XVIII; Rozaki 2004, 3). However, Madurese people are also known for their magic skills (Soegianto 2003).[15] The seemingly contradictory cultural features of Islamic orthodoxy and adventurous bandit culture as well as magic practices are comprehensively expressed in Abdur Rozaki's (2004) concept of Madurese society as a twin-system of kyai and *blatér* (religious leader and bandit), who both remarkably shape Madurese society. Yanwar Pribadi (2018) sees these two informal leaders—kyai and blatér—as being more influential than *klébun*, the village heads, who occupy a formal leadership position.

The famous SuraMadu Bridge between Madura and the megacity of Surabaya, which is located only five kilometers from Madura, was intended to modernize Madura and enhance economic development. However, some scholars argue that the bridge made Madura even more dependent on Surabaya since the number of Madurese working in Surabaya increased and the import of goods and food via the bridge began to compete with local production. Moreover, the kyai fear that the connection to Surabaya will limit their authority and open Madura to negative influences from the "morally decadent" city (Rifai et al. 2013; Wiyata 2013, 83).

My interest in Madura was triggered by the label "Arab" that often came up in jokes and stereotypical accounts about the Madurese when my Javanese interlocutors argued that there was a high "Arab" affinity in Madura. This "Arab affinity" relates to the role of the kyai who emphasize their spiritual, historical, and contemporary connections to the Arabian Peninsula as the Holy Land, among others through the use of Arabic language and Arabic clothing style. Symbols of "Arabness" are omnipresent in Madura in many regards, such as Arabic script on street signs; a Middle Eastern-inspired music style; everyday language and clothing style; Arabic names and the overall presence of Hadhrami communities; and their sale of cosmetics, holy water, dates, and other items from the Middle East. Many *pesantren* maintain connections to the Middle East and send their pupils through informal channels to Saudi Arabia and Yemen to study with associated sheikhs there.

The infamous figure of Shaikhona Kholil, or Kyai Kholil (born in 1820 in Bangkalan), whose grave site in Bangkalan in the western part of the island is a popular pilgrimage site, illustrates the connection to the Arab world. Shaikhona Kholil is considered to have been the forefather of almost all present-day influential Muslim figures in Indonesia and his lineage is traced back to the *wali* Sunan Gunung Jati and thus to Yemeni origin (Ma'arif 2015, 150; Rozaki 2004,

129). The numerous miracle stories about Shaikhona Kholil's years studying in Mecca and later trade and spiritual connections to the Holy Land are popular in everyday life and religious education in Madura. In contemporary depictions, he is shown in a white turban and Arab dress that his present-day offspring and admirers adopt.[16]

While the families and religious scholars in the tradition of Shaikhona Kholil maintain Sufi spiritual Arabness and a connection to the Holy Land, other religious figures assert their connections to the Middle East through the introduction of religious rules and in some cases through affiliation with Saudi Arabian Wahhabism, though this appears to be a minority. Arabness, religious symbols, and connections to the Middle East are prestigious, and thus other public figures try to access this capital, as can be seen in the introduction of *PerDa Sharia* (or *Gerbang Salam = Gerakan Pembangunan Masyarakat Islami*) in Pamekasan in 2010,[17] which is regarded as an elite project that has little impact on ordinary people's daily lives and was used by secular parties to gain votes (Ubaidillah 2010).[18]

The Madurese are famous as enthusiastic *hajjis*, and the pilgrimage waiting lists in East Java are among the longest in Indonesia. Moreover, due to the lack of work opportunities on the island, in addition to the domestic *merantau* migration, international migration, especially toward Malaysia and the Gulf, is very common in Madura.

My research in Madura focused primarily on two regencies: on Bangkalan in the west of the island, and on Pamekasan, located in the middle of the island (see map 2). In Bangkalan I lived in the subdistrict Kamal, which is a semiurban area characterized by its proximity to the city center of Bangkalan and the harbor with ships commuting between Surabaya and Madura. Moreover, the state university, Universitas Trunojoyo Madura, is located in Kamal, which means that many students live in the area. Nevertheless, Kamal is a rural area, and when there it is almost difficult to believe that the megacity Surabaya is only a twenty-minute ferry ride away. In Bangkalan, the research activities focused on labor migrants and pilgrims in nearby villages and on the Qur'anic School Shaikhona Kholil, which is run by descendants of Shaikhona Kholil.

The main research location in the center of Madura Island was a village in the rural interior of eastern Pamekasan regency which I will call Ladangtembakau.[19] Through my stay with the family of my research assistant Mala, I came to understand the meaning of hajj farewells and returns for the whole community, the relevance of religious knowledge and religious schools and the honoring of religious leaders. In the family compound was a mushollah, which was financed by a Saudi Arabian foundation, which also triggered conversations about Saudi and Wahhabi influence in Madura. Therefore, the compound was frequented by neighbors for evening prayers and Qur'an reading groups, especially during Ramadan.

Outline of the Book

Following this introduction, chapter 1 provides a historical overview of ambivalent encounters between Indonesia and the Arab world. Here I build on findings from the current state of the art, showing that the relationship between Indonesia and the Middle East has, in fact, always been ambivalent. From the earliest encounters with Arab traders in the seventh century, through encounters with Indo-Persian Sufi, the period of the Dutch colonial authority, independence struggles, nation building and autocracy, up to the current democratization process, Indonesians' attitudes toward the Arab world have been marked by contradictory dynamics. Arabs have been acknowledged as teachers of Islam, as brothers and sisters in faith, and as allies in the postcolonial nonbloc movement, but the Arab world was also a gloomy counterimage against which Indonesian officials and religious leaders drew the picture of a tolerant, pluralist Indonesian Islam. Historically, mobility across the Indian Ocean has played a key role in the formation of Islamic culture in Indonesia, and there have been attempts to control and restrict this connection (e.g., by the Dutch colonial authorities), and to enhance it (e.g., in postcolonial solidarity and in the current pilgrimage business). Today, the transnational connections within the Muslim world are more contested than ever. I show that globalization—in particular the globalization of Islamic terrorism and Islamophobia—poses new challenges to Indonesian positioning toward the Arab world. In light of these historical evolvements and current controversies, I analyze how labor migrants and Mecca pilgrims make sense of their encounters with the Arab world in chapters 2, 3, and 4.

Chapter 2 characterizes the nature of today's mobility from Indonesia to the Arabian Peninsula. For migrants and pilgrims, the journeys are "beaten tracks" that are loaded with meaning and direction through previous travelers' narratives, institutional guidance, and intermediaries' navigation. Moreover, the prospect of return significantly "leads" migrants and pilgrims in what they make of the journey. Only in reference to norms and values that are valid in their home context can the returnees exploit different types of capital from their migration or pilgrimage. This chapter culminates in the analysis of "success stories" of migrants and pilgrims as an outcome of their experience of guided mobility. Ethnographic accounts from the local level illustrate how popular ideas of success and images of the Arab world guide migrants and pilgrims in how they represent their journeys.

Chapter 3 tackles ambivalence in the representations of Indonesian selves and Arab Others and explains the broader sociopolitical dimensions of images of Arab Others. Here I include an excursion into popular culture. This reveals, among other things, how cultural boundaries provide orientation and guide identity formation in contemporary Indonesian Islamization trends. Through engagement with these current inner-Indonesian controversies about "Arabization" and competing religious lifestyles, lessons from the collective mobilities of migrants and pilgrims take preference over their individual biographies.

In Chapter 4 I return to the microlevel of individuals' processing of migratory experiences and explore the particularities and exemptions in the overall appropriation, rejection, and Othering of Arabness. I sketch out two special cases, namely Javanese labor migrants' rejection of Arabness in favor of East Asian styles and Madurese peoples' vivid localizations of Arabness. A closer look at these disparities and local features reveals that changes in Islamic lifestyles cannot be generalized in a culturally heterogeneous country like Indonesia. Regarding the ambivalence of Indonesian engagements with the Arab world, I unravel the question of why migrants and pilgrims in Madura and migrants in Central Java apparently follow different guiding narratives. This question is expanded to more general discussion about reasons for following a particular normative guidance. Reflection about deviations and adherence to guidance leads to the theoretical consideration of conditions for cultural (ex)change or continuity, critically assessing the nature of cultural translations and localizations.

Evidence of the determining force of guidance in mobility culminates in discussion of the conditions under which sociocultural changes and religious (re)orientations happen in the course of Indonesians' transnational mobility to the Arabian Peninsula. Drawing all aspects of guided mobility together, the reciprocal demand-supply logic of guidance, the profitability of guiding, and the prospect of capitalizing on mobile experiences appear to determine the effects that migration and pilgrimage have for social change in Indonesia. My conclusion seeks firstly to complement studies which show that the conservative turn in Indonesia is highly complex, regionally diverse, and has underlying local social tensions, and secondly to speculate more generally about the functioning of features of mobility that are not perceived as restraints and that enhance sociocultural continuity rather than change.

1

INDONESIA AND THE ARAB WORLD, THEN AND NOW

Ambivalent notions lie at the heart of the relationship between Indonesia and the Arab world. The ambivalences are historically grown and inspired by recent events. Mona Abaza argues that "for the Southeast Asian world, the Middle East has been the object of much anxiety, hatred and fear and, paradoxically, an increasing curiosity since the dramatic events of 9/11" (Abaza 2007, 419). Contemporary observations of increasing conservatism, or what is called a "conservative turn" in Indonesian Islamic traditions, are often associated with connections to the Middle East. The encounter with the Arab world has been and continues to be constitutive and inspirational for Indonesian people. However, the historical experiences show that local social structures have always had a guiding function in the way Indonesians perceive the Arab world, be it through colonial control or the transregional ties of local religious networks.

Above all, a glimpse into the historical interactions between Indonesia and the Middle East shows that today's complexities are rooted in historical experiences. On the one hand, Middle Eastern Muslims have been honored as the "earlier" Muslims in light of the Middle East's role as a historical birthplace where the Prophet Muhammad received the revelation of the Qur'an (Bowen 2008, 34; van Bruinessen 2013c, 47; Burhani 2010; Chaplin 2014, 223; see also Kahn 2015). Concomitantly, Arabic language as the language of the revelation and Arabic culture and customs inherent in the words and deeds (the *sunna*) of the Prophet are recognized as central and prestigious in Islamic practices (von der Mehden 1993, 4). On the other hand, Arabness has been denounced as harsh, violent, and radical, especially in reaction to the Wahhabi conquest of Mecca in 1926 and in the aftermath of the 9/11 terrorist attacks in 2001 (see Abaza 2007). After 9/11, there has been what Lewis (2004) calls a "crisis of Islam," in which Muslims face accusations that claim an inherent violence of Islam. In Indonesia, some Muslims respond to this "crisis of Islam," by differentiating between religion and culture, and by arguing that reasons for radicalism are rooted in culture and not in the religion of Islam.

As outlined in the introduction of this book, in this regard the Arab world must be understood as an *imagined center* that goes beyond geographic borders, being intrinsic in Muslims' religious practices and at the same time representing an image of the Other. This means that Indonesians see aspects of Arabness as part of their own religiosity and heritage while they also look at the Arab world as a place that is different and distant from indigenous lifeworlds. Such representations are not congruent with Arab peoples' self-perception, nor do they reflect the ethnic and cultural diversity of the Arab world (see introduction). They are guiding images for defining Indonesian selves in differentiation from Arab Others.

In line with considerations about guided mobility, this chapter focuses on the question of how Indonesians have been guided in their encounters with Arab Others over time. But I will first give a brief introduction into Islamic conceptions of travel and the Turnerian idea of a ritual community.

Sacred and Structured Journeys

Following Arnold van Gennep's theory on *rites de passage* and its further development by Victor Turner, pilgrimage aims at transformation, contemplation, spiritual renewal, and change of the pilgrims' social status. The Turnerian differentiation of the ritual process describes a preparatory stage that is marked by structure, a medium stage that is marked by the absence of structure (antistructure) with the experience of a community of equals, and a stage of restructuring after the rituals. Individuals experience liminality, a transitional state between the different stages of a ritual, and *communitas*, the community of equals during the ritual stage of antistructure.

With a methodological approach that focuses on the pre- and postpilgrimage and migration structuring, I am more interested in the reestablishment of structure. Yet the research participants' representations of liminality and communitas are relevant for this restructuring. Migrants' and pilgrims' accounts show that liminality and communitas matter—not only in terms of actual experiences but also in their representation and relation to historical metanarratives. The idea of unity or communitas also corresponds with Islamic doctrines about travel and pilgrimage.

Pilgrimage in Islam means the hajj to Mecca and Medina, which is one of the five pillars of Islam and obligatory for those who are physically, financially, and spiritually capable of going on the journey. In addition to the Holy Mosque (*al-masǧid al-ḥarām*) with the Ka'aba in Mecca and the Prophets' Mosque in Medina (*al-masǧid an-nabawī*), a hadith by al-Bukhari names Al-Aqsa mosque in Jerusalem as a third pilgrimage destination.[1] Apart from pilgrimage to Mecca, Medina, and Jerusalem, Muslims practice *ziarah*, which means visiting holy shrines. Along with the Islamic concept of *rihla*, travel in search of knowledge, pilgrimage and ziarah are related to the *hijrah*, exodus from un-Islamic regions to Islamic ones (Eickelman and Piscatori 1990, 5). Thus the Islamic concept of mobility carries a transformative notion and social change. In fact, the idea of an Islamic communitas, the *ummah,* is linked to the story of exodus in Islam and the end of *ǧāhilīya*, which defines the pre-Islamic time of ignorance, ethnic division, and war.[2] The unification of Arab tribes and the claim of universal rights regardless of ethnic and religious affiliation was regarded as a great achievement (Laffan 2003, 120). However, soon after the death of the prophet Muhammad, the *ummah* split into competing confessions and sects, among others into Sunni and Shi'a, two competing parties in the question about the rightful successor to the prophet Muhammad. Ever since, the idea of one global *ummah*, the unity of all Muslims, has been something that many Muslims have longed for, and many pilgrims claim that the hajj provides a taste of the satisfaction of this longing. The historical overview of encounters between Indonesia and the Arab world shows how the communitas that Muslims experience in Mecca informs a metanarrative among believers. It is rooted in historical accounts of the Prophet Muhammad's revolutionary restructuring of society and is reproduced over time. Throughout history, the unity of all Muslims has repeatedly emerged as an important political demand. These are some of the crucial theological conceptions and historical experiences that have guided Indonesians and Arabs in their encounters and in mental mappings of centers and peripheries. The research at hand takes these underlying factors into consideration when it follows the line of anthropological hajj research that has revealed the multifarious social meanings and aspects of "lived religion" in the context of the hajj (see Buitelaar 2015).

Centers and Peripheries of the Muslim World

Indonesia, along with sub-Saharan Africa, Central Asia, and South Asia, is commonly perceived as the periphery of the Muslim world, while the Middle East, especially the Arabian Peninsula, is located at its center (Woodward 2011, 64). John Bowen argues that Indonesia faces struggles in bringing together Islamic and local values:

> Indonesia offers a critical case in our efforts to reorient how we understand Islam. As the largest Muslim society, and at the same time the most distant, in space and in ways of life, from the Arabian heartland (or even from the broader Arabian-Persian-Turkish one), Indonesia is a site of particularly marked struggle to bring together norms and values derived from Islam, from local cultures, and from international public life. (Bowen 2003, 19)

In line with this observation lies the perception of Islamic purity and authenticity related to its roots in the "center" and modifications and syncretism located at the "periphery." These hierarchizations between center and periphery are prevalent among both Muslims and non-Muslims in academia and in everyday mappings of the world. The Arabian Peninsula, especially the Hejaz with the holy sites in Mecca and Medina, are the reference point toward which Muslims from all over the world orient themselves physically five times a day during the ritual prayer, in their sleeping position, and in burial. The pilgrimage to Mecca is the ultimate emphasis of the region's centrality and the connection that believers maintain to the Holy Land (Metcalf 1990, 100). Other important centers of the Sunni Muslim world are likewise located in the Arab world, such as old and prestigious Islamic universities, like Umm Al-Qurra University in Mecca, Saudi Arabia, and Al-Azhar University in Cairo, Egypt.[3]

Mona Abaza has argued that the idea of the so-called "Islamic periphery," in differentiation from the "center," implies that "the dissemination of knowledge, religious and secular, has been a one-way relationship," in which the Middle East "seems to play a hegemonic role as a donor of authentic culture and religious supremacy exemplified in a domineering orthodox discourse while Southeast Asians remain cast as its syncretistic recipients" (Abaza 2007, 427). Abaza criticizes that Middle Eastern Muslims, as well as Western scientists, do not attribute to Southeast Asian Muslims a creative potential (Abaza 2007, 421). However, besides empirical evidence that in some cases there has been mutual exchange between Arabs and Indonesians (see Abaza 2011; Azra 2004), the persistent perception is epitomized by the image of a one-way relationship. While many Muslims in Southeast Asia highly value Arabic language and Arabic intellectual production, hardly any note is taken of Southeast Asian Muslim scholarship in the Middle East, and the "Islamic centers perpetuate an Arabic-centric vision towards the peripheries" (Abaza 2007, 427). As a result of the ideas of "center" and "periphery," many scientists attribute binary oppositions to the regions.

Abaza observes that the Middle East is associated with orthodoxy, the harsh and arid climate of the desert, with high culture, textual and scriptural knowledge, *ulama*, and with Azhar-Wahhabi-Saudi trained scholars with Arab habitus, dress and lifestyle and the primacy of Arabic language. Southeast Asia, in contrast, is associated with heterodoxy, rainy weather, monsoon, prolific soil, popular Islam, laxity, local and oral traditions (*adat*), syncretism, Sufi culture (perceived as low culture), prayers in local language (Bahasa Indonesia), and the perception of Arabic language as magical (Abaza 2007, 428). However, as Abaza argues, these dualisms can be found *within* every Muslim society and are the subject of controversy in domestic negotiations between competing Muslim groups. As an example, in Indonesia these binary oppositions are adduced as distinction criteria between the so-called *abangan* Muslims, nominal Muslims with a strong element of Sufi tradition, and the *santri*, more orthodox ones (ibid. 428).[4]

This exemplifies that boundaries between center and periphery, or authenticity and deviations, apply to different levels and are prevalent in domestic as well as international contestations between different Islamic traditions. Regarding points of orientation in Indonesians' engagement with the Arab world, there are several historical examples of a multiplicity of centers and reference points, which are not at all only located outside Indonesia but often combine elements from outside and inside Indonesia.

A prominent example of this is the legend of the nine saints, the Wali Songo, who are seen as bearers of Islam and who came from various cultural backgrounds. In missionary activities, the Wali Songo combined their religious and cultural backgrounds from India, Persia, China, and the Hadhramaut in today's Yemen with the Hindu-Buddhist heritage of precolonial Mandala states. These states were in trade relationships with Arab, Chinese, and Portuguese traders from the fourteenth century onward (Azra 2004; Chaudhuri 2007; Reid 1988).[5] In addition to trade, systematic Islamization apparently came not only through the Wali Songo but also from other religious leaders and merchants from Bengal, Coromandel, Gujarat, and from Persians and Kurds (van Bruinessen 1987, 43; von der Mehden 1993, 1).

Orthodoxy and Heterodoxy

The influence of diverse Islamic traditions from different parts of the world and differing incorporations into indigenous lifeworlds in the archipelago gave rise to various streams of Islam. As Abaza (2007) has argued, both orthodoxy and heterodoxy characterized Indonesian ways of being Muslim. These differing Islamic traditions have coexisted in the archipelago since the first encounters with Islam and neither can be regarded as more original to Indonesia than the other. Nevertheless, the influence of Arab traders is described as a rather orthodox, scriptural tradition of Islam known as *santri Islam*, the scholarly Islam, or *Islam pesisir*, the Islam of the coastal regions with trade centers. Sometimes this form of Islam is referred to as *Islam Arab*, taking into consideration its roots in the Arabic tradition of Islam, even though it was "filtered through India" (von der Mehden 1993, 2). The different character of Islamization in coastal regions and inland is considered a major distinction criterion between Islamic streams in Indonesia in this period.[6] The mystic Sufi tradition of Islam that was apparently more prevalent inland is associated with the above-mentioned Wali Songo, who are honored as initiators of a distinctive Javanese version of Islam. Today their heritage is promoted by Nahdlatul Ulama (NU), Indonesia's largest Muslim organization, as *the* authentic Indonesian Islamic tradition in the discourse on Islam Nusantara, the Islam of the archipelago (see below). However, as much as the Wali Songo are associated with local authenticity, they are perceived and honored as foreigners.

The Arabness and the Javaneseness of the Wali Songo

Accounts of the origin of the Wali Songo vary. While some sources stress their descent from the Prophet Muhammad himself, others suggest that only one of the nine *wali*, namely Maulana Maghribi (born 1419 CE), also known as Sunan Giri, was actually an Arab (Laffan 2011, 8). However, as his name suggests, he was not from the Arabian "heartland" of Islam but from the Maghrib (North Africa). Besides Arabia, the origins of the wali, some of whom were born in Java, have been traced to India, Persia, and China. The location of Southeast Asia on the trading routes between Arabia, India and China explains the influence of Chinese Muslims as there was an established Muslim presence in Canton from the ninth century onward (Laffan 2003, 12). Some Javanese narratives about Maulana Maghribi and the other wali suggest that they relied on trade links with China. Zheng He (1371–1433), a Ming admiral, stands out as a potentially influential religious scholar in the tradition of the Hanafi school of thought, who is sometimes considered to have been the driving force of Islamization in Java, potentially predating the mission of the Wali Songo (Laffan 2011, 8).[7] While some of my research participants emphasized the Asian nature of Islam in Southeast Asia, others lamented the Sinicization of the history of the Islamization of Indonesia and stressed the Arabness of the Wali Songo. This indicates that references to the past are filtered in contestations over the originality of contemporary religious worldviews and practices in which Arabness, as well as Asianness and, moreover, Javanesesness, are prominent labels, guiding people in their lifestyle choices.

Regardless of the actual origin of the Wali Songo and their role as "Arab adventurers or as handlers of Chinese business" (Laffan 2011, 9), they are certainly considered to be the founding fathers of *Islam Jawa*, Javanese Islam, especially because of their use of extant cultural traditions, such as the wayang shadow puppet play and the *gamelan* percussion orchestra, to transmit their message (Woodward 2011, 180). They are perceived as malleable, syncretistic, adopting Hindu and Buddhist cultural elements, as multivoiced, and are celebrated as saints, healers, and magicians (Geertz 1968, 12; Laffan 2011, 8). Their graves, which are mainly located on the northern coast of Java and in East Java, are popular destinations for ziarah, local pilgrimage (Ziemek 1983, 229; Mas'ud 2006, 222). Pilgrimage to these tombs is booming and sometimes it is attached to, or even performed instead of, the pilgrimage to Mecca (Quinn 2004, 2008).

The Wali Songo heritage and Javanese traditions constitute ideas about Java as the center of not only the Muslim world but of the world in general. A legend transmitted by Clifford Geertz about one of the wayang figures, the clown Semar, illustrates this:

> Nabi (i.e., Prophet) Adam married Babu Kawa (Eve) and had children Nabi Sis and Sajang Sis (Semar). Nabi Sis gave birth to all the Prophets, such as Nabi Ibrahim (Abraham), Nabi Nur (Noah), Nabi Muhammad, and Nabi Isa (Jesus); and the various Western peoples descended from their nabis (The Arabs from Muhammad, the Dutch from Jesus, and so on). Semar gave birth to the Hindus and the Javanese. Thus all people are the same and all religions are the same. (Geertz 1976, 276, translations in original)

Apart from the idea that the Javanese figures Nabi Sis and Semar are the ancestors of all world religions, this legend interestingly subsumes Arabs and Europeans under the same category as "various Western peoples," whereas Javanese people are seen as being closer to Hindus. This is an example of the filtering within subjective systems of knowledge and situated representations. Apparently, the people who recounted this legend to Geertz referred to a context in which the Javanese tried to make sense of the encounter with foreigners who geographically came from the west of the archipelago: most prominently the Dutch, as the colonial authority, and Arab traders. Mona Abaza (2011) shows that interestingly, some Middle Eastern intellectuals, like Taha Husayn, have also expressed that Arab civilization, or specifically Egyptian culture, is closer to the West rather than the East or Orient.[8]

In any case, Indonesian conceptions of spirituality do relate to metaphysical experiences with the Arab world, involving encounters with the Prophet Muhammad. However, as in the example of the wayang figures, indigenous interpretations of how and where these encounters took place challenge the Eurocentric or Arabcentric mainstream narratives about the history of Islam. Another heroic figure in Java, King Merah Silu, "dreamt that the Prophet had spat in his mouth, thus enabling him to recite the Qur'an upon waking" (Laffan 2011, 5). Thus, before moving physically to Mecca, there was already a spiritual ownership of this meaningful place and culture in Indonesia. The spiritual significance of Arabic and the miraculous powers ascribed to it are evident in these accounts. This might be the reason why historical figures who Islamized Southeast Asia are sometimes referred to as "Arab" in a spiritual sense and can be seen as being essentially Javanese at the same time. In this regard "Arab" is a reference to an attachment to the Holy Land of Islam as a spiritual concept, regardless of geographic origin.

Indonesian Communities in Cairo and Mecca

Apart from the spiritual and mystical connections to the Holy Land and the existence of local religious centers, Southeast Asians began to move to the Middle East physically as well. The South-South transregional linkages between Southeast Asia and the Middle East were a mixture of spiritual endeavors and educational, economic, and political aspirations. The hajj served as a primary trigger for people to undergo the arduous journey across the Indian Ocean.[9] During the fifteenth century, when pilgrimages from Indonesia to the Hejaz started, the voyage was more of an individual endeavor, reserved to those who could afford the journey and who organized it by themselves (Tagliacozzo 2013, 7). Due to the distance involved, the first people traveling from Indonesia to the Hejaz in order to do the pilgrimage stayed there for longer periods of time, studying in the Muslim student circles in the region (Tagliacozzo 2013, 34). Bowen (2008) speaks of "intellectual pilgrimages" (ibid., 33) and "study pilgrimages" (ibid., 34) in this regard. Apparently, some Muslims from the Indonesian archipelago became permanent residents in the Middle East as religious teachers. Azra describes the community of *ulama* in the *haramayn* region (the region of the two holy mosques) in the sixteenth and seventeenth centuries as an international community of fruitful cross-cultural exchange (Azra 2001, 87). However, he also concedes that apart from exchange with fellow *ulama* from other places, the Malay *ulama's* audience were pilgrims from their homelands and not an international or Arab audience. Some of these pilgrims likewise became teachers back in the Malay world and corresponded with their teachers in the Hejaz when they experienced problems while teaching in their local home communities. The provision of guidance through these *ulama* networks stands out as a characteristic feature of international Islamic education during these times (Azra 2001, 111).

In the eyes of the Arab people, the Malay travelers were a rather homogenous group. Among other things, the homogenizing label jawi, under which all Southeast Asians were subsumed by the Arabs, is evidence of this (Abaza 2004, 3; Laffan 2011, 4; Laffan 2003, 13). Their origin was referred to as "lands below the winds" (Laffan 2003; Reid 1988), representing them as arbitrary dots of land (islands), that are swept by monsoons, as can be seen in early maps like those of al-Idrisi (Laffan 2003, 11). From the seventeenth century onward the growing number of jawi travelers mainly consisted of scholars who established scholarly networks centered in Mecca, Medina, Yemen, and later, also in Cairo (Abaza 1991, 1993, 1994, 2003; Bowen 2008; Laffan 2004; Roff 1970; Tagliacozzo 2009; van Bruinessen 2012, 122).

During the period of Ottoman influence in the Hejaz, jawi travelers came into contact with Turks and Kurds who practiced Islam in the Hanafi tradition (van Bruinessen 1987). Besides this, Sufi orders like the Qadiryya and Naqshbandiyya exerted a profound influence on jawi journeyers to Arabia, which is reflected in the establishment of local branches of these orders from the mid-1880s in Central and West Java and West and North Sumatra (van Bruinessen 1990).

At the end of the eighteenth century, Wahhabi influence became more dominant on the Arabian Peninsula, and the power struggles in the Middle East, which broke out in the Saudi-Ottoman war in 1814 along with other conflicts, influenced the jawi in the region and had an effect on the diversification of Islamic streams in the Indonesian archipelago, as can be seen in the Padri movement in West Sumatra that propagated Wahhabism between 1807 and 1832 (Laffan 2003, 30). Besides direct interconnections between Southeast Asia and the Middle East, there was indirect interaction through the role of Europeans and East Asians in the course of their expeditions, trade, colonization and war.[10] In Indonesia, the Dutch colonial administration significantly framed the relationship between Indonesia and the Middle East through classification and regulation, which indicates how dependency on a superior counterpart determines adherence to guiding factors. During colonialism, the movement of jawi to the Middle East became more common and simultaneously more controlled and channeled.

Colonial Control of Orientations toward the Middle East

In the Dutch East Indies (1800–1945),[11] the colonial administrators were particularly concerned about the ideological side effects of Indonesians' journeys to the Middle East, and after their strategy of restricting physical and ideological orientation toward the Hejaz had failed, they began to sponsor and thereby utilize it as a means by which to control the travelers' activities abroad and to make economic profit from them (Tagliacozzo 2013, 7; von der Mehden 1993, 3). This case is yet another example of the interdependent relationships of guidance and the interest in extracting capital from mobility.

The Dutch management of the hajj and the invention of the steamship in the nineteenth century transformed the hajj into a mass travel event (Bianchi 2004, 49; Tagliacozzo 2013, 7). The annual number of pilgrims increased from two thousand in the mid-nineteenth century to eleven thousand by the end of the century (von der Mehden 1993, 3). The Dutch noted that the performance of the hajj gave local Muslim leaders significant symbolic power. Similarly to the hajji,[12] which is a title of honor for hajj returnees who thereby have a connection to the Holy Land, persons of Arab descent were honored because of their "ability to speak Arabic, and the holy place from which they came" (ibid., 4). This indicates the symbolic capital that was attributed to Arabness and the economic capital that the Dutch extracted from the travels.[13] The Dutch classification of different societal groups residing in the Dutch East Indies enforced the perceived superiority of persons of Arab descent and at the same time this colonial strategy of "divide and rule" might have fueled ambiguous feelings toward the Hadhrami, the Arab diaspora community in Indonesia. According to the colonial differentiation between "Europeans and their Christian allies, the Foreign Orientals (*vreemde oosterlingen*) and natives," indigenous Muslims were the absolute underclass (Laffan 2003, 45, emphasis in original).[14]

Concerning the intertwinement of connections to the Middle East and political movements, it appears to be especially noteworthy that while in the late nineteenth century Pan-Islamic political movements were dominated by the Hadhrami, as well as by Turks residing in the Dutch East Indies, from the turn of the century onward, indigenous nationalists led the movement (von der Mehden 1993, 8).[15] Their spatial movement toward the Holy Land of Islam became intertwined with political movements from the 1920s onward—at least from the perspective of the Dutch, who were especially concerned about these movements. As indicated in the introduction, such fears can motivate endeavors to establish guidance and control. For Indonesians, on the contrary, there were ways to circumvent Dutch control.

Indonesian residents in the Middle East formed inter-Indonesian political circles whose thoughts traveled back to the archipelago through people or writings, such as the monthly journal *Seruan Aazhar* (Call of Azhar). These "political remittances" mobilized their home community to fight for independence (Bowen 2008, 36; Laffan 2003, 213; Roff 1970, 73; von der Mehden 1993, 5).

Anxiety about subversive powers being strengthened by these study circles and returning pilgrims was termed *hajiphobia* in the Dutch administration (von der Mehden 1993, 3), even though, as von der Mehden argues (1993, 11), the actual political influence of the hajj returnees was overestimated. Because of such anxieties the Dutch orientalist Christiaan Snouck Hurgronje was appointed to report on "whether Southeast Asian *Hajjis* constituted a danger for the Dutch East Indies" (Abaza 2007, 423; emphasis in original).[16] Snouck Hurgronje (1857–1936) on his part propagated a so-called "Islamic policy." On the one hand, he doubted that pilgrims from the Dutch East Indies would be fanatical enemies of the government (Tagliacozzo 2013, 157), while on the other hand he indicated that some *hajjis* were attracted to Pan-Islamic nationalist ideas and that the pilgrimage was transferring not only religious but also militant ideas and thus inspiring independence movements (Abaza 2007, 424; Tagliacozzo 2013, 157).[17] While previously the Dutch had tried to reduce the numbers of pilgrims in 1825, Snouck Hurgronje argued that by supporting and managing the hajj, the Dutch could better control the pilgrims and establish diplomatic relations and espionage in Mecca. As a result, the Netherlands became the first non-Muslim country to have a hajj bureau in Jeddah (Bianchi 2004, 43).

Dutch control of and business involvement with the movement toward the Middle East, as well as the political agitation of the hajj returnees, reveals the intertwinement of competing forms of guidance and of sacred and profane aspects in the context of the hajj (Tagliacozzo 2013, 195). Finally, the movement to the Middle East and Pan-Islamic independence ideologies contributed to the independence of the Indonesian people from the Dutch. Apart from the amalgamation of religious and political education in the Middle East, the period between World War I and World War II was characterized by the overall bureaucratization of encounters with the Arab world and the institutionalization of and growing tensions between different streams of Islam—both in the Middle East and in the archipelago.

Anticolonial Movements and Competing Streams of Islam

While the Dutch, like the Arabs, considered Southeast Asian travelers a rather homogenous group, there is historical evidence of frictions within the group of Southeast Asians in Mecca, Medina, and Cairo, especially since the early twentieth century. In his comprehensive analysis of the social transformative character of jawi journeys to and residence in the Middle East, and their significance for the establishment of Islamic nationhood in colonial times, Michael Laffan (2003,

11–36) differentiates between an *ecumene*, as a heterogeneous community of jawi in Mecca who established a heightened sense of their "situational ethnicity" due to their experience of diaspora, especially prevalent in the nineteenth century, and the establishment of the idea of an Indonesian national entity that emerged in the early twentieth century in Cairo (ibid., 232).

Snouck Hurgronje reported that the jawi in Mecca remained much among themselves because of a kind of inferiority complex. Laffan (2003) argues that "through the communitas engendered by Jawi ecumenism in Mecca, some Jawa were increasingly sensitized to their shared characteristics" (ibid., 75, emphasis in original). Due to experiences of alterity, the jawi identified as a community, yet without blurring ethnic differences (ibid., 233).[18] The larger the jawi community grew, the more persons embraced their ethnic rules and customs, gathering around local guides (Laffan 2003, 75). Apparently, joint residence abroad with other jawi had a bonding effect, or what Bowen (2008, 35) calls a "cohort effect," for scholars who studied together. These ecumenical networks valued the Arab world as their spiritual heart, but they found different meanings in this spiritual center, depending on religious leaders who emphasized alterity on different levels, namely the local ethnic identity, the jawi joint identity, and the overarching Muslim identity (Laffan 2003, 232). Their utmost aim was the Islamization of their home community.[19] These Muslims were later referred to as *kaum tua*, meaning the "old clan," also referred to as traditionalists, as a stream of Indonesian Islam. In contrast, the Cairene community of Muslims who came from the Dutch East Indies was referred to as the "younger clan," the *kaum muda* and was more homogenous, united by the idea of an independent Indonesia (Laffan 2003, 233). The kaum muda were inspired by reformist thinkers in Egypt like Rashid Rida and Muhammad Abduh (Laffan 2003, 234; van Bruinessen 2013c, 50) and criticized the centrality of religious leaders in the older clan, promoting the religious learnedness of individuals. Moreover, they were strong spokespersons of independence, which was reflected in the establishment of the organizations Sarekat Islam and Muhammadiyah (Laffan 2003, 167; von der Mehden 1993, 10). The trade union Sarekat Islam, which was founded on the initiative of the hajj returnee Samanhudi in 1912 in Surakarta, became an important player in the independence movement (Laffan 2003, 167) and intersected with the reformist organization Muhammadiyah that was founded by Ahmad Dahlan in Yogyakarta, also in 1912 (ibid., 168). Through these organizations, modernist/reformist interpretations of Islam came to Indonesia at the beginning of the twentieth century (Ricklefs 2008, 120).[20]

The formation of anticolonial movements triggered reorientations within the kaum tua as well. One of the most important jawi religious leaders of this time, Agoes Salim, apparently began to consider Mecca and Cairo as secondary centers only, as he advised a fellow believer that although Mecca and Cairo were "suited for worship" one should rather seek science and wisdom in schools back home (Steenbrink 1994, 131, in Laffan 2003, 233). This inspired adherents of the kaum tua to establish their own organizations, not least as a statement against the Wahhabi domination of Mecca. Looking at this historical event through the lens of Graeber's theory on interpretative labor, the situation could be seen in terms of Indonesians being in a potentially underprivileged, inferior position—both against Arab counterparts and Dutch colonial authorities—from which they established an interpretative surplus, questioning their superiors' views of the world and, in this case, interpretation of Islam. As a result of these developments, in 1926 the Muslim umbrella organization Nahdlatul Ulama (NU) was founded by Hasyim Asy'ari in Jombang (van Bruinessen 2013c, 50).

The kaum muda and the kaum tua, represented by the organizations Muhammadiyah and NU, have continued to argue about the "right" interpretation of Islam up to the present day. Interestingly, even though the kaum tua emphasized the importance of traveling to the region of Islam's origin in the nineteenth century, in fact still valuing this connection highly today, and though the kaum muda were known to be more nationalist-oriented in the early twentieth century, the kaum tua referred to the kaum muda as "Mecca people," "Arabs," or even "Wahhabis" (Laffan 2003, 236–37). This divide was probably due to the traditionalists' emphasis on local ethnicity, while the modernists emphasized the importance of studying Arabic and sought to establish Arabic as a uniting Pan-Islamic language (ibid., 236–37), this being perceived as Arabcentric (ibid., 236).[21] In any case, the classification of these streams of Islam compounds the confusion caused by earlier ideological distinctions concerning the meaning of the label "Arab," as the above-mentioned differentiation between coastal Islam as Islam Arab and inland Islam as Islam Jawa is not congruent with later labels of "local" and "Arab" attributed to traditionalist and modernist streams. Martin van Bruinessen shows that the term *Arabization* is used with great inconsistency, as the potential Arabness of the reformists, represented by Muhammadiyah, is oriented toward reformist thinkers in Egypt, while the potential anti-Arabness of the traditionalists, represented by Nahdlatul Ulama, seeks to oppose Wahhabism from Saudi Arabia (van Bruinessen 2015, 61–85), thus referring to two very different Arab traditions of Islam.

The controversy about Arabness as a defining feature and orientation point of authentic Islam remains topical today. Among others, traditionalists keep accusing modernists of carrying out an "Arabization" of Indonesia. Yet it must be said that today more players engage in this controversy and NU and Muhammadiyah sometimes oppose new conservative streams together or keep competing with each other, while simultaneously there are deep frictions within the two large mainline organizations. NU has more than 40 million members (Nahdlatul Ulama 2019) and Muhammadiyah has around 30 million members (Muhammadiyah 2019), which makes them the largest Muslim organizations in the world.

The proliferation of different streams of Islam and their institutionalization established a plurality and competition of different narratives, guiding religious leaders and institutions. The element of competition emerges as a characteristic feature in relationships of guidance. Ambivalent labels like "Arab" or "conservative" are used to denounce or affirm within this competition.

Reorientation toward Asia?

These competing tendencies were overshadowed by the Japanese attempt to (re)orient Indonesians toward Asia rather than the Arab world during their occupation of Indonesia in World War II. In their endeavor to make Islam "'Asian-centered' and to substitute the 'Greater East Asian Co-Prosperity Sphere' for Pan-Islam" (von der Mehden 1993, 86), they banned the teaching of Arabic language and promoted the use of vernacular languages in prayer. Even though contact with the Middle East was limited in the postwar years due to domestic conflicts (von der Mehden 1993, 86), all in all experiences in the Middle East had a constitutive effect on Indonesia's independence movement, even though the modernists failed in their attempt to establish an Islamic constitution in Indonesia.[22] Although Sukarno, the first president of independent Indonesia, favored Pan-Islamic movements as part of the anticolonial, nonbloc alliance, he was mainly supported by national and communist activists, and thus political Islam lost its influence.

Centralization and Bureaucratization in Independent Indonesia

Although anticolonial Pan-Islamic ideas exerted some influence during the independence movement and in the early years of the young nation-state, the notion that Indonesians should look to the Middle East for ideas lost significance as the Communist Party gained greater power, and later as the alignment with Western countries, in particular the United States, became popular during the Cold War. Concomitantly the number of people traveling to the Middle East decreased.

Guided Democracy

Sukarno's attempt to harmonize national, religious, and communist ideologies, which he famously voiced in his concept of NASAKOM, failed in 1957 when he introduced "Guided Democracy" in order to realize his idea of the Indonesian nation-state.[23] While the Sukarno administration was struggling to "guide" the nation into a prospering democracy, mobility toward the Middle East continued to be guided by the Dutch, who owned the majority of available ships (Tagliacozzo 2013, 206). Because of shortcomings in governmental capabilities, during that time hajj management was a private business, in which the Dutch, small private firms, and the large Islamic organizations Nahdlatul Ulama and Muhammadiyah played leading roles. However, due to a lack of logistic guidance, shortages of foreign exchange, and confrontations between Muslim groups, between 1950 and 1968 the number of Indonesian pilgrims hardly grew at all and never exceeded fifteen thousand pilgrims per year, the lowest hajj participation rate worldwide at that time, far lower than neighboring countries including Thailand and the Philippines, where Muslims are a minority (Bianchi 2004, 180). The poverty and uncertainty of wartime allowed the suggestion that going abroad for the hajj was not feasible practically and not attractive in terms of its social meaning. In fact, the hajj was considered to be "extravagant religious tourism" (Bianchi 2004, 179). Thus pilgrims could hardly extract prestigious social and cultural capital from the pilgrimage.

Autocratic Vacillation between the West and Islam

After the attempted coup and its bloody aftermath in 1965 and 1966, in which an estimated 1 million alleged communists and ethnic Chinese were killed, Sukarno's Guided Democracy was replaced by the New Order of General Suharto. Administratively, the Suharto regime reclaimed the authority to govern the pilgrimage affairs that since 1968 had been under the control of the Ministry of Religious Affairs, making the state the main provider of transport, lodgings, and information, and controlling the millions of dollars for hajj services (Bianchi 2004, 180). The number of Indonesians traveling to the Middle East slowly began to increase. However, in Suharto's Western-oriented autocracy, religious activities were firmly controlled and political Islam was restricted. Taking control of hajj management was also a strategy to undermine NU influence in Indonesia. In fact, Suharto even deprived NU of a symbolic attachment to the hajj when he forced NU's political branch, the party Partai Persatuan Pembangunan (PPP, United Development Party) to replace the Ka'aba as their party logo with a five-pointed star (Bianchi 2004, 209). This restrictive atmosphere was probably the reason why hajj participation rates stagnated and political Islam, as well as ideological orientation toward the Middle East, disappeared from the public sphere.

Only in the mid-1980s when Suharto's power began to crumble did hajj participation rates increase again. This can be seen in conjunction with Suharto's strategy to gain the support of Islamic groups (Bianchi 2004, 209). According to Robert Bianchi, Suharto identified the state more and more with the hajj, and "most desperately, with himself" (Bianchi 2004, 209), staging his own hajj in 1991 as a "warm-up for the campaign trail" (ibid., 176). In the 1990s, along with the growing prosperity of Muslim middle classes and the Islamization of the Suharto government, hajj participation rates exploded, becoming the largest in the world (Bianchi 2004, 184), and they have remained so ever since. While in the 1950s 117 pilgrims per million Indonesian Muslims accomplished the hajj, during the 1990s it was 965 pilgrims per million Muslims (Bianchi 2004, 185). The most remarkable feature of Indonesian mobility toward the Middle East during the Suharto era was the massive bureaucratization of the religion (Evers 1987) and the government's control of the hajj, which continue today (see Bianchi 2015, 65–84). Hooker argues that Indonesian Muslims must surrender to the state in order to perform the hajj and thereby the event becomes an encounter with the nation-state (Hooker 2008, 206).

Apart from the government's investment in the pilgrimage, the Suharto administration also started to recruit Indonesian labor migrants, mainly women, as domestic servants for the Gulf States in the 1980s. Due to crumbling support from the West, Suharto began to lean toward the Middle East, strengthening bilateral ties and discovering labor migration as a potential trigger for economic development, in line with the development paradigm during that time. While Indonesian mobility toward the Middle East had been intertwined with trade and labor as well as education, since the 1980s these spheres have become increasingly separated and bureaucratized. Moreover, female labor migration was a new element in the relationship between Indonesia and the Middle East. However, while first celebrated as a development trigger, labor migration came to be seen in an increasingly negative light. The women being recruited as national foreign exchange heroes and lured into labor migration with promises of religious fulfilment often experienced the Arab world not so much as a Holy Land but as a place of hardship, exploitation, and injustice.

Suharto's turn from the West to an Islamic strategy shows how those who guide—like the leading regime—engage in a swapping of guiding reference points and allies, considering which one will be more profitable or switching from one point of orientation (e.g., cooperation with Western governments like the US government) to alternative ones (e.g., cooperation with Arab countries).

Migration to and Remittances from the Middle East

The relevance of remittances is an example of the variations in adherence to guidance and the different socioeconomic effects of spatial mobility. Labor migration, as a new form of Indonesian mobility to Arab countries, was from its beginnings in the 1980s regulated by the state and inspired by modernization theories that saw remittances as enhancing the local economy.

However, as I have mentioned in the introduction, financial remittances have *not* enhanced sustainable growth and economic development but are spent on daily necessities (IOM 2010), which is contrary to the intended guidance provided by the government and nongovernmental organizations.[24] Adams and Cuecuecha (2010) explain for Indonesia that remittances have a beneficial effect on poverty reduction but lift households just above the poverty line, rather than actually enhancing development. Additional income is mainly spent on food and not on investment in human or physical capital because many remittance-receiving households are too poor to go beyond basic needs.

Nevertheless, since the 1980s the Indonesian government has continued to support international labor migration in the interest of financial remittances that are meant to enhance the economy (Silvey 2006). As a result, in Indonesia as well as in many other developing and newly industrialized countries, there are discourses and bureaucratic structures that are meant to provide guidance for the sustainable usage of remittances, and labor migrants and their families are either celebrated as foreign exchange heroes or criticized as selfish and status-hungry consumers (Chan 2014; 2015; Silvey 2006). In my analysis of what labor migrants in Indonesia make of their journeys to the Middle East, I show that there is significant deviation from the guidance on how to invest financial remittances and the relevance of other guiding factors, like the local communities' interests and public pronouncements about making the "right" investments. Moreover, financial remittances have had a remarkable impact on family structures. For instance, female labor migrants in Indonesia have become the main breadwinners for their families, which has effected gender roles and marriages (see Dinkelaker and Grossmann 2010). The sending of financial remittances strengthens the migrants' attachment to their home community and responsibility for their families, as remittances are "part of an intertemporal, mutually beneficial contractual arrangement between migrant and home" (Lucas and Stark 1985, 904). In this context, labor migrants are sometimes acknowledged as the carers of their families and of the nation (see Silvey 2006). Moreover, the consumption desires of labor migrants, especially those desires that diverge from societally desirable investments, reflect labor migrants' wishes to partake of middle-class lifestyles (see Lindquist 2009), which serves as another pull-factor or guiding feature. This is one a reason why remittances are often spent on prestigious consumer goods like satellite dishes rather than being invested sustainably (Chan 2014, 2015) and why institutional guidance conflicts with personal desires and family commitments.

The communities' expectations, public discourse about appropriate and desirable usage of remittances, and the social responsibilities of labor migrants reveal that the spatial flow of money is guided by both social and normative aspects and "translated" into material and immaterial values that are meaningful in the home context. That this does not always happen smoothly and can entail contradictions in guidance becomes strikingly clear in the analysis of migrants' and pilgrims' "success stories" in chapter 2.

Apart from financial remittances, the transformative effect of social remittances (Levitt 1998), cultural remittances (see Lindquist 2012), political remittances (Rother 2009; Kessler and Rother 2016), and religious remittances (see Johnson and Werbner 2010) are relevant.[25] Derived from the economic concept of remittances, these concepts deal with the mobility, transferal, and transformation of nonmaterial remittances.

Research on political remittances (Kessler and Rother 2016) reveals that the social embeddedness of migration, and migrants' personal backgrounds, and their opportunities to organize their movement are decisive for what they actually "transfer" home. The comparison of different landscapes of political remittances reveals that diverging experiences and personal backgrounds lead to diverging political remittances and a situation where remittances travel not only from destination countries to origin countries but also the other way around.[26]

The historical overview has shown that ideational remittances are not a new phenomenon. Indonesians' historical mobility toward the Arab world is a telling example of this. In the twentieth century, Mecca, Medina, and Cairo became places where Indonesians who resided in these Arab cities could form political movements outside the Dutch colonial sphere of influence. The Middle East became "a hotbed of nationalist fervor" (von der Mehden 1993, 5). Indonesian residents in the Middle East not only exchanged political ideas with Muslims from other places but also formed inter-Indonesian political circles whose outspoken aim was the dissemination of political ideas toward their homeland. The Indonesian community in Cairo formulated these ideas in the *Seruan Aazhar* journal, which was specifically intended to stir political mobilization of the home community and promoted the new idea of an Indonesian nation (Bowen 2008, 36; Laffan 2003, 213; Roff 1970, 73; von der Mehden 1993, 5).

These observations provoke the question of what circumstances determine the different forms of sociocultural and political remittances, or their absence. Given the significance of preconditioning for the traveling of norms, it is necessary to revisit the question of whether the term *remittances* is appropriate for these normative (ex)changes or whether we should rather speak of *normative circulations*.

The historical evolution of these normative circulations reveal the influential predeterminative role of the state. Yet the agency of migrants is obvious in the fact that financial remittances are not used in the way the government intended them to be used. Amitav Acharya argues that local agents actively promote norm diffusion in which they borrow and modify transnational norms in accordance with their preconstructed normative beliefs and practices (Acharya 2004, 270). Acharya states that "many local beliefs are themselves part of a legitimate normative order, which conditions the acceptance of foreign norms" (ibid., 239). This enforces the need to evaluate the conditions under which they establish interpretative skills and modify situated representations in a translational manner.

Contemporary Concerns: Politics and Commerce

In Indonesia's history, spatial mobility has often coincided with sociocultural change: Islam came through trade to the archipelago, the Wali Songo were not only saints but also travelers, independence movements and competing religious groups were inspired by Indonesians who resided abroad. However, the examples also show that all sociocultural changes in the course of transregional mobility happened in close intertwinement with local conditions: the fear of the Dutch colonial administrators, the prestige of returnees in their home communities, ideas of success and social prestige or the decline of movement toward the Arabian Peninsula during the New Order dictatorship. Such local factors determine the impact of Indonesians' encounters with the Arab world. Profit, prospect of extracting financial and sociocultural capital, loyalties and social hierarchies characterize the local guidance of experiences of mobility.

In recent years, three tendencies in the relationship between Indonesia and the Middle East have been crucial: (1) the increasing regulation, bureaucratization, control, and guidance of Indonesians' mobility toward the Middle East; (2) the increase in actors who seek to guide, which goes along with; (3) the democratization of the political system, the marketization of Islamic lifestyles, and the politicization of religious identities.

Islamism and Politics

As I stated in the introduction to this book, the Islamization of Indonesia's public sphere is one of the most significant social changes since the end of the Suharto regime in 1998. For some observers, it seems to be contradictory that increasing Islamization goes hand in hand with the process of democratization and some see increasing conservatism as influenced from the Arabian Peninsula. Martin van Bruinessen (2012, 2013b, 2015) has assessed these claims of Arabization critically, highlighting the above-mentioned differences in various Arab influences and contradictory meanings of the term *Arab* itself. Furthermore, a comprehensive book about sharia laws in Indonesia by Michael Buehler (2016), an edited volume on democracy and Islam in Indonesia by Mirjam Künkler and Alfred Stepan (2015), and the nuanced works of John Sidel (e.g., 2008), John Bowen (2015), Muhammad Wildan (2013), Ahmad Najib Burhani (2013), and Greg Fealy (2004, 2016, 2019) complicate and question simplistic explanations of why there is growing conservatism, or conservatisms, in today's Indonesia. These authors show that conservative Islamization is not a monolithic development, and that there are indeed a large number of competing Muslim actors and interpretations of Islam—including various competing versions of conservatism.

When looking at Islamic organizations, such as the Majelis Ulama Indonesia (MUI) (Ichwan 2013), the mainline organizations Muhammadiya (Burhani 2013), and NU (van Bruinessen 2013c), it is obvious that there are different versions of conservative Islamic practice in today's religious landscape in Indonesia, some of which are puritanical and traditional and a minority which is radical. Increasing Islamization of Indonesia's public sphere results from internal power struggles between liberal, moderate, and puritanical representatives of Muslim organizations. Martin van Bruinessen (2013b, 2) argues that most of the recent developments toward increasing conservatism "appear to have been temporary responses to the tremors of the political landscape rather than indications of a pervasive change of attitude of Indonesia's Muslim majority." Similarly, with regard to violence in the name of Islam, John Sidel (2008, 344) has shown that Islamist violence shifted from local Christian targets to those representing the Western world, following the proclaimed war against terrorism after the September 11 attacks on New York and Washington, DC, and a shrinking political influence of Islamists in Indonesia. Sidel (2008, 345) has argued that Islamist violence of foreign targets "is part of an attempt to restore visibility and viability of Islam at the very moment of its relegation to a minor, compromised role in Indonesian politics."

Furthermore, some of the initiators of Islamic conservatism are politicians from secular political parties. Michael Buehler (2016) has shown how old elites from the New Order regime attempt to remain in power through the support for Islamist movements. Since in the democratic system these elites are now more dependent on mass support and more receptive to pressures from below, their policies coincide with Islamic movements' demands. While Islamist political parties have experienced a decline since 1999, Islamist movements outside the official political sphere do influence politics through pressure on political elites. This has led to the seemingly contradictory situation that primarily secular local governments have issued sharia regulations (Buehler 2016, 2–3). Secular parties, such as GOLKAR, seek to forestall their Islamic rivals and make these parties' election campaign topics their own (see also Ubaidillah 2010). Greg Fealy (2019) described the last elections in 2019 as a "pitched contest between competing forces within Islam," where Prabowo, the competitor to incumbent and reelected president Joko Widodo, more widely known as Jokowi, was backed by "new, trendy forms of Islamic pietism, such as the hijrah movement, a revivalist phenomenon which has drawn in tens of thousands from the young urban middle-classes" and by Islamists such as the vigilante grassroots movement the Islamic Defenders Front (Front Pembela Islam, FPI). None of these groups is organized as a political party, and yet their recent influence on political agendas is immense.

The most obvious example of this is the "Ahok case." In 2016, the then-governor of Jakarta, who is of Chinese ethnicity and a Christian, Basuki Tjahaja Purnama, better known as Ahok, was accused of blasphemy due to a reference he made to a Qur'anic verse. On September 27, 2016, Ahok referred to Surat al-Maidah, verse 51, which speaks about the guidance of Allah and advises Muslims not to take Jews and Christians as allies. Ahok hinted at potential misuse of Qur'anic verses to mobilize people not to vote for a non-Muslim leader like himself. A few days later, a slightly modified video of the speech was systematically disseminated over online social media by Ahok's opponents, leading to accusations of blasphemy from Muslim organizations including the Indonesian Ulama Council (Majelis Ulama Indonesia, MUI), which issued a fatwa against Ahok. Out of this incident an alliance of various Muslim organizations formed the so-called National Movement to Defend the MUI Fatwa (Gerakan Nasional Pengawal Fatwa-MUI), with Habib Rizieq Syihab from the FPI as its key figure. This movement organized protests against Ahok under the slogan "Aksi Bela Islam" (Islam Defense Action). The level of participation in these *Aksi Bela Islam* protests grew rapidly, with a few thousand participants in the first demonstration on October 14, 2016, an estimated 300,000 participants on November 4, 2016, and about 750,000 on December 2, 2016. After the third rally on December 2, the trial against Ahok began and on May 9, 2017, he was sentenced to two years in prison (IPAC 2018, 2, 3). In reference to the protests on December 2, the alliance of Islamic organizations is referred to as the 212 Movement and follow-up demonstrations that have been taking place until the present day are usually advertised with a three-digit number for the date of the demonstration. Even though the Aksi Bela Islam demonstrations continued and gained new popularity during the presidential elections in 2019, the initial alliance fell apart. Observers from the Institute for Policy Analysis and Conflict recapitulate:

> The Islamist alliance that brought down the Jakarta governor in 2016 has broken up but it has made a major mark on Indonesian politics in two ways. It has left many politicians convinced that they need conservative Muslim support to win elections, and it has convinced many Islamists that they can achieve their social and political goals by working through Indonesia's democratic system. Still, the disunity in Islamist ranks suggests that hardliners may be a less potent force than is sometimes feared. (IPAC 2018, 1)

In the course of these events, Muslim parties and organizations such as the PKS (Partai Keadilan Sejahtera/Prosperous Justice Party), HTI (Ḥizb at-Taḥrīr Indonesia/Party of Liberation Indonesia), and FPI have enjoyed increasing popularity even though in elections Islamist parties have not experienced vote gains. Their leading figures, such as Habib Rizieq, perform in Arab attire—a style that many of their followers adopt—and relate to what they refer to as Muslim brothers and sisters around the world. And yet what some observers see as an overall conservative turn, or "Arabization," within Indonesian society can be evaluated in more nuanced ways as a phenomena of clientelism, elite contestation, and complex internal power struggles (see among others Buehler 2016; Künkler and Stepan 2015; Sidel 2008; van Bruinessen 2013c; Wildan 2013).

My study complements these observations on Islam and politics by adding insights on how ordinary Indonesians relate to these political negotiations. I shall show that clientelism not only determines political decisions but also affects the everyday lives of Indonesians. Yet, different from the manifestation of Islamist agendas in laws and policies, the negotiations on the ground are more multifarious. One of the few studies which explores the situation on the ground is David Kloos's (2017) analysis of Muslim identity making in Aceh, a region on the northern edge of the island of Sumatra that is famous for its sharia regulations. Kloos shows that Acehnese Muslims deal in ambivalent and diverse ways with Islamic regulations, finding individual answers to what it means to be ethically good people or moral Muslims. Their responses to public controversies are marked by personal fears of failure and ambitions to become morally good Muslims.

Similarly, migrants and pilgrims with whom I researched related to various local reference points and structures that turn out to be more relevant than ideological questions. State guidance often happens in a "state in society" (Migdal 2001) constellation, where the state acts through semiofficial intermediaries and is thus embedded in society through clientelism (see van Klinken and Barker

2009). Trust and loyalty, emotive bonds, neighborhood alliances, and family relationships often carry much more weight than official regulations, and local social values are more meaningful to migrants and pilgrims than Islamist agitators' ideological agendas.

Besides the observations of Islamists' influence in politics and competition to access the symbolic capital of "Islam," there are also observations of Indonesian peoples' interest in unpolitical forms of Islamic traditions. Upwardly mobile middle classes are often not interested in political Islam but in Islamic-styled fashion, wellness, healthcare, finance, entertainment, business training, self-help groups, meditation, and spiritual therapy (van Bruinessen 2013d, 225). Their lifestyles are seen as being beyond Islamism.

Post-Islamism

One of my research participants from Nahdlatul Ulama claimed that people followed Islamist movements because they teach religion in easily digestible Twitter messages. He further argued that this type of "fast-food-religiosity" has little impact as people "tweet and go to the mall" without serious political follow-up. In her opinion, capitalist Islamic religiosity is the dominating feature of today's Islamic traditions and lifestyles in Indonesia. This corresponds with the insights from studies on Islam and consumerism in Indonesia (see, among others, Abaza 2004; Fealy 2008; Fealy and White 2008b; Heryanto 2008a, 2011, 2014a, 2014b; Hew 2012; Hoesterey 2012; Jones 2010; Muzakki 2012; Rudnyckyj 2009, 2010; Sutton 2011; Weintraub 2011b).[27] Borrowing the term *post-Islamism* from Asef Bayat (2007), Ariel Heryanto (2014a) argues that contemporary religious piety among ordinary Indonesians, as a new middle-class lifestyle in Indonesia, can be seen as a fusion of Islamic religiosity and individual choice, entertainment, freedom, and ideas of modernity that are relatively nonpolitical (Heryanto 2014a, 142–43).

Islamism and post-Islamism are apparently two parallel developments in Indonesia. Using terms like *conservatism*, *Salafism*, or *Arabness* in a homogenizing manner disguises the ambivalent and diverse Islamization trends. As an example, the new middle-class lifestyles, as well as ideological convictions like Wahhabism, are likewise labeled as "Arab" in emic Indonesian and international discourses, even though the two do not go hand in hand and do not necessarily have anything to do with Arab culture. A popular Arab-style headscarf fashion does not allow a conclusion about its owners' or its designers' ideological views. As Hew (2012, 179) has shown for Chinese cultural markers, popularized outward appearance must be seen as a "symbolic commodity" rather than an ideological statement.

In fact, among many fashionable middle-class Muslims there is a widespread perception that the "ills of Islam," like violence, terrorism, and radicalization, come from outside Southeast Asia. Miichi and Farouk (2015, 1) argue that some Muslims in Southeast Asia "warned of the influences of transnational Islamic movements." In chapter 3 I suggest that globalized Islamophobia manifests as "Arab-phobia" among some Indonesians.

This Arab-phobia is evident in the popularly voiced propagations of an "Islam of the Archipelago" (Islam Nusantara), as an international role model of a peaceful, democratic, and pluralist Islamic tradition, in which Arabness is demonized (see Lücking 2016). Strikingly, persons of Arab descent, as well as labor migrants, pilgrims, and students who travel to the Middle East, are sometimes considered to be vessels that are infiltrated by Wahhabi teachings abroad and are Arabizing Indonesia upon their return (Abaza 2007, 420; Rodemeier 2009, 55; Slama 2008, 4; Stahlhut 2015).

However, despite being labeled as forms of Arabization, middle-class lifestyles, migration, pilgrimage, education, Arabic descent, political Islam, and radicalization do not necessarily have much in common. In some cases, they overlap, while in others they are quite contrasting. The ambiguous use of the term *Arab* itself is a strong example of this.

Who and What Is "Arab" in Today's Indonesia?

Summing up the historical and contemporary ideas of the Arab world, there are the following uses of the term *Arab* in Indonesia: Geographically Indonesians speak of Arab in reference to Saudi Arabia. Yet Arab can also more generally mean the region of the Arab world, encompassing the Arabian Peninsula, the Middle East, North Africa, and sometimes even Iran/Persia, as I mentioned above with regard to the Wali Songo. Even more generally the term *Arab* is used as an equivalent of "Islamic." Moreover, Arab is used to refer to Arabic ethnicity, especially referring to the Hadhrami community of Yemeni descent. Arabic language is referred to as Arab, or as Bahasa Arab ("Arabic language").

As an attribute, the term *Arab* is also used in reference to habits and can be translated as "being Arabic" or as "Arabness" and "Arab mannerism." As an example, someone or something is called "Arab," for example "dia Arab" (he/she is Arabic), or "dia punya gaya Arab" (she/he has an Arabic style), "pikiran**nya** Arab" (his/her thinking is Arabic), but also in a merged form with prefixes or suffixes like "Arab**nya** kental sekali" (her/his Arabness is intense) or "**ke**-Arab-Arab-**an** mereka" (their Arabness/their Arabic manner). The term is also used in verb form, for example related to Arabization, which is called "Arabisasi" in Indonesian, the complementary verb for which is in its passive form "**di**arab**kan**"

(Arabized) or in its active form "**meng**arab**kan**" (Arabizing), like "**meng**arab**kan** diri" (self-Arabizing).

Pious and orthodox Muslims are attributed an "Arab" style and likewise fundamentalist or Wahhabi-oriented persons are described as "Arab." Especially in recent debates about the legitimacy and authenticity of Islamic practices that are regarded as distinctively Indonesian, "Arabness" is related to fundamentalist ideologies, exclusive versions of Islam in contrast to the pluralist Indonesian ones (Abaza 2007; Slama 2008; van Bruinessen 2013b). In this regard, "Arabness" as a mindset is not only located in the Middle East but also within Indonesia, as I will show in greater detail in chapter 3.

Thus the local conceptions of the term *Arab* are multilayered and contradictory. It must be noted that the geospatial, ethnic, linguistic, religious, and ideological connotations in the emic use of the term *Arab* are mixed and combined, making it a very vague term. While "Arab" is used interchangeably with other terms, for instance with "Islamic," "conservative," or in some contexts with "fundamentalist," it is often used in an ambiguous sense. The situation is especially complicated when different meanings of the term *Arab* are somehow related—for instance, when Arabic ethnicity is related to fundamentalist ideologies (see Slama 2008).

Because of the multiple connotations of local attributes of Muslim characteristics in Indonesian lifestyles, like the term *Arab*, there have been efforts to define sharper analytical terms, some of which I have mentioned above, like the "traditionalist Arabness" of the kaum tua, or *santri* Islam (Geertz 1960, 1976), Wahhabi Arabness and Salafi Arabness (Chaplin 2014; Geertz 2001; Rodemeier 2009), the "modernist Arabness" of the kaum muda reformist Islamic streams (Woodward 1989; Laffan 2003, 236–37), Arab ethnicity for people of Arab descent like the Hadhrami (Mandal 2009, 2011; Gilsenan 2003; Slama 2008, 2014), and moreover the "Pop Arabness" of the urban middle classes (Eliyanah and Lücking 2017; Lücking 2016), which relates to the labels of "Pop Islam" (Heryanto 2011, 60), "lifestyle Islam" (Hew 2012, 179) and "Islamic chic" (Abaza 2004, 173; Heryanto 2011, 60) that describe Islamization trends in Indonesia. The study at hand aims to engage with these analytical differentiations and also to provide further examples of emic Indonesian ways to use the term *Arab*. Among other things, research participants described Arabness in contrast to Islam Nusantara.

Islam Nusantara

The mainline organization NU continuously propagates the legality of local Indonesian Islamic practices and has emphasized the superiority of a distinctive Indonesian Islam in the *Islam Pribumi* (Islam of the Natives) discourse of the 1980s (see Slama 2008) and, more recently, the Islam Nusantara discourse (see Lücking 2016). Islam Nusantara is advocated as pluralist, tolerant, moderate, and peaceful, originally grown from historical experiences (Sahal and Aziz 2015). Prominent proponents of the discourse are NU intellectuals like Musthofa Bisri and former minister of religious affairs Lukman Hakim Saifuddin.

Throughout 2015 there have been public controversies about the authenticity of religious rituals like Qur'an readings in local styles. Another example is an image that was widely shared on online social media during the research period showing Indonesians in traditional dress from all over the archipelago entitled "Busana Asli Nusantara. No Arab Look! This is Indonesia" ("Original Archipelago Clothing. No Arab Look! This is Indonesia), contrasting potentially authentic Indonesian clothing with Arab styles from outside the archipelago (Lücking 2016, 7). Abaza (2007) analyses how today Arab Islam is portrayed as fundamentalist Islam and is perceived as a "threat to an Indonesian 'local,' syncretistic religious culture" (Abaza 2007, 422).

Apart from understanding the Islam Nusantara discourse in the context of the rivalry between NU and Muhammadiyah, it must be seen as a state-sponsored project against radical streams of Islam. As there is no terminological distinction between so called "Arab" style or ideology and Arab ethnicity, the Hadhrami are sometimes included in the stereotypical conceptions of Arabness.

Indonesian Arabs Today: Hadhrami Popularity

The equation of ethnic Arabness with fundamentalism is sometimes racialized by focusing on Hadhrami involvement in terrorist acts, in particular the Hadhrami descent of Osama Bin Laden and of leading figures in Islamic Jihadist groups in Indonesia like Ja'afar 'Umar Talib, Habib Rizieq Syihab, and Abu Bakar Ba'ashir. Abaza (2007) and Slama (2008, 2014) critically reflect on the stigmatization of Hadhrami people in the course of promoting an indigenous Indonesian Islam. In the context of locating the roots of Islamic fundamentalism and terrorism outside Indonesian society, the Hadhrami are sometimes represented as scapegoats and are accused of fundamentalist tendencies. However, the 5 million Indonesian Hadhrami exhibit diverse ideological orientations. While the majority of Hadhrami practice Islam in a tradition that resembles Shi'a Islam and elements of mystical Sufi Islam, very similar to Javanese traditionalist Islam (Abaza 2004, 202), smaller branches of Hadhrami are becoming scriptualist and conservative, as seen, for example, in figures like Habib Rizieq Syihab (Abaza 2004, 202). Thus, even though Hadhrami people have been part of Indonesian society for centuries, they experience the repercussions of racial accusations (Abaza 2007; Slama 2008), and it remains an open question whether Islam Nusantara will accommodate the ethnic and cultural diversities of the Arab and Chinese diasporas in Indonesia in its discourse of plurality.

At the same time, all over Southeast Asia there appears to be a rediscovery of Hadhrami Arabness, with increased use of Arabic language, the popularity of the Arabic gambus orchestra, and Arabic food (Abaza 2004; Gilsenan 2003; Mandal 2011, 2012, 2014).[28] Therefore, it is worth considering both the recent tendency of Othering Arabs and the contemporary popularity of the so called *habaib* (singular: *habib*), or *sādah* (singular: *saīd*), the descendants of the Prophet Muhammad, in entertainment and politics. Examples of the increasing popularity of Hadhrami are da'wa activities and Islamic gentrification in Jakarta (Abaza 2004), performances of traditional Arab music (Abaza 2004; Berg 2011), Hadhrami celebrities like televangelists (Barendregt 2010; Muzakki 2012), and politicians. One of the most prominent examples is Anies Baswedan, a Hadhrami intellectual who was elected governor of Jakarta after the blasphemy accusations against Ahok.

Moreover, Hadhrami communities are active in the pilgrimage business, especially for the upper-middle class in Jakarta, where the prospect of performing the hajj in the company of a descendant of the prophet or with a *sādah* travel agency is a selling point (Abaza 2004, 199). One very recent trend is that of pilgrimages to the Hadhramaut, in which non-Hadhrami Indonesians participate (see Alatas 2016).

Recent Arab Interests in Southeast Asia

Mobility between Indonesia and the Middle East has not increased in only one direction. Recently there has also been Middle Eastern interest in Indonesia, especially in the fields of tourism and education. This development must be seen against the backdrop of the 9/11 terrorist attacks, as people from the Middle East have difficulty obtaining visas for travel to North America and Europe (Mandal 2014, 809). As with the Indonesian imaginings of the Arab world, Arabs views on Asia are "tainted by Middle East-centric visions" (Abaza 2011, 23).

Students who face the difficulties of obtaining visas for European countries study in Malaysia and more recently also Indonesia (see Killias 2015). NU is in fact investing in educational institutions for Middle Eastern students to promote certain interpretations of Islam (tho Seeth 2019). At the same time, Saudi Arabia seeks to promote other forms of Islam and invests in higher education in Indonesia (Kovacs 2014; tho Seeth 2016) and in mosque buildings. During my investigations in Madura, research participants drew my attention to several Saudi-funded mosques and mushollahs, either financed through official government channels or private foundations. Apart from financing the construction of mosques, Saudi Arabia donates Islamic literature of Wahhabi interpretation. This also plays a role in the context of the pilgrimage to Mecca, where Saudi Arabia distributes Wahhabi literature in various languages.

Moreover, the number of tourists arriving in Indonesia and Malaysia from the Middle East has been increasing. This leads to another form of perceived Arabization in some areas in Indonesia and Malaysia. Mandal (2014) points out that in the Bukit Bintang area in Kuala Lumpur, the business of supplying Arab food and staging performances of traditional Hadhrami music is flourishing. The Hadhrami are seemingly rediscovering their Arabness as a result of the increasing numbers of Arabs arriving in Malaysia, while Arabs from the Middle East discover their Muslim "brothers and sisters" and thereby see Southeast Asia as a favorable new destination for Islamic tourism and education (Killias 2015; Mandal 2014). In Indonesia this new Arab interest manifests especially in tourism. Arab tourists' needs are for instance accommodated in Puncak near Bogor in West Java, where a halal sex tourism industry is growing. Indonesian news coverage frequently expresses outrage about the practice of contract weddings that are meant to legalize prostitution for Muslim tourists from the Middle East, though there continues to be no political action on this issue.

Furthermore, refugees from the Middle East, especially from Iran, Pakistan, and Afghanistan but also from Iraq and Syria, have been arriving alongside tourists. The tourists from Saudi Arabia remain the majority, representing about 90 percent of the 1,500 tourists per day that were counted in Puncak in June 2016 (Triana 2016). Another region where Arab tourism is growing is the island of Lombok, where Saudi investors are seeking to promote a halal tourist industry. According to a report by TEMPO magazine (2016), former Lombok labor migrants who have been working in Saudi Arabia are engaged in building up this tourism sector, which is accommodated via bilateral governmental agreements. In 2016, Saudi Arabia provided 2.4 billion rupiah ($182.160 USD) for an Islamic Center in Mataram, the capital of Lombok (Khafid 2015). Indonesia's presence at a tourist fair in Saudi Arabia in 2015 underlines the increasing importance of this sector for the two countries. At the fair, Indonesia was awarded the prizes of "World's Best Halal Tourism Destination" and "World's Best Halal Honeymoon Destination" (Khafid 2015) and at a ceremony of the World Halal Tourism Awards that was held in 2016 in Abu Dhabi, Indonesia won twelve awards out of sixteen categories (Indonesian Ministry of Tourism 2018).

Yet in academic and political spheres, Indonesia is still treated as peripheral. Machmudi (2011, 225) concludes that in the past Indonesians were at least to some degree respected as intellectuals while "at the present they are humiliated as domestic workers." In his analysis of Saudi Arabian print media, Machmudi detects a negative image of Indonesians in Saudi Arabia.[29]

The lack of recognition of Indonesian religious scholars seems to equal Middle Eastern disinterest in Indonesian political achievements. Fealy (2014) describes how Indonesians were trying to provide political consultancy for politicians in the Middle East and North Africa after the Arab Spring, as there was an assumption that the Arab countries could benefit from Indonesian experiences of political transition from autocracy to democracy, with Indonesia acting as a model for a democracy in a majority Muslim society (Fealy 2014, 233). Fealy concludes that "many Arabs continue to regard Indonesian expressions of Islam as inferior to their own and are thus disinclined to devote attention to studying Indonesia's reform trajectories" (ibid., 245). The Indonesian attempt to act as a model was sponsored by Western development agencies like USAID and AusAID, and prominent politicians like Hillary Clinton and Barack Obama expressed desires that Indonesia's version of Islam be exported to the Middle East (ibid., 239). However, the Indonesian delegations that were sent to Egypt were met with little appreciation (ibid., 240). And yet, the Arab or Middle Eastern interest in Southeast Asia is a dynamic field that keeps changing with changing economic constellations. As an example, the booming business for Mecca pilgrimages had an effect on other religious travels from Indonesia to the Middle East. Therefore, travel agents and tour guides in Egypt, Jordan, Israel, and Palestine engage with Indonesian language and culture (Lücking 2019, 200).

Different Levels of Communitas

The historiography of the interaction between Indonesia and the Arab world reveals that from the early encounters with Arab traders in precolonial times, the region and culture west of the Indian Ocean became an important reference point for Indonesians. This reference point is imagined in many ways, becoming a source of prestige and symbolic capital. Most accounts and analyses have in common that they focus on foreign influence in Indonesia—be it Arabic, Persian, South Asian, East Asian, or Western. And yet there is also evidence of Indonesians' influence in areas outside Indonesia and internal Indonesian dynamics like the incorporation of various cultural influences and the significance of local religious and cultural centers. Mobility between Indonesia and the Arab world became meaningful through local social embeddedness, or as Laffan (2003, 3) describes it, the journeys "fostered seemingly contradictory ideas of both local and Islamic identities—indeed two different levels of what Victor Turner called *communitas*." Most important, the overview shows that labels like "Arab" or "conservative" describe diverse traditions and are often used in a legitimizing or delegitimizing manner. Claims of authenticity are related to the origin of Islam, yet labels like "Arab" function in the local context and say little about Arab societies, which are very diverse in themselves.

Five key periods appear to be crucial in the multifarious interactions between Indonesia and the Arab world and Indonesians' localizations of (imagined) Arabness: (1) Arab, Indian-Persian, and Chinese influences and the creation of local centers of Islam; (2) exchange with Turks and Kurds during the Ottoman influence on the Arabian Peninsula; (3) anticolonial movements and the twentieth-century frictions between different streams of Islamic tradition, most notably the Wahhabi ideology that became hegemonic in the Hejaz and the Islamic modernism that flourished in Cairo; (4) bureaucratization and orientation toward the West during the Suharto era, including Suharto's later turn to alliances with Muslim countries and the establishment of bilateral agreements for labor migration; and (5) a competitive environment in politics and economy, with political elites gambling to access the symbolic capital of Islam and a mélange of neoliberalism and consumerist Islamic lifestyle in democratic Indonesia.

All in all, from the historical overview there is evidence that spatial mobility across the Indian Ocean triggered self-identifications and cultural exchange, and that the foreign counterparts have repeatedly been labeled as "Arab," despite culturally diverse backgrounds. The synopsis has indicated that references to the past are a matter of perspective and that there is diverging emphasis on the different periods and spheres of influence. Contemporary controversies and anxieties about Arabness are most likely the reason why NU and the government on the one hand promote Islam Nusantara and locate sources of Islamism outside the archipelago, and on the other hand simultaneously give in to some demands from Islamist factions.

Thus generalizations about the Arab world are prevalent throughout time. These generalizations clearly guide people in making sense of their world. Considering what role the Arab world plays in these ideas of self and Other, this leads to questions about todays' identification with others, as a larger communitas of fellow Muslims, or differentiations from others, identifying with a local or national communitas. Moreover, I will explore in greater detail what the representations of self and Other, and the Arab world, mean for ordinary Indonesians who travel to Arab countries. Or, putting it more generally: In what way is the guidance of mobility toward the Middle East related to social change and to cultural and ideological reorientations?

2

THE BEATEN TRACKS AND EMBEDDED RETURNS OF MIGRANTS AND PILGRIMS

The paths from Indonesia to the Middle East on which migrants and pilgrims move are beaten tracks. Labor migration and pilgrimage are not pioneering adventures on "the road less traveled." In contrast, it is because others have traveled on the same routes before that the movements become meaningful, especially concerning pilgrimage. The spiritual engraving of the routes to Mecca comprises a collective connection through shared physical experiences of moving on the same paths, reciting the same Qur'an verses, bowing in prayer toward the same direction. By following their predecessors' footsteps, pilgrims are connected across cultures and across time and space. These physical movements become meaningful through the stories that accompany them. Metanarratives about the pilgrimage become orientations and are reproduced again and again.

One story is the ultimate metanarrative of all hajj experiences: the story of Ibrahim and Hajar that is referenced in the Qur'an in surah 2, verse 158, and surah 37, verses 101–11.[1] Indonesian pilgrims introduced me to it as a story of anxieties, doubts, and temptation, as a story of a search for orientation, and a happy ending with the affirmation of being on the right track, emerging from mobile experiences with strengthened faith in God. When a person becomes a pilgrim, the ritual mobility in the hajj and umrah are an enactment of the experiences of Ibrahim and Hajar.

In addition, the hajj also relates to the story of the Prophet Muhammad clearing the House of God, the Ka'aba, of polytheist idols and bringing enlightenment to the people who are believed to have been stuck in *ǧāhilīya*, the pre-Islamic time of ignorance. The emphasis on *tawḥīd*, the singularity of God, and the renunciation of polytheist beliefs is central in both Muhammad's and Ibrahim's quests and is prominent in Indonesians' hajj narratives.

Differing emphasis on the respective guiding narratives reveals the interchangeability of travel narratives, which can give the same destination and the same patterns of movement different meanings. It is thus not only physical adherence to the ritual itself that makes the pilgrimage, or any kind of mobility, meaningful.

Metanarratives that provide physical and emotional orientation and produce meaning are not only found in pilgrimage. Labor migrants are equally inspired by certain guiding narratives that make them move and make their movement meaningful. Strikingly, despite the different character of pilgrimage and migration, these two forms of mobility from Indonesia toward the Middle East exhibit remarkable similarities in the way the journeys are guided. Yet, despite having the same destination and involving similar patterns of guidance, the different narratives related to the journeys mirror the significantly differing meanings of their mobility.

The Beaten Tracks of the Pilgrimage

Besides all aspects of the more mundane guidance that constitute a large part of my analysis, for devout Muslims, the guidance of God appears to be the determining guidance. This applies especially in the context of pilgrimages to Mecca and Medina, but also to Muslims' lives more generally. When talking to Indonesian Mecca returnees, a common response to the question of how they came to the decision to undertake the pilgrimage was that they had received *hidāyah*. The Arabic term *hidāyah* happens to mean "guidance" and describes the theological concept of being guided by God. In Indonesian the term is used in combination with the verb "receiving." *Mendapat* hidāyah means "to receive guidance," indicating that the practices resulting from this guidance are believed to happen not because of one's own will, but because of God's guidance. Regarding the pilgrimage, this usually concerns the conviction of having been called by God to go on hajj. The pilgrims to whom I spoke had traveled in the belief that once one receives the hidāyah, guidance from God, everything will go smoothly. In other contexts, for instance, explaining a change in lifestyle habits like starting to wear a headscarf, the term is deployed similarly, and it is argued that this does not happen out of personal motivation but because of an intuition, inspired by God's guidance.

Thus, as with the mentioning by pilgrims of Qur'anic stories, spiritual and ritual guidance lead Mecca pilgrims. The synopsis of hajj and umrah rituals is based on research participants' narrations and on the contents of pilgrimage preparation courses. It does not represent a scholarly Islamic viewpoint on the ritual process and its meaning, but a summary of how the pilgrimage was presented to me—a non-Muslim Western researcher. In addition, I provide examples of pilgrims' personal interpretations of God's guidance.

Collective Pilgrimage Rituals

It is believed that Ibrahim and Hajar's trust in God was challenged when they feared for the life of their son Ishmael. In the Qur'an it says that when Hajar, alone in the desert, was desperately searching for water for her son, a well, known as the *zamzam* well, miraculously came into existence. Furthermore, it says that when God demanded that Ibrahim sacrifice his son, Ibrahim experienced an inner struggle and was tempted by the devil. Eventually, on proving his readiness to make the sacrifice, God ordered Ibrahim to slaughter a lamb instead. In gratitude, Ibrahim and Ishmael constructed the Ka'aba, the "House of God." It is believed that Ibrahim turned away from polytheist practices.

Nevertheless, the Ka'aba became the destination for pilgrimages in a polytheist tradition in pre-Islamic times. In Muslim belief, it was through the revelation of the Qur'an that the Prophet Muhammad was appointed to give the Ka'aba back its original meaning as a site for the worship of Allah as the only God. Being in conflict with his own tribe, the Quraish, who made profit from the pagan pilgrimages, Muhammad migrated to Yathrib, which became known as the city of the Prophet, in Arabic simply called "the city" (Medina), in the year 622 CE/1 AH. In 630 CE/9 AH, Muhammad returned to Mecca and destroyed the polytheist idols. Two years later, in 632 CE/11 AH he instructed his followers on how to perform the hajj in remembrance of Ibrahim and Hajar's struggle and declared it the fifth pillar of Islam, concomitantly performing it himself shortly before he died.

Thus pilgrims do not only enact the story of Ibrahim and Hajar, but also perform the pilgrimage in remembrance of the Prophet. The hajj is the complete pilgrimage, consisting of the rituals introduced by the Prophet Muhammad, while the umrah encompasses only one key element of the hajj rituals and is considered a minor pilgrimage. The Ka'aba is located in the middle of the Holy Mosque, *al-masǧid al-ḥarām*, with the zamzam well close by. The second holiest place in Islam is the Prophet's Mosque, *al-masǧid an-nabawī*, in Medina. Today, these holy sites, which are also known as *al-ḥarāmayīn,* the two sanctuaries, are administered by the Kingdom of Saud, specifically King Salman bin Abdulaziz Al Saud as the official custodian.

The pilgrimage rituals begin by entering a state of ritual purity, the so-called state of *iḥrām*, which is established through prayers, ritual washing, and a special dress of nonsewn white pieces of cloth for men and white robes for women, indicating the equality of believers before God. When pilgrims enter the Holy Mosque, they shout a prayer verse called *talbīyah* that is used numerous times during the hajj and umrah to assert the pilgrims' intention to worship God alone. The talbīyah, which is sometimes also referred to as *labbayk*, which is the first word of the verse, is widely known and for many Muslims its words and the sound of its recitation carry strong emotions. The Arabic text (in transliteration) of the talbīyah is:

> *Labbayk Allāhumma Labbayk. Labbayk Lā Šarīka Laka Labbayk. Inna l-ḥamda, Wa n-Ni'mata, Laka wal Mulk, Lā Šharīka Lak.*
>
> Here I am Allah, responding to Your call, here I am. Here I am at your service, You have no partners, here I am. Indeed all praise, grace and sovereignty belong to You. You have no partner.
>
> (see Bukhari, Hadith 621, translation adapted from Qur'an-Explorer 2016)

The joint recitation of the talbīyah as it happens in Mecca is for many Muslims the sound they associate with the hajj and it features in videos and music. After this affirmation, pilgrims perform the first of seven circumambulations of the Ka'aba, the so called *tawāf*, which is done anticlockwise, starting from the eastern corner of the Ka'aba. During tawāf, pilgrims aspire to get as close as possible to the Ka'aba, especially to the black stone at its eastern corner, which they desire to touch and kiss. I was told that this has become a lucrative business for members of what was referred to as the "Madurese Mafia" in Mecca who help pilgrims to channel their way toward the black stone.

The commemoration of Hajar's desperate search for water happens in the *sa'i* ritual, which involves running or walking between the hillocks of Safa and Marwah that are located close to the Masjid al-Haram. Sa'i is the central activity for the umrah pilgrimage and during the research many women said that they found this part of the ritual crucial because as mothers they identified with Hajar's struggle. In today's construction of the holy compound, the distance of approximately 450 meters between Safa and Marwah consists of a roofed, multistory walkway called *mas'a*, which enables millions of people to perform this ritual at the same time. Pilgrims walk or run seven times back and forth between the two hills. After sa'i the pilgrims' hair is cut, which symbolizes the spiritual transformation.

The sa'i ritual can be performed at almost any time of the year, while the other hajj rituals have to be performed on designated days between the eighth and the twelfth of the month of Dhu al-Hijjah. Apart from the sa'i ritual, the hajj rituals include the *wuquf 'arafah*, an overnight stay in Muzdalifah, a location near the mountain Arafah, and the symbolic stoning of the devil at Mina. Wuquf means standing and refers to the standing of all believers before God on the plain of mount Arafah. By gathering at this place from noon to sunset on the ninth of Dhu al-Hijjah, pilgrims commemorate the last sermon of the Prophet Muhammad in 632 CE/11 AH, in which he demanded that his followers live in peace and harmony. During their overnight stay in Muzdalifah, pilgrims collect forty-nine pebbles which they use for the symbolic stoning of the devil, throwing them at the three pillars (*jamrat*) in the valley of Mina near Mecca. In today's construction of the ritual site in Mina, the three pillars representing the devil, who tempted Ibrahim not to sacrifice his son, are shielded in order to enable everyone to throw pebbles.[2]

Remembering God's grace in ordering Ibrahim to sacrifice a lamb instead of his son, pilgrims as well as Muslims all over the world slaughter sheep, goats, camels, and cows on the day of *'id al-aḍḥā*, the festival of sacrifice, on the tenth of Dhu al-Hijjah. After the feast of sacrifice, pilgrims usually travel to Medina, where they visit the tomb of the Prophet and the Prophet's mosque and then return to Mecca one more time, for the farewell tawāf.

In Indonesia, pilgrims rehearse all the steps of the hajj and umrah in pilgrimage preparation courses. Many pilgrimage agencies and local governments put up a model of the Ka'aba for rehearsal, and in Yogyakarta the practice was done at the beach, as it was argued that the pilgrims could thereby prepare for the heat and drought of the Saudi Arabian desert. The rituals are performed as a group. Individual movement is channeled through the physical sensation of joint reciting, walking, circumambulating, throwing, touching, standing, and bowing. Research participants described this embodied guidance as eliciting strong emotions and a spiritual proximity to God. The experiences of five pilgrims from different social backgrounds exemplify this.

Hidāyah: Guided by God

Qur'an recitations are an integral part of Indonesian pilgrimage preparation courses. One of the Qur'an verses refers to Ibrahim's trust in God's guidance (hidāyah):

> No reason have we why we should not put our trust in Allah. Indeed, He has guided us the ways we follow. We shall certainly bear with patience all the hurt you may cause us. For those who put their trust should put their trust in Allah. (Surah 14, 12, Qur'an translation by Abdullah Yussuf Ali, *The Meaning of the Holy Qur'an*)

The subsequent five examples of how pilgrims describe their feelings of being guided by God are exemplary snapshots providing a range of narratives, indicating that this aspect of guidance is intimate and collective at the same time, given its strong emotional component and the reproduction of metanarratives.

BEING CALLED BY GOD: THE UNEXPECTED PILGRIMAGE OF DEWI

Mbak Dewi was one of the first Mecca returnees whom I met at the beginning of the research in early 2013.[3] At that time, she was a student at Gadjah Mada University and, aged twenty-five, one of the youngest hajj participants of 2012. First of all, she explained that her hajj had been different. Withdrawals by other pilgrims had led to a sudden jump in the waiting list and only one week before the departure date she was informed that she was on the list of participants for the hajj in 2012. Mbak Dewi expressed her amazement about this unexpected luck in being allocated a seat for the hajj at such a young age and recounted that she could not explain how this had happened, as some of her relatives had registered earlier and were much older than herself but had not been contacted to fill free places. She talked about her excitement and the last-minute preparations, all of which were done at very short notice. In retrospect, she reflected that if anyone had told her in advance that she would be able to process all the administration issues within a week, let alone processing her passport and visa in the Indonesian administration, and on top of this doing all the essential shopping and packing, organizing a last minute farewell and spiritual counseling, she would not have believed it. All of this had felt astonishing. That everything went smoothly despite the adverse circumstances and the suddenness of her departure filled her with the deep conviction that God would guide her way and that the pilgrimage would proceed smoothly. Throughout the hajj, she had felt very calm and confident, having come to the conclusion that it must have been God's plan for her to perform the hajj in that year, for reasons that she did not know, maybe to care for all the elderly pilgrims, or maybe because something important would happen in her life. It was hidāyah. She concluded: "It was really 'wow,' overwhelming, to have made it there [to Mecca], ya Allah. That's why the prayer that we use, the recitation when going on hajj, is to express thanks for God's grace in inviting us to His house" (Mbak Dewi, January 25, 2013).

ANXIETIES AND REPENTANCE: MAS EKO'S PRAYERS FOR FORGIVENESS

Not everyone is as convinced of having received hidāyah at the time of their pilgrimage. When I talked to Mas Eko about his experience of having accomplished the umrah, he related to the feelings that Ibrahim and Hajar must have had, as he put it. He was filled with doubts and anxiety because of not adhering to God's guidance on a daily basis.

Mas Eko is an enthusiastic young man who runs a travel agency in urban Yogyakarta. He started his business by organizing trips to nearby tourist attractions, like the famous Borobudur temple or the Merapi volcano. Recently, he had reflected on the possibility of including religious tours in his offer. He was himself a devout Muslim and a member of a group of young entrepreneurs who were inspired by Yusuf Mansur, a popular consultant for Islamic business ethics. The group started from the members' own initiative with the aim of sharing ideas of how to lead their lives, including their business activities, as good Muslims. The group, called the Tawhid Community, consisted of around fifteen men and women at the time of inquiry. They shared interests in business and Islamic lifestyle.[4] His search for a more pious everyday life led Mas Eko's thoughts to his own business, and he came to the conclusion that offering religious tours in his agency would be an ideal combination of doing business and promoting religious practices like the pilgrimage by making them more accessible. He considered this a form of *da'wa*, which means the invitation to Islam. He deemed it important to do the pilgrimage himself before selling it to others. Thus he signed up for an umrah tour together with his father. When they departed for the pilgrimage, he began to feel afraid, reflecting on his sins and constantly praying the *istiġfār*, the prayer for forgiveness. He described his feelings during the journey as follows:

> I was afraid. When we arrived at Soekarno Hatta Airport, I was totally limp, my feet, my arms, everything was limp. I did not dare to speak to my father and fell silent. If you had recorded it, there would have only been my silence and in my heart, I was praying *istiġfār*. Remembering my sins, you know, asking Allah for forgiveness, over and over again. And at the airport, I felt the need to perform a prayer of repentance, a prayer to ask for forgiveness. I had to perform the prayer of repentance before I set off. In the mushollah at the airport, during the noon prayer time, I was performing the prayer of repentance and I really meant it. I prayed for forgiveness, "Ya Allah, I am repenting towards you. I ask for forgiveness, for all my past mistakes, everything that has happened, I bring it before you." (Mas Eko, October 17, 2013)

Mas Eko recounted that the feelings of shame and fear persisted throughout his stay in Mecca, but that in the end he felt relieved and since his return to Indonesia, he has wanted to lead a more pious life. He had signed up for the hajj, was on the waiting list and was eager to prepare himself spiritually. Before his departure, estimated by the Ministry of Religious Affairs to be in 2023, he wanted to become a good Muslim, aspiring not to have any reason to be ashamed by then.

He decided to include umrah trips in his travel agency's offer as a first step in spreading the message of Islam.

SEEKING THE PATH OF THE PROPHET: CAK NUN'S CRITICISM OF THE HAJJ BUSINESS

Hajj narratives are also prevalent among those who have not gone to Mecca or who prefer not to *physically* go there. Emha Ainun Najib, also known as Cak Nun, is a popular Muslim intellectual in Indonesia, famous for his poetry, his preaching, and his performances with a group of musicians called Kiai Kanjeng, playing the traditional Javanese *gamelan*, an ensemble of percussion instruments, which they combine with Western and Arabic musical traditions. Cak Nun performs with Kiai Kanjeng in front of audiences of thousands of people with regular events in Jakarta, Yogyakarta, and Jombang. During one of these events, he criticized the current pilgrimage boom and the economic exploitation of the event by various actors, in particular by the Kingdom of Saudi Arabia, which he considered as having fallen back into the time of ignorance, the *ǧāhilīya*. In an interview that Ubed and I conducted with him, he specified his criticism and contextualized it by arguing that there was a conspiracy by a Zionist-American-Saudi capitalist world order. While Mas Eko does not see a conflict in the combination of spiritual and business activities and considers the increase of pilgrimage tourism as a form of *da'wa*, Cak Nun harshly criticizes the marketization of the pilgrimage. His criticism corresponds with other Islamic intellectuals who lament the commercialization of the pilgrimage, which they consider to be just the same as the Quraish tribe's practice of making money through pilgrimage that the Prophet Muhammad had denounced. Today the Holy Mosque is surrounded by big, modern skyscrapers, of which the Abraj Al Bait Towers and the Mecca Royal Clock Tower Hotel, which is an imitation of London's Big Ben, have become an integral part of Mecca images. Critics' opinions range from denouncing this as a symbol of capitalism to conspiracy theories that are especially popular on the internet. Cak Nun's position is the following:

> Saudi Arabia is a puppet, isn't it? What's the difference between Arabia, America, and Israel? The Saudi's market has the biggest travel agency in the world, and it is called hajj. The Ka'aba is a commodity that does not lose its value. They will not give it to anyone, except this Bedouin tribe. . . . The Prophet had already Islamized the Arabs, but now the Arabs dominate Islam. The Arabs return to the time of Abu Ǧahal. The dominance of the ǧāhilīya there is not easy to estimate, is it? . . . The distance between Islam and Arabness is now even larger than the distance between Islam and the West. . . . They conquered Islam and

> now they exploit the religion for tourism and capitalism. That's why the Ka'aba, Mecca, Medina should belong to all Muslims around the world, it should not be allowed that it is dominated by the Saudis. In the logic of a global Islam, it should be in the ownership of all Muslims, not of the Arabs. (Cak Nun, May 21, 2014)

For Cak Nun, to join the pilgrimage boom, especially for umrah tourism, is to follow the path of ǧāhilīya and capitalism rather than the path of Muhammad. Nevertheless, many Muslims experience religious fulfillment in Mecca, as the following examples show.

FULFILLMENT: THE EXPERIENCES OF IBU AND PAK SETIONO

Ibu and Pak Setiono live in urban Yogyakarta where they both worked as teachers until their retirement four years ago.[5] They accomplished the hajj in autumn 2012 and I met them about half a year later, in March 2013. Pak Setiono described how, together with pilgrims from around the world, he did the first tawāf of the Ka'aba, shouting the talbīyah, and that he could not hear his own voice in the joint shouting of a million voices around him that seemed to become one single voice. When he repeated the phrase *Labbaika-llahumma labbaik,* to demonstrate and remember the experience, he could not hold back his tears.

As emotional outbursts are uncommon in Java, I was surprised by this. His wife stayed relaxed and explained that her husband often cried when he remembered his closeness to God during the hajj and that it was all good, because these were tears of fulfillment. Obviously, for this couple the feeling of closeness to God is related to the collectivism of a Muslim ummah that Pak Setiono described as one of the most fascinating and precious experiences of the hajj. From that moment on, he never wanted to forget this experience and he described feeling a new affection for all fellow human beings as creations of God (Ibu and Pak Setiono, March 15, 2013).

PAK MARIADI'S EXPERIENCE OF COMMUNITAS

A very similar experience was described by Pak Mariadi, a pilgrim from rural Yogyakarta who had also accomplished the pilgrimage in 2012. I was introduced to Pak Mariadi by another pilgrimage returnee, Pak Raharjo, a farmer in rural Yogyakarta. Pak Raharjo had been keen to introduce me to Pak Mariadi, arguing that Pak Mariadi was more knowledgeable and had been the head of their travel unit of fifteen persons. As a university lecturer and because he had been on his own for the hajj, Pak Mariadi appeared to be the most eligible candidate for the position of group leader. When he had registered for the hajj many years earlier, he had not yet married. Because his wife could not jump the waiting list, he departed for the hajj on his own. Pak Mariadi argued that in Mecca, people become aware of the fact that all differences vanish before God; he was especially excited about the fact that this feeling of unity even included Shi'a Muslims when he explained:

> The differences vanished, zero . . . zero. Null, there were no differences at all. Even towards Shi'a people, those from Iran for example, yeah, the groups from Iran. . . . The differences disappeared, different characteristics and even principles didn't matter, even principles like Shi'a, they vanished. So, there we were brothers and sisters. There were no differences at all. (Pak Mariadi, February 24, 2013)

Confessional and cultural differences seem to be wiped away during the hajj. Pak Mariadi's statement echoes a famous metanarrative of the longing for a united Muslim ummah.

These testimonies are representations of personal experiences and interpretations of God's guidance. Emphasis on differing aspects indicates people's overall moral and cultural orientation and their lifestyle preferences. They must be seen as part of enactments of lifestyle changes, aspiring to become a better person, starting an Islamic business, or spreading religion. Some of the statements are not only personal, but also political. Cak Nun's criticism especially indicates that personal views on how to lead a life in adherence with God's guidance are not only a matter of interpretation but also of contestation. In chapter 3, I will come back to such frictions in situated representations, in particular in representations of Arab Others. Apart from being guided by God, pilgrims are also guided by more mundane aspirations that are related to the pilgrimage and which are evident in a range of rituals that are not officially designated as hajj and umrah rituals, but that have become important common practices among Indonesian pilgrims. Research participants explained that without these practices, the pilgrimage would not feel complete.

Favored Pilgrimage Activities among Indonesians

When Mbak Dewi showed me the photographs of her pilgrimage, she introduced me to the meaningful places on the pictures, which I rediscovered in other pilgrims' video and photo documentation. They showed not only the sites for the official pilgrimage rituals but also other places, some of which turned out to be favored motifs for posts on Facebook. Apparently, there is a range of activities that complement the official pilgrimage rituals and that were described as being especially favored by Indonesian pilgrims. This does not imply that pilgrims of other nationalities do not share these tastes, only that Indonesian pilgrims presented them as typically Indonesian preferences.

MAGICAL MEDINA, NEW NAMES, AND THE HILL OF GRACE

While the initial statements about hajj experiences mostly confirmed the overwhelming experience of entering the Holy Mosque in Mecca and seeing the Ka'aba, the place of eternal orientation, in the course of pilgrimage accounts, returnees conceded that they considered Medina to be the more peaceful of the two holy sites. The mosque of the Prophet was described as particularly aesthetically pleasing. One of the motifs that is most frequently uploaded on online social media is the forest of high tech, automatically unfolding umbrellas in Medina that many of my informants described with amazement. Pak Raharjo, the Mecca returnee from rural Yogyakarta, cheerfully recounted that he had noted the exact time of the unfolding of the umbrellas in order to see them unfold every day because he was so amazed by this spectacle. Furthermore, in Medina, the visit to the Prophet's grave is particularly important for Indonesians. During recent years this has been a controversially discussed issue, as Saudi Arabia wants to close the grave site in order to prevent it from being worshipped. Especially in Madura this issue was a topic of heated discussion and the Madurese reinforced the importance of maintaining the accessibility of the grave site.

Praying at graves is in general very common in Indonesia, though not equally acknowledged by Muslims of all streams: for instance, most adherents of Muhammadiyah consider this practice to be a heretical innovation (*bid'a*) or syncretistic practice stemming from pre-Islamic polytheist beliefs and ancestral worship. Stories about supernatural experiences related to this practice divide believers. Thus such stories were not among the first statements about the pilgrimage, and they were evidently not shared with everyone because they do not correspond with officially desirable stories of pilgrimage, or maybe my interlocutors were not sure how much their Western visitor could relate to their supernatural experiences. Nevertheless after some time, I did hear stories about mystical incidents occurring during the pilgrimage, including the appearance of visions, meaningful dreams, strong emotional sensations, healing, and contact with ghosts or deceased people.

Another important destination for Indonesians is Jabal Rahma, or the hill of grace, which is said to be the spot of the encounter between Ādam (Adam) and Hawa (Eve). At the hill of grace pilgrims pray for love. The lower part of the white pillar on this hill is covered with hand-written poems, prayers and names of all those longing for love or praying for friends and relatives to find the love of their life or their determined match (*jodoh* or *pasangan*), to accept their match, to experience a blessed marriage, to conceive a child, or settle a quarrel. Stories about visits to the hill of grace were very lively, becoming an excuse to innocuously inquire about the love lives of others. Dewi was giggling when she showed images of the spot and told me about her hopes related to her visit to the hill of grace. As she had been the youngest pilgrim in her group, the elder women had encouraged her to bring her longings before God. Dewi also recounted that her friends had requested that she pray for their romantic hopes at the hill of grace, and in Madura I observed how the relatives and neighbors of pilgrims prepared small pieces of paper with prayers or names on them, printed photographs and entrusted these items to pilgrims in order that they be carried to the Holy Land and in particular to the hill of grace. These intimate hopes and wishes are shared in more private conversations and make the pilgrimage an arena for strengthening interpersonal relationships. In a way this is where pilgrims *leave the guided paths*—at least mentally—and secretly follow their deepest longings.

Another unofficial ritual common among Indonesians is the changing of names after the hajj. This practice is especially popular among Madurese pilgrims. Pak Imam, a Madurese member of the government delegation of the hajj in 2014 who had previously performed the hajj numerous times, explained that through changing their names, the pilgrims assert their changed social status. Moreover, changing a Madurese or Javanese name that often carries a notion of social class derived from the Hindu caste system into a Muslim one makes social hierarchies more egalitarian. He indicated that in Madura, people from lower classes had no "proper names," as it was considered pretentious for parents to give their children names that are reserved for persons of nobility. Therefore, they sometimes were given names of kitchen equipment or other ordinary items. An Arabic-Islamic name would improve their status significantly. Furthermore, he informed me that the provision of name certificates had become a business for hotel owners in Mecca. Previously, I had been told that the new names were given to the pilgrims by sheikhs, but Pak Imam argued that it was just the hotel owners who appeared as sheikhs and printed nice certificates, making a business of the Madurese desires (personal communication, October 15, 2014).

WORLDLY RITUALS

While these activities are still more or less related to religious activities, more mundane activities of the pilgrimage are important rituals as well. Seemingly of great significance were two aspects: shopping and taking photographs. Apparently, Indonesians are famous for their shopping and many pilgrims and guides told me that Indonesian pilgrims represented the most important spending power in Mecca and that Saudi Arabians hired Indonesian shop employees in order to make the shopping smoother, or that they would learn basic Indonesian bargaining phrases and advertise their products in Indonesian.

Sometimes this was proudly considered to be a creeping "Indonesianization" of Mecca. In an interview with Ustadz Wijayanto,[6] who is one of the most well-known Muslim celebrities in Indonesia, starring in TV shows, providing Islamic business consultancy, running a philanthropic network of schools in Yogyakarta, teaching at a university and traveling to Mecca several times per year as a guide for exclusive umrah trips, he joked, "If I lose a group member, I will not look for him in the mosque, but in the mall" (Ustadz Wijayanto, March 12, 2013).

Among the items that pilgrims purchase in Mecca are headscarves, cosmetics, jewelry, bracelets, dates and raisins, fragrances, and zamzam water. Strikingly, certain items, like rings with a so-called *akik*, a stone attributed with supernatural powers, are apparently shipped from Indonesia to Mecca where Madurese vendors sell them to fellow Indonesians. Even though the customers know of the origin of the rings, it seemed to be special to have purchased them in Mecca. The importance of shopping is related to the expectations of relatives, friends, and neighbors of pilgrims of receiving a souvenir upon the pilgrim's return.

Shopping is not just a fun activity but a way of thinking about those at home, choosing presents for them. Sometimes, bringing these items back to Indonesia can become an endeavor that demands commitment and bravery. This was evident in stories about smuggling zamzam water onto airplanes, as some of my interlocutors reported that they wanted to take more of the "real," "original" zamzam water from Saudi Arabia, which they considered to be of higher quality than that being sold in Indonesia. Demand for original zamzam water increased after reports surfaced of fake zamzam water being sold. Pilgrims argued that the official allowance of five liters was not enough to meet the demands of their home community. Pak Raharjo therefore hid additional bottles of water under his clothes.

Furthermore, taking pictures is an important ritual during the stay in the Holy Land and the selfie stick, or *TongSis*, which is the Indonesian abbreviation for *tongkat narsis*, the narcissistic stick, has become an important piece of travel equipment. Taking a Mecca selfie, which can be uploaded on Facebook, Instagram, or Twitter, is especially favored among urban middle class umrah pilgrims. Taking such a selfie is, however, a rather challenging undertaking as cameras are, according to research participants, not permitted inside the Holy Mosque. One of my research participants recounted how she had managed to sneak her camera inside the mosque and succeeded in taking some pictures. The other two most frequently recurring motifs in visual pilgrimage documentation are the umbrella forest in Medina and the hill of grace.

INDONESIAN FAVORITES

These Indonesian favorites of pilgrimage activities reveal that apart from the beaten tracks of the official pilgrimage rituals, there are Indonesian side paths and rituals of nonconformist Muslim traditions. In some contexts, this can mean leaving the beaten tracks and following very intimate longings or semilegal actions, as indicated by the cases of the love prayers at the hill of grace and the smuggling of zamzam water. In these practices, Indonesian pilgrims are not only connected to fellow pilgrims with whom they share the embodied ritual experience, but also to their social network back home. Their vision is not only directed toward the Ka'aba and the global Muslim communitas, but also toward their lifeworld back in Indonesia, where neighbors expect them to share souvenirs and where their social status increases, for which a certificate of a name change or a Mecca selfie can be a handy manifestation. Pilgrims are thus also guided by their communities' expectations and values that are valid in the existing normative structures on the local level. Finally, yet importantly, these practices distinguish Indonesians from other pilgrims and by proudly informing me that these are Indonesian habits, the pilgrims exhibit their identification as Indonesians (or Javanese and Madurese), indicating the significance of shared experience with an Indonesian communitas. Further inquiry showed that, in fact, Indonesians seem to spend most of their time in the Holy Land in Indonesian-only environments.

Indonesian pilgrims' worldly needs are satisfied by the supply of Indonesian food and Indonesian-speaking employees in their accommodation, as well as Indonesian guides and helpers, quite often Indonesian students who study in Cairo, Mecca, or Medina and who work as volunteers and guides during the hajj season. Every pilgrim is obliged to carry five kilograms of rice as a contribution to the food supply and many carry additional dry food and instant noodles to secure their well-being abroad. With great excitement pilgrimage returnees informed me that their concerns about food had been unnecessary as there was in fact a lot of Indonesian food in the Holy Land. Madurese residents sold Indonesian street food and the catering that was provided in the hotel was prepared by Indonesian cooks as well. For the transportation there were shuttle buses that were divided by country and overall there had been no reason to worry as everywhere in Mecca there were Indonesians and Indonesian- or Malay-speaking people. Because they traveled in groups and relied on travel guides for full guidance and complete care, Indonesians seemed to leave little room for interaction with people from other parts of the world or with Saudi Arabian culture. Moreover, the Indonesian way of doing the pilgrimage exceeds the pilgrimage rituals that are performed at the holy sites. Pre- and postpilgrimage rituals in Indonesia, especially preparatory activities, farewell rituals, and return celebrations, complete the journey.

Pre- and Postpilgrimage Rituals in Indonesia

PREPARATION

The practical guidance of Mecca pilgrimages begins with a preparatory period. In so-called *manasik* preparation courses, pilgrims rehearse the sequence of rituals and discuss practical matters like clothing and food supplies. Moreover, during these sessions there is an introduction to Arab culture and customs (*adat istiadat orang Arab*). A guide informed me that this section is meant to prepare Indonesians for the encounter with "loud and coarse" Arabs. In a break in one such *manasik umrah* course, some elderly widowed women told me that they had heard about Arab men being particularly interested in Indonesian women and that there had even been incidents of rape.

Pilgrims sometimes complement the official preparation courses with personal preparation by reading guidebooks, which are published in large numbers in all forms and formats in Indonesia. Furthermore, some pilgrims visit the tombs of the Wali Songo and deceased family members before their departure and arrange interpersonal counseling with local religious leaders. Quinn argues that "the steady rise in the number of pilgrims undertaking the hajj to the Holy Land seems to be having a flow-on effect into local pilgrimage" (Quinn 2008, 67), not only as preparation for the hajj but also for those who cannot afford to accomplish the hajj or umrah.

During the hajj season of 2014, I witnessed that the travel preparations in Madura involve endowment with special clothing. In addition to uniform clothing for the hajj and umrah, like Batik dress, with a new nationwide design for each year, the pilgrims also buy personal clothing, mainly in white, as well as outfits which they intend to wear upon return. When I accompanied pilgrimage candidates to so called "Arab stores" in the *kampong Arab*, the Arab compound, in Pamekasan where many Hadhrami reside, I learned that during the hajj season business was good as pilgrims equipped themselves for the journey and even more so for their return, as they bought the bulk of their souvenirs, which they would share with neighbors and relatives, in advance. My interlocutors explained that pilgrims could not possibly carry all souvenirs from Saudi Arabia to Indonesia. While the Arab shops offer many products that are imported from the Middle East, like cosmetics and zamzam water, my interlocutors joked that certain "Arab" souvenirs were made in China, like small electronic *tasbih* prayer counters, which traditionally consist of a chain of prayer beads.

Pilgrims who accomplish the hajj under the official government program stay in Saudi Arabia for forty days, and it is believed that the angels of Mecca will sit for the same period on the shoulders of the returnees. Therefore, postpilgrimage visits and celebrations usually last for forty days after their return. In rural areas, especially in Madura, the scope of these events is more extensive than in urban contexts and wealthier pilgrims are under greater pressure to share their wealth during that time.

DEPARTURE

During the hajj seasons in 2013 and 2014, I observed several hajj departures in Central Java and Madura and got an impression of the festive atmosphere that involves the whole nation. The way people expressed their best wishes for departing pilgrims revealed the special status of the pilgrimage and many peoples' longing to participate in the hajj themselves, which was mentioned as a reason to ask pilgrims to carry one's picture to the Holy Land, as once the picture had made it there, the real person would hopefully receive hidāyah, being called to perform the pilgrimage.

An example of the departure rituals is the farewell of Ibu and Pak Sukis, a senior couple in Ladangtembakau—a small Madurese village. Ibu and Pak Sukis belong to the better- off families in the village. Their children are meanwhile working in the city, in Pamekasan, but they had taken time off from work to help their parents with the farewell celebrations. Putri, Ibu and Pak Sukis's daughter, told me how busy she had been in the preceding days, accompanying her mother to do the shopping and coordinating the neighbors in helping with the cooking. She took me inside the house and proudly presented the 500 souvenirs that they had acquired to give to neighbors and relatives after her parents' return. Seeing my puzzled expression, she explained that the people knew that these items, like headscarves and prayer bracelets, were purchased in Indonesia, but it did not matter too much as the important thing was sharing the joy of having completed the pilgrimage. She further informed me that the celebrations before and after the pilgrimage would double its cost of approximately three thousand US dollars for one person. She added that fortunately, visitors were contributing to the costs by bringing and making gifts, and I remembered the bag of sugar and the sack of rice that my hosts from the village and I had carried to Ibu and Pak Sukis's house. Later on, I found out that in other villages in Madura people record the form and quantity of gifts in order to return similar gifts on the next occasion, making these events occasions of reciprocal exchange.

Putri's eyes were swollen. She had been crying and explained that a hajj farewell is happy and sad at the same time, as completing the hajj means being *ikhlas*, having fulfilled all religious duties and, after all, many people would die during the hajj.[7] The farewell evening was spent consuming food, coffee, and cigarettes, singing songs and telling jokes, taking pictures and exchanging wishes and prayers.

The next day was Friday and at noon, when most of the men were in the mosque performing the Friday prayer, we returned to the house of Ibu and Pak Sukis, where a lot of women in festive clothing had already assembled, amongst them Ibu Sukis in the uniform Batik dress of the 2014 Indonesian national hajj clothing collection, with a government ID badge and hand luggage with the

FIGURE 2.1. Festival-like atmosphere during hajj departure, Pamekasan, October 2014. Photo by the author.

FIGURE 2.2. Waving hajj candidates goodbye, Pamekasan, October 2014. Photo by the author.

Indonesian flag and a name tag. Three decorated cars parked in front of the house and soon the sound of numerous motorcycles announced the return of the men from the mosque. Pak Sukis hurried into the house, where he changed into the uniform pilgrimage clothing and then all visitors fell silent, lined up in front of the house before Ibu and Pak Sukis, who stood next to each other and closed their eyes as the Imam standing behind them started to recite a Qur'an verse. After the recitation the Imam began to sing a song. As everyone joined in with the song, the Imam guided Ibu and Pak Sukis toward the car and to the sound of car horns and cheers they drove toward the city center of Pamekasan accompanied by a convoy of around ten cars and numerous motorcycles. On that day, fourteen coaches departed from Pamekasan to transport the pilgrims to the Asrama Haji, the hajj dormitory, in Surabaya, where they would spend the night before the flight to Saudi Arabia. People from all over Pamekasan regency met in the festival-like atmosphere, in food stalls and cheering crowds.

During the pilgrims' absence, their relatives commemorate them, during daily prayer gatherings, among other ways, in which the *sūrah yā'-sīn* is used, indicating the pilgrimage's ultimate significance for fulfilling all duties in Islam and the risk of dying on the journey. The sūrah yā'-sīn, the thirty-sixth surah of the Qur'an, which is usually recited during funerals and in remembrance of the deceased, is

FIGURE 2.3. Listening to stories from Mecca, Pamekasan, November 2014. Photo by Khotim Ubaidillah.

recited in evening gatherings by the pilgrims' family members. Moreover, departing pilgrims are sometimes washed, imitating a last washing before death, and they are invoked with the *azan*, the call to prayer, as is done with people who pass away. Even though these rituals remain important during the preparation, farewell, and remembrance of Indonesian, or in this case Madurese, pilgrims while they are abroad, in fact most Indonesians expect to return from the pilgrimage, not only viewing the hajj as the ultimate fulfilment of Islamic duties and the path to becoming *ikhlas*, but also having excitement about their return. In contrast to the claim that going on hajj means being ready to die, many Indonesian pilgrims appear to "depart in order to return," as one of my informants put it, hinting at the prestige of having completed the pilgrimage (cf. Frey 2004).

RETURN

When Ibu and Pak Sukis returned in November 2014 the convoy of cars and motorcycles that picked them up exceeded that of their departure. On their way to the village, they first stopped at the local mosque, where they performed a prayer of thanks. In the following days, they hosted a big celebration with *haddrah* or *rébanah* music, which is labeled as Arabic music, and with food and prayers. Pak Sukis, sitting on a stage, gave a report about their experiences in Mecca and Medina. Behind him was a larger than life photoshopped picture

FIGURE 2.4. Telling stories from Mecca, Pamekasan, November 2014. Photo by Khotim Ubaidillah.

FIGURE 2.5. Marking the return: House decorations, Pamekasan, November 2014. Photo by Khotim Ubaidillah.

FIGURE 2.6. Rébanah drumming for the Mecca returnees, Pamekasan, November 2014. Photo by Khotim Ubaidillah.

FIGURE 2.7. Transferring the blessings of Mecca: Asajère visits, Pamekasan, November 2014. Photo by Khotim Ubaidillah.

FIGURE 2.8. Transferring the blessings of Mecca: Asajère visits, Pamekasan, November 2014. Photo by Khotim Ubaidillah.

showing Ibu and Pak Sukis in front of the Ka'aba, and the slogan "Semoga menjadi Haji Mabrur," meaning "May you become virtuous Mecca returnees."

Many visitors hugged them, as it is believed that blessings are transferred through physical contact and through objects like souvenirs from Mecca. In Madura, this visiting of Mecca returnees is called *asajère*, which also means pilgrimage, and makes the visits of returnees a kind of pilgrimage as well (field notes Khotim Ubaidillah, November 15, 2014). My research partner Ubed's photographs illustrate the scope of the celebration and the Arab-inspired decoration, clothing, and music, which symbolizes pilgrims' transformation into hajj returnees.

Similar celebrations happen in a less extensive way for umrah returnees. The imagery of pilgrimage completion frequently involves markers of Arabic culture and even months after the completion of the pilgrimage, pilgrims dress differently. In urban areas, many middle-class Muslims perform the umrah numerous times and mark their status as virtuous pilgrims through a pious Pop Islamic lifestyle. They draw on the popular and commercial features of an urban middle-class Muslim lifestyle, especially regarding clothing style. Their fashionable headscarves and colorful *abaya* are obviously inspired by an Arabic clothing style and are sometimes referred to as "*gaya Arab*," meaning "Arab style."[8] This trend is similar among Malaysian female pilgrims, where the abaya—an Arab-style long robe for women—is a symbol of modern Muslim lifestyle (see Thimm 2018).

Compared to the extensive celebrations at the village level, the arrival in the transit area of the Asrama Haji is rather formal and sterile. Nonpilgrims are not usually allowed to enter the Asrama Haji, and my research partner Nuki and I had to apply for permission to enter. Apart from the opportunity to buy last souvenirs in a designated area with so-called Arab market stalls and the possibility of performing the first prayer back home, transit through the Asrama Haji mainly serves administrative purposes, like health checkups. After a brief note of welcome from a government representative and a joint prayer, the pilgrims went back onto the buses and continued toward their hometowns.

Labor Migrants' Invisibility in Mecca

Compared to the eventful weeks of the pilgrimage, labor migrants recount that they experience a rather monotonous everyday life of domestic work. While pilgrims travel to Saudi Arabia in large groups and for the special purpose of the pilgrimage, labor migrants often travel alone. Apart from the preparatory time that they spend with other migrants in training camps, where they learn Arabic and household skills, their mobility is a lonelier undertaking. In contrast to pilgrims who mainly move in Indonesian environments during their journey, knowing Arabic culture and customs mainly from the introduction provided by their preparation courses, female labor migrants who work as domestic workers in the Gulf experience Arab culture and customs in the intimacy of private homes, where they usually reside as live-in domestic helpers.

It is noteworthy that many migrants actually do perform the pilgrimage to Mecca and Medina during their stay in the Gulf. Quite often this is a recruitment strategy of migrant agencies and it is part of their contract that they would be enabled to perform the pilgrimage while working abroad. However, their pilgrimage is not always acknowledged as the equal of a pilgrimage that has been accomplished with a departure from and immediate return to Indonesia. This is another indication that what makes the journey meaningful is not only the mere adherence to ritual processes, use of prayers, and the same destination, but the overall social embeddedness of it. The pre- and postpilgrimage rituals that take place in Indonesia, traveling in a group, wearing the uniform Indonesian batik clothing, and adhering to the hajj management of the Indonesian government make the hajj an Indonesian hajj. Last but not least, the involvement of those who remain at home fosters social relationships and reciprocity that migrants miss out on when they perform the hajj during their stay abroad, which happens unnoticed.

In the Madurese village Batu Bintang in Pamekasan regency, which is known as a labor migrant village, I learned that Indonesian labor migrants often return to Indonesia in order to depart for the hajj from their home villages. A pilgrim from Batu Bintang explained that rituals at home, especially in rural areas, were more exciting (*lebih seru*). Without these rituals that notify everyone of a person's journey to Mecca, the hajj would not feel complete. This signifies that it is not simply the physical movement from Indonesia to the holy sites that makes someone a pilgrim, but the ritualized and embedded departures and returns.

This reveals another nuance of meaning of the pilgrimage, namely the significance of the hajj as a national event, considering that government guidance can become a ritual act as well. In this regard, the guidance that takes place in labor migration is strikingly similar. Pilgrimage and migration, as well as their respective aftermaths, are not individual undertakings. They involve people and parties that do not go on the journey themselves but nevertheless are somehow related to it. Both labor migrants and pilgrims experience the journey as something managed by various actors, including government and nongovernment agencies, village communities, families, and friends. Many of these actors play intermediary roles in the guidance of the physical movement toward the Middle East as well as the potential upward social mobility.

Profitable Navigation and Government Guidance

Apart from feeling guided by God, by collective embodied experiences, social networks, and local values, migrants and pilgrims are guided by the Indonesian government, primarily by its bureaucracy. A juxtaposition of research findings by Killias (2014) and Hooker (2008) reveals similarities in the guidance by the state:

> Islam means surrender [to] God, but in the context of the hajj the Indonesian Muslim also surrenders to the state. It is not possible, once the decision to make the pilgrimage has been made, to undertake it without complying with the laws of the state. (Hooker 2008, 206)

> Indonesian women do not simply leave the country as individual, independent migrants: they are recruited, trained, certified and briefed by a vast array of institutionalized actors even before they leave Indonesia. Interestingly, it is precisely by planning to move across national borders that they come under closer scrutiny of Indonesian state authorities—as increasingly pervasive techniques of state control . . . illustrate. (Killias 2014, 890)

In addition to regulating the physical mobility of pilgrims, the government guides them in their identification as Indonesian pilgrims. Through uniform pilgrimage clothing, national emblems on travel equipment, state-sponsored paraphernalia, and farewell and return addresses by government officials, the hajj becomes an encounter with the nation-state. It is almost impossible to leave the guided government paths during the pilgrimage and the government guidance evokes a cohort feeling among the Indonesian pilgrims, which labor migrants who equally accomplish the hajj cannot share with them.

While labor migrants are primarily instructed by their employers during their stay abroad, before and after the migration they are subject to government regulations in a similar way to pilgrims. Especially when they migrate with officially certified agencies, they remain in government-controlled channels during the preparation process. The government stresses its intention to protect migrants by regulating their movement, but it certainly also has an interest in inspiring migrants to identify as national citizens and to care for their families and for the nation by sending home remittances.

However, as the state channels the movement of migrants and pilgrims through regulations, laws, and fixed procedures, this form of guidance creates confusion among many migrants and pilgrims. Incomprehensible bureaucratic procedures and regulations evoke the need for additional guidance, which migrants as well as pilgrims find being supplied by intermediary actors such as private migration and pilgrimage agencies, local elites like teachers and religious authorities who act as informal brokers. Their service of navigating the odyssey through the bureaucratic jungle is a profitable undertaking. A look at the striking similarities of government guidance and brokerage in migration and pilgrimage reveals the guiding role of these intermediaries and the need for guidance in bureaucratic procedures.

Guiding Regulations and Government Permits

Upon having decided to become a labor migrant or a pilgrim, the first quest is to obtain a license proving legal status as a migrant or pilgrim and authorizing physical mobility. The license for labor migrants is the Overseas Workers Card, referred to as KTKLN (Kartu Tenaga Kerja Luarnegeri). Its equivalent for pilgrims is the SPPH, the Surat Pendaftaran Pergi Haji, or Letter of Hajj Registration. These bulky abbreviations are well known among migrants and pilgrims and obtaining a KTKLN or an SPPH is a quest. While government officials emphasize the utmost importance of these licenses, migrants and pilgrims lament the administrative burdens. Having obtained a KTKLN or SPPH is an achievement and the bureaucratic procedure becomes a kind of ritual process in itself.

The initial requirements to start this ritual process are similar for migrants and pilgrims, apart from age and gender. Most vacancies in the Gulf are for domestic workers and recruitment focuses on unmarried women between the ages of twenty and thirty. The other conditions for registration for migrants and pilgrims alike basically concern adherence to Islam and the possession of official identification papers. Fulfilling this latter aspect can be quite a complex undertaking, as the required citizenship documents include not only ID cards but also birth certificates and the infamous *kartu keluarga*, the family card, which is one of the most important identification documents in Indonesia. Processing an ID card or renewing one and updating the family card can be challenging and is in many cases related to journeys across the country as some people are only registered in their birthplace. In Indonesia possession of these documents, let alone a passport, is not entirely common. Processing the passport is one of the first stages of the bureaucratic ritual process to come closer to the goal of obtaining a KTKLN or SPPH. This means that in order to travel to the Middle East, Indonesians first have to officially become Indonesian citizens. As Killias points out aptly in the quote at the beginning of this chapter, they become Indonesian citizens when they plan to move across national borders (cf. Killias 2014, 890). However, the passports that migrants and pilgrims receive cannot be used for any other border crossing than that related to pilgrimage or migration. Concerning labor migrants, Parreñas (2001) therefore argues that they are only granted partial citizenship.[9] Hooker argues that in the course of processing identity documents and submitting to government guidance "the individual is reduced to a passive object to be put through the appropriate process, becoming totally dependent on possessing the correct forms required by the bureaucracy" (Hooker 2008, 210). Again, this quote equally applies to labor migrants. Pak Raharjo, the farmer from rural Yogyakarta who accomplished the hajj in 2012, lamented the fact that there is no opportunity to do the hajj more individually, as a backpacker, which would have been his preferred method of travelling to Mecca. The jungle of bureaucracy through which migrants and pilgrims have to navigate their way is dense.

ADMINISTERING LABOR MIGRATION

Officially, documented labor migration is managed under the authority of the Ministry of Manpower (Kementerian Ketenagakerjaan Republik Indonesia), formerly known as the Ministry of Manpower and Transmigration (Kementerian Tenaga Kerja dan Transmigrasi) and by local service units like the Service Unit for Manpower and Transmigration (Dinas Tenaga Kerja dan Transmigrasi). My inquiries concentrated on a subdivision that focuses on labor migration and that issues the KTKLN, the BP3TKI (Balai Pelayanan Penempatan dan Perlindungan Tenaga Kerja Indonesia, Service Unit for the Placement and Protection of Indonesian Labor Migrants).[10] Apart from approving labor migrants' legal status and registering them through the provision of the KTKLN, the BP3TKI assists with the placement of labor migrants as well as the coordination of training and preparation courses and reintegration of returnees. From the government employees' point of view, their guidance ensures protection of migrant workers. They complained that many migrants do not understand the importance of licenses like the KTKLN and the official procedures. They said migrants were lured into undocumented labor migration by dubious agencies that made it sound easier and faster. Billboards at the entrance of the BP3TKI advertised the significance of obtaining a KTKLN, warning of fraud and exploitation in labor migration through unauthorized agencies.

Apart from the migrants themselves, who found the process of obtaining the KTKLN time consuming and intimidating, labor migrants' rights activists denounced the KTKLN as a medium of control, an impediment for migration candidates, not ensuring the protection promised. Therefore, they launched a petition to abolish the KTKLN.

Besides fulfilling the requirement of possessing citizenship documents and a personal background that suits the vacancy descriptions, migrants have to fill out numerous forms and submit photocopies of the identification documents, their high school certificate, ID pictures, and previously processed documents from the immigration department, the police, local health community centers (*puskesmas*), the Dinas Tenaga Kerja, letters of confirmation from their parents (or a death certificate if parents have passed away) and spouse (if married), and proof of having paid for insurance. All of these documents need to be verified by the village head in the area of the migration candidate's residence before they are submitted to the BP3TKI in order to issue the KTKLN. This means that the family and in many cases, the whole village could be notified about a person's plan to become a labor migrant.

PILGRIMAGE BUREAUCRACY

The main actor in pilgrimage administration is the Ministry of Religious Affairs (Kementerian Agama Republik Indonesia), with the General Directorate of Hajj and Umrah Management (Direktorat Jenderal Penyelengaraan Haji dan Umrah) being responsible for pilgrimage issues. In bilateral cooperation with its Saudi Arabian counterpart, the ministry manages the mass mobility, the allocation of places for the hajj, and the waiting lists.

Due to the large numbers of pilgrims, the Indonesian government stretches their departure and return over a period of two months, which means that only on the essential days for the key rituals, between the eighth and twelfth of Dhu al-Hijjah, are all Indonesian pilgrims in Mecca. The government clusters pilgrims in so called "flying groups," *kelompok terbang*, abbreviated as *kloter*. One kloter consists of approximately four hundred persons. Every kloter is structured in an organizational hierarchy consisting of regional divisions and subdivisions, the smallest of which consist of ten to fifteen people. The subdivision head, like Pak Mariadi who was elected head of a subdivision from rural Yogyakarta, is responsible for keeping track of his group members and reports to the head of the regional division. In 2014, the 168,000 Indonesian pilgrims were organized into 375 kloter. The departure of the 375 airplanes was stretched from September 1 to 28, with approximately thirteen hajj charter planes each day.[11]

Furthermore, the ministry authorizes private travel agencies for the umrah and hajj, and provides spiritual guidance through its publications and ministerial Islamic scholars. The government's direct interaction with pilgrims happens through the ministries' local subdivisions, the Department of Religion, Departemen Agama (DepAg), and the Cluster for Hajj Guidance, Kelompok Bimbingan Ibadah Haji (KBIH). The KBIH mainly provides theological guidance, while DepAg is responsible for logistics and administration. Recently, the government has earned much criticism for its management of the hajj, because of accusations of corruption and frequently changing regulations.

Many of my interlocutors claimed that state-administered hajj funds are misapplied and that the whole preparation and registration procedure is very complicated. There is a vast array of frequently changing regulations on the hajj in the form of laws, presidential decrees, ministerial decrees, and resolutions concerning various topics like hajj finance, registration requirements, health issues, visa regulations, the allocation of participants, transparency of waiting lists, and the overall logistics.

The two different forms of hajj journeys that are managed by the government are the regular hajj (*haji regular*) and the special hajj (*haji khusus*). Moreover, a limited number of hajj places are marketed by private travel agencies as *haji plus* travel, offering superior standards of accommodation, transportation, and sometimes celebrity hajj guides.

About 90 percent of the pilgrims depart through the program for the regular hajj and approximately 10 percent depart on the special hajj program, which includes government delegations and guides (Indonesian Ministry of Religious Affairs 2016d). Law 34/2009 (*undang-undang* 34/2009) on hajj finance opened up the possibility of registering with the government for the hajj with a down payment (*uang muka*). Furthermore, according to this regulation pilgrimage candidates are obliged to use a special hajj savings system at a bank to finance their hajj, usually referred to with the abbreviation ONH (*ongkos naik haji*, travel expenses for the hajj). Validating a registration through down payment means that people can register before they possess the full amount of money needed for hajj expenses.

Many research participants criticized these new laws, saying that they caused an explosion of hajj registrations. In some regions, like East Java (including Madura) or Aceh, the waiting times for participation in the hajj grew to longer than twenty years (Ministry of Religious Affairs 2016e).[12] In order to elucidate the administration procedure, the Ministry of Religious Affairs provides a video guide entitled "Haji Pintar" (The Clever Hajj). The video explains that

> in order to register at the local branch of the Ministry of Religious affairs in the regencies or cities, hajj candidates have to fulfil the following conditions: 1) adherence to the religion of Islam, 2) age above twelve years, 3) no hajj participation in the last 10 years, 4) possession of a valid ID card with the correct address, 5) a family card, 6) a birth certificate, 7) a bank account for hajj savings. At the ministerial office they have to fill in registration forms, take a photo and fingerprints. Furthermore, the pilgrims have to open a hajj savings bank account at a bank that is approved by the ministry. In order to open such an account, they have to make a down payment of the minimal deposit [the video does not give numbers here]. This down payment needs to be transferred to the Ministry of Religious Affairs. Proof of this down payment BPIH [*biaya penyelengaraan ibadah haji*] and of its transfer needs to be submitted to the Ministry of Religious Affairs within five days and validates the registration. The hajj candidate then receives an official confirmation of the registration which is called *surat pendaftaran pergi haji* [letter of hajj registration], abbreviated as SPPH. The SPPH contains the *nomor porsi* [portion number], which indicates the position in the waiting list. Once a hajj candidate has proceeded in the waiting list, the payment of the full cost for the hajj is due to secure one's place for the next hajj season. (Ministry of Religious Affairs 2016c, my summary and translation)

Animated comic figures illustrate these explanations and the well-known song "Pergi Haji" (Going on Hajj) by the artists Pipik and Uje plays in the background, with the talbīyah as its underlying motif. In addition to the documents mentioned in the video, pilgrimage candidates also need a health certificate and proof of a meningitis vaccination. The concluding slogan of the video says "mudah dan transparen" (easy and transparent), though aspiring pilgrims with whom I talked found the procedure anything but easy.

Next to videos and banners, which express the importance of adherence to government procedures, brochures illustrate the process. Strikingly, the government brochures that are intended to guide migrants and pilgrims look quite similar, with arrows, cartoons and text fields, explaining the sequence of administrational duties. However, the government's attempts to make its guiding intentions, the complicated regulations, abbreviations, and specific jargon more accessible does not always succeed, and many migrants and pilgrims seek further guidance in order to understand the administrative "rituals" of becoming a migrant or pilgrim.

Guidance through Intermediaries

Because of the complicated bureaucratic procedures, the assistance of brokers is much appreciated among migrants and pilgrims alike. Contact with brokers can be established by actively approaching a travel agency for pilgrimage travels or a labor migrant agency. In many cases, however, it is not even necessary to search for intermediaries' assistance by going to the agencies' bureaus as there are intermediary actors who live in migrants' and pilgrims' neighborhoods or who are friends of friends, someone a distant relative has recommended, or a reliable public figure like a teacher in a local school (cf. Lindquist 2012). That brokers are not strangers appears to be essential with regard to the trust that is put in their ability to guide. Therefore, some agencies, especially for labor migration, officially or unofficially cooperate with local elites for the recruitment of migrants, which makes them resource persons who are continuously consulted during the administrative process.

Thus, even if brokers are informal, when they are well-known in the local context, from their clients' perspective, they appear to be official and reliable. Personal relationships in recruitment and consultation are highly valued, and these brokers are perceived as being more accessible than government institutions. For some labor migrants, this leads to the assumption that it can be safer to migrate through informal channels as undocumented migrants.

In Madura some migrants informed me that the government was not reliable at all. If there was a real emergency, one could wait forever for the embassy to act. Yet migrating with the "mafia"—as it was labelled in Madura—would ensure security. If, for example, one were harmed, sexually abused, or exploited by employers, one phone call to the "Madurese mafia in Mecca" would be enough, and I was assured that the mafia was ready to take *every* necessary step to guarantee the inviolacy and honor of Madurese women working abroad (see Lücking 2017).

When I unintentionally met a member of this so-called mafia, I learned from the caring motherly figure in pastel robes about the importance of intermediaries' empathy and sense of responsibility, their ability to understand people's situations, and to establish trust. The woman I met was a teacher in a neighboring village of my hosts and knew the lack of prospects for people in the rural areas of Madura. In the beginning, she recounted, she did not want to get involved with labor migration. However, due to her broad social network, people had approached her many times, asking her to introduce them to the labor migrant recruitment mafia, which she knew through family relations. Thinking how easy it was for her to simply connect someone with her relatives in Saudi Arabia, one day, when a woman was begging her to help, she gave in. Initially, she only introduced women to labor migrant brokers. Over time, she got more knowledgeable and more involved in intermediary activities. Now, people consulted her on various issues, seeking advice and help, as she was considered an experienced and influential person. That's how she slowly became a broker. She recounted that the women for whom she had arranged labor migration were thankful and had been successful. They had been able to support their families, build a house, and invest in the education of their children. Apart from recruitment, her brokerage includes assistance with financial transfers, as some persons do not own bank accounts or seek undocumented methods of money transferal.

Remarkably, in the strategies for circumventing state control, labor migration and pilgrimage are often intertwined as some pilgrims use migrant passports and vice versa. Such forms of "mixed migration" or undocumented labor migration are considered a welcome way to get around the official bureaucratic procedure and, most important, the waiting list for the hajj. One of the loopholes in the hajj regulation is the so called *umrah sandal jepit*, which literally means "umrah in flip flops," describing the strategy of using an umrah visa to enter Saudi Arabia and then staying there until the hajj season begins. Reportedly, this practice is often intertwined with labor migration, as these pilgrims work in temporary jobs while waiting for the hajj season (see Lücking 2017).

Migrating with the so-called mafia and doing the *umrah sandal jepit* or arranging travel through the official government channels are just two poles in a continuum of various possibilities for becoming mobile. In most cases, there is no black and white contrast, but only shades of grey, as even in the government bureaucracy there are sometimes informal aspects involved, and informal brokers make use of official channels too. Many agencies are authorized by the government and cooperate with it officially, while some operate more informally and semilegally. To identify the difference between a state-authorized agency and an undocumented (labeled by the state as "illegal") one is apparently hard for migrants and pilgrims, and ultimately the overall feeling of trust and knowing the brokers personally is considered more important than their legal status. Brokers know the legal situation very well and bridge the gap between bureaucracy and people, for which many migration and pilgrimage candidates are grateful and willing to pay. Thus brokerage becomes a profitable business.

Another interesting aspect of guidance through brokerage is that having had a personal experience as a migrant or pilgrim is considered beneficial, as these persons have gained an insiders' understanding. As the example of Mas Eko's aspiration to offer pilgrimage tours indicates, it can even be considered an indispensable requirement for travel agents to have experienced pilgrimage themselves. The process of becoming a broker oneself can start rather informally and subtly, by encouraging others to register with the same agency, asking others to come along (*mengajak*), providing information, or letting fellow migrants or pilgrims use one's own resources, ranging from bank accounts and mobile phones to social networks.

If this activity of recruitment and brokerage becomes more professional, the respective migrants and pilgrims become business partners of the agencies, or at least enjoy certain privileges or discounts for their own journeys. Guided customers can thus become guiding business partners. Some agencies use the offer of financing migration or pilgrimage through business partnership as a selling point. Again, the similarities between guidance as business in migration and pilgrimage are remarkable.

Accessing the Capital of Guidance

Benefits to some are costs to others.[13] The hajj costs about US $3,000 per person for the regular program.[14] In 2014, the costs for a nine-day umrah trip varied between promotion prices of US $2,000 and five-star hotel accommodation for US $4,000 per person.

Compared to an annual average income of US $3,475 per person (World Bank 2014), the umrah and the hajj are both costly undertakings for most Indonesians. The packages that pilgrims purchase for these prices include airplane tickets; the costs of passports and visas; an allowance of twenty-five kilograms of luggage; travel insurance; transportation and tours in Saudi Arabia; a team of assistants to carry luggage and so called *mutawwif*, helpers who guide the tawāf; preparation courses; five liters of zamzam water; three meals per day (often advertised as Asian meals); and accommodation. Additional payments are due for airport taxes, umrah clothing and equipment, meningitis vaccinations, food during additional tours, overweight luggage, additional worship activities at sites other than the official pilgrimage sites, and a certificate of a *muhrim*, which means a male companion, ideally a relative, for women under forty-five years who travel alone.

The minimum required balance pilgrims need to have in their hajj account to obtain the SPPH was 25,000,000 rupiah (US $1,845) in 2014. When the savings are sufficient, the "start deposit" (*setoran awal*) is transferred to the ministry and with proof of this the customers can obtain the SPPH. Research participants calculated that with around 200,000 pilgrims completing the hajj each year and the rough estimations of an average waiting period of fifteen years, the Ministry of Religious Affairs administers the down payments of around 3 million pilgrimage candidates. Along with these calculations, people expressed suspicions about the trustworthiness of the ministry and accusations of corruption.

In the private sector, the umrah business promises to be much more profitable than the hajj business, which is mainly managed by the government and because the limitation of hajj pilgrims by the quota means that there is not much room for expansion in the hajj business, whereas umrah travel keeps expanding. Critics argue that the travel agencies misuse peoples' aspiration to go on hajj and lure them into umrah journeys that are almost as expensive as the hajj, promising them that it would be worth postponing the hajj rather than risking being unable to go to the Holy Land at all due to long waiting periods. Considering the amounts paid by an estimated 1 million umrah pilgrims in 2013, paying an average of US $3,000 per trip, US $3 billion were spent on umrah trips, which gives an idea of the travel agencies' turnover.

Some travel agencies promote their packages by offering customers the opportunity to become business partners. The intertwinement of business and religion happens in the form of what is advertised as multilevel marketing, in which potential umrah candidates become partners as recruitment agents. These methods of multilevel marketing are criticized because fraud is widespread and travel agencies are especially interested in securing down payments, which they can invest and make profit in the form of interest. A down payment of about US $350 (approximately 3.5 million rupiah at the time of research) looks affordable in contrast to the full price of around US $2,000 for an average standard umrah trip. By administering the assets from the down payments alone, the travel agencies can make a profit from interest, something forbidden according to Islamic legal thought. Many financing systems that are advertised as "business partnerships" rely on Ponzi schemes, promising shares and benefits but in fact turning out to be unprofitable for most participants and causing economic bubbles. The Ministry of Religious Affairs warns citizens of these frauds.[15] However, it is equally accused of making profit from interest accrued from hajj funds.

In the context of labor migration, it is much more difficult to find exact numbers about brokerage fees, costs for administration, and preparation. The statements of my research participants indicate that the costs of recruitment, training, visas, vaccinations, insurance, flights, and placements vary between three and six monthly salaries that are usually automatically cut from the migrants' income. The minimum wage in Saudi Arabia was 1,450 SAR (US $387) per month in 2014. My findings suggest that the placement fee paid to the recruitment agency and the additional charges levied for the services of informal brokers can mean that women are in debt before their labor migration begins.

Selling Dreams

These examples of public and private navigation indicate that despite the different character of pilgrimage and labor migration, guidance happens in recurring patterns. Most obviously, the government seeks to guide through its legal tools of laws and regulations, by building organizational hierarchies and clustering travel units, making masterplans and itineraries. In this context, guidance not only leads mobile people toward their destination but also controls them and uses the opportunity to strengthen feelings of nationality. Informal brokers who have discovered a business opportunity in guiding others through the bureaucracy and private agencies intermingling in the guidance demonstrate that guidance can become a contested arena. In the example of labor migration and pilgrimage, the reasons for the contestations over guidance appear to be economic ones. The profitability of providing guidance indicates that mobility not only entails capital for those who move, but even more so for those who navigate.

While for the government and for private guides and agencies guiding constitutes a business opportunity, for mobile actors it entails significant costs. Migrants and pilgrims depend on the guidance, advice, and brokerage of agencies. However, those supplying guidance are also dependent on the level of demand from migrants and pilgrims, which confirms that guidance happens in interdependent relationships, as I argued the introduction of this book.

In order to keep demand stable, or even to increase it, the government as well as private agencies use advertisements that relate to their customers' aspirations. The most central buzzword in advertisements and guidebooks—for pilgrimage as well as labor migration—is the term *success*. Interestingly, government brochures for the hajj exhibit similarities with the travel agencies' advertisements, as there is a use of similar vocabulary, a mixture of English, Indonesian, and Arabic language, with the prominence of terms like *success* and *clever* inspiring desirable behavior. The ministry equally advertises models of hajj finance, investment strategies for hajj funds, spiritual guidance, and organizational matters, representing ideas of a successful, smooth pilgrimage economically and spiritually. A closer look at the representations of success allows conclusions about how guidance determines the local impacts of mobility.

Success Stories: Foreign Exchange Heroes and Virtuous Pilgrims

The return from Mecca marks the beginning of a new period in life. Successful pilgrims are expected to act as responsible members of society. Figure 9 shows the return of Ibu and Pak Sukis. They are escorted to their house in a convoy of cars, some of them decorated. Policemen and volunteers from the local boy scouts group in rural Madura direct the convoy. Their route is lined with food stalls, cheering people, and colorful banners. The banners express wishes that they become *haji mabrur*, which literally means that the hajj is accepted by God but can roughly be translated as becoming "virtuous hajj returnees." The banners also indicate the name of the sponsors of the warm welcome, in this case a local Qur'anic school and the government, in other areas, I saw posters of mobile phone companies and banks.

Given this lavish welcome, how could a Mecca returnee not become a haji mabrur? The great attention given to Mecca returnees by the local communities, by public figures, politicians, and media coverage puts them under pressure to live up to the expectations of the community that they become more righteous people and share their material wealth and spiritual gain.

FIGURE 2.9. Guiding the successful returns from Mecca, Pamekasan, November 2014. Photo by Khotim Ubaidillah.

Even though labor migrants usually depart and return in a less spectacular way and their sojourns are not related to a nationwide festival-like event, their migration is equally related to public and private expectations of returning as a responsible member of society, which is expressed in celebrating labor migrants as *pahlawan devisa*, as foreign exchange heroes and heroines.

In the expectations of the social responsibility of haji mabrur and foreign exchange heroines, the juncture of spatial and social mobility is evident. Conceptions of responsible returnees are related to the concept of success as an intertwinement of materiality and morality.

From the very beginning when persons consider migrating or going on a pilgrimage, their social network is involved in the undertaking of going abroad and the expectation of success becomes a guiding orientation in their decision to migrate or perform pilgrimage. In order to make the movement meaningful in retrospect and to access the social capital it entails, the right postmobile representations are essential, especially regarding the prospect of upward social mobility.

In my inquiries about what people make of the journey, the absence of stories of failure was remarkable. While news coverage does report problems in migration and pilgrimage, on an individual basis almost no one admits failures or inconsistencies and deviations from the norm. If failure is discussed, it is through self-mockery or by blaming others—those who manage the journey, like the government, or through representations of cultural Others, like Arab Others, as I will show in chapter 3.

The Nīya—Pilgrims' Sincere Intentions

For pilgrims, having a sincere personal intention is the first part of the pilgrimage ritual. In Islam, the *nīya*, meaning the intention to perform a ritual, concerns the inner state of heart and mind of believers. Only if believers have a conscious and committed intention to perform a ritual will the religious act be valid and meaningful. Ritual acts must be preceded by the performers' declaration of conscious intent to perform the act. This declaration might be pronounced audibly or mentally (Wensinck 2012, EI2).

The guidebooks provided by the government and travel agencies define conditions of how to become a virtuous pilgrimage returnee—a haji mabrur. According to the ulama that are cited in these guidebooks, the most important condition for becoming a haji mabrur is the nīya, the basic intention to do the hajj. This intention has to be *ikhlas* and *halal*, which is interpreted as having established sincere relationships with all friends, relatives and colleagues and leading a halal lifestyle, meaning to follow food restrictions, avoidance of alcoholic beverages, and modest clothing.

In accordance with Qur'anic and hadith recommendations for behavior during the hajj, these manuals characterize a haji mabrur as a person that cares less about worldly and material issues, and considers life beyond death, seeking to establish a good relationship with God and with fellow human beings, a person that will take on responsibility and educate family members. Besides these instructions, ulama also elaborate on the societal responsibilities of a haji mabrur, which include a general higher social concern and sense of responsibility, politeness, and increased piety that serves as an outstanding example for fellow believers (see Wajidi in Wisata Kahlifa 2015). The research with pilgrimage candidates revealed that the establishment of good relationships can also expand to those who have deceased, as the visiting of graves before the departure to Mecca was common.

This means that for pilgrims their prepilgrimage condition is crucial for the successful and sustainable completion of the pilgrimage. Guiding clerics explained that the establishment of a sincere nīya was not so much a personal decision but more an inner readiness to fulfill this fifth pillar of Islam and the hidāyah one would receive. Concerning this vocation, it was argued that if one was not ready for the hajj, one would usually feel it and then there were often unexpected obstacles that kept one from performing the hajj.

Of course, similar to the case of labor migrants, it must be taken into consideration that these motivations are the official and desirable reasons for performing the hajj. These were the reasons that were mentioned by guides, pilgrims, or pilgrimage candidates themselves, while other people, especially those who are critical of the recent pilgrimage boom, and also experts like anthropologists, sociologists and public figures, including religious leaders, argue that the strongest motivation to perform the hajj is the potential uplift in social status. They point to the prestigious character of the pilgrimage and the title of honor Mecca returnees hold after the completion of the hajj, women being addressed as *hajja* and men as *hajji*.

For the umrah, intentions are similar when spiritual renewal and upward mobility go together. My research partner Nuki Mayasari (2014) uncovered the social reasons for repeated umrah trips among urban middle-class women for whom the umrah was treated as method of recharging their faith and came in line with charity activities. Also, Mas Eko's statement at the beginning of this chapter indicates that umrah pilgrims aspire to become better Muslims.

Becoming a Haji Mabrur

At the time of their return pilgrims are greeted nationwide as "virtuous returnees." On TV shows, in newspapers, advertisements, and public speeches, on

Facebook and Twitter, in shopping mall decorations and on street banners, on gift cards and house decorations, the slogan "semoga menjadi haji mabrur," meaning "may you become an accepted/virtuous haji," is prominent. This wish or request illustrates that the hajj is not an individual endeavor, but that it is related to social responsibility and the expectations of the community. Even though first and foremost the concept of a haji mabrur means that the pilgrim is accepted by God, in everyday life it also means being accepted by the community. Virtuous pilgrims are expected to be honest, lead a halal lifestyle, and take on responsibility in their community, acting as role models for others. Through engagement with these expectations, Indonesian pilgrims assert their social status. Thus the pilgrimage is not only an engagement with Muslims from all over the world during the rituals in Mecca and Medina, but also with the community back home. The extensive pre- and postpilgrimage rituals and celebrations in Indonesia indicate the transformative character that the pilgrimage bears for the pilgrims. Through the completion of the pilgrimage, they boost their social status and upon return they inherit a new position. In their role as a haji mabrur, they have new privileges and responsibilities. Including the community in the rituals of preparation and return, and sharing the blessings of Mecca, are crucial in order to fulfil expectations.

Accordingly, alongside their actual experiences, pilgrims are eager to represent an image of the pilgrimage that suits the expectations of the community. Besides spiritual/religious aspects, postpilgrimage representations of success include material aspects. That Ibu and Pak Sukis had prepared five hundred souvenirs to be shared after their return indicates the need to share material wealth as well as blessings from the Holy Land. Interestingly, on a narrative level, virtue is also exemplified through the Othering of Arab people and other pilgrims one meets abroad. In retrospect, many pilgrims argue that Asians are the "better Muslims" and that this was obvious during the *hajj*, where they had met what they described as "uncivilized" people from Africa and harsh Arabs. Through the Othering of fellow Muslims, Indonesian Muslims affirmed their own moral superiority. Thus, among others, their self-representation as haji mabrur was also visualized through a rather gloomy portrayal of Arab culture (see chapter 3). Ironically, however, at the same time religious symbols, many of which look Arabic and are labeled as "Arab," are prevalent as a medium through which to represent being a haji mabrur. Indonesian pilgrims take off the uniform batik dresses that identify them as members of the Indonesian communitas after returning home and display their increased spirituality through a new clothing style that often uses Arabic cultural markers, like a Saudi Arabian *jubbah* or the checkered *kufiyah* cloth. As a result, the image of Arabness becomes an ambiguous one.

Aspirations of Labor Migrants

During my stay in Ladangtembakau, one of the young women in the village informed me that before her marriage she also had wanted to become a labor migrant. She had just finished school and could see few future prospects in Madura. What an adventure it would have been to go abroad, see something new and earn some money with which she could have supported her family in Madura. She had begged her mother to allow her to register for a labor migrant program. Yet her mother was skeptical. She told me that she even consulted with a *dukun* (a spiritual guide or healer) and eventually her parents decided that it was best for her to get married and to stay in Madura. When we got to know each other, she had settled with her husband and children, farming tobacco fields like so many people in Madura. "Watering tobacco on and on"—that's how she described her daily activities to me, repeating the word "watering," in Indonesian *(me)nyiram*, several times—"nyiram, nyiram, nyiram," emphasizing the dullness of this labor.

Evidently, many young people in rural areas in Indonesia, in this case Madura, dream about a brighter tomorrow. They have been left out of the country's economic growth. On TV and during visits to urban areas, they witness the change of lifestyle of the urban middle classes, and they long to take part in modernity (Wiyata 2002, 84; Rifai et al. 2013, 186).

Going abroad as a labor migrant appeals to many people as a promising way to quick economic gain. Wages in the Middle East or neighboring Southeast Asian countries are higher than in Indonesia, and there is a widespread assumption that labor abroad is not as hard or dull as work on the fields back home. The comprehensive studies of Silvey (2004, 2006, 2007) show that the motivations that women identify for going abroad are mostly in line with the socially accepted reasons, while some personal motivations are perceived as being less legitimate. As Silvey argues, female labor migrants represent their migration as "having been prompted most basically by the needs of the family, particularly the needs of children" (Silvey 2006, 32). However, "some women also wanted to escape marriages that were violent or unfulfilling; some were curious to visit foreign countries and felt bored staying in Sunda; and some also wanted to make the holy pilgrimage to Mecca" (ibid., 32). Except for the potential opportunity to complete the pilgrimage, these latter reasons are rarely mentioned openly. The discrepancy between socially accepted reasons to migrate and personal ones that are not desirable reasons for migration also feature in postmigration narratives and representations of success. Thus making mobility successful begins with the representation of the "right" reasons for migration.

About Fate and Morality among Labor Migrants

The term *sukses* bears a general centrality in emic conceptualizations of migration in Indonesia. In Gunungembun in Central Java, migrant women were often divided into the categories of "success" and "failure" by neighbors who hardly knew any more about their migration experiences. My host in Gunungembun, Ibu Nani, who had been one of the first labor migrants from her village in the 1980s, introduced me to many other female labor migrants in the area. Each time we approached a house she would give me some preparatory information in which the question of whether the person we were about to meet had been successful in her labor migration was very central. Sometimes Ibu Nani just said "dia sukses" ("she was successful"), or, "now we are visiting the house of Ibu Anisa, Thank God [*Alhamdulliah*] she was successful" and "I will introduce you to Ibu Lastri, unfortunately she was not successful." When we walked through the village, she would stop at newly built and freshly painted houses and mention that these were the houses of successful labor migrants.

Johan Lindquist's (2009) analysis of migration from Batam to Singapore confirms this emic dichotomy between success and failure. In order to characterize the regions' role as a hub for Indonesians who aspire to migrate to Singapore to benefit from booming economic development abroad, the letters of the island's name (B.A.T.A.M.) are transformed into various acronyms, among others: "Bila Anda Tiba Akan Menyesal—When You Arrive You Will Regret It"; and "Bila Anda Tabah Akan Menang—If you Endure You Will Succeed" (Lindquist 2009, 8, emphasis in original). This indicates the ambivalent attitude toward migration in search of success, the fear and risk of failure, and the perceived dichotomy of these two outcomes of migration. The reaction to failure is, as Lindquist analyses, a feeling of *malu*, which means an emotional state of "shame," "embarrassment," and "shyness" (Lindquist 2009, 7). In Madura as well as in Central Java, I was repeatedly informed that some labor migrants' fear of feeling malu makes them take on debt to pretend that they had been successful and to fulfil expectations. A Madurese who had settled in Yogyakarta, in his case the *rantau*, the destination of *merantau* (migration), recounted that he could not go home for Idul Fitri, the celebration at the end of the fasting months of Ramadan, because he couldn't afford to buy or rent a car for the return home. He explained that he wasn't exactly poor and that his business ran well but he couldn't meet the expectations of his family back in Madura, which he described as exorbitant and unrealistic.

MAKING THE RIGHT INVESTMENTS

Evidently, the representation of success relates to certain material expectations. While there is empirical evidence that the majority of remittances are actually spent on daily consumption (see introduction), during my stay in Central Java and Madura I observed that labor migrants are expected to invest in building houses, which are considered the most visible proof of success. Some of these houses look quite luxurious and I was often astonished to stand in front of two-story houses with spacious entrance areas and monumental pillars, painted in bright colors or yellow, pink and green in some very remote areas. Many people have to migrate numerous times in order to achieve this goal, which results in the phenomenon that there are newly built houses that are not yet inhabited. An extreme example of this is the labor migrant village Batu Bintang in Pamekasan regency in Madura, a village of beautiful new houses on the slope of a hill that resembles a ghost town as the dwellers are still abroad, mainly in Malaysia.

Building a house is regarded as an investment, along with the education of children, investment in land and in small-scale businesses. Whether remittances do enhance a nations' economy is questionable (see Adams and Cuecuecha 2010). Investments in education, land, and business are regarded as a sustainable and development-enhancing usage of remittances. In contrast, consumption is denounced as unsustainable. Based on these development theories, the Indonesian government as well as some private companies try to promote sustainable usage of remittances and support migrants in starting small-scale businesses after they return home. In Gunungembun, almost all returned migrant women had started chipboard cottage production. The chipboard company had targeted rural areas with a high percentage of labor migrants for production assistance. The migrants invested remittances in buying the equipment for the cottage production and the material to produce chipboards, which they later sold to the chipboard company. Apart from this, women in the village had experimented with cow and bird breeding, small retailing businesses, and cookie production. Labor migrants invest significant amounts of their financial capital and at times draw on credit to start businesses, as doing this is considered a sign of success and promises further success.

While chipboard production in Gunungembun appeared to be comparatively successful, other businesses turned out to be completely unprofitable and the disappointed migrant returnees considered going abroad again, where the wages are much higher, eventually becoming "trapped" in circular migration. A woman who had received seed capital to open a *warung* (snack bar) and a guesthouse for tourists in a government reintegration program meekly conceded that the large numbers of tourists that the region was hoping to welcome hadn't come and that so far she hadn't earned much from her business.

In other cases, labor migrants are lured into potential "businesses" that turn out to be strategies to exploit them. In Madura some migrant returnees were working for the Chinese multilevel marketing company TIENS, selling cosmetics online. The company provided expensive presents, like motor scooters, for migrants who were willing to become members, declaring their program a support project for labor migrants. However, in the course of their membership, members have to reach sales achievements or pay off debts and the system is just like the Ponzi schemes that pilgrimage travel agencies use to attract customers.

The representation of sustainable investment contrasts with evidence that remittances are mainly spent on daily needs like food, fuel, and electricity (cf. IOM 2010). Moreover, the vast number of jewelry stores that caught my attention in Madura and Central Java appear to be much frequented by labor migrants. Gold bracelets, new motor scooters, and satellite dishes hint at the fact that, beyond well-intended investment plans, remittances are spent on the prestigious consumer goods of a middle-class lifestyle to which many migrants aspire, or perhaps on a search for reliable assets like gold. This is, however, a controversial issue. In public discourse, migrants, especially female labor migrants, are celebrated as foreign exchange heroes and government and recruitment agencies try to condition migrants to sustainably invest remittances and send as much money home as possible. This includes the warning not to waste their income on consumer goods for personal pleasure, especially not during their time abroad (see Chan 2014, 2015).

The image of foreign exchange heroes applies on the ground as well. In Gunungembun, the village head, Pak Estiono, explained that the village had been built through the remittances of migrant women. Besides investing in their own houses and children's education, the women had also supported the construction of a new school building and the mosque. He explained that he admired the women for what they had done and reflected that he was malu that he, as a man, could not contribute to the prosperity of the village in the same way. He recounted that he was willing to migrate as well, but that there weren't many working opportunities for men abroad. In fact, he had accompanied his wife to Saudi Arabia because he did not want to let her travel there alone. However, he admitted that he could not endure living in Saudi Arabia. "Saya tidak tahan" ("I couldn't stand it"), he said. He described how harsh and violent the Arabs were and that he hated them; in the end he decided to leave after a year, before his contract as a driver terminated. Pak Estiono concluded that he admired the women of Gunungembun for their persistence and their sacrifice (personal communication, March 19, 2014). His statement mirrors general public opinion that the migrant women make sacrifices for the well-being of their families and the nation. My host, Ibu Nani, often joked "duit pulang, tapi orangnya tidak pulang-pulang," meaning "the money comes home but the people do not," referring to the circular migration of many women. They would not see their children growing up, but they could support them financially. She remarked that the women themselves could not enjoy their success, as they lived very modestly abroad in order to send as much money home as possible. However, Ibu Nani lamented that the women's families, especially their husbands, did not honor the sacrifice they made. In fact, many men would spend their wives' remittances on gambling, alcohol, and prostitution.

Clearly, the emic concept of success involves ideas of morality. It is not only the financial outcome of migration that makes a labor migration successful. It is also the "right" usage of remittances and personal modesty and faithfulness. Pak Estiono's remarks about not being able to stand the hardships indicate that the portrayal of Arab culture comes into play in the representations of hardship.

The discrepancy between statistics about the usage of remittances and labor migrants' representations is similar to the representation of acceptable reasons to migrate or more personal, not openly presented ones. The discourse about success promotes an image that migrant women are "frugal, non-social, and save almost all their earnings for their family at home" (Chan 2015). Silvey (2004, 2006, 2007), Killias (2017, 2014), and Chan (2014, 2015) show how the Indonesian government, travel agencies, and partly even human rights and women's rights NGOs construct the image of submissive, modest, and pious migrant women that need to be protected. These narratives serve as reference points for migrant women's representation of the experiences abroad. Thus, the guiding factors determine the outcome of migration. Silvey argues that the "migrant female body is constructed as a vessel and emblem of the nation itself, thus extending and reimagining the territory in which the state is held responsible for its citizens" (Silvey 2004, 260).

As Lindquist shows, many migrants feel guilty about potentially becoming immoral, or wild, as the emic term *liar* (wild) is frequently used with reference to life in the *rantau,* the destination of migration (Lindquist 2009, 7). In public discourse and also at the village level, women are criticized if they spend money on clothes, makeup or leisure, and enjoying life abroad (Chan 2014, 6956). In addition to potentially selfish consumption and free-time activities, women are also not conceded any social or emotional needs. Migrating men, in contrast, are excused for spending money on cigarettes, food, accommodation, and commercial sex as "these were 'biological necessities,' or needed for the men to adapt to foreign cultural norms and cope with the pressures of living and working overseas" (Chan 2015, 6956). Men who are left behind in the village are excused in a similar manner. Silvey describes that most migrant women react in an understanding way when they find out about the infidelity of their husbands and do not blame them for having spent the remittances carelessly and selfishly while they were abroad. Many migrant women regard divorce as "inevitable after such long separations because male sexual needs required fulfillment that could not be provided from a distance" (Silvey 2006, 31). My observations indicate that men are not always excluded from moral judgements. In Gunungembun, Pak Estiono was one of the people under suspicion. In fact, there were rumors about his mysterious material gain in Saudi Arabia. Reportedly, he had found a wallet full of money and thereby financed his election as village head. But in fact no one knew if that was the true story of the sudden material luck. Some villagers also characterized him as a *preman* (a gangster), and he obviously did not fit in the category of a morally unobjectionable successful labor migrant. His harsh criticism of Arab people seemed to be a way to resolve doubts about the legitimacy of his material gain in Saudi Arabia. Apparently, the representations of labor migration revolve around constructions of morally unobjectionable success that involve the representation of hardship, constructed by Othering Arab culture as a particularly hard to endure context.

REPRESENTATIONS OF HARDSHIP

Enduring a difficult situation is considered a crucial condition for success. In training and preparation courses it is impressed on labor migrants that they must endure difficult situations, remain patient (*sabar*), and avoid conflicts and problems. Patience and humility would protect them from trouble. Trouble seekers, in contrast, would encounter trouble.

Representations of hardship are guided by public discourse about the legitimacy and illegitimacy of success. Chan identifies three categories in public representations of migrant women: national heroines, who contribute to Indonesia's economic development; exploited victims of an unequal global labor economy; and "immoral victims" that are represented as personally responsible for their tragic fate because of immoral behavior (Chan 2014, 1950). She touches indirectly on a forth category, namely the immoral, materially successful migrant women who potentially gained their money through immoral activities. Even though the categories of "hero" and "victim" appear to be contradictory, they are constructed along similar "gendered moral assumptions" (ibid., 6949). Similar to Chan's observations, the narratives of appreciation of success in Gunungembun were usually followed by representations of hardship. Migrant women who were able to remit significant amounts of money home carefully emphasized how hard their time abroad had been and how much they had sacrificed. Moreover, they evoked images of harsh and violent Arabs and emphasized their own moral superiority. Through the othering of Arab culture, migrant women invoke the image of enduring hardship and superior morality. This justification of their success is crucial, as there was gossip about migrants whose financial success was seemingly unjustified, such as in the example of Pak Estiono.

Unexpected material gain is called *rejeki* in Indonesian. Rejeki is shared and since it is regarded as unexpected luck and not the result of individual labor, there is no obligation to return the gift. Yet with regard to labor migration, rejeki causes suspicion. My observation corresponds with Chan's analysis of perceptions of immorality in the context of labor migration. The migrant women in Gunungembun indicated that the amount of money that some women remitted home was not equivalent to wages abroad. Everyone knew what the average wage of a domestic servant in the Middle East, Hong Kong, and Taiwan was. According to other migrant women, the houses that some families of migrant women built and the goods they consumed far exceeded the financial capacity that they could have earned through domestic work. Consequently, they concluded that these women must have been involved in some additional work or side activities, hinting at sex work. After further inquiry, it was admitted that there was still the possibility that these women had very generous employers and were just lucky to get this rejeki. Obviously, the representation of success is a matter of negotiation and an emphasis on personal piety and a representation of the time abroad as a time of hardship and personal sacrifice increased the acceptance of material gain. Migration agencies invoke these ideas of rejeki and fate by emphasizing that humility, modesty, and piety would foster a good fate (Chan 2015; Silvey 2004, 2006, 2007).

If migrant women do not remit significant amounts of money and are thus perceived as having failed, a similar moral evaluation applies. An innocent victim is perceived as having done no wrong and simply having had a bad fate. The "innocent migrant woman" is portrayed as a victim in media coverage and sometimes also in activists' rhetoric about labor migration and the government's claim to care for these victims (Silvey 2007, 269). Yet there is also the category of the immoral victim as "uneducated, untrained and naïve, . . . as psychologically ill, morally ambiguous or suspect" (Chan 2014, 6958). Chan observed that morality is also questioned when there aren't any remittances from migrant women: "If women do not send money home regularly, villagers are quick to accuse them of immoral behavior overseas, such as loose sexual behavior, adultery, and abandoning familial duties" (Chan 2015).

In the end, having failed would mean that migrants' *nasib* (their fate) had not been good, and this view would probably make them even more upset. I realized that it is widely assumed that a labor migrants' success or failure is their own personal responsibility and that there is little solidarity among labor migrants. Even among activists, success and failure are often individualized and they portray labor migrants as victims needing protection, rather than criticizing the system itself. In her overall evaluation of labor migration in Gunungembun, Ibu Nani said: "Well, many are successful, and many aren't. You never know how your fate is, you can just pray that your fate is good, be a good person, don't do wrong, a good person will encounter a good fate and experience success" (personal communication, March 21, 2014).

It was probably in order to assure others of their own moral righteousness that labor migrants told stories about situations in which they had resisted temptation, remained innocent and loyal to their moral values, even though others wanted to drive them into trouble, dealt patiently with accusations from their employers, and increased their adherence to Islamic rules. They recounted how they dealt with unjustified accusations of stealing and lying by their employers or that the employers would test the domestic workers by putting expensive jewelry as a temptation in a room that the helper should clean. As a domestic worker, one would have to remain patient and trustworthy and not do wrong. Eventually a good person would encounter a good fate.

NONREPRESENTATION OF EXPERIENCES ABROAD

Although representations of hardship were common, more comprehensive representations of migrants' experiences abroad, especially regarding more positive experiences, tended not to be shared. In Gunungembun, who had been successful and who had not was common knowledge. Ibu Nani also knew about investments and consumption, as well as divorces and rumors about debt or conflicts in a family. However, she didn't know much about the exact income of fellow labor migrants or their experiences abroad. She obviously concluded from their investments and consumption, from small talk with neighbors and fellow labor migrants, and from what she had overheard about success and failure. Ibu Nani recounted that when a successful labor migrant returned to the village, there was sometimes a small celebration but no lengthy talking. The return of unsuccessful migrants could occur without any notification of their arrival and they would not investigate too much about the reasons for failure. It also took quite some time during interviews to actually come to talk in more depth about experiences of migration. Conversations and interviews often began with expressions of gratitude for a good fate and success resulting from this. While some conversations remained rather superficial, others became quite lively, especially with the women whom I got to know better and met several times. They would even state that they were happy to tell someone about their experiences as there was little interest in them among family and friends.

On the rare occasions when relatives talked, they showed little knowledge about their daughters', mothers', and wives' experiences abroad. When engaging with teenage girls in Gunungembun, I learned that they felt alienated from their mothers and would not spend much time with them when they came back home. Migrant women explained that their families did not ask much about their experiences and they did not impose their stories on them in order avoid making a bigger issue of the migration than it was already. This included avoiding showing off with language skills in Arabic and Mandarin, even though many migrant women were proud of their skills and indicated that they regretted slowly forgetting them over time. However, after return, their utmost desire seemed to be to go back to a normal life. Their endeavor to return to normality and foster harmonious relationships within the family conflicted with newly gained experiences, consumption desires, and emotional ties to the people they had met abroad. Thus there was a general tendency to describe time abroad in a rather gloomy light, as a time in which the labor migrants were fully dedicated to their work and lived modestly to send as much money home as possible.

However, livelier accounts of experiences abroad that cropped up in some interviews indicate that there might be a discrepancy between the representations of hardship and actual experiences abroad. Even though the time abroad was often described as a time of hardship, many women indicated that there had been experiences of joy and relationships that they cared about. The problem of how to represent these experiences seemed to be their complexity, which evoked ambivalent feelings. This is especially relevant in the context of care work.

Personal care complicates the affiliations and feelings of belonging and not belonging, or even ostracism, experienced by labor migrants. Estrangement from their own children troubles migrant women, creating feelings of guilt and loss, as they feel that they belong with what they called their "real family" in Indonesia. This appears to be one of the reasons why there is little talk about emotional entanglements abroad after migration. The women appear to be emotionally troubled, as their emotional ties to people abroad are rather ambivalent. Killias analyses how a migrant woman describes how she missed a handicapped man she had cared for and how, at the same time, she had hated him in a way, and was always keen to leave (Killias 2014, 895). Similarly, Ibu Anisa, a migrant returnee in Gunungembun who had worked in Saudi Arabia, recounted how she had established a feeling of solidarity with the young Saudi generation. She criticized Arab people harshly, but she excluded the youth from her criticism. She complained about the bad treatment of women in Saudi Arabia, pitying Arab girls: "I was not happy to see the youth there. Especially the girls and how they know they have to behave themselves. Even though they are still small children, they know they have to behave in a certain way. You become afraid [for them], even the adults, and the small children know that harassment happens often" (Ibu Anisa, March 21, 2014).

Furthermore, she described that she had told these girls about Indonesia and that many of them said they would like to live in Indonesia, which reveals that migrants do engage with the people they meet abroad. Ibu Anisa's differentiation between Arab youth and Arab society in general indicates that labor migrants experience the circumstances abroad not as "black and white," like the simplifications of success and stereotypes of Arab culture, but as more complex and sometimes also disturbing because they do not fit into the schematic representations.

Interviews revealed that the migrant women had observed a lot about habits in their destination countries. Their cohabitation with the families they worked for gave them insights into family life, culture and customs. The reasons for reducing representations of Arab culture to stereotypes nevertheless seemed to be due to the lack of room afforded for more complex stories and the ambivalences they entail. In a few exceptions, especially among siblings, there was more exchange about experiences of migration. Ibu Nani's daughter, for instance, had learned some Korean language from her older sister who had worked in Korea. From my observations in Gunungembun, I got the impression that the family still represents the most open environment for exchange of experiences. Even though labor migrants explained that fellow labor migrants would understand them best, as they shared similar experiences and they sometimes joked about having secret languages, there seemed to be little in-depth exchange about the time abroad, and in some cases there was even distrust and suspicion. Ibu Nani explained said that she was happy to accompany me because thereby she could eventually hear their stories as well. Obviously, rather than sharing stories about their experiences; cooking food that they liked to eat in the Middle East, Hong Kong, Taiwan or Malaysia; speaking in the languages they had learned; or describing the people they had met and the challenges they encountered, migrants mainly reduced the representation of their experiences and of the cultural Others they had cohabited with to stereotypes and representations of success (in most cases) and failure (in some).

Guidance of Social Mobility

Personal ambitions to complete migration and pilgrimage successfully, as well as communities' expectations of sharing in this success, reveal how public discourse about norms and morality influence migrants and pilgrims and guide them in what they make of their mobile experiences—or at least what they represent thereof. It is remarkable how similar the norms and values in the two contexts are, indicating that the different experiences of migrants and pilgrims abroad are not so significant for the impact of the journeys. Representations of success after a pilgrimage or work abroad are oriented toward existing social values and expectations rather than new inspiration from abroad. In both cases, social pressure and social control mark the guidance. Migrants' and pilgrims' ability to evoke the approved images of their journeys to the Middle East and to share their newly gained wealth and spirituality ultimately determines the prospect of upward social mobility.

The leading discourses concern Indonesian, or more precisely Javanese, values like modesty, the caution of managing or avoiding feelings of shame (malu), accepting one's fate, and not acting selfishly but establishing reciprocity and considering what is best for the family and the broader community. Furthermore, representations of success draw on ideas of modernity, exhibited through consumer goods, even though for migrants this is not always evaluated positively by their community. The pilgrims' use of Arab-style clothing and souvenirs as symbols of success in spiritual regards appears to remain an outward cultural marker. This last aspect—spiritual renewal—is where the representations of success of migrants and pilgrims differ. The symbolic capital that the portrayal of "Arabness" entails for Mecca returnees is not equally present among labor migrants. In chapter 4 I shall discuss the reasons for this difference, considering why the symbolic capital of Arabness is not equally accessible.

Guided Mobility in Spatial and Social Spheres

The synopsis of migrants' and pilgrims' experiences of guided mobility highlights how guidance determines the impact of mobility. The juncture of physical and social mobility is characterized by guiding narratives like moral discourses that accompany migrants and pilgrims. The various forms of guidance, such as guidance by God, guidance through collective practices, embodied sensation of rituals, institutional guidance through laws and regulations, intermediaries' navigation, social networks, and local values lead migrants and pilgrims. However, it is obvious that certain forms of guidance are more intentional and have a more significant impact on the outcome of mobility than others. While the physical mobility of migrants and pilgrims is enabled through interpersonal and institutional guidance, their social mobility only becomes possible through adherence to the moral values of their home context. Only through migrants' and pilgrims' engagement with this normative guidance can their spatial mobility be related to social mobility. Besides sharing materiality, migrants as well as pilgrims engage with the social and moral systems of their home societies. Thus the paths of migrants and pilgrims are prepared by the overall guidance of the journey and their returns are embedded in the social context back home.

The juxtaposition of labor migration and pilgrimage reveals how the different outcomes of mobility depend to a significant degree on guidance in local social contexts. Social (im)mobility as a potential effect of spatial mobility does not result from spatial movement per se, but from the migrants' and pilgrims' ability to make their movements meaningful. Pre- and postpilgrimage rituals, an inner intention, or nīya, and success stories reveal that the outcome of mobility depends tremendously on social embeddedness back home. Pilgrims are under pressure to share their potential wealth and spirituality in extensive celebrations that make the pilgrimage complete, as well as act as pious role models and responsible members of society. Labor migrants are equally expected to share their material wealth and care for their communities. The context-bounded returns indicate that for Indonesian migrants and pilgrims, Javanese and Madurese values and national discourses can be more significant for their experiences abroad—which are a black box for their relatives and for the researcher. Interestingly, it is through the discursive Othering of Arab culture that loyalty to local values can be assured.

An assessment of the impact of mobility, through remittances or through migrants and pilgrims as "change agents," must include the home context. Pilgrims and migrants do not go to the Gulf as empty vessels, their vision is not only directed toward their destinations, and they do not spend their time abroad as curious adventurers. In contrast, they travel in order to return and considering that their vision is much oriented toward their home context, the change that occurs in the context of migration and pilgrimage must be seen as circulation, rather than as a one-way flow of financial and cultural, religious and political remittances. An illustrative example of this are the akik rings that Indonesian pilgrims buy in Mecca. Their circulation in being shipped from Indonesia to Saudi Arabia and then taken home again by the pilgrims can be seen as metaphor for a similar movement of norms and ideas. The mobility has a transformative effect, but this effect only becomes effective through social embeddedness.

Considering this, anxieties about an Arabization being carried out by migrants and pilgrims appear to be misconceived. As the examples of returnees' lifestyle preferences indicate, ideas about Arabness and Arab style primarily become an outward cultural marker, symbolizing economic and spiritual success. On the level of normative structure, however, peoples' self-identification, the values they adhere to, and their behavior and loyalties exhibit Indonesian, Javanese and Madurese culture and customs such as reciprocity, humbleness, collectivism, and local religious rituals that would in fact conflict with Wahhabi norms.

Finally, mobility has different meanings for labor migrants and pilgrims: pilgrimage is highly prestigious, while labor migration has a rather undesirable image in society. This also means that spatial mobility does not automatically imply social mobility, or at least not the same social mobility. In fact, many labor migrants experience social stasis. Even if they can accumulate significant financial capital, they do not experience the same boost in their social status as pilgrims do.

However, not everything is predetermined through various forms of guidance. The examples presented here have also indicated that there are contestations and that there is often more than one path indicated by guidance. That migrants' and pilgrims' unequal possibilities for upward social mobility depend on diverging normative discourses, and images associated with migration and pilgrimage is a vivid example of this. Even though the choice of what guidance one adheres to is not arbitrary, there are indications of creativity and deviation from the main road of the leading normative discourse, as pilgrims' side excursions to places like the hill of grace and supernatural experiences, as well as migrants' personal engagement with their employers abroad, suggest. When people leave the beaten tracks, this is probably not represented as prominently as the experience of having followed them. Yet in some cases, the choice between competing guiding discourses becomes a public debate, as indicated by Cak Nun's criticism of the pilgrimage boom. In the following, I shall describe the different and frequently competing representations of Arab Others, showing in what ways competing guiding narratives mirror internal Indonesian frictions.

3

ARAB OTHERS ABROAD AND AT HOME

The insights about patterns of guided mobility in social, spatial, and cultural spheres reveal the guiding function of situated representations. Migrants' and pilgrims' experiences, as described in chapter 2, reveal that moral values, social relationships, and public discourses give them orientation in the overall process of going abroad and returning home. Context-bounded cultural representations include, for instance, migrants' representations of success that relate to ideas of morality in their home context. Apart from the administrational infrastructures, which mainly guide spatial mobility, these representations guide the social mobility of migrants and pilgrims.

The following analysis of situated representations is narrowed down to representations of Arab Others, drawing on migrants' and pilgrims' narrations on Arab Others and on the more general media representations of Arab Others in Indonesia. In order to understand how migrants and pilgrims relate to general discourses in society, I include the perspective of non-Muslim groups and of popular media representations.

On the basis of Salazar's definition of "cultural mobility" as the movement of knowledge, ideas, norms, habits, and "mobility imaginaries" (Salazar 2010a, 64), I seek to unravel how representations of Indonesian selves and Arab Others in the context of migration and pilgrimage indicate changes in cultural and religious orientations in Indonesia—in particular what is perceived as the conservative turn. The discussion relates to the questions that resulted from the historical overview in chapter 1 and leads them further, regarding recent controversies about the authenticity of Islamic lifestyles and the competing promotion of

Arabness as an authentic feature of Islam and local Islamic culture in the Islam Nusantara discourse. This also concerns the distinction between the Arab "heartlands" of Islam and Indonesia at the periphery of the Muslim world. Interestingly, Indonesians do not only locate Arab Others abroad in reference to their migration and pilgrimage but also find them at home. This shows that the making and functioning of guiding narratives concerning Arab Others is contradictory and contested. Situated representations are subject to controversies and personal interpretations.

The analysis primarily focuses on data from investigations in Java and on nationwide media representations. Engagement with Arabness in Madura differs significantly from the Central Javanese context, as I shall show in chapter 4.

Representations of Arab, the World and the Self

Pak Mariadi, the fellow hajj returnee of Pak Raharjo from rural Yogyakarta, described Arab people in a negative light. In his evaluation, he referred not only to firsthand encounters in Saudi Arabia but also to holy books, which led him to the following conclusion:

> But really, the Arab people are just crazy, aren't they? The Arabs are harsh. It's not me saying that the Arabs are crazy; it's the holy books. The holy books say that *al-Arabīyūn*, the Arabs, are people that really like to argue and are hypocrites. It's the holy books that state that. That's why all the prophets were sent there, because they need that there. Here we do not need a prophet, you know. Because we are just good. (Pak Mariadi, March 1, 2013)

This statement is exemplary of recurring postpilgrimage evaluations of Arab Others in contrast to a morally superior self. Pilgrimage returnees describe their distaste for the encounters they had with Arab "harshness." Similarly, labor migrants lament the "coarse" culture they had to cope with. My summary of these narratives considers in what ways they are based on actual encounters with Arab peoples, bearing in mind the different character of migrants' and pilgrims' experiences: female domestic workers cohabiting with their employers and pilgrims retaining a tourist's perspective.

In order to give an idea of how the narratives are embedded in personal lifeworlds, I mainly focus on interviews with Pak Raharjo and Pak Mariadi, representing pilgrimage returnees' narratives, and on conversations with three sisters from Gunungembun, Ibu Anisa, Ibu Dian, and Ibu Laksmi. Ibu Anisa had been a domestic worker in Saudi Arabia and Oman, Ibu Dian had worked in Oman and

Malaysia, and Ibu Laksmi in Hong Kong. The narrations about Hong Kong and Malaysia show that in Gunungembun migrant women's representations of Arab culture are made in comparison with Asian destination countries.

The stories of Pak Raharjo, Pak Mariadi, Ibu Anisa, Ibu Dian and Ibu Laksmi are exemplary of others' individual interpretations, especially the Javanese ones. To underline general patterns, I complement them with references to other research participants' statements. Furthermore, I shall describe both differentiation *from* Others and identification *with* Others, the latter being especially prominent in the metanarrative about the communitas of a global Muslim ummah.

Communitas and Cultural Differences among Pilgrims

Previous studies on Indonesian hajj returnees have shown that in the context of the hajj ritual, there are different levels of communitas (see chapters 1 and 2). Feener argues that Indonesians' perception of their position in the global ummah is sharpened by the mobile experience of the hajj:

> Contemporary Indonesian pilgrims, each with his or her own perspective, return from hajj to their local mosques and neighborhoods with an enriched sense of their participation in the worldwide Muslim community as well as of their own identity as Indonesian Muslims. (Feener 2004, 205)

As discussed in the historical overview in chapter 1, it is not only pilgrims' self-positioning in the global ummah, but also in the local one. When they return to their local mosques and neighborhoods, they are inspired not only by the journey to Mecca, but also by local social relationships, norms, values, and hierarchies. As an example, Ibu and Pak Sukis from Ladangtembakau stopped at the local mosque on their way home as the first step of acting as a *haji mabrur* with newly gained piety. There is identification with various in-groups and experiences of communitas on different levels.

BEING PART OF THE GLOBAL, REGIONAL, AND LOCAL UMMAH

Umrah and hajj returnees described joint worship with pilgrims from all over the world as one of the most impressive and precious experiences during the pilgrimage (see chapter 2). For the hajj, this aspect appears to be more central than for the umrah, as the umrah is accomplished in smaller travel groups throughout the year, while the hajj is a unique annual mass event, with specially hired charter flights, and a nationwide overarching management. This guided mobility is one of the first aspects of the communitarian experience of pilgrims. Being part of umrah travel groups and hajj divisions conditions the whole setting of the pilgrimage as a collective one. From the preparations onward, Indonesian pilgrims move in groups. As I mentioned in chapter 2, Pak Raharjo, who wanted to go on hajj individually, as a backpacker, was incapable of withdrawing from the governments' guidance and control. His first inquiries about traveling alone made him aware of the fact that there is no individual way to Mecca, not even for the umrah. While this was something of a drawback for Pak Raharjo, most of the other research participants were not bothered by it. Their criticisms of government management mainly concerned financing, waiting lists, and corruption. State control and the obligation to travel in groups was not a pressing concern.

The equality of all believers before God—men and women, old and young, different ethnic groups and confessional divisions—unites believers. The joint worship, the clothing and prayers, and the sharing of food and space are part of this experience. Consequently, when talking about pilgrimage experiences, most of my interlocutors talked about collective experiences—not only coming together with Muslims from all over the world but also traveling collectively with fellow Indonesians. The pilgrimage has a bonding effect for the pilgrims who travel together. Even though he initially wanted to travel alone, Pak Raharjo enthusiastically informed me about the regular postpilgrimage meetings he attends with fellow pilgrims, and in retrospect, he was pleased that he had accomplished the journey collectively. When I asked him about the reason for having found his peace with collective travel rather than an individual backpacker's hajj, he pointed out that community is highly valued in Islam, as a collective prayer always weighs more than an individual one. Thus the communitas aspect is relevant beyond the pilgrimage experience.

In Indonesian, the community prayer is called *sholat berjemaah*, and when there is an opportunity to pray in community with other Muslims, people do so. Mas Eko, the travel agent with Islamic business aspirations, indicated that since his return from Mecca, he had been trying to perform the daily prayers in a community setting, ideally in the mosque, whenever possible. Thus the pilgrimage not only strengthens the feeling of a global communitas, but inspires pilgrims to engage more in communal ritual back home. Especially in rural areas and particularly in Madura, neighbors assemble in nearby mushollahs, or mosques, to perform the daily prayers as a community.

However, according to Turner (2005, 96), after a ritual experience of a communitas of equals, the actors return to the structures of daily life with a reemphasized, new social status.

Among the pilgrims who participated in the research, differences were reemphasized and newly manifested in reference to several in-groups. In line with Laffan, these pilgrims returned to their societies "with a fresh view of the world" and at the same time maintained a "homeward vision" (Laffan 2003, 33). Yet I would add that this homeward vision inspires Indonesians to identify with more than the two levels of communitas that Laffan makes out for the eighteenth-century jawi pilgrims. While Laffan speaks of "local" and "Islamic identities" as two levels of communitas (cf. Laffan 2003, 33), I would argue that in contemporary pilgrimage experiences five different levels of communitas can be identified, at least from the analysis of postpilgrimage representations that give more evidence about the restructuring, rather than the actual experience of communitas that possibly took place. Besides communitas with a global ummah and the national Indonesian ummah, there are further identifications with what are perceived as a larger Asian ummah, a Southeast Asian ummah, and a local ethnic, for example Madurese, ummah.

In the course of their narratives about cultural differences, Indonesian pilgrims identify themselves along cultural and religious lines at global, regional (national), and local levels. Besides the unity with Muslims from all over the world, many of my interlocutors were particularly excited about the fact that Asians were widely visible as the largest group of Muslims in Mecca. They recounted that at the holy sites, Asian faces were everywhere, with many Chinese, Indian, Sri Lankan, and Pakistani Muslims, with Southeast Asian Muslims from the Philippines, Malaysia, and, of course, Indonesia, also in attendance. This awareness that Asians are the majority of Muslims in the world obviously filled Indonesian Muslims with pride. This excitement about the large number of Asians was qualified with emphasis on Southeast Asian Muslims in particular. The idea of a Southeast Asian ummah is striking, since identification as Southeast Asian is a rather recent phenomenon in Indonesia (see Schlehe 2013b, 497).[1] What appeared to hold more weight than identification as part of the (Southeast) Asian ummah was belonging to the Indonesian ummah as the largest national group. Thus local belonging as Indonesians appears to be of the highest relevance. I have described this in the following way:

> *Hajjis* proudly recount how easy it was to recognize other Indonesians in Mecca because of their uniform clothing—Indonesian travelers wear the same traditional batik-style clothing, white *ihrom,* and the same leisure clothes, which make them visible as the biggest group of pilgrims. This dominant presence obviously fosters the self-confidence of Indonesian pilgrims. (Lücking 2014, 141–42)

Apart from national identification, it is often the respective ethnic belonging that is reemphasized in the course of the hajj, especially regarding specific local rituals before and after the pilgrimage. For Madura, the extensive pre- and postpilgrimage celebrations and the *asajère* visits are labeled as uniquely Madurese and examples from Aceh and Sulawesi indicate other famous local traditions.

Moreover, through the government's organization of hajj divisions, there is a cohort effect for the respective groups that travel together. As I observed during meetings with Pak Raharjo and Pak Mariadi, getting together was special for them and they enjoyed recalling the experiences of joint travel. Many Indonesians hold annual meetings with their fellow pilgrims, even years after the pilgrimage. The grandfather of Dewi, the young pilgrim from Yogyakarta, recounted that he met up with his fellow pilgrims on a regular basis and that they kept in touch even though it had already been twenty years since they went on the pilgrimage. Furthermore, the fact that his granddaughter had accomplished the pilgrimage strengthened their bond. Dewi recounted that her grandparents had been very supportive of her pilgrimage and were reminded of their own pilgrimage twenty years earlier; they had taken out old pictures and told Dewi about their pilgrimage prior to her departure, as well as inquiring about her experiences thereafter. Thus the pilgrimage unites Indonesian Muslims, especially those who travel in the same group, but also as a larger community, sometimes even stretched over generations, as in the example of Dewi and her grandfather. The defining feature in these feelings of togetherness is culture and the location of cultural boundaries varies in pilgrims' mappings of the world—with Arab Others being placed in the larger picture.

MAPPING THE WORLD

Even though there was a general excitement about the unity and equality of all people before God, after longer conversations and when I inquired about differences, pilgrimage returnees could elaborate on cultural differences at length. They exhibited astonishment and sometimes even disgust at people and customs that they perceived as being foreign.

One of the groups that they seemed to perceive as extremely different from their own Indonesian culture was people from Africa. Using racial stereotypes my interlocutors recounted that they were frightened by what they described as "dark," "coarse" people from Africa. During the tawaf, the circumambulation of the Ka'aba, they were afraid of falling down and being trampled by them and when there was free food, especially after the feast of sacrifice, Africans would cut into the queues and Indonesians stated that they felt too small and weak to oppose them. Pak Mariadi argued that African people were "wild," "dirty," and "uncivilized" in his view. The racism was sometimes extended to South Asians (Indians and Pakistanis in particular), who some of my interlocutors described as "smelling different," "having no sense of cleanliness" and "being rude."

In contrast, encounters with Western pilgrims were described in a more positive light. For some Indonesians, it seems to have been rather a surprise that there were so many Muslim Westerners. My presence as a Westerner might have caused these positive evaluations and in any case, accounts about Western converts were frequently used to promote the benefits of conversion. Even though everyone emphasized that the hajj was the prime choice for travel, many pilgrims also admitted that they had an interest in traveling to other parts of the world and Western countries were ranked highly as travel destinations, especially for higher education. As the umrah guide Ustadz Wijayanto pointed out, umrah plus Europe journeys were a new trend. Even though the West is not generally recognized positively, as Westerners are perceived as lacking religion, spirituality, and morality (cf. Schlehe et al. 2013), Western converts are obviously regarded as an ideal harmonization of Western modernity and Islamic religion. The umrah plus packages might well represent certain tastes. I was informed by Ustadz Wijayanto and other travel agents that umrah plus Istanbul was one of the bestselling packages. At the time of inquiry, Turkey was praised as a democratic Muslim country in contrast to Arab countries. Turkey was clearly considered to be a well-functioning symbiosis of Orient and Occident. More recently, umrah plus Al-Aqsa packages to Jerusalem have gained in popularity.

Concerning identification with a larger Asian community, there was fascination with the realization that most Muslim people are actually East- or Southeast Asian. Furthermore, many interviewees described their excitement about meeting so many people from China as, due to the majority of Chinese Indonesians' adherence to Confucianism, Buddhism, and Christianity, the combination of Chineseness and Islam was something rather new to them.[2]

While the statements about Africans, South Asians, Westerners, East Asians, and Southeast Asians were relatively forthright, comments on Arab people were often more equivocal.

Pilgrims' (Non-)Encounters with Arab Others

Package tourism, like pilgrimage group travel, allows only limited actual encounters with people that do not belong to one's own travel group. Of course, during the pilgrimage rituals, Indonesian pilgrims pray side by side with pilgrims from other countries, but the encounters are restricted to the time of prayer and rituals, as the rest of their time is mainly spent in Indonesian-only contexts, in their hotels, travel groups, and on buses. Free time activities like shopping are the most flexible time slot, allowing some opportunities for encounters with Saudi Arabian culture. Most pilgrims describe the pilgrimage as a bonding experience primarily with fellow Indonesians. Meeting pilgrims from other Indonesian regions was an event in itself. Sometimes one would meet distant relatives or friends of friends, which many of my research participants found particularly exciting.

Moreover, the pilgrimage can be an opportunity to get in touch with important Indonesian public figures.

Pak Mariadi recounted how he had used the opportunity of the hajj to mingle with Indonesian government officials and important *kyai*, and that they had even invited him for dinner. Evidently, meeting with Indonesian authorities—from the governmental as well as the religious sphere—was a meaningful encounter for Pak Mariadi, something he mentioned when I asked him about his favorite events in Mecca. Pak Imam, a member of the government delegation in 2014, confirmed that many Indonesian pilgrims were excited about meeting the government delegation and he had been very busy in Mecca giving speeches and counseling.

Ibu and Pak Sukis from rural Madura recounted that they wanted to meet a sheikh who teaches students from Madurese Qur'anic schools in Mecca, but unfortunately it had not worked out as the sheikh had been very busy meeting Indonesian pilgrims (field notes Khotim Ubaidillah, November 15, 2014). For the umrah, some travel agencies, especially those for five-star elite pilgrimages, advertise doing the pilgrimage with a special kyai or a celebrity such as Ustadz Wijayanto.

Considering these in-group experiences, the bonds among Indonesians and inter-Indonesian encounters appear to be more meaningful than encounters with Arab people and people from other parts of the world. Pak Raharjo represents an exception in this regard. From the beginning, he aspired to do the hajj more individually, as a backpacker, and even though in the end he joined a government-organized travel unit, he sought opportunities to wander around and was curious about other people. His video documentation and his detailed descriptions of the habits of Arabs, Africans, Europeans, Americans, and other Asians indicated that he had observed them in a different way than the majority of the other pilgrimage research participants.

Yet even Pak Raharjo's observations were limited to interactions at the pilgrimage sites. Getting any insight into the everyday life and private sphere of Arab people is very unlikely. Pak Imam recounted that the delegation of Indonesian government officials had been invited to the private houses of their Saudi colleagues. Yet this is of course an occasion with a formal character and reserved to a small elite. The following narratives about Arab Others suggest that pilgrims reproduce images of Arab Others that are prevalent in public discourse, media, politics, and the pilgrimage business, like in preparation courses.

HOW AUTHORITIES DEFINE IMAGES OF ARAB OTHERS

In the quote at the beginning of this section, Pak Mariadi is mocking the Arab people, which is quite typical for Indonesian pilgrims' narratives about Arab

Others. Being an academic but living in a rural area makes Pak Mariadi somewhat exceptional, as most villagers work as farmers or run small-scale businesses. Due to his education and his position as a lecturer, Pak Mariadi is a highly respected person in his village and even though he is still quite young, he inhabits leading positions in the village context. As an example, he was elected as the R.T., the *rukun tetangga*, or neighborhood chief.[3] People seek his advice because of his potential *savoir-vivre* that they relate to his education and experiences outside the village.

Even though Pak Raharjo was very enthusiastic to talk about the hajj experiences and share his stories, photos and videos with me, revealing his fascination and detailed observations as a curious traveler, he relativized his report and repeatedly indicated that the head of his travel group, Pak Mariadi, knew much more about the hajj and about Arab culture and that he was sure Pak Mariadi could answer my questions in a more qualified way.

The first meeting with Pak Mariadi took place in the company of Pak Raharjo. They enjoyed recalling their pilgrimage experiences and exchanged humorous anecdotes from their joint travel. Jokes and laughter accompanied their stories. A second meeting with Pak Mariadi was calmer but he reemphasized the statements of the first meeting. Pak Mariadi kept mocking Arab people. This motif in his account served as a contrast against which he claimed the superiority of Indonesian Muslims. Pak Raharjo was infected by Pak Mariadi's jokes about Arab Others, even though his own more detailed observations had not been equally negative.

Pak Mariadi labeled Arabs as harsh and impolite in a deprecating tone. However, he was not really describing their behavior. His gestures and laughter stressed his reluctance to give more detailed descriptions of Arabic culture and customs, and Arab peoples' characteristics. He was waving my questions aside by claiming that the Arabs were "just crazy." As a legitimization of his denouncement of Arab culture and customs, Pak Mariadi referred back to other authorities, emphasizing "it is not me saying this" and referring to holy books that he mentions in the introductory quote. He also referred to opinions of Indonesian ulama and kyai as well as politicians like the former Indonesian president Abdurrahman Wahid, who had been a prominent spokesperson of the *Islam Pribumi* discourse (Slama 2008), to affirm that his opinions were backed by other authorities, while he himself was an authority for Pak Raharjo, for whom the knowledgeable estimations of Pak Mariadi were more valuable than his own observations and his video documentation. Thus the following narratives about rather stereotypical characteristic features of Arab Others are most likely oriented by guiding meta-narratives that authorities shape.

HARSHNESS AND ARROGANCE

In reaction to my questions about possible reasons for Arab people's harshness, Pak Mariadi tried to explain his evaluation, suggesting that it was probably because of the hot climate that they had such hot temperaments and stronger physical appearances, being generally bigger than Indonesians. One of his main criticisms referred to what he described as Arabic racism. The Arabs would privilege their own people, as well as Westerners, for residence and work in Saudi Arabia. He criticized that the Arabs would not take Indonesians seriously, not even educated Indonesians, and would only allow them to work in inferior positions. He explained:

> I see the Arab people as, ah, it's hard to say (*laughing*). I can illustrate it like this: the person who does the call to prayer in our local mosque here is a graduate from Universitas Gadjah Mada with the best grades. He got *cum laude* in almost everything. Then he went to Saudi Arabia for two years and became a driver. Even though he is a technical engineer, he became a driver there! I asked him why he did not get a work permit as an architect. Why? Because the Arabs said: "Sorry brother, the work permits for architects and technical engineers are only given to Arabs, French people or Russians," that's what they said, "No work permits for Indonesians!" So Indonesians become labor migrants. He became a driver, and now he has returned home. Even though he is an engineer, *cum laude*. (Pak Mariadi, March 1, 2013)

Many of my interlocutors described similar situations, indicating that Arabs looked down on Indonesians in professional issues related to working opportunities and regarding religious learnedness. They viewed Indonesia as one of the many poor Muslim countries, as a supplier of domestic workers, and did not acknowledge the authenticity and legality of Islamic practices in Indonesia. Research participants located Arabs' feeling of superiority particularly in the religious sphere. One of them criticized that the Saudis never appointed an Indonesian to lead the prayers or perform the call to prayer in the Holy Mosque in Mecca, even though Indonesians always won the Qur'an recitation competitions. In another conversation, Pak Mariadi argued that Arabs would only ask Indonesians to do the prayers for funerals and concluded that it was an ugly attitude to treat Indonesians like this. The Arabs' feeling of superiority was branded as arrogance and racism, leading to the conclusion that Arabs were fanatical about bloodlines.

In other interviews and conversations with pilgrimage returnees as well as working migrants, the topic of arrogance was central. My interlocutors described the Arabs as careless and reckless, as selfish and arrogant, and as treating

Indonesians and people from other parts of the world as inferior. This was often related to wealth and foreign workers in Saudi Arabia. Many returned pilgrims suggested that it was because of the Gulf States' wealth that they were so arrogant. They drove recklessly, because no one cared about a scratch on a car, they threw rubbish everywhere, because they would not have to collect it, they shouted at others because they were used to bullying people. It was widely assumed that Arabs would work either in white-collar jobs or they would not work at all. With sarcasm, Pak Mariadi argued that the Saudi government could actually be evaluated positively because it supplied its citizens with everything without making them work hard because of the wealth from oil exports.

AUTHORITARIANISM AND VIOLENCE

Similarly, the Arabs' feelings of superiority and their wealth were sometimes seen as related to the autocratic political system there. Yet most of my interlocutors argued that even though Saudi Arabia was technologically advanced and, in a way, hypermodern, it was also somewhat backward regarding the lack of democracy and human rights. Speaking of the latter, labor migrants mainly referred to reports about the ill treatment of Indonesian labor migrants in Saudi Arabia and to draconic penalties in the context of sharia law.

Again, criticisms of Arab people were contrasted with Indonesian softness and good manners. In the course of this, it was highlighted that Indonesia is a democratic country, being compared to Turkey, which was equally considered as a democratic Muslim society at the time of inquiry. In many cases, questions of appropriate behavior were related to religion. Indonesian pilgrims admitted that the Arabs possessed a high degree of piety, which was one of the few positive attributes mentioned. Yet they also criticized religious fanaticism, and what they considered to be outdated religious customs. Dewi recounted that an Arab man had asked her if she would like to be his second wife. "I thought he was crazy" she said, laughing, further explaining that from her point of view polygamy was not acceptable and fortunately not common in Indonesia.

GENDERED IMAGES OF ARAB OTHERS

Narratives about Arab Others are gendered. As pilgrims observe Arab people from a rather passive standpoint on the guided journeys, from a tourist perspective, one of the most frequently mentioned differences between Indonesian and Arab culture concerned gender segregation, as this was seemingly the most significant aspect that pilgrims observed in public interactions. They described women as being veiled and hidden, staying in the private sphere inside houses most of the time and only going outside in a full body veil. Thus Arab women were described as "absent," "weak," and "passive," and sometimes also as arrogant, as some pilgrims suggested that Arab women were either too arrogant to show their faces and talk to other people or they were too weak to oppose the men who might instruct them to cover their faces. Many pilgrims mentioned with surprise that there were no women in the markets in Saudi Arabia like in Indonesia.

Arab men were perceived as being very pious and many pilgrims described how Arab men would stop all activities and immediately rush to the mosques when they heard the call to prayer. The idea of Saudi Arabian Islam as more authentic or original is personified in the image of the pious Arab man. However, even though Arab men's piety and adherence to religious rules was represented in a positive light, my interlocutors described other characteristics of Arab men very critically. Pilgrims argued that Arab men were coarse and impolite, they were loud, big, and tall, and always had high libidos and therefore approached women constantly—including Indonesian women, who were advised during preparation courses to beware of Arab men.

The pilgrims' narratives about Arab people echoed the introduction to Arab culture and customs that is given in pilgrimage preparation courses remarkably closely, sometimes in almost exactly the same wording. This indicates that some leading discourses are merely reproduced in postpilgrimage representations of the Arab world and that either their pretravel anticipations were congruent with their actual encounters or that actual encounters occurred only in a limited scope. Another explanation could be that the actual encounters differed but that nevertheless, the representations stuck to the leading discourse about Arab Others.

INDONESIANS' SUPERIORITY

Lamenting the fact that Arabs regard Indonesians as inferior, Pak Mariadi in turn depicted Arabs as inferior, emphasizing Indonesian superiority. The positive picture of the self-depicted Indonesians as wise, tolerant, soft, patient, and polite. Tolerance and religious pluralism appeared to be of high relevance for him, as he talked about them repeatedly, informing me about the history of the Islamization of the archipelago through the Wali Songo, which did not abolish local culture but harmonized it with Islam. He explained that the temples of Borobudur and Prambanan were important heritage sites for Indonesian Muslims too and that Hindu-Buddhist values were combined with Islamic ones. While he emphasized that Indonesia was a notably open and tolerant society, he claimed that Islamic fundamentalism and terrorism came from Malaysia and from the Arab world—in any case from regions outside Indonesia. He explained that these radical people also dressed in an Arab way, for example with turbans and *gamis* (a long white robe).

Like in the introductory quote of this book, he argued that God had sent his prophets to the Arab region because the people there were in need of a prophet to teach them how to behave, while Indonesians were good already. Maybe out of politeness, because he was talking to me, or maybe because he also considered the West to be superior, he argued that if God had located the Ka'aba in Germany or in Indonesia, pilgrims would never have wanted to leave these beautiful, pleasant places. Locating it in Saudi Arabia, where it is extremely hot and dry, ensured that people would leave after the pilgrimage as no one could stand to stay there longer. In his own words:

> I can imagine if, let's say, the Ka'aba was relocated. For example, why is it that the Ka'aba is located in an extremely hot place? Why was it not placed in Indonesia, where it's pleasant? (*laughing*) You know, Mecca and Medina become the most crowded spots on Earth. But it's because it's pleasant *here*, isn't it? If you build a building with a hundred floors, it's still pleasant in Indonesia, but there, it's so hot. The majority of people who travel there cannot stand it for a long time, cannot live there.... Imagine if the Ka'aba were placed in *your* town, goodness, your town would be overwhelmed by the crowds. But Mecca today, people always think about whether they would really want to live there. They aren't capable physically and it's not pleasant. (Pak Mariadi, March 17, 2013)

This is not the only time that Pak Mariadi and others portrayed the West as preferable to the Arab world. Among other reasons, this was underlined by his desire to do his Ph.D. in a Western country and his perhaps surprising interest in traveling to important religious sites in the West like the Vatican. Besides the harsh climate in Saudi Arabia, pilgrims mentioned another reason for the differences between Indonesia and Saudi Arabia, or the Islamic periphery and the centers of Islam in general: namely, adherence to the five principles of Islam. While in Indonesia the hierarchy of the five pillars is first: the creed; second: the daily prayer; third: giving alms; fourth: fasting in the month of Ramadan; and fifth: the pilgrimage; Pak Mariadi argued that the Saudis would exchange pillars 4 and 5, making the pilgrimage the fourth pillar and fasting the fifth. He claimed that Indonesians would fulfil the first four pillars before considering going on hajj. Adherence to the first four pillars was regarded a basic condition of inner readiness for the pilgrimage. Because of the great distance to Mecca, the hajj is the most difficult pillar to fulfill, while fasting is rather easy. As Indonesian Muslims earnestly adhered to the first four pillars before going on hajj, they were considered the better Muslims, showing great willpower and an inner spiritual readiness. In contrast, Arabs, it was argued, could easily do the pilgrimage, and fasting in the month of Ramadan was more difficult for them, demanding greater discipline. Therefore, they were not trained in controlling their desires and being patient.

Drawing a connection between climate and geographical location of the Arab world and Arab peoples' characteristic features was a recurring theme among pilgrims as well as labor migrants. Alongside speculation about the link between the harsh climate and harsh people were opinions about the different food being the reason for the hot temperament of the Arabs. It was suggested that because the Arab region was too hot to grow vegetables and it was far from the sea, Arabs ate lots of meat rather than fish and vegetables like Indonesians. Their consumption of sheep and camel meat was believed to cause high blood pressure, making them more aggressive than people who consume fish and vegetables. In this context, my interlocutors also differentiated between "cold" and "hot meat," the latter one being attributed to goat meat for example.

These views on Arabness concerned the culture and people of Saudi Arabia and other Middle Eastern countries—often with little or no distinction. Besides the *manasik* preparation courses for the pilgrimage, similar narratives are prevalent in popular media such as TV, cinema, prose, and news reports. The media representations in which these narratives about Arab Others are evoked concern hajj and umrah accounts, like the pilgrimage experiences of celebrities or written pilgrimage diaries, but also other encounters with Arab people in the course of educational migration and labor migration. Furthermore, such views are widespread in public discourses like the Islam Nusantara discourse.

Sisters of the Same Fate: Solidarity among Labor Migrants

Narratives about identification as Indonesian and Asian are of similar relevance for labor migrants as for pilgrims. In fact, the narratives about selves and Others, especially concerning characteristic features, exhibit great similarity. Even though labor migrants do not base their feelings of belonging on ritual communitas, they do mention a communitas of women with whom they share the same fate. Furthermore, there are several other relevant in-groups, like their family in Indonesia and their employers' family. Their mentioning of these in-groups rarely included Indonesian pilgrimage groups—to which they did not belong even if they had a chance to do the pilgrimage to Mecca. As I have shown in chapter 2, they do not depart with the travel groups and delegations from Indonesia and therefore do not share the same experience of traveling in a group and hosting pre- and postpilgrimage rituals in Indonesia.

Just as for pilgrims, for migrants the identification with an Indonesian national identity relies on government guidance and control. Migrants' training camps become an arena of identification with the nation-state and with a community of fellow migrants (cf. Killias 2017, 2014). The national propaganda stylizing female labor migrants as the nation's carers and foreign exchange heroines triggers their identification as national citizens (cf. Chan 2014). However, while state propaganda portrays the women as a homogenous group of nationals who care only about their country and their families, personal accounts reveal that many domestic workers also feel attached to their employers' families. The migrants' emotional struggles over belonging are more complex. My research confirms the observations of Killias (2017, 2014), Lindquist (2009), Silvey (2006), and Chan (2014) who have indicated that the question of belonging among labor migrants is accompanied by social pressure, feelings of guilt, personal desires, and in-between-ness. While Indonesian society expects them to be responsible foreign exchange heroines, many labor migrants, especially migrant women, are also emotionally entangled with the families they care for as domestic servants and are estranged from their own families due to long stays abroad.

For the case of Indonesian maids in Malaysia, the ambivalence of belonging is comprehensively described by Killias (2014). While Indonesian and Malaysian diplomats stress the cultural proximity of the two "kin states," Malaysian employers, the Malaysian government, and Malaysian recruitment agencies emphasize cultural differences between Indonesia and Malaysia, warning Malaysian employers against establishing close relationships with their Indonesian maids (Killias 2014, 885). Agents advise employers to keep a professional distance from their maids through language and clothing, equipping maids with uniforms for work, and avoiding idioms of kinship between employers and maids (ibid., 893). The maids themselves, however, do use kin terms in reference to their employers' families. Apparently, many maids are especially attached to the children they look after, while they are alienated from their own children. Thereby they refute the rhetoric of industrialization and depersonalization, challenging the leading discourses in Malaysia and Indonesia (ibid., 894). The example of Indonesian maids in Malaysia not only exhibits great similarities with the Saudi Arabian case, it also shows how relative the perception of cultural similarities or differences can be.

While recruiters for labor migration to Saudi Arabia often stress religious proximity, emphasizing brotherhood (or sisterhood) in Islam, the migrant women's experience is that they are not welcomed as sisters of the same faith but are often treated as second-class citizens and servants. One of my interlocutors explained that her initial preference for migration to an Arab country was related to the argument of being among Muslims, as there had been rumors about domestic workers in non-Muslim countries like Hong Kong having to do *haram* things like cook pork. However, after having lived in Saudi Arabia and other Gulf states, she concluded that the people there "weren't real Muslims," a recurring narrative that I will further illustrate below. Nevertheless, the distinctions were not total generalizations. Congruent with Killias's observations about Indonesian migrants' emotional ties to their Malaysian employers' children, my interlocutors described emotional ties to the people they cared for.

Ibu Anisa and her sisters Ibu Dian and Ibu Laksmi can together draw on working experiences in Saudi Arabia, Oman, Malaysia, and Hong Kong. They juxtaposed their evaluations of these countries and argued that caring for children was the nicest part about working as a domestic worker. Because they took care of the children, maids were often invited along on trips. These trips made Dian's bond more strongly with them and when she left, the children cried. She explained:

> If you look after a child from an early age on, if the child is with the maid all the time, if she leaves, they will cry the whole trip. But if you look after a child, the work never stops. And they were terribly stubborn, but their parents didn't care. You always have ups and downs, that's for sure. And with small children, yeah, of course, small children cannot understand when the maid has to leave. I was looking after them from the time they woke up in the morning until they went to bed again at night, the one person who is on standby is the maid. The parents rarely did that. They [the children] were crying for several days, and I loved them a lot. When the child was still small, eight months old, she slept with me, did everything with me. Even when her father wanted to hit her, I defended her, I said, "Hit me instead." She was already like my own child. Every time, in the few months before I wanted to return to Indonesia, my employers would always be worried, wondering what they would do if the children could not stand it. So what I did, when they missed me, I gave them a book. Eventually, the child even began to write letters. Back then, there was no phone, just writing letters, from here to there and back. (Ibu Dian, March 21, 2014)

Ibu Dian describes that establishing these emotional bonds was not always easy, that there were "ups and downs" and that the parents were concerned about their children's strong affections for their maid. I heard similar stories from Ibu Dian's sisters, Ibu Anisa and Ibu Laksmi, and from other migrant women. These stories mainly related to care for children and sometimes for elderly people.

The migrant women's feelings and aspirations of belonging to their family in Indonesia, to parts of the families abroad, to the nation, to the ummah, and to the middle class are ambivalent and often unfulfilled. In many cases they encounter boundaries and are not able to be part of the community they want to belong to. As a result, solitude is most obvious in their isolation during their work abroad, as many of them cannot leave the private households they are working in. However, their longing and their struggles within "economies of emotion" (Lindquist 2009, 150) challenge the exclusiveness of the communitas of other parts of society, like middle-class lifestyles that draw on popular Arab style, which labor migrants labeled as ridiculous in the face of their in-depth experiences with "real" Arab culture.

Aside from being torn between emotional ties to their families back home and to the people they care for abroad, a communitas is the one thing connecting fellow migrants. Talking about people of the "same fate," "se-nasib," as many of my interlocutors put it, they feel united with women from the same recruitment and training camp units. Later on, during residence abroad, there are only limited opportunities to meet with fellow migrants, not only Indonesians but also Filipinos, Pakistanis, Sri Lankans, and Indians, who are considered sisters of the same fate (rather than the same faith like the employers). Many of my interlocutors described how they used to meet other domestic workers at the dustbins, sharing a quick chat, expressing solidarity and togetherness, contrasting their solitude during work. Sometimes they would also meet other domestic workers during festivities when the employers took them along. Many women who had worked in Saudi Arabia recounted that there were big family gatherings every Thursday night—a good opportunity to meet other domestic workers. On these occasions, cultural differences seemed to become less important. Some features of a communitas are prevalent, like the blurring of religious, ethnic, or national boundaries. Yet, similar to the pilgrims, in retrospect the labor migrants also talked about cultural differences, restructuring their perceptions of boundaries, even though previously they had emphasized solidarity. Many women recounted that they had met Christian Filipinos and that religion had not played any role at all. Their retrospective ideas about people from Sri Lanka and India were more critical. Many migrant women argued that people from South India had a different sense of hygiene, that they smelled different and were more arrogant. Nevertheless, Ibu Anisa recounted that during her residence in Saudi Arabia, one Indian labor migrant had become her sincere friend, her sister, and that she still kept a stitched Jasmine flower that the Indian woman had given to her, remembering their friendship. Ibu Anisa's account of her friendship expresses these feelings of solidarity with other migrants:

> It was when we threw the garbage away in the afternoons, that's where we would gather with our friends, at the dustbins. We made appointments for that, "Tomorrow we'll meet again when we bring the garbage down, yeah." Later we would meet, talking for a moment, chatting. At those dustbins . . . the people there would say, that's the "Indonesian center" [*laughing*]. So, we would just talk. Between us, you know, we did not differentiate maids according to their origin, we were all friends. People from India, Pakistan, Sri Lanka, the Philippines. They were like

> us, it was exciting whenever we met. Even if we had nothing there, we would try to contact one another. Now of course there are many maids who have mobile phones, it's possible to have a phone now. Even though some employers do not allow their maids to have mobile phones. They are afraid that something will happen, but in fact, you can always use a friend's phone. I used a friend from India's phone, behind the house. We talked about what we had cooked and stuff. We would exchange food and later she would even come and eat at my house. My employer was okay with that. And later I would go there, even if there was no food, it didn't matter. She was my sister there. Even though she was Indian, nevertheless, I never differentiated. What matters is that the one who shares the same fate as mine is my sister. We would even share clothes.... We shared stories, talking, for example, about potential marriage candidates. She told me how it is in India and so on. They also have boyfriends and girlfriends before marriage in India, in Arab countries they don't. There are only arranged marriages in Saudi Arabia.... The Indians are Hindu. But we were just the same, when I prayed for example, she was just like me. Indians like jasmine flowers, you know. She made one for me. She stitched it for me during the night. Later, when I came, she put it on my headscarf, it was so nice! She often made things like that for me. But it seems like the Indians are dirtier, you know. Less cleanliness. Yeah, they are not clean. That's why the people there, the people abroad, the Arabs, they like Indonesians. Because Indonesians are cleaner. (Ibu Anisa, March 21, 2014)

Ibu Anisa's account of her friendship with the Indian woman reveals feelings of community and solidarity. They shared many things in a time when they had little scope to move and only modest belongings. They shared the short excursions to the dustbins and the limited free time, they shared stories, important ones about marriage and banal ones about daily cooking duties. They shared their mobile phones, their clothes, and their food, and even if there was no food, as Ibu Anisa stressed, they would meet, and felt like sisters. Similar to pilgrims' experiences of communitas, the feeling of sisterhood between Ibu Anisa and her Indian friend was most relevant during their residence abroad, while later on, in retrospect, Ibu Anisa described how she feels appalled at having established such close ties to a person from India, considering the differences between Indians and Indonesians. Knowledge about these differences is more nuanced than among pilgrims, who have only limited encounters with people from other countries. Thus, in conclusion, the in-group feelings of female labor migrants concern the Indonesian nation, their family, and the local community and, during their time abroad, also fellow labor migrants as well as people whom they cared for.

Labor Migrants' Intimate Observations

Even though labor migrants' observations are more intimate, their representations of Arab peoples' traits and characteristics correspond with the stereotypes that are prevalent in the pilgrims' narratives, as outlined above. Unlike pilgrims, labor migrants could report in more detail on Saudi women, who were their main counterparts from their employers' families. In contrast, they seemed to have had only limited interaction with Arab males. And yet, in their families and neighborhoods there was not much detailed talk about Arab peoples but rather a representation of common stereotypes.

Like the pilgrims, they represented Arab men as harsh, loud, coarse, arrogant, and violent, while the component of piety, which pilgrims named, was rarely mentioned. Migrant women recounted that they had observed Arab men treating their wives badly and that they had several partners, some of them legal second or third wives and some of them adulterous relationships. Many migrant women also talked about the advances made by Arab men, expressing their fears of being harassed. They criticized Arab men for being driven by sexual desires and emphasized that they could not imagine having a relationship with an Arab man. This statement was probably also evoked in order to reassure their husbands back in Indonesia that they would remain faithful. Reports about Arab-looking children in so-called labor migrant villages and the creation of an orphanage in Jakarta for children of migrant women conceived during their stays abroad contradict these claims. Yet whether these children are the offspring of consensual sexual relationships is another question.

ARAB MEN AND WOMEN

The Arab men's alleged harsh and violent attitudes and their potentially bad treatment of women were not only represented as accusations against these men but also as a critical reflection on Arab women. Some migrant women seemed to perceive Arab women as being partially responsible for the bad attitude of their husbands; they wondered why they did not oppose their husbands and indicated that many Arab women had resigned themselves to this reality, restricting themselves to the domestic domain and to material luxury and letting themselves go.

Ibu Anisa and her sisters were particularly animated when they described Arab women as arrogant, lazy, never working, stingy, suspicious, and jealous. They contrasted this image with the ideal beauty and morality of Indonesian women, suggesting that this was one of the reasons why Arab men made advances on Indonesian maids. The sisters endorsed each other in their evaluation of Arab women until they were laughing loudly about their own accounts. As an example, here is a quotation from our conversation:

> Yeah, it's because the Indonesian women, they are sexy, strong and tight, you know. There, they [the Arab women] do not take care of themselves; the women there, they just sleep and eat, so their physical appearance isn't good. They never work, so they become loose and slack. They never do sports. They are just at home. Men do the shopping and everything, the daily needs. There is nothing that the women do. Just sleep and have children (*laughing*). (Ibu Anisa, March 21, 2014)

In addition to descriptions of Arab women's loose bodies, many Indonesian migrant women expressed how they felt appalled about a lack of morality among Arab women. They argued that Arab women had no feeling of shame (*malu*), that they would wear immoral underwear, which they saw when doing the laundry, and that they would dress in an embarrassing way inside their houses and in female-only areas during festivities. For example, Ibu Endang, a fifty-year-old woman in Madura who had repeatedly migrated to Saudi Arabia over a period of twenty years, described how Arab women danced during festivities in female-only areas. She recounted that they would shake what she described as "big loose bellies and breasts" (Ibu Endang, June 28, 2014). And she shook her upper body to illustrate how she had seen Arab women dancing. In conclusion, having observed the lifestyle in Saudi Arabia and other Gulf States, many Indonesian migrant women saw Arab women as hypocrites. Their full body veil, they argued, had no meaning at all because beneath this black veil there was an "immoral person." Moreover, many migrant women argued that Islamic conventions about veiling concerned modesty more generally and that the Arab women's luxurious lifestyle made their full body veils meaningless. Ibu Tati, a young woman of about twenty-five years from Gunungembun who had worked in Dubai and in Saudi Arabia, concluded that Indonesians had more balanced attitudes; they dressed modestly in public and also at home, and there was no stark contrast between an extreme use of veils outside and an immodest or vulgar clothing style in the private sphere.

Viewing these statements against the background of the interview situations as well as the overall social context of the women, it appears to be very likely that apart from actual observations and experiences abroad, the migrant women's statements were also provoked by the hierarchy between employer and employee and by the moral judgments within their own society as well as, during interviews, my presence and how they wanted to present themselves to me as a Western woman.

LABOR MIGRANTS' MORAL SELF-PERCEPTION

Like pilgrims, migrants display their own moral superiority in demarcation against cultural Others. In this regard, they contrast the self not only with Arab Others but also with labor migrants from other countries, even though they had previously emphasized their solidarity with them, as I outlined above. Even though on the one hand, they described their reluctance with their Arab employers, on the other hand they seemed to be proud that Arabs liked Indonesians, which they illustrated by describing the contrast between themselves and migrant women from other countries. Ibu Anisa, for example, described Indonesians' beauty not only in contrast to Arabs but also in contrast to Indians and Filipinos:

> The Arab men, they say that Indonesians are exceptional, that they have natural beauty. Indonesians are, for example, humble and polite, and have a good degree of tolerance. . . . Because Indonesians are exceptional, that's all. They take it as exceptionality, maybe because they see Indonesian peoples' bodies, soft and strong. Indonesian people are tight and strong, do you know what I mean? That's what it is, natural beauty. Clean. Different from Indians, who are black and dirty. (Ibu Anisa, March 21, 2014)

Furthermore, Indonesian migrant women described themselves as having superior morality, and being honest and faithful. Ibu Dian, for example, describes Arab employers' suspicions and indicates that they trusted Indonesian employees more than employees from India and the Philippines:

> There was often a feeling of suspicion. For example, if my employer wanted to go out, and my sisters from the Philippines and India were there, she would give the room keys to me. . . . They trusted me. That was because, for example, whenever I found something, even the smallest earring, I would tell them. We were often tested like that there. They test . . . honesty. (Ibu Dian, March 21, 2014)

She further explained that Arab people liked Indonesians because they were honest and faithful and also, she claimed, because they were modest, polite, soft, and submissive:

> Indonesians know their position, they reflect: *who am I*, they can accept different [social] positions, know who the employer is and who the

> maid is. This is different to the Filipinos, whose culture is maybe more 'hooray-hooray.' Employers do not actually like that; Filipinos move freely there, going out and stuff. Indonesians cannot do that, it's not possible, not allowed. (Ibu Dian, March 21, 2014)

Even though the experiences of labor migrants differ remarkably from those of pilgrims, there are significant parallels in the representation of Others and the concomitant representation of the self as morally superior. Just as pilgrims represent affiliation and rejection on different levels, labor migrants exhibit a feeling of unity with fellow labor migrants in some regards, but in other regards differentiate themselves from them. Such multilayered practices of Othering are far more complex than a dichotomy between self and Other. This provokes the question, under what conditions is there identification and solidarity with cultural Others and under what conditions do representations foster rejection and alienation? When do people stress cultural commonalities and when do they emphasize cultural differences?

Discursive Boundaries

The recurring patterns in reflections after a trip or work abroad about selves and Others have a guiding function, becoming an orientation for migrants' and pilgrims' self-identification. The discursive boundaries between different in- and out-groups are not rigid, but flexible, depending on the respective function of this kind of guidance. While identification with a larger communitas seemed to be essential during their stays abroad—for pilgrims as a ritual experience and part of their spiritual proximity to God, and for migrants as a coping strategy during precarious solitude and emotional struggle—upon return to Indonesia, the former fellows of this communitas are Othered through narratives that draw boundaries along cultural distinction criteria. Here the discourses guide migrants' and pilgrims' self-identification as (Southeast) Asian, Indonesian, Javanese, and Madurese. Claims of moral superiority refer to familiar values. Contrasting with conceptions of the self are visions of Arab Others, as well as other Others, like Africans and Indians, which are gendered, rather stereotypical and quite often racist.

This reveals a perception of a hierarchization of countries and cultures. Indonesians who have traveled to Arab countries seem to be convinced of Indonesian cultural superiority, especially in the realms of morality and spirituality, including Islamic religiosity. They emphasize Indonesian softness in contrast to Arab harshness and mention numerous values, characteristics, and customs that are superior to those that they encountered abroad. Sometimes other

Asians, especially Southeast Asians, are included in the celebration of superior values, wisdom, and spirituality, which can echo the state-sponsored Asian values discourse of the 1990s. Westerners appear to rank above Arabs but below Indonesians. The ideal seemed to be a Westerner that had converted to Islam. This conviction was underlined by the numerous attempts, wishes, and prayers intended to make me convert to Islam, or references to Turkey as a combination of Islam and modernity. Concerning this "mapping of the world," Indonesians challenge hegemonic Westerncentric as well as hegemonic Arabcentric ideas of the world to a certain extent. They do not consider the West as the ultimate reference point for modernity, nor do they consider the Arab world as the exclusive center of authentic Islam—what they criticized was Arab culture in differentiation from Islam. Yet the contradiction of hegemonic mappings of the world is not entirely radical, as other regions such as Africa and South Asia are Othered along orientalist and racist stereotypes that are common in colonial and neocolonial worldviews. In fact, even Indonesians' Othering of Arab culture can be regarded as being in line with a Western discourse of Islamophobia, in which Indonesians emphasize their distinctiveness from Middle Eastern Muslims.

Yet the discourses do not only have a guiding function, serving as orientation, but are obviously also guided. The making of discursive boundaries appears to underlie opinion-making processes and obedience to authorities. Pak Raharjo's hesitation to elaborate on my questions and his suggestion that I should consult with a more knowledgeable person indicate that there is a reliance on authorities in interpreting situations. Moreover, the labor migrants and pilgrims I talked to did not articulate ground-breaking or surprising evaluations about Arabness, the world, and the self, and the great similarity in their narratives hints at a more general leading discourse. What they represented were discourses that are common and socially accepted. The guidance of mobility in practical terms (chapter 2) is stretched to the guidance and framing of discursive boundaries. Guiding actors who shape these discourses are travel agents, government representatives, and the media. In order to understand how migrants and pilgrims refer to the broader societal discussions, the following sections concern public discourses about Arabness in Indonesia and media representations in particular. Furthermore, I look at the practical level of representations of Arabness, pointing to a discrepancy between discursive boundary making and practical adoption of Arab style.

Contested Images: Arabness at Home

In chapter 1, I problematized the multiple meanings inherent in the contemporary emic use of the term *Arab* in Indonesia. In this section, I come back to the ambiguities around these terms with a special focus on ideas surrounding Arabness *within* Indonesian society, as this came up during my investigations. Thus I extend the analysis to actors who are not directly involved in pilgrimage and migration but to whom migrants and pilgrims relate, or vice versa.

Arab-Phobia in Indonesia

My residence in proximity to convents and churches and the Catholic University Universitas Sanata Dharma in Yogyakarta revealed insights about non-Muslim Indonesians' views on Arabness. Many interlocutors from my neighborhood mentioned the *Arabisasi* of Indonesia, explaining their concerns about increasing conservatism and an influx of what they perceived as Arabic and as prone to violence in the name of religion.

VIOLENCE IN THE NAME OF ISLAM

Like my Catholic neighbors, Hindu, Buddhist, and Protestant interlocutors as well as Muslims, especially those with a strong affiliation to NU, articulated their concerns about Arabization. In this regard, the term *Arab* was used specifically in reference to Wahhabi ideology, Salafi lifestyles, and violence in the name of Islam, and more generally and arbitrarily to Islamic lifestyle fashions. Many non-Muslim people recounted that over the last decade Islamic lifestyles had become more present in public life in Indonesia. This observation was frequently illustrated by claims about the clothing style of Indonesian Muslims, especially female Muslims, which, according to my interlocutors, had changed remarkably throughout the preceding decade. Many non-Muslim interlocutors argued that this was a process of Arabization as an outside influence from the Arab world, rather than changes from within Indonesia.

The new Islamic chic was regarded as un-Indonesian by virtually all non-Muslim interlocutors and also by some Muslim ones. It was frequently argued that in former times Islam had been different in Indonesia, when it was more mixed with the joint Hindu-Buddhist heritage of all Indonesians. The newly "Arabized people" were seen as lacking loyalty and having no commitment to the constitution and its preamble, the Pancasila. It was feared that they would want to turn Indonesia into a Muslim country where sharia law was obligatory for all citizens. Many non-Muslims mourned that Islam had become too dominant in all parts of public life and criticized that the changing lifestyle was also affecting them as, for example, the dress code for school children had changed and headscarves and long skirts had become almost obligatory in some areas, segregating non-Muslim children from the majority of Muslim peers.

The recent propagations of Islam Nusantara were valued highly by these people who were anxious about Arabization, yet there was a tendency to doubt the influence of government and NU discourse and worry that the government would give in to fundamentalists' demands too easily and lose control. In their anxieties about Arabization, the criticism of a generally more Islamized public sphere was mixed with fear of fundamentalism, radicalism, violence, and terrorism. When violent incidents occurred, interlocutors highlighted the perpetrators' Arab style and voiced suspicion about Arabness itself. Also, in news reports, the outward Arab appearance of radical groups and potential financial and ideological support from the Gulf was pointed out.

This perception of increasing Islamist violence is not in line with the empirical evidence, which in fact shows a decrease of Islamist influence in Indonesia (Sidel 2008, 245). Sidel (2008, 350) observes a de facto decline in violence in the name of Islam and argues that the terrorist acts that did happen around the 2000s resulted from frustration about decreasing political influence. The reasons that the popular public and international perception differs in this regard may lie in the government's concessions to Islamist demands. Buehler (2016) has shown this for sharia bylaws, and during the time of my research such symbolic conservatism rose in the election campaigns for the 2014 presidential elections, for example, in stricter laws on alcoholic beverages. In the 2019 presidential elections such symbolic politics were even more vivid and yet, as Fealy (2019) has shown, the actual influence of Islamist actors remained marginal, with the leading competitors both having a secular background. Furthermore, the perception of increasing Islamist violence might also result from a general international Islamophobia since the 9/11 terrorist attacks in 2001.

ARAB-PHOBIA

In Indonesia, this globalized fearful view on Islamic terrorism is ethnicized, and often terrorism is attributed to Middle Eastern Muslims. Different from Western Islamophobia, in which the religion of Islam is identified as the source of violence, many Indonesians differentiate between culture and religion, and brand Arab culture as the reason for violent acts. By locating the roots of Islamic terrorism in the Middle East, Indonesians outsource the problem. This Arab-phobia can be seen as a strategy for coping with fears of Islamism by maintaining local harmony and not risking open conflict through accusations against fellow citizens. The making of Arab enemy images varies from gloomy demonization to mockery and is congruent with the narratives about Arab Others among migrants and pilgrims following their sojourns abroad. A vivid example of the mockery is the common abbreviation ALKACO, standing for *Aliran Kathok Congklang*, meaning the "short trousers faction," referring to the Salafi style of wearing trousers that go just to the top of the ankles, looking too short for the common standard. Along with this "short trousers faction," "goat beards," *gamis* or *jubbah* garments (ankle-length robes for men), and full-body veils for women are associated with the ALKACO groups of Salafi orientation. The mockery of this style makes the groups appear ridiculous rather than dangerous. In the Islam Nusantara discourse such mockery is contrasted against Indonesian and local ethnic styles.

Interlocutors who adhere to *kejawén,* the Javanese worldview, many of whom are officially Muslims but who also practice Javanese rituals, were especially in favor of the Islam Nusantara discourse and emphasized the distinction between culture and religion, between Arabness and Islam. With a strong confidence in their spirituality, dedication to patience and wisdom, they were quite relaxed when it came to the questions of Arabization of the country. Mockery of Arabness dominated their statements and they were convinced of the persistence of what they called the Islamic message of peace and harmony. One of my interlocutors was a custodian at the royal cemetery in Imogiri. He explained with a self-confident smile that the pilgrimage boom to Mecca and the Pop Arabness of the middle class was just hype. He argued that politicians might put the label *Pak Hajji* or *Ibu Hajji* on their election campaign posters and publicly testify about their piety, documenting their Mecca pilgrimages, but in fact, important politicians never declined to visit the graves in Imogiri either: politicians would often come to Imogiri secretly, during the night, to ask for the deceased kings' fortune for their claim to power. He was sure that this was what really mattered. It might not be in vogue to admit it publicly, but the fact that politicians kept coming reassured him of the relevance of kejawén.

These examples suggest that the mere visibility of cultural markers, in this case Arab-Islamic ones, does not always provide insights into the actual cultural and ideological orientation of the actors and that there are back roads and side roads in addition to the main road of guiding discourses. This aspect also relates to the rather hushed stories about mystery, miracles, and supernatural incidents in Mecca (see chapter 2). It is clearly not regarded as appropriate to include it as part of an official representation of pilgrimage experiences, but in private there were vital exchanges about this among some people.

It seems that representations of a strong Javanese/Madurese/Indonesian self-confidence and anxieties about Arabization are two sides of the same coin. Reassurance of self-identity and the scapegoating of a potential outward influence as a reason for problems eases the mind and is a way of avoiding accusations within society. However, this strategy is contradicted by the fact that many people in Indonesia who adopt an Arab style, including Mecca pilgrims, are not necessarily ideologically oriented toward a Middle Eastern tradition of Islam. Thereby, the Arab-phobia, as an outsourcing of problems becomes contradictory. Where persons who have a nonideological liking for Arabness, or a personal background of Arabic ethnicity, feel denigrated by generalizations about Arabness, the Arab-phobic attitudes create frictions. Unpolitical Pop Arabness is especially prevalent among the urban middle-classes and in popular media representations.

Popular Media Representations of Arab Others

Despite, or probably because of, Arab-Phobia, many contemporary media representations in Indonesia engage with the Arab world. Migrants' and pilgrims' narratives mirror the general debates concerning Islam's proximity to Arab culture. Insight into the media interests of research participants sharpened my awareness of on-screen representations that presumably inspire off-screen representations. The following examples from TV, literature, news coverage, fashion and beauty magazines, music, internet platforms, and cinema blockbusters were relevant to research participants.[4] Yet, the examples are only a snapshot and not a complete coverage of Arab world themes in the rich variety of Indonesian popular culture.

TRAVELING AND ARABNESS IN CONTEMPORARY INDONESIAN CINEMA

The two-part film *Ketika Cinta Bertasbih* (*When Love Glorifies God*, Umam 2009), a box office hit in Indonesia in 2009, illustrates the representation of Indonesian selves and Arab Others in Indonesian cinema. A description of a sequence from the film gives an idea of this:

> Azzam, an Indonesian in his twenties, clean-shaven and neatly dressed in long trousers and shirt, cleaves his way through the busy, crowded streets of Cairo. In fluent Arabic he purchases soybeans at the market, which he uses for his cottage production of *tempe* (fermented soybeans), a small side-business while studying at Al-Azhar University. From the taxi on his way home, he sees two desperate looking Indonesian women at a bus stop. He recognizes one of them, Anna, as the young woman who had asked him for directions on the bus earlier that day and with whom he eventually falls in love. When he halts to check their condition, the young women, who are dressed in light pastel-colored *abayas* (full-body garments) and colorful matching headscarves, report that one of them has lost her belongings, presumably through pickpocketing, on the bus. Azzam offers to give them a lift and after a short fare-bargain with the taxi driver, they depart, holding their breath because of

> the breakneck driving style of the cab driver. (*Ketika Cinta Bertasbih 1*, sequence from the film min. 49:25–50:15, Umam 2009, my description)

Anna and Azzam, the protagonists of the film, are depicted as polite and righteous; they are the faces of a modern Indonesian Islam. As "good Muslims," both of them study hard at al-Azhar University and on top of this, care for their families back in Indonesia, for example by sending home money from the small *tempe* business.

Cinematic representations of self and Other in this and other Islamic themed blockbusters in Indonesia are gendered. In the sequence at hand, Azzam emerges as the hero who saves Anna and her friend on the dangerous roads of Cairo; he is supportive in an unobtrusive, polite way. His politeness and softness mark a stark contrast to the harsh and coarse Egyptian cab driver. Anna is represented as equally soft and modest, being dressed decently, her clothing style inspired by Middle Eastern clothing but in a more colorful and fashionable way. Throughout the film, she is depicted as an intelligent, independent, patient, and friendly woman. The producers of *Ketika Cinta Bertasbih* portray Anna and Azzam as the ideal Indonesian Muslim woman and man and concomitantly define the ideal relationship between men and women. Anna and Azzam appear to have equal rights, both pursuing education at the most prestigious Islamic university in the world, Azzam as a caring, responsible man and Anna as a humble yet intelligent woman. This portrayal engages with a counterimage of Arab Others. Most of the villains in the films are Egyptians, pictured as stupid, harsh, lower-class citizens like the cab driver, criminals, or terrorists. Only the teachers at al-Azhar are an exception. However, in fact, as Evi Eliyanah discovered, the production politics behind the scenes reveal that the producers' portrayal of a morally superior Indonesian Islam did not primarily aim to criticize Arab Muslims, but rather those Indonesian Muslims who propagate fundamentalist versions of Islam. Yet by placing the story in Egypt and creating Arab Others as counterimages, the producers avoid a direct critique of Indonesian Muslims. In an interview that Evi Eliyanah conducted with Faozan Rizal, the director of photography of *Ayat-Ayat Cinta* (*The Verses of Love*, Bramantyo 2008), another Islamic-themed film, Rizal described his frustration at a growing Arabness in Indonesia, arguing that this was one of the reasons why he presented alternative versions of Islamic lifestyles on-screen (Eliyanah and Lücking 2017, 8).

The Muslim filmmakers and non-Muslim producers of *Ayat-Ayat Cinta* and *Ketika Cinta Bertasbih* obviously share concerns about changes in Islamic lifestyle in Indonesia and promote a vision of a modern, tolerant, pluralist Islam as their mission for a better Indonesia, offering solutions to the "crisis of Islam" in a post-9/11 world, albeit that they may not necessarily agree with each other in every regard (Heryanto 2014b, 64–65).

In an ambivalent manner the films criticize Arabness on the one hand and engage with it on the other. While female clothing style seems to be inspired by Arab styles and the education at Al-Azhar is depicted in a romantic way, Indonesian men interestingly dress in a Western style. Ariel Heryanto (2014b, 54) shows that apart from Islamic themes, these films promote Western and Indian cultural elements. Indonesian protagonists are presented as harmonizing various cultural elements. This idea of adopting only good cultural inputs and combining them with the ultimate moral superiority and politeness of Indonesians exhibits great similarities with the narratives of labor migrants and pilgrims. Furthermore, the female protagonists' Arab style resembles the lifestyle of some middle-class pilgrims. It thus seems very likely that on- and offscreen representations of Arab Others mutually influence each other.

Apart from Arab Others, Islamic-themed films also engage with Western Others. Similar to films set in Egypt, the two-part *99 Cahaya di Langit Eropa* (*99 Lights in the European Sky*, Soeharjanto 2013, 2014) depicts the story of students in Vienna. In this film the counterimage is not the Arab world, but Europe, in this case Austria. The filmmakers rewrite the history of Europe, highlighting the Islamic heritage of the continent and tracing the protagonists' discoveries of Islam's alleged superiority. A French convert is presented as the ideal harmonization of Western culture and Islamic religiosity.

Another Islamic-themed film, or *film islami,* that inspired Pak Raharjo is *Haji Backpacker* (Rifki 2014). *Haji Backpacker* tells the story of a young man who is desperate after a series of losses and misfortunes in his life, who feels abandoned by God and turns his back on religion. Eventually, he decides to set off on a journey to experience freedom and search for a new purpose in life. Once abroad, he rediscovers his religion, which becomes his refuge and saves his life in dangerous situations. Several romantic encounters with Muslim women in foreign countries inspire him to return to Islam, finally leading him to Mecca. The emotion of the story is underlined by the sentimental song "Pergi Haji" (Going on Hajj) with the *talbīyah* as recurring motif throughout the film. It thereby draws on the existing emotion that this phrase connotes for Muslims all over the world and reproduces and stylizes the redemptive tendency of the protagonist's return to God.

The fact that the two films feature the discovery of Islamic culture in other countries like Austria, France, Turkey, Spain, China, India, Pakistan, Afghanistan and Iran stimulates a general interest in travel and corresponds with travel agencies' promotion of *umrah plus* journeys as a way to get to know Islamic cultures in other parts of the world. Thus travel agencies can include new destinations in their segment of religious travels. Though for some travelers these small excursions turn out to be rather disappointing, as the frequent umrah stopovers in Colombo, for example, appear to be related to cheaper flight offers rather than cultural tourism. Films like *99 Cahaya di Langit Eropa* and *Haji Backpacker* stimulate this interest further, especially by suggesting that Islamic culture is the key feature of modern civilization around the world.

The films relate Islam to images of love, brotherhood, peace, personal transformation, modernity, and gender equality in contrast to the images of Islam as related to war, terrorism, violence, and discrimination against women. Thereby, the films not only represent Islam as compatible with modernity, but by suggesting that the values of modern civilizations like democracy, freedom of opinion, human rights, and gender equality have Islamic roots, they also make these values their own.

These films inspire and support Indonesian middle-class Muslims' travel aspirations. For labor migrants, it is more difficult to identify with film characters, as their stories are rarely depicted in cinema blockbusters. A noteworthy exception is the film *Minggu Pagi di Victoria Park* (*Sunday Morning in Victoria Park*, Amira 2010), which tells the story of two sisters in Hong Kong. One of them represents the unfortunate fate of labor migrants, trapped in a vicious cycle of debt and prostitution, while the other is rather successful, working as a maid for friendly employers. By presenting a morally good labor migrant in contrast to her sister, who experiences a bad fate and left Indonesia for selfish reasons, the film reproduces Indonesian stigma toward labor migration that I described in chapter 2. The motifs of endured hardships, the propagation of morality, and hope for eventual morally victorious returns correspond with other popular representations of working and studying in the Middle East.

PILGRIMAGE, MIGRATION, AND STUDYING IN NOVELS AND GUIDEBOOKS

Many contemporary Indonesian movies are based on novels, most prominently those written by Habiburrahman El Shirazy. El Shirazy, an alumnus of Al-Azhar himself, set many of his stories in Cairo, focusing on Indonesian students' lives there, including *Ayat-Ayat Cinta* (*Verses of Love*, 2004), *Pudarnya Pesona Cleopatra* (*The Fading Charm of Cleopatra*, 2005), *Ketika Cinta Bertasbih* (*When Love Glorifies God 1*, 2007a), and *Ketika Cinta Bertasbih 2* (*When Love Glorifies God 2*, 2007b) among others. Some other novels are set in other parts of the Middle East, for example *Langit Makkah Berwarna Merah* (*The Sky of Mecca is Red*, 2011) and *Bulan Madu di Yerussalem* (*Honeymoon in Jerusalem*, 2012). Besides cinema adaptations, El Shirazy's novels have also been adapted for television. El Shirazy's representation of the Arab world is a passionate one, depicting it as a romantic region of Islam's roots, but also, as in the film adaptations, positioning Indonesians in these contexts as the morally superior Muslims.

Another type of literature that presents journeys to Arab countries is that of travel accounts by migrants, pilgrims, and students. One of the most famous pilgrimage accounts is Danarto's novel *Orang Jawa Naik Haji* (published in English as *A Javanese Pilgrim in Mecca)*, which portrays Javanese pilgrimage experiences in humorous self-mockery (Danarto 1984; Danarto and Aveling 1989). More recent hajj and umrah accounts are posted on online blogs and frequently concern spiritual experiences and personal transformation.

One of the especially illustrative student travel accounts is the bestselling trilogy *Notes from Qatar* by Muhammad Assad (2011, 2012, 2014), who studied engineering in Qatar. Each subtitle of the three volumes of *Notes from Qatar* is an alliteration of a moral triad: (1) *Positive, Persistence, Pray* (Assad 2011); (2) *Honest, Humble, Helpful* (Assad 2012); (3) *Dream, Do, Deliver* (Assad 2014). As one can guess from the titles, these alliterations suggest that being positive, virtuous, dutiful, persistent, humble, and of course, a good Muslim, ensures success in the Middle East. The necessity of enduring hardships is obviously related to the representation of the Middle East as a region in which Indonesians encounter hardships. Yet by patiently enduring them and sticking to one's own values, one will eventually succeed. Thus the portrayal of one's own moral superiority as the key to success goes hand in hand with a rather gloomy representation of Arab culture. While the books are written in Indonesian, their English titles invoke a touch of the cosmopolitanism associated with studying abroad.

Besides travel accounts, travel guidebooks are another source of knowledge about Arab Others. Hajj and umrah guidebooks like *Catatan Perjalanan Haji Seorang Muslimah* (*Notes of a Muslimah's Hajj Journey*) provide practical information, in this case especially for women. The advice covers emotional, hygienic, spiritual and organizational matters (Meutia 2009). Almost every travel agency publishes its own travel guides and prayer handbooks, which can also be found online. Besides prayers, many of these guidebooks include an introduction to Arabic culture and customs, as is given during the *manasik* preparation courses. A fancy comic guidebook entitled *Cara Mabrur Naik Haji dan Umrah* (*How to Become a Virtuous Haji and Umrah Pilgrim*, Luqman 2000) portrays Arab people as harsh, loud, and tall in a chapter entitled *Adat Orang Arab* (*Customs of Arab People*) and suggests that Indonesians adhere to the rules in Saudi Arabia and patiently adapt to Arab peoples' customs in order to make the pilgrimage smooth and successful (Luqman 2000, 100).

ARABNESS AND ASIANNESS ON INDONESIAN TELEVISION

Television is probably the most important form of mass media in Indonesia today. While residing with some of my research participants, *nonton TV* (watching TV) was a daily evening activity. Remarkably, even though there are soap operas, talk shows and documentaries that relate to the Arab world on Indonesian TV, the most prominent TV series at the time of inquiry was the Malaysian animation series *Upin and Ipin*, featuring the adventurous everyday life of twin brothers *Upin* and *Ipin* in a fictional Malaysian *kampong* (village/urban subcompound). During my research visits, I found the series flickering on TVs almost everywhere, in rural Madura as well as in urban and rural Central Java. Despite the differences between migrants and pilgrims, rural and urban areas, Madura and Java, everybody seemed to like *Upin and Ipin*. Research participants explained their liking for the fictional twin brothers by saying that they were cute and funny and related to everyday realities: the food that was discussed, the culturally specific jokes and the religious morals.[5] Besides the traditional rivalry between Malaysia and Indonesia, many Indonesians emphasized the cultural, religious, and linguistic similarities between the two countries.

While *Upin and Ipin* features Islamic Asianness with traditional Malay clothing, language, food, culture, and customs, numerous other TV broadcasts relate more to the Middle East and to Arabness. On several TV channels Muslim scholars spread various interpretations of Islamic theological concerns, differing in their use of cultural markers such as clothing style, language, and titles (see Barendregt 2010; Fealy 2008; Howell 2001, 2010; Muzakki 2012; Thomas and Lee 2012). Most of the televangelists appear to use the title *ustadz* for male preachers and *ustadzah* for female ones, who also sometimes appear on television. The Arabic term literally means teacher or master and is a common form of address for younger teachers in *pesantren*, in differentiation to the more prestigious title kyai.

Famous for their television-based sermons are K. H. (Kyai Hajji) Abdullah Gymnastier (known as Aa Gym,) K. H. Zainuddin MZ, Ustadz Muhammad Arifin Ilham, Ustadz Jefry Al-Buchory, Ustadz Yusuf Mansur, Ustadzah Qurrata A'yun, Ustadzah Mamah Dede, Ustadz Ahmad Al-Habsyi, Ustadz Nur Maulana, Ustadz Soleh Mahmud and Ustadz Wijayanto, whom I have already mentioned several times. Many of the shows featuring their sermons include dialogic elements in which viewers can ask questions. Love and family life are among the issues of concern, in addition to business issues such as the promotion of halal businesses and topics surrounding Islamic lifestyle (Muzakki 2012, 45). Arab words in the names of the programs, like *qalbu*, and the titles of *ustadz/ustadzah* mark the Islamic character of the shows, and in the sermons Arabic expressions are in vogue beyond the core Arabic Qur'an recitation and prayers. Many of my interlocutors argued that these preachers have an Arab style, *gaya Arab*. Sometimes, this Arab style is related to the content of the teaching, as it is sometimes regarded as promoting Salafi ideas, which are labeled as an Arab mindset. However, Muzakki (2012) argues that the way Indonesia's Islamic televangelists preach actually exhibits parallels with the traditional teaching methods of the *pesantren*. Moreover, that women appear as preachers is rather "un-Arabic," given the fact that this would be rather unusual in most Arab countries. A remarkable difference to traditional religious authorities is, according to Muzakki, that televangelism downplays the role of the religious authorities. In contrast, marketization and mediatization promote autonomy and autodidacticism among viewers (Muzakki 2012, 57). Observations by Julia Howell (2001, 2010) confirm that traditionalism does not lose its importance in mediatized and popularized transmissions of Islamic teachings. With reference to Howell, Bubandt argues that even though all televangelists promote an image and theology of an orthodox, pious, and Salafi brand of Islam, they "actively incorporate numerous Sufi elements into their televised ministries and 'do-it-yourself' spiritual guidebooks" (Bubandt 2013, 60). Rituals like *ḏikr* (commemoration of God's names), *khalawat* (spiritual retreats), and *zuhud* (simplicity and abstinence), as well as the concept of *hakekat* (the hidden inner meaning of the reality of all things), are prevalent in televangelists' talks, which is striking as most televangelists are regarded as modernist or even Salafist, closer to Muhammadiyah or PKS, while these rituals and concepts are regarded as part of NU's domain (Bubandt 2013, 60). Therefore, the Arab appearance of the televangelists does not necessarily reveal their scholarly opinion or confessional affiliation.[6]

An example from my own research is Ustadz Wijayanto, who happens to also be a travel guide for umrah-plus journeys. Many research participants claimed that Ustadz Wijayanto, similar to other TV *ustadz*, had an Arab touch, regarding his style, teachings and, moreover, his frequent travels to the Holy Land. Yet in interviews Ustadz Wijayanto relativizes this image, reflecting very critically on Arabic culture and customs, and his scholarly opinion is far from Wahhabism or Salafism. In his *pesantren* in Yogyakarta, he fosters Javanese traditions and gender equality.

For *some* preachers, Arabness simply serves as selling point. They use style to make up for a lack of religious education (Barendregt 2010, 41). Arabness—regarding style as well as descent—appears to entail a certain symbolic capital in this realm, as the popularity of Hadhrami in the business of televangelism reveals.[7] Besides TV series, talk shows and televangelists, TV documentaries about the umrah and hajj are prominently featured, especially when celebrity pilgrimages are documented in popular gossip/variety shows.

All in all, regarding televised representations of the Arab world, Arabness on TV appears to be a marketing strategy in the first place, especially during Ramadan, symbolizing Islamic religiosity but not necessarily revealing the ideological affiliations of the people appearing on TV and even less the credentials of those who are responsible for the production and broadcasting process.[8]

ONLINE-BASED DIALOGIC REPRESENTATIONS

Another important media sphere is the internet.[9] The internet is an arena for representations as well as interactions. Muslims in Indonesia communicate with each other and with religious leaders online, among them some of the abovementioned televangelists (see Slama 2017). While television has been a very important form of media in Islamic da'wa, the mobile phone has become even more important (Muzakki 2012, 52). There is even a neologism for religious studies via telephone, merging the syllables tele- with the Arabic term *taujih*. *Taujih* itself means "direction," "guidance," or "sermon" and *teletaujih* means "telecommunicated religious guidance" (Muzakki 2012, 53). In fact, in the overall consideration of guidance, smartphones stand out as tremendously important guides of Indonesia's middle classes.

Many research participants used various communication devices such as mobile phones, tablets, and computers to access information and entertainment online. Furthermore, they regularly use internet-based communication services such as WhatsApp or WeChat and above all, of course, the social media platforms Facebook and Twitter, which are for many irreplaceable tools when traveling or migrating. The American marketing association eMarketer ranked Indonesia, with 60 million Facebook users, as the fourth largest national group on Facebook in 2014 (Statista 2014) and the third largest in 2015 after the United States and India (eMarketer 2015).[10]

Pilgrims document their journey on Facebook or Instagram and some of them create their own online blogs. This indicates that the intersection between media representation and personal offscreen and offline representation is fluid: the internet provides a platform that can be used by anyone to upload representations and make them accessible to a wider community.

Among labor migrants, using Facebook and other internet-based social media and communication services appeared to be a rather new trend, as some of them used these sites with great ease, while others seemed to be less familiar with the technology. This reflects a digital divide related to social class. Moreover, rather than representing their journeys, labor migrants mainly accessed internet services for communication, especially to keep in touch during their time abroad. Furthermore, migrants used their phones and the internet to search for information, some of which was especially targeted at them, such as advertisements for the Chinese multilevel marketing company TIENS, mentioned in chapter 2, or mobile phone companies' special offers for internet tariffs abroad. In any case, unlike pilgrims, for migrants accessing information and communicating appeared to be more important than representing stays abroad or images of themselves.

While most of the internet-based religious activities appear to concern emotional issues, like family life, and aim at a more pious lifestyle generally, sometimes statements in this realm become political and competing guiding communication emerges. Research participants showed me hashtags like *#ShiaBukanIslam* (Shia is no Islam) and *#SolidaritasSharia* (Sharia Solidarity). Some social media partly disguise ideological affiliations. And as the hashtags show, global discourses, like the propagation of Islamic jurisprudence and Sunni-Shi'a hostility, are among the guiding narratives in a competitive environment.

Evidently, opinion making and lifestyle are subtly intertwined. While for many Indonesian internet users, a certain portrayal of Arabness in social media appears to be a fashionable feature of their modern, media-based lifestyle, for other groups it is part and parcel of their ideological affiliation. This is the reason why NU and some government representatives oppose trends of what they see as "Arabization," making competing use of social media. While the public debate about Islam Nusantara was more differentiated, on Twitter and Facebook it was sometimes reduced to slogans that stigmatized Arabness, as in a widely shared image that engaged with the Arabness of the Hadhrami community: the photo montage showed a historical photograph of a group of Hadhrami women in traditional Javanese clothing in contrast to a more recent picture showing female graduates of doctoral training at the Infaq Dakwah Center, who were all wearing full-body veils and face covering chadors.[11] It stated that Arabs from the Hadhramaut were humble when they came to Indonesia and adopted Indonesian culture, while now some Indonesians hated their own archipelagic culture and were Arabizing themselves.[12] Facebook and other communication services are battlefields of competing internal Indonesian groups.

MEDIATING ARABNESS

This exemplary cross-section of the productive contemporary Indonesian film and TV industries, a glimpse into novels and guidebooks, and the consideration of the increasingly important role of internet-based communication reveals that migrants' and pilgrims' narratives about selves and Others are not individual ideas, but are situated in broader societal discourses. The guidance of mobility is accompanied by negotiated processes that feature prominently in different media spheres. Yet migrants and pilgrims are not merely passively guided by the mediatized narratives, reproducing them or following them, but they engage with them more or less actively. In the mediatization of the engagement with the Arab world and Arabness, the boundaries between on- and offscreen are blurred. This becomes especially evident in online representations, but also in the complex offscreen negotiations of filmmaking and publication procedures. Thus representations of Arabness are not only mediatized but also mediated, as the diverging representations and negotiations reveal. Various actors seek to make use of media influence, and individuals have to make sense of the often contrasting and competing representations: as customers, they choose and combine. And Arabness is not the only selling point, as the popularity of the TV series *Upin and Ipin* indicates. In fact, it seems to be the flexibility and the interchangeability of things that drive media consumption.

Like in the Arab-phobic discourses that I described above, popular media defines Middle Eastern culture in a differentiation between culture and religion. Indirectly, the political undercurrents of media representations do also criticize Arabness at home by depicting Indonesians in contrast to Arabs. The feeling of needing to emphasize the compatibility of Islam and human rights, and especially women's rights and gender equality, appears to be related to a global crisis in Islam. Media representations are another form of easing the mind by providing easy solutions. However, these easy solutions are contradicted by many peoples' taste for Arabness as the cultural markers of televangelists and the adoption of globalized discourses like the Anti-Shi'a discourse indicate.

Media representations of Arabness reflect the overall ambivalence in contemporary Indonesian engagement with the Middle East. Cinema representations are an illustrative example of how the Middle East is portrayed as a place where Muslims long to go, very likely becoming a booster for travel agencies' umrah offers, yet by depicting Indonesian Muslims as superior, consumers are guided in the direction of Indonesian self-confidence. The presence of Indonesian Muslims at the holy sites and prestigious universities is represented as self-evident and the portrayal of Indonesians' capability to combine features of Western, Islamic, and to some extent, Arabic cultures, that is also prominent in travel accounts promotes Indonesianness. The ultimate advice is to encounter Arabness with Indonesian patience and persistence. The transition between mediatized and mediated popular representations and lived Pop Arabness is fluid, which can be seen in embodied Pop Arabness.

Indonesians' Arabness

Contemporary Arab-phobia in Indonesia concerns a perceived new Arab influence. However, thus far, the discourses surrounding Arabness, show that there is no such thing as uniform, homogenous Arabness. Based on the examples in this book, we can identify "traditionalist Arabness" in the tradition of NU, the "modernist" Arabness of Muhammadiyah, the "ethnic Arabness" of the Hadhrami peoples, the "Pop Arabness" of the urban middle-classes, and a "hajji Arabness" among Mecca returnees with specific local features of adopting prestigious Arab style that could also be labeled according to ethnicity like "Madurese Arabness" (see chapter 4). All these different ways and versions of adopting a certain Arab style are "made in Indonesia." In contrast to the Arab-phobia proponents who subsume some of these forms of Arabness into one category with Wahhabi and Salafi streams, the examples at hand indicate that these features of Arabic cultural elements are often not related to any ideology but rather to social status. Furthermore, they are not exclusively inspired by Middle Eastern culture but can be seen as Indonesian creations.

Thus when I argue that various forms of Arabness, as they feature in daily practices, habits, language, music, names, food, and fashion, are Indonesian phenomena rather than Middle Eastern ones, I intend to look beyond the surface of Arab theming and consider what the respective form of Arabness means within the Indonesian context and how it came into existence. NU's and Muhammadiyah's engagements with Arabness differ and the two organizations may likewise label one another as Arab-oriented, with NU's alleged focus on Islamic teachers who have studied in the Holy Land and Muhammadiyah's supposed affinity with Arabic modernist teachings (cf. chapter 1). The ethnic Arabness of the Hadhrami can be a source of discrimination in the course of Arab-phobia. And, as discussed in chapters 1 and 2, *hajji Arabness* marks a prestigious change in clothing and habits by haji mabrur upon return from pilgrimage. The category of "Pop Arabness" yet demands further analysis regarding its relation to the above-described media representations and other localized versions of Arabness.

As the comprehensive studies on popularization and commercialization of Islamic culture in Indonesia indicate, there are various cultural themes in today's Pop Islamic landscape in Indonesia. Derived from the concept of "Pop Islam" (Heryanto 2011, 60–82), I define the Arab cultural markers in modern, popular Islamic lifestyle as Pop Arabness. Pop Arabness is one type of Islamic lifestyle in Indonesia and is mainly found in the urban middle class. It is characterized by its popular, commercial, and modern features. Heryanto highlights that today's Islamic culture and lifestyle in Indonesia is celebrated as a symbol of wealth and modernity by the growing educated urban middle class (Heryanto 2011, 2014b). "Lifestyle Islam" is thus often a symbol for seemingly mundane social, economic, and political values, rather than a specific Islamic teaching—nevertheless it can entail separation from non-Muslim Indonesians and changes social togetherness, which is probably one of the reasons for non-Muslims' fear and uncertainty.

Popular media representations of Arabness and the Arab world are intertwined with the lived elements of what is labeled Arabness. Engagement with Arabness on a practical level is in itself a representation of Arabness, especially regarding style, fashion, and lifestyle trends but also certain habits. In the case of embodied cultural representations, the term *Arab* is often employed primarily by outside observers. The label *Arab* is used with hesitation by those who do adopt Arab style and, remarkably, many of my research participants who exhibited what was labeled as Arab style from an outside perspective distanced themselves from Arab culture and people on a discursive level, labeling their style as Islamic, rather than Arabic. Here, they would usually refer to the sunna and explain that their habits and clothing were inspired by revelation and Prophetic tradition. They do not see a discrepancy between their discursive demarcation from Arabness and their lived Pop Arabness.

One of the most frequently recurring categories in my data was the differentiation between Arab and Islam, between culture and religion. What is remarkable is that everyone seems to support this differentiation. The difference is where people draw the boundary between things considered to be religion and those considered to be culture. While persons who have a liking for Middle Eastern traditions, wearing short trousers or growing a beard, for example, argue that this is in line with the Prophet's recommendation for appropriate Muslim behavior, thus considering it sunna and not culture, the opponents of this style consider it culture. They mock these Arab practices, arguing that these people have misunderstood what the sunna is, as one would not also start riding camels just because the prophet did so, when there are no camels in Indonesia.

Many research participants from urban middle classes, especially those that had repeatedly performed the umrah, dressed in a fashionable Islamic style, using fashion elements inspired by Arabic clothing, like long abaya robes for women, jubbah robes for men, and headscarves of various styles. Besides clothing style, their Islamic lifestyle included da'wa activities and living as devout Muslims themselves was considered a crucial step in spreading the values of Islam. This leads to a change in daily interactions. As an example, in the interaction between men and women, they avoid physical contact like shaking hands. Moreover, many of them try to establish a more Islamic and halal lifestyle in general, not only concerning clothing style but also other forms of consumption, eating habits, knowledge of Arabic language, business, and education, as well as religious rituals in everyday life, like strict adherence to prayer times or dedication to Qur'an recitation and prayer group meetings, as for example, in the business self-help group Tawhid Community, in which Mas Eko was engaged.

Fellow Indonesians who are not in favor of these changing daily practices brand them as Arab practices. Yet one of my interlocutors, the owner of a pilgrimage travel agency and Muslim fashion store, explained that Arabic style was only an inspiration and that it was adjusted to Indonesian tastes, saying: "Arabic Islam is black and white, but Indonesian Islam is colorful." Furthermore, she explained that Indonesian fashion labels were very successful and that they might soon export to the Middle East. Therefore, she was confident that the Arab touch was not a one-way influence but a mutual inspiration and exchange with great creativity coming from Indonesia.[13] Throughout our conversation, she positioned herself as being fond of the "rise" of Islam, arguing that soon people around the world, including the Western world, would begin to be enlightened by Islam. She supported her argument by informing me about the breaking news that she was reading on her tablet while I interviewed her, which claimed that Pope Benedict XVI had converted to Islam. This attitude of self-confidence and an apparently strong conviction that Islam would enlighten the world, particularly the Western world, corresponds with the narratives in the above-mentioned films, especially *99 Cahaya di Langit Eropa*. This reveals that besides fashion and an appropriation of Pop Arabness, Islamic lifestyle *can* be accompanied by ideas about the world and certain ideological convictions. Yet these ideas stem from Islamization tendencies within Indonesia. For this young, fashionable businesswoman, Islamic lifestyle was a cosmopolitan notion, a global idea about the future, an integration of Western elements with business and thus not a one-way influence from the Middle East.

This encounter indicates that engagement with Arab style is for some people related to a general change in their perspective on the world. However, it remains an Indonesian perspective, rather than a Middle Eastern one. The overall message is not the superiority of Arab culture, but that of Indonesian-Islamic culture. Labeling these Islamization trends and their underlying worldviews as "Arab" falls short of providing deeper understanding. This Islamization trend must also be seen in relation to social segregation. By claiming that Islam was "on the rise," with even the pope converting to Islam, the fashion store owner also asserted her status as potentially knowledgeable and being on the right track, both toward me, a Western researcher, and toward her customers. On the other side, Islamic scholars, people from lower classes, and pilgrims from rural areas, as well as labor migrants, often criticized this Islamic chic as hypocritical and arrogant, denouncing the commercial interests of fashion labels as well as those related to the pilgrimage as a *jalan-jalan* activity (making a trip). Pak Mariadi, who mocked the Arab people whom he met during the hajj, similarly mourned Indonesians who appropriate Arab style, subsuming the traditional Arabness of the kyai, Pop Arabness, and the popularity of people of Arab descent in his criticism:

> In Indonesia, there are many religious adherents who overemphasize Arabness. Islam and being Arab, those are two different things, aren't

> they? Not everything that comes from Arab countries is Islam. They overdo it, like many people who wear Arab clothing, kyai who wear Arab clothing excessively, that definitely conveys the message to their *santri*, their students, that culturally there is a special honoring of the Arab race from Indonesian people. So these so-called *habib* people appear more and more often as TV preachers. (Pak Mariadi, March 17, 2013)

While some people understand many Arabic cultural traditions as intrinsically Islamic, Pak Mariadi and others make a sharper distinction between Arab culture and Islam. His statement reflects the generalizing denouncements of Arabness. Quite interestingly, his Othering of Indonesian Arabness and his Othering of Middle Eastern Arabness serve the same purpose: self-affirmation and legitimization of his preferred way of life and interpretation of Islam. The very same holds true for the fashion store owner, except that for her the same aim is realized through Pop Arabness as lifestyle. This reveals that identification with or rejection of Arabness is a distinction criteria that is only meaningful in its relation to internal Indonesian social frictions, such as Pop Arabness being associated with middle-class lifestyles, traditionalist Arabness of the kyai being associated with the influence of religious authorities, or Hadhrami Arabness being related to their recent popularity. Thus when Pak Mariadi claims that these factions "overemphasize Arabness," at first sight it seems as if he only criticizes their notion of treating Arabness as especially authentic when the undercurrent of his criticism is about middle-class exclusiveness, kyai leadership, and Hadhrami popularity. Ideological orientation, in contrast, does not really seem to matter.

To a certain extent, Arabness and controversies about it can be considered a surrogate conflict, in the sense that the discourse about Arabness entails underlying social frictions. Weintraub (2011b, 4–5) shows this for the example of the headscarf. He grasps the complexity of interpreting embodied cultural symbols like the headscarf, highlighting their multiple meanings that are sometimes not directly related to a religious message but might, for example, be deeply rooted within social identity politics, like middle-class identity or in the Suharto era as one of political protest.

Concerning the Indonesian creation of Pop Arabness as a symbol of middle-class affiliation, wealth, and piety, as well as cosmopolitanism and modernity, the umrah must be seen as part and parcel of this lifestyle. Interestingly, Pop Arabness appears to be interchangeable with other cultural markers in Islamic popular culture like "lifestyle Chineseness" (Hew 2012) or Asianness more generally. Diverging lifestyle features are in competition. Another example of this is the mélange of various cultural influences in Cak Nun's gamelan ensemble Kiai Kanjeng whose engagement with Arabness in the musical sphere appears to be creative and playful. Cak Nun criticized the consumerist appropriation of Arab style and argued that his engagement with Arabic music was different. With regard to middle-class Pop Arabness he states:

> But it is not oral, not music. It's a trend, a way of dressing and a certain jargon, the *jilbab* [Indonesian: headscarf] is now called *hijab* [Arabic: headscarf], people use the [Arab] terms *anthum* [you] and *ana* [me], so that's the middle class, not the villagers. Village people aren't like that. . . . About this Arabization, I think it's important to have parameters to analyze the differences between Arab and Islam. (Cak Nun, May 21, 2014)

Cak Nun and Kiai Kanjeng don't want to fit in. Their criticism of capitalist Pop Arabness and Islamic consumer culture are an encouragement to their followers, many of whom appear to come from rural areas, to remain self-confident. As Cak Nun himself put it in Javanese: "Jowo digowo, Arab digarap, Barat diruwat" (Cak Nun, May 21, 2014), which means that Java or Javaneseness is the stable foundation, Arabness is incorporated and Westernness is adjusted to Javanese culture. This engagement with Arabness reveals another facet in the Indonesian way of localizing Arabness, and it highlights that popular localizations are not singular but plural and often playful and creative as well as contested and in competition with each other.

Lifestyle Boundaries

This overview of the perceptions of Arabness within Indonesia, or Indonesians' Arab worlds, indicates that despite the discursive demarcations in the context of pilgrimage and migration that I have described above, there is an engagement with Arabness on a practical level that results in incorporation and representations of Arab style and sometimes also certain ideologies in media, popular performances, and in everyday life.

The analysis shows that the Indonesian creations of Arabness are in most cases not related to Wahhabi or Salafi ideologies so much as being interchangeable symbols through which various underlying social frictions are communicated. Non-Muslim views on Islamic lifestyle indicate that Arab style and what is seen as an "Arab mindset" are often subsumed under the label "Arab" due to anxieties that demand easy answers, which are found through the identification of scapegoats. However, similar to the movies' narratives, by outsourcing the problems of violence in the name of Islam or the increasing Islamization of public life and exclusivity, the critics avoid attacking fellow Indonesians directly, but formulate their worries indirectly, by naming outward influence as the problems' source.

Sometimes these generalizations are even racialized, as doubts about the Hadhrami indicate.

Yet the popular localization of lifestyle Arabness, or Pop Arabness, reveals that these popularized, commercialized features are often interchangeable and are not solely related to religious ideologies but also to other parts of life, such as class affiliation, modernity and cosmopolitanism, or entrepreneurship. This corresponds to the variety of media representations of Arabness. Representations and localizations of Arabness are mediatized, mediated, adjusted, filtered, and challenged.

Contested Guiding Discourses

The normative discourses and practices that revolve around ideas of Arabness and of the Arab world become guiding reference points for the positioning of the self and the legitimization of lifestyle choices. Furthermore, these *situated representations* are a medium of communication. They communicate affiliation and demarcation; they express aspirations and articulate social hierarchies. As images of cultural Others reveal more about those who make these images than those who are the subject of them, Indonesian portrayals of the Arab world must be considered in the light of their function within local communities and nationwide social dynamics. The example of migrants and pilgrims shows that individuals—even those who can draw on firsthand encounters with cultural Others—look for leading discourses, which guide their self-positioning. Consequently, their narratives mirror national and international leading discourses, some of which are in competition. These narratives about Arab Others do not only concern people and culture in the Middle East and the positioning of Indonesian Muslims globally; they also relate to cultural orientations and trends at home. The ambivalent dynamics of self-Other discourses in the context of Indonesians' relationship with the Arab world are evident in this regard.

Partial Othering: Arab Others Abroad

Concerning Indonesians' narratives about Arab Others abroad, especially those of migrants and pilgrims, I identify three key aspects: (1) the Othering of fellow Muslims, (2) the differentiation between culture and religion and the concomitant assertion of cultural boundaries, and (3) the function of Othering from a peripheral perspective.

Concerning the first aspect, it must be noted that the Othering of what is considered Arab happens only partially. Sharing the same religion and being subsumed in the same category of a "Muslim world," Indonesians identify with the Arab world while simultaneously Othering it. The Arab world is a place of longing, depicted romantically in popular media representations, and Indonesians stress their rightful presence in the Holy Land, which obviously boosts the pilgrimage business. This is also evoked by travel agencies and reveals changes from differing approaches within history, as for instance the decline in pilgrimage travels to Mecca during the early years of the Suharto regime.

Yet Arab culture and ideologies from the Gulf are also the subjects of anxieties. The different levels of communitas indicate how affiliation to a group varies according to the respective context. Especially during ritual practice, there seems to be a strong identification with a larger ummah. However, in postritual narratives, cultural differences appear to stand out even more. The identification with fellow Muslims that pilgrims experience during ritual practice does not occur in the same way for migrant workers. Yet migrant workers equally relativize their demarcation from Arab people, as they are emotionally attached to their employers' families, especially to those for whom they cared, like children.

The second aspect refers to the prominent differentiation between culture and religion as a key feature of Indonesians' partial Othering of the Arab world. They carefully emphasize that it is not Islam, but Arab culture that is the difference between Indonesian and Arab Muslims. Identifying with different in-groups is a process of selection and filtering. Lastly, Indonesians claim to combine the positive features from various foreign cultures. Here the overall mapping of the world shows that cultural proximity is to be considered a more bonding criterion than sharing the same religion. Asianness, especially Southeast Asianness and Indonesianness are the defining features of the alleged moral superiority of the self, emphasizing Asian politeness, humbleness, guarding a feeling of shame (*malu*), being patient and persistent. This praise of Asian, and in particular Javanese, values is prevalent among migrants and pilgrims alike, as well as in media representations of Indonesian encounters with the Arab world in which these Asian values are promoted as a strategy for coping with the harsh Arabs.

This aspect of the affirmation of moral superiority relates to the third aspect, the function of Othering between Indonesia and the Middle East in the center-periphery divide. Indonesians' evaluation of cultural differences are also a reaction to the stigma of being labeled as the periphery of the Muslim world. There seems to be a feeling of needing to emphasize the legality of local practices, the claim of being the better Muslims, and presenting solutions to the global "crisis of Islam" (Lewis 2004), as famously voiced in the Islam Nusantara discourse and in popular media representations.

Surrogate Discourses: Arab Others at Home

As a distinction criterion, Arabness refers to ideological orientation, clothing style, moral values, daily habits, lifestyle trends, and class affiliation. While those who have a liking for Pop Arabness do not label it as such, instead arguing that they live in accordance with the sunna, the critics of this lifestyle denounce their practices as infiltrated by *foreign* Arab culture. The simultaneity of discursive rejection of what is described as an "Arab mindset" and Arab style does not represent a contradiction for those who are in favor of this style, as they do not perceive it as foreign influence.

With the exception of a minority's ideological orientation toward Wahhabism and Salafism, the various forms of Arabness in Indonesia, like traditionalist NU Arabness as well as the modern Pop Arabness or *hajji Arabness* use Arabness in a merely symbolic way, conveying differing meanings. Concerning Pop Arabness, identification as middle class appears to be most crucial. Furthermore, the symbiosis of business activities and piety becomes important. While for some people exhibiting an Arab style is a form of communicating their affiliation to a pious middle class and an Indonesian self-confidence of combining neoliberal modernity and Islam, for the critics of this lifestyle, the Arab features are considered to be either hypocritical or dangerous, associated with radical ideologies. However, many critics do not directly attack the lifestyle of the pious middle class and the proceeding Islamization of the public sphere but brand them as an outward influence from the Middle East. By outsourcing reasons for increasing conservatism, including fading interreligious tolerance, there is no actual discussion about the Indonesian makings of the various forms of new conservatism.

Furthermore, Indonesian society appears to be much divided about the question of the extent to which Arab practices are part of the sunna and therefore an authentic part of Islamic religiosity. Interestingly, besides their competition, the competing streams consider their Indonesian Muslim religious practice as superior, either because of becoming better Muslims and refining sunna practices or because of claiming that Asians have always been the better Muslims, which they name as the reason that God did not send his prophets to the archipelago.

Cultural Mobility

Thus, in conclusion, contemporary cultural orientations in Indonesia, including new conservative orientations, are a form of cultural change or cultural mobility.

This cultural change is—as I have shown—not first and foremost inspired by spatial mobility to the Middle East. In contrast, this cultural mobility is much determined by competing guiding narratives that are relevant in domestic gambling over influence and economic gain. The experiences of labor migrants and pilgrims who actually did visit Arab countries, are an especially strong example for this: Even though they can draw on firsthand experiences abroad, they follow guiding narratives. The guiding narratives have a homeward vision and relate to social frictions and contestations over public influence within Indonesia. Like in the personal accounts of pilgrimage and migration, the potential movement of knowledge, ideas, norms, and habits appears to be not so much triggered by the experience of spatial mobility itself, but by restructuring in the domestic context.

Transferring anxieties about growing conservatism in Indonesia to talk about influence from the Middle East, and journeys to the Middle East as inspiring this change, is a method of simplification. Apart from locating the reasons for cultural change elsewhere and thereby easing the mind, discourses about Arab Others are a surrogate conflict between competing directions concerning convictions about the right interpretation of Islam and the most appropriate path for Indonesian society. Elites are keen to promote their preferred guiding narratives and there is an indication of obedience to authority.

However, individuals do not follow the leading discourses blindly. Authorities are dependent on the loyalty of their followers and must adjust their guidance. The interdependent leader-follower relationship of guidance exhibits similarities with a market logic of demand and supply. As I argued in the introduction, the search for guidance facilitates its supply. It seems that in the changing social landscape of Indonesia and the context of global Islamophobia, orientation is much appreciated among Indonesians, yet they choose and filter in the competitive market of guidance.

One of the currently leading discourses about the Arab world in Indonesia challenges hegemonic discourses by promoting Indonesian Islam as an international model. While apparently internationally there is little acknowledgement of this aspired model character of Islam Nusantara, it is likely that this discourse is also not actually directed to an audience abroad but to opponents within Indonesia. Thus the dynamics of the conservative turn are highly complex and subject to competition over political and economic gain as well as new consumption patterns and the demand and supply of guidance.

The discursive and lifestyle boundaries indicate that besides having a guiding function, representations of Arabness can also become a commodity. In contestations over public influence and power gambling, and in social hierarchies more generally, affiliation with and rejection of Arabness becomes a symbolic capital for the respective message the actor seeks to convey. On the local level, in migrants' and pilgrims' homes, the relevant representations of Arabness can be a pragmatic way of proving one's loyalty to family and relatives or one's moral integrity. Moreover, for travel agencies as well as labor migrant agencies, romantic images of the "Prophet's Land" and the need to set foot there become a narrative that can be transferred into economic capital. The transferability and transformability of Arabness as a commodity is the focus of the next chapter, indicating that certain interpretations and translations of connections to the Arab world complicate Indonesian engagements with Arabness and nuances of the conservative turn even more.

4

ALTERNATIVE ROUTES IN MADURA AND TRANSLATIONAL MOMENTS IN JAVA

The aforementioned differentiation between various types of Arabness, such as Pop Arabness or traditional NU Arabness helps to elucidate the complexity of Indonesians' ambivalent engagement with the Arab world. The analysis of situated representations in chapter 3 has shown that migrants' and pilgrims' representations of the Arab world are not only inspired by their experiences abroad but also to a significant degree by nationwide public discourses about Arab Others. Media representations (chapter 3) and the administrational and interpersonal guidance of public and private actors (chapter 2) shape a guiding "main road" among research participants. Their engagement with guiding people, structure, norms, and images is complex and their firsthand experiences in Arab countries do not make their representations any less ambivalent or contradictory. And yet, overall, migrants and pilgrims appear to follow the "main road" guidance. Their social mobility, which can follow spatial mobility, is guided by local and national norms and values.

However, long-term research revealed that beneath this adherence to what looks like overarching guidance, there are also deviations from the mainstream. These deviations became particularly obvious to me in the Central Javanese mountain village that I call Gunungembun and in Madura. In the analysis of representations of Arab Others and identification of different forms of Arabness, I have already mentioned that labor migrants would extend their critical statements about Saudi Arabian Arabness to their compatriots' Pop Arabness. This was a first small indication of further inquiries into how migrant women in

Gunungembun make sense of dominant guiding elements, their own transnational experiences and their opportunities for upward mobility.

For Madurese research participants, even though Madura is an NU stronghold, the dominant guiding discourse of Islam Nusantara and its demonization of Middle Eastern Arabness has little appeal. The Madurese, who from a Javanese perspective are themselves labeled as having "Arab characteristics," find their own way of incorporating Arabness into Madurese identity. Moreover, apart from omnipresent Arab-Islamic symbolism, the Madurese are especially active as brokers in the pilgrimage and labor migration business. Ustadz Wijayanto argued from his perspective as an umrah guide that a pilgrimage tour would only run smoothly if the travel agency included Madurese brokers who live in Saudi Arabia. With pride in their intermediary roles, the Madurese make Arabness their own, joking that due to Madurese influence in Mecca there has been a "Madurization" of Saudi Arabia.

These two deviations from mainstream guidance provoke the question of what makes people follow? And furthermore, how do they choose between competing offers of guidance? David Graeber's concept of interpretative labor provides a useful tool to understand how individuals do not follow authoritarian or "mainstream" guidance blindly but establish agency. I shall show under what conditions this interpretative labor is established and enacted.

The two examples from the microcosm of Indonesian society reveal how people on the ground make sense of what it means to be Muslim, finding their own answers to themes of the conservative turn and features of Arabness. This corresponds with the analysis of Kloos (2017) for Aceh, where people are not passive receivers of official norms but actively negotiate these norms. For the Acehnese people, a sense of failure triggers personal reflection and the endeavor to become "better Muslims" (Kloos 2017, 161). For the Madurese and Central Javanese research contexts, it was more aspiration for success rather than fear of failure that appeared to lead individuals in their choices of and demand for guidance or their personal interpretations. In any case, the fear of failure and hopes for success go hand in hand.

An understanding of local differences in the vast variety of Islamic lifestyle choices in Indonesia shows that claims of increasing conservatism must consider peoples' individual agency. The analysis in this chapter focuses on data that was generated through participant observation and cohabitation with research participants.

Labor Migrants between K-Pop and Piety

During my first few days in Gunungembun I met Ayu, the daughter of a female labor migrant who had worked in Saudi Arabia. Ayu was wearing a white T-shirt featuring a brightly colored image of a K-Pop girl group.[1] When I admired her colorful T-shirt, I was very surprised to learn that her mother had brought the shirt from Saudi Arabia for her. A K-Pop T-shirt was the last thing I would have expected as a souvenir from Saudi Arabia. Throughout my stay in Gunungembun, I noticed that East Asian fashion, souvenirs, TV series, and music were quite popular among female labor migrants and their families. Moreover, it transpired that countries in East Asia were favored destinations for labor migration and knowledge of Mandarin and Korean was in vogue.

This observation was striking for me and I wondered why East Asian culture was popular among female labor migrants who had traveled to various places. Wasn't Arabic culture more prestigious, as it showed that they had traveled to the land of the Prophet Muhammad? Especially if these women aspired to belong to the middle class, which I assumed to be the case because of their material desires and the consumer goods they purchased, why did they not adopt the middle-class lifestyle of Pop Arabness?

In contrast to migrant women in Gunungembun, labor migrants in Madura exhibit Arabness upon return, just as Mecca returnees in both regions do. Why, then, was there a different attitude toward Arab style in Gunungembun? Why was K-Pop a more favored cultural marker than piety? A juxtaposition of the different outcomes of travel experiences among labor migrants in Central Java and Madura sheds light onto this puzzle.

About Cultural Bonds and Cleavages

In Gunungembun, it is not just that the migrants in the village have traveled to multiple destinations, but quite often an individual migrant will have migrated to more than one place. As women from Gunungembun had not just migrated to Arab countries but also to Malaysia, Singapore, Hong Kong, Taiwan, and Korea, there were ideas circulating about all these countries. Knowledge about other cultures resulted from personal experiences as well as the gossip and information that fellow labor migrants shared. Some women were virtually cultural experts, informing me about the differences between Arab, Southeast Asian, and East Asian culture. Along with these comparisons, there was talk about preferred and less-favored destination countries.

During my first inquiries into how migrants chose their destination country, I found that female labor migrants in Gunungembun frequently reproduced the agencies' recruitment pitches. Migrating to Arab countries opens up the chance to do the pilgrimage to Mecca and Medina and one is not confronted with handling pork, as might happen in households in Hong Kong or Taiwan. One can express one's religiosity freely: wear a headscarf, do the daily prayers, and eat halal food. My interlocutors often named these religious factors as initial reasons for signing up for labor migration to Arab countries. As I got to know the women better, I learned that their hopes and expectations were not fulfilled. After having traveled to Arab countries, they often found that these arguments weren't as relevant as the agencies suggested. The Arabs in Saudi Arabia were not like they had imagined brothers and sisters in faith, and in other Gulf States, the employers were in fact very often foreigners themselves and not necessarily Muslim.

Most of the female labor migrants in Gunungembun were highly critical of Arab culture in their reflections and representations of travel experiences (see chapter 3). It turned out that countries in Southeast Asia and East Asia were preferred destination countries, with cultural proximity and higher salaries mentioned as the most important reasons for this. The countries favored were Hong Kong, Singapore, and even more so, Taiwan and Korea. Taiwan and Korea are considered rich countries, and it was argued that working conditions for labor migrants are secured by labor rights. Moreover, in these countries, there are training opportunities and employment in skilled or semiskilled sectors, like care for the elderly or in beauty salons. This probably marks the most significant difference to Saudi Arabia and other Gulf States like the United Arab Emirates, which were also labeled as rich but would treat foreign laborers badly and mainly employ female Indonesian labor migrants in the informal sector as domestic workers. Strikingly, the country that appears to be the most similar culturally and linguistically, Malaysia, was named as the least favored destination, together with Saudi Arabia. That this is the case marks the relevance of structural factors, as working opportunities and labor rights are precarious in Malaysia and Saudi Arabia. Moreover, there is a revived hostility between Malaysia and Indonesia that is depicted in public discourse about labor migrants.[2]

Thus, aside from the argument of sharing the same religion that was raised in response to initial questions about destination countries and in which the recruitment arguments of migrant agencies are reproduced, the most important factors in choosing a destination country seem to be structural ones like higher salaries, better rights for labor migrants, and working conditions. Interestingly, even though the decisive factors appear to be structural ones, in their narratives, migrant women in Gunungembun boiled them down to cultural aspects, with an emphasis on Asian cultural proximity. They tended to differentiate between religion and culture and often came to the conclusion that cultural proximity was more significant than sharing the same faith. The women's own juxtaposition of Arab and Asian cultures illustrates their argument.

HOW TO GET ALONG WITH ARAB PEOPLE

Labor migrants who had worked in Arab countries recounted that prior to the journey, they had expected that they would get along well with their fellow Muslims in Saudi Arabia and the other Gulf States and that religion would be a uniting force. However, in reality the cultural and hierarchical differences proved more significant than religious commonalities. In addition to the narratives of Othering that I have already summarized in chapter 3, further complementary examples of migrant women's evaluation of Arab culture reveal their sentiments about engagements with Arab culture and customs.

The most notable difference between Arab and Indonesian or more general Asian culture in the opinion of migrant women in Gunungembun was gender segregation. In chapter 3, I have already described how Ibu Anisa pitied Arab women. Similar statements were made by other women. Research participants explained that women in Saudi Arabia could not move freely and that men and women could not sit together and have a relaxed chat like in Indonesia. Women always had to be accompanied by male family members and remained inside the house most of the time. Pitying women in Saudi Arabia, Ibu Anisa stated that they lived "like a bird in a cage" (Ibu Anisa, June 7, 2014) inside their houses, surrounded by high walls.

Indonesian migrant women primarily presented their own moral superiority against images of immoral Arab women. Exemplary for their moral evaluations was their denouncement of the full body veil as ridiculous and hypocritical. The women in Gunungembun themselves wore headscarves when they went on trips to the city but rather sporadically in the village and almost never at home. Remarkably, their criticism of what they saw as "Arab hypocrisy" was extended to the Pop Arabness of the Indonesian urban middle classes.

This Othering of Arab employers might be a coping strategy by which to become more resilient in the context of precarious labor. However, Johnson and Werbner (2010) show that unequal power structures, social exclusion, and marginality do not always result in the demonization of and disinterest in a foreign culture. In fact, labor migrants often travel again and establish a general interest in traveling (Johnson and Werbner 2010, 208) and emotional relatedness. This holds true for the labor migrants' interest in traveling to East Asia and to Arab countries, for the pilgrimage or even for holidays. So engagement with an Other does not result in a complete condemnation of their way of life but rather an increase in knowledge about other cultures and partial Othering.

There was an undertone of knowing Arab culture, understanding how family life works, and how people behave and being able to react to this. The best strategy for getting along with Arab employers was described as sticking to one's personal religious conviction, putting one's trust in God and patiently enduring the hardship. Concerning their faith, many women argued that what makes a good Muslim is a good heart, not the most fashionable or most covering headscarf. Asian values were particularly esteemed in this regard. Indeed, Asianness was the most significant counterimage in the distancing from Arab culture. A glimpse into the popularity of East Asian culture in Gunungembun indicates how praise of Asian characteristic traits is concomitant with the popularity of East Asian cultural markers.

ASIANNESS AND MODERNITY

The women's clothing preferences and the general popularity of Western and East Asian products go hand in hand with generalized positive opinions of Asian culture. Women in Gunungembun explained that it was nicer to work for fellow Asians (*sesama Asia*) and stressed that cultural proximity was more relevant than religious commonalities. This holds true for preferences in destination countries as well as solidarity with other (Southeast) Asian labor migrants in Saudi Arabia and other Gulf States.

The most explicitly expressed view on favoring engagement with Asian rather than Arabic culture was about potential relationships with Asian or Arab men. During talks about the attributes of Arab men, female labor migrants explained that they could never imagine having a relationship with an Arab man. East Asian men were, however, favored among some women. One labor migrant from Gunungembun married a Taiwanese man and the family was rather proud of this, even though they emphasized that he had converted to Islam. In another case, the child of one of the women was considered as "Asian-looking." No one really spoke frankly about the question of whether this girl had a Taiwanese father, but many people joked about the mother having had dreams about Taiwan during pregnancy. Potential sexual relations with East Asian men were not condemned or looked down on in the same way as relations with Arab men, which quickly led to rumors about prostitution or sexual harassment. The overall positive evaluation goes hand in hand with the engagement with East Asian cultural features.

Ayu's K-Pop T-shirt was only one of many markers of an affinity with Asianness that I encountered in Gunungembun. As I mentioned above, this concerned music, TV series, language, and fashion. Quite interestingly, clothing and styling preferences were not only based on Asian beauty ideals but also on Western markers. The women dressed casually in jeans and a T-shirt. The popularity of Asianness, represented by K-Pop, Asian beauty ideals, such as white skin, large eyes, and long black hair, and other products labeled as Asian fuse with symbols of Western culture like for instance pop-music or fashion features like a suit and tie for men. As Ariel Heryanto argues: "Instead of 'de-Westernising' Asia, in the strictest sense of the word, the process of Asianization involves a significant shift and refashioning of what were previously considered stereotypically Western cultural attributes" (Heryanto 2014b, 168). Heryanto points out that K-Pop and other elements of Asian popular culture are already products of the engagement with elements of Western popular culture that has been Asianized. For female labor migrants and their families in Gunungembun, Korean style, or East Asian style in a broader sense, spreads a certain air of cosmopolitanism and a partaking in globalization and modernity. Through their interest in other cultures, in this case East Asian culture, the migrant women in Gunungembun contrast recruitment agencies' strategies of promoting culturally and religiously similar countries, like Malaysia and Saudi Arabia, as destination countries. Moreover, their preferences conflict with the Eurocentric perspective and class bias that sticks to ideas of cosmopolitanism and modernity. Open-mindedness and a willingness to engage with the Other are often attributed to travelers from wealthier parts of society that "feel at home" in the world (Werbner 1999, 17). Yet cosmopolitanism "does not necessarily imply an absence of belonging but the possibility of belonging to more than one ethnic group and cultural localism simultaneously" (Werbner 1999, 34). Feelings of belonging to more than one cultural environment result in ambivalent representations of cultural Otherness. The female labor migrants of Gunungembun engage in cosmopolitanism in this sense. Encounters with Others, knowledge about other cultures, languages, and international conventions are inherent in their international experiences, and they stressed this by using English, Arabic, Korean, and Mandarin in our conversations and engaging with foreign culture, in this case Korean culture, which becomes part of their lifestyle and which they self-confidently evaluate. Nevertheless, in the interaction with their local social network many women distance themselves from these other cultures, from Arabic culture even more than from East Asian culture. However, this does not mean that there is no interest in these cultural Others, but that migrant women might formulate demarcations to show their loyalty to their families and their country, as is expected by their social environment.

In addition, labor migrants linked ideas of modernity to human rights and democracy. Even though Saudi Arabia was acknowledged as a rich and technologically modern country, it was denounced as backward due to undemocratic activities and human rights violations. Activists' discourses probably have an influence here as the village is in contact with NGOs from bigger cities in Java that advocate labor migrants' rights.

The evaluative juxtaposition of different cultures in Gunungembun indicates that the women actively reflect on their experiences. As a result, they represent a feeling of superiority because they are experts in understanding how different cultures work. This corresponds with Graeber's (2012) argument about the prevalence of "interpretative labor" within employment relationships that are marked by structures of inequality. As domestic workers in Saudi households, the women have to know how family life works in order to complete their duties in accordance with the employers' expectations. Their interpretative labor and reflexivity ultimately give them a feeling of self-determination and being able to choose Indonesian and Asian habits, which they consider superior. The arguments for an affinity with East Asian culture can be boiled down to cultural similarities, even though Malaysia was excluded from this positive evaluation, which hints at the fact that these cultural arguments are related to the structural reasons for their preferences. However, the popularity of East Asian culture in Gunungembun does not only result from the women's experiences abroad, but apparently also from the opportunity to translate experiences of mobility into symbolic capital.

The Translatability of Travel Experiences

The analysis of "success stories" among migrants and pilgrims showed that labor migrants relate to public discourse in which migrants are stylized either as victims, including victims who are responsible for their own fate, or as foreign exchange heroines. In accordance, they represent themselves as frugal and self-sacrificing, and primarily mention reasons for migration that are widely accepted, like investment in children's education. Arab cultural markers appear not to be prominent in contrast to pilgrims' representations of a successful *haji mabrur* (see chapter 2). To bring home a K-Pop T-shirt from Saudi Arabia might be related to access to the symbolic capital of Arabness. Apparently, the translatability of mobility toward the Middle East varies. Differences in the translation of travel experiences are most obvious in a juxtaposition of migrant realities in Gunungembun and Madura. The following two stories of return illustrate the importance of the local context for making overseas experiences meaningful. The first is an encounter with Ibu Tati, a twenty-seven-year-old labor migrant in Gunungembun, whom I met in March 2014.

PROUD TO BE FAMOUS

> Ibu Tati welcomes me in fluent English and invites me into her brand new house, made of concrete, painted in a cheerful yellow and equipped with new furniture. She leads me to the sitting room, where guests are usually received, and offers me a seat in the nicely arranged wooden suite. I notice the embroidery, showing camels and pyramids on the big cushions that lie on the sofa. On the walls, there is more decoration,

> obviously souvenirs from her time in the Gulf States, including a picture of Mecca as well as an imitation sandal of the Prophet and golden teacups. Smiling, she says, "Well, this is the reward for becoming a labor migrant." She wears a neat black shirt with glittering letters that read "proud to be famous," as well as a thin golden necklace and matching earrings. She introduces her husband to me, who is wearing an "I love Dubai" shirt. I learn that Ibu Tati has been working for eight years in different Gulf States (Kuwait, Oman, Saudi Arabia and Dubai). When I inquire about Arab culture, she laughs and states that in her opinion the Arabs were a bit narrow-minded and very jealous. That's why they never allowed other men to see their wives, daughters and sisters. If a wife got jealous, then the graceful household maids from Indonesia had to wear a chador veil even inside the house. These wives were often fat, doing nothing except eating and sleeping. They had no feeling of shame (*malu*) and no pride, she said, letting themselves go like that. No, she had not liked Saudi Arabia much. But her time in Dubai had been great. That's where she bought some of the souvenirs and sent them back home. She would love to go back to Dubai for a holiday. For now, they were trying to invest the money from labor migration into bird breeding. Who knows, she might get the chance to show Dubai to her children one day. (field notes, March 30, 2014)

THE RETURN OF A RESPECTED HAJJA

In June 2014, I met Ibu Endang in the village of Ladangtembakau, in Madura. My companions and I waited for a while before the forty-year-old woman, wearing a long black *abaya* (traditional Arabic dress), hurried toward the mushollah we were sitting in.

> Ibu Endang waves toward us, indicating that she will join us in a while, rushing into the house next to the mushollah. She returns with a tray of tea and apologizes for being late: there was a sick neighbor and she had to pray for her, she told us. Ibu Endang recounts that she worked in Saudi Arabia for almost twenty years, earning money for the well-being of her family and not seeing her children grow up, not even returning back home for her son's wedding. There had been a huge celebration when she returned, of course. For years, she had sent her earnings back home and the family had invested them in the children's education and in building the mushollah we were sitting in. When I ask her how it feels to be back home after such a long time abroad, she states that on the one hand she feels strange in her own country, that she misses

> speaking Arabic and eating Arabic food and that she is sticking to wearing Arab clothes like the black *abaya*. But then, on the other hand, she is happy to be back in Madura, where she belongs. After all, the Arabs were a bit strange, she reflects. She was often embarrassed seeing Arab women dancing almost naked at wedding parties (of course out of sight of Arabic men), they had no feeling of shame (*malu*), these women, wasn't it haram to dance like that? Officially men and women were not allowed to talk to each other, maybe because they could not manage to be well mannered. She had been approached by Arab men countless times she says, rolling her eyes. In Indonesia people were free, but they knew their limits and they had morality. That's what she had told her employer's children and she was sure that these children longed to live in Indonesia, where people were more sincere. Besides that, of course, it had been great that she was able to do the minor pilgrimage (umrah) every year and she had done the hajj six times. While on pilgrimage, she often met people from Madura and sent home clothes, pictures or dates and raisins through these fellow Madurese. Now back home, she was teaching the Qur'an in evening gatherings and, thanks to her excellent knowledge of Arabic, teaching the language to the children in the nearby Qur'anic school. (field notes, June 28, 2014)

These field notes from encounters with Ibu Endang and Ibu Tati signify noteworthy differences in the translation of travel experiences. While Ibu Tati and Ibu Endang share similar evaluations of Arabic culture on a discursive level, in postmigration everyday life their engagement with Arabness, as well as consumption and investment preferences, are quite different.

Ibu Tati spent her earnings on constructing a big fancy house, like most of the female labor migrants in Gunungembun. Moreover, she invested in starting a bird breeding business and also in gold and jewelry. The things she bought in Dubai can best be described as souvenirs, like the T-shirt for her husband, the imitation sandal of the Prophet and the decorations. Symbols of piety, like headscarves, were less prominent. It seems that living in the hypermodern environment of Dubai had been more thrilling than residence in the Holy Land. Her experiences abroad certainly influence her postmigration lifestyle choice. The conclusion that Arab people are hypocritical Muslims might have led to the decision not to wear Arabic-Islamic clothing and the experience of going on holiday with her employers in the Gulf seemingly triggered her aspirations to show Dubai to her children. However, Ibu Tati's lifestyle is not an exception in Gunungembun. Postmigration lifestyle is not only inspired by experiences abroad, but also depends on the possibility of translating these experiences to the home environment. In Gunungembun, the prominent cultural symbols among returned migrant women are those of Western and East Asian modernities in terms of fashion trends, music preferences, languages that are in vogue, as well as consumer goods like motorcycles and satellite dishes, which are perceived as connecting households to the world through TV, and prestigious belongings like gold assets and big houses. In Ibu Tati's case, the Arab souvenirs that she did bring from Dubai likewise symbolize popular tourist culture and cosmopolitanism rather than piety. The souvenirs in Ibu Tati's house are proof of having traveled. She is proud of her English skills and does not bother to recount anything about religious events during her journey. Only when I directly asked her about it did I learn that she had done the hajj while she was in Saudi Arabia.

Ibu Endang, in contrast, is proud of being a hajja and wears traditional Arabic clothing in everyday life. Her Arabic skills and her religious knowledge are acknowledged in the village community. She is appointed to pray for sick neighbors and takes on responsibility in teaching the Qur'an and Arabic language. Religion is a crucial factor in her lifeworld. Consequently, she has invested in building a mushollah, which increased her family's social status significantly. In her criticism of Arabic people, she stylized herself as being more pious than the Arabs, who were mere hypocrites in her eyes. Besides her critical view of Arabic culture, Arabic style is a meaningful symbol of piety and entails social capital in Madura.

Ibu Tati's and Ibu Endang's evaluations of Arabic culture are similar. Yet their engagement with Arab cultural features differs remarkably. While it might be related to their actual experiences abroad, it also seems to be related to their preconditioning through their social environment at home. Most obviously, the social home context of migrants determines their status upon their return, which leads to the discussion of why Madurese labor migrants are automatically acknowledged as hajji/hajja, while Javanese labor migrants are not.

Being or Not Being a Hajja

The stories of Ibu Endang and Ibu Tati do not only show differences in individual personality but are exemplary of the different life realities of migrant returnees in Madura and Gunungembun, Central Java. Clearly, being or not being a hajja or hajji is not only a matter of the actual completion of the pilgrimage and physical presence at the holy sites. This is another example of how normative guidance determines social (im)mobility.

The process of "translating" travel experiences among labor migrants in Gunungembun does not entirely follow guided paths, as these paths do not lead to upward social mobility. Migrant women are trapped in narratives that depict them as the carers of the nation and their families, the label of being proletarian sticks to them. Practically as well as socially they cannot emerge from this category, especially when they are involved in circular migration. Thus in order to boost their social status, they contradict the leading discourse and find their own way through interpretative labor (cf. introduction; Graeber 2012). In their interpretations they distance themselves from Arab Others—those abroad and the pious middle-class at home. As Robinson (2007, 14) argues, labor migrants' engagement with the Other, their *savoir-vivre* and cosmopolitanism, reveal that they are "not acted upon, 'subjected to' global processes, but are active agents in self-fashioning in the culturally, politically and economically expansive social fields of the cosmopolitan world we live in." Due to their experiences abroad, some migrant returnees appear to be more cosmopolitan than pilgrims who do not leave their guided paths and travel units. The women in Gunungembun who migrated to various countries have especially cosmopolitan ideas about the world, even though the labels "rural poor," "laborers," and "victims" stick to them. To overcome the stigma, they engage with Arabness, Westernness, and Asianness and make their own lifestyle choices. Their counterimage relates to lifestyle features of Western and East Asian modernities, symbolized through the K-Pop trend or, as in Ibu Tati's case, through touristic souvenirs and prestigious consumer goods. For the Madurese, in contrast, access to the social capital of Arabness is a driving force in labor migration as this is the cultural marker that is the most readily acknowledged in society. Nevertheless, this choice is a reaction to exclusion from others' identity construction and the different versions of religious and cultural orientations mark inter-Indonesian social frictions and boundaries between different groups, classes, and regions.

The case of female labor migrants in Gunungembun indicates the exclusivity of contemporary middle-class piety in Indonesia. The Islamization of society not only leaves Indonesians divided over the question of the right interpretation of Islam, it also manifests the divide between the rich and the poor. Some new Indonesian Muslim ideals are related to class. Even though migrant women in Gunungembun aspire to belong to the middle-class, they do not try to imitate middle-class Pop Arabness, but instead challenge the discourse of a modern, economically successful "Glamour Islam," mocking both Middle Eastern Arabness and Pop Arabness at home. Ibu Tati and the other women denounce Arab style, *gaya arab* or *gaya islami*, of long headscarves and *abayas* as hypocritical—both the perceived original that they found in Saudi Arabia as well as the pop version of the urban middle class in Indonesia. The reason for this appears not to be just their firsthand experience with Middle Eastern culture, but also the fact that middle-class Pop Arabness is exclusive and its symbolic capital is not easily accessed. In a very subtle way, migrant women's lifestyle choices challenge the imagined solutions and dreams of the middle class as well as Arab-phobia, revealing that Pop Arabness and recent Islamization trends are also related to middle-class demarcations from the rural poor that originate from domestic social structures.

This is another vivid example of the significance of social context in Indonesia for the processing or translatability of travel experiences. Migrants and pilgrims are predetermined in what they (can) make of their journeys. This leads to the situation that even seemingly similar experiences abroad, like those of Ibu Tati and Ibu Endang, result in different outcomes. The personal interest that migrants and pilgrims have before their journeys, their family and educational backgrounds, as well as the commodities that are exploitable in their home context guide the mobile groups in the translations of their travel experiences.

What does seem remarkable, however, is the difference between Madura and Gunungembun/Central Java. The analysis of what migrants and pilgrims make of their journey has so far indicated that there are leading discourses that guide them on a "main road," sticking to the social roles attributed to them. Underlying social tensions do not create radical deviation from the guided tracks but only modest side excursions, like in Gunungembun. The reasons to follow appear to lead back to the prospects arising therefrom.

Such regional characteristics, as here presented for Madura and Central Java, can look very different in other regions of Indonesia. Central Java is one of the most advanced regions in Indonesia, and Yogyakarta is the country's educational hub and cultural center, drawing young people and tourists to the region. However, this does not mean that there are no underprivileged and poor people in Central Java. In fact, rural and urban populations remain rather separated. Along with the divide between rural and urban populations, there is a divide between the new middle classes, those who are among the beneficiaries of modernization, and those who are left out. Additionally, there is greater cultural heterogeneity in Central Java than for instance in Madura or West Java and possibly easier access to labor migrant agencies for migration to East Asian countries.

As labor migrants in Gunungembun are among those who are left out by economic growth and modernization, who feel trapped in circular migration, and are disappointed that the promises of travel agencies and the government were not fulfilled, they search for alternative routes. Interestingly, their reaction to the feeling of being left out does not provoke greater adherence to guidance but rather a reflexive selection of different guiding narratives. As in Central Java, middle-class Pop Arabness and piety are not the only labels of modernity; migrant women switch to other cultural markers. Though the K-Pop trend is not the most prominent in mainstream contemporary cultural orientations in Indonesia, it is prevalent in the heterogeneous environment of Central Java. Thereby, migrant women in Gunungembun are in a position to choose their lifestyle and by denouncing Pop Arabness and Middle Eastern Arabness as hypocritical, they overcome exclusion from the symbolic capital that journeys to the Middle East and the completion of the pilgrimage entail. Thus, to strengthen a precarious position, the plurality of guiding narratives and the possibility of switching to another form of cultural orientation establishes resilience.

In Madura, the situation is different. First of all, the choice between different cultural orientations is rather limited. Being a homogenous, predominantly Muslim, society, with majority affiliation to NU, symbols of Western and East Asian modernities are not equally appreciated in the social environment of migration returnees. However, there is also a less pressing need to engage with alternative cultural orientations, as migrants in Madura are not similarly excluded from opportunities to make journeys to the Middle East meaningful as journeys to the Holy Land. The example of Ibu Endang indicates that migrants' completion of the pilgrimage is acknowledged and their experiences in the Middle East are an asset in the religious sphere.

Apparently, in the religiously and culturally more heterogeneous Central Java, nationwide discourses like government guidance and popular media representations are more determining factors of the guidance of social mobility than in Madura. Yet in the midst of these nationwide discourses, there are alternative guiding narratives or "side roads" for migrants. In the homogenous environment of Madura, the religious sphere conditions social structures and religious authorities are the main orientation. What is more, in Madura there is not a similar divide between rural and urban populations. The whole island is rather rural and so densely populated that there is no sharp distinction between village and town. In contrast, identification with one's village is crucial among the Madurese, and migrants return to their villages and keep supporting them. There is a distinctive pride in Madurese *merantau* (migration) culture and migrants enjoy a higher status. The vast majority of Madurese people (16 million) live away from the island and many of the 4 million inhabitants of the island are dependent on relatives' remittances. This explains why migrants are not marginalized but celebrated: labor migration is a more natural part of Madurese culture and society, occurring in all families. Moreover, in Madurese society, the nationwide mainstream discourses and government guidance are challenged by the guidance of religious authorities and Madurese intermediaries in the pilgrimage and labor migration business, who make alternative routes more attractive to Madurese people.

In conclusion, the translatability of travel experiences into various forms of capital seems to be a condition that makes people follow. Guidance can be limiting as well as enabling. The mainstream guidance in Central Java excludes migrant women from the symbolic capital of Arabness, yet they can make use of other guiding symbols. In Madura, guidance enables migrants to capitalize on their experiences of mobility to the Arab world but at the same time they have little opportunity to switch to other paths.

In the subsequent section, I further describe the alternative routes from Madura to the Middle East, which represent an exception in the national context, but are a common feature within Madurese society.

Alternative Routes from Madura to the Middle East

The omnipresence of labor migration in Madurese society and the intertwinement of labor migration and pilgrimage is especially obvious in housing arrangements and labor migrant villages like Batu Bintang, a village that is located in Pamekasan regency. The atmosphere in Batu Bintang is that of a ghost town, as most of the newly built houses are not permanently inhabited; some of them are only guarded (*dijaga*) until the owners return from abroad. Interestingly, a large number of houses showed signs of hajj return decorations. Colorful festoons and pictures of the Ka'aba as well pictures of the pilgrims indicated that the dwellers of the respective houses had accomplished the hajj recently.

An elderly man who was guarding his son's house recounted that his son was in *bère* (in the west), referring to the Holy Land, which is located westward from the Indonesian perspective (cf. Introduction). However, in fact, his son was not in Saudi Arabia, but in Malaysia—which is also west of Madura.

Apparently, the term *ka bère* (toward the west) is used as a more general reference to residence abroad. As the hajj is an extremely prestigious event for Madurese people, Madurese migrants seek to finance it with earnings from migration. Therefore, they relate labor migration toward Malaysia, which is the main destination for migrants from Madura, to the hajj. The construction of a house and the completion of the pilgrimage are taken as evidence of a successful migration. Throughout my investigations I was repeatedly informed that circular migration and accumulation of financial capital would continue at least until one had achieved the ultimate goal of accomplishing the pilgrimage. Labor migrants in Batu Bintang are considered especially successful, and their hajj celebrations appear to be the most extensive on the whole island. Naturally, Madurese migrants aspire to return from migration in order to engage in pre- and postpilgrimage rituals. However, even those migrants who had accomplished the pilgrimage during residence abroad are acknowledged as hajji and hajja.

The distinction between pilgrims and labor migrants that is prevalent in Central Java does not exist in the same way in Madura. The symbolic and social capital of being a hajj returnee is, different from Central Java, accessible for labor migrants in Madura. In fact, many labor migrants are addressed as hajji or hajja in everyday interactions, even if there is no information about the actual completion of the pilgrimage. As a sign of honor, migrant returnees are attributed the status of a pilgrim, assuming that they must have accomplished the pilgrimage, given that it is part of the aspirations related to labor migration.

Ibu Endang's story indicates that migration to the Middle East entails economic, social, and symbolic capital. Her case also shows that, similar to social obligations of nonmigrant *haji mabrur*, migrant returnees in Madura take on similar responsibilities in their community back home. Ibu Endang herself invested in building a mushollah, where people from her neighborhood assemble for prayer, and she engages in religious and educational activities in her village.

Due to the dominant role that religion plays in Madura and the long history of connections to the Middle East as well as contemporary Madurese involvement in intermediary positions in pilgrimage and migration, every journey to the Middle East is valued highly. Interestingly, Madurese mobility toward the Middle East follows somewhat different guidance than that in Central Java. The institutional guidance is officially in the hands of the government, but traditional religious authorities influence it significantly and often occupy positions in the government themselves. Moreover, from Madura there are some back roads to the Holy Land, as pilgrimage and migration can be accomplished through the alternative channels of what was introduced to me as the "Madurese mafia" (see Lücking 2017 and chapter 2).This also hints at possible limitations in the accessibility to documented labor migration to East Asian countries.

Besides spatial mobility, social and cultural mobility also follow slightly different logics. Concerning social mobility, the divide between migrants and pilgrims is less significant in Madura than in Central Java, and the hajj is central in boosting peoples' social status. This is reflected in hajj waiting times of more than twenty years, among the longest in the country, and the extensive pre- and postpilgrimage rituals like those I described for Ibu and Pak Sukis's departure and return (see chapter 2). Cultural mobility, or cultural change, in Madura looks like an increase in piety, which is symbolized through Arab clothing among other things. However, many of the cultural markers that are labeled as "Arab" in Madura are neither new influences nor imports from journeys to the Middle East. According to research participants, clothing items like the jubbah from the Arabian Peninsula, have been present for decades in Madura. Madurese people buy these clothing items in local markets and shops, which are run by the Hadhrami population. Furthermore, what is called "Arab" style

FIGURE 10. Pious clothing for Friday prayers, Sumenep. April 2014. Photo by Khotim Ubaidillah.

FIGURE 11. Wearing jubbah and sarong on the way to the mosque, Sumenep, April 2014. Photo by Khotim Ubaidillah.

is combined with local styles, especially with the sarong (a skirt like cloth), which is the most widespread clothing item in Madura. The importance of the sarong became especially clear to me, when I saw people apologizing for wearing pants when meeting religious authorities unexpectedly. The pictures above show young Madurese men and boys who combine the white jubbah from the Gulf, the checkered kufiyah cloth, and the sarong. The colorful sarong (figure 10) peers out under the white jubbah, which people put on for special occasions and Friday prayers. Cultural elements that are related to Middle Eastern traditions are integrative parts of Madurese traditions. The intensified movement of labor migration and pilgrimage can be a trigger for engagements with these traditions, but this new intensification of movement to the Middle East is not their source, as I will further discuss below.

Madurese Connections to Mecca

The pilgrimage to Mecca and Medina is extremely prestigious and highly valued in Madurese society, rooted in historical connections to the Gulf and flourishing through the current pilgrimage boom. In light of the potential increase in a person's social status, the hajj can be seen as an investment. It becomes a medium through which to transform economic into social and political capital.

Everyone who is accumulating financial capital in order to do the hajj is considered a hajj candidate. Thus labor migration is understood as getting closer to the Ka'aba, financially, physically, and spiritually. Going to the Holy Land or somewhere close to it, is linked to the idea of getting closer to God and closer to spiritual enlightenment. Considering the long-term aim of migration, many migrants consider themselves to be pilgrimage candidates—even if the hajj is still in the distant future. This intertwinement of pilgrimage and migration in Madura is not only a spiritual one but also a practical one. It materializes in mundane administration procedures of using pilgrimage visas to work and work visas to do the pilgrimage.

MIXED MIGRATION: UMRAH IN FLIP FLOPS

While many Madurese labor migrants are future pilgrims, some Madurese pilgrims actually become labor migrants. In what is knowns as *umrah sandal jepit,* meaning umrah in flip flops, people use the umrah visa to enter Saudi Arabia and eventually stay to work. This practice of mixed migration appears to be more common in Madura than in Central Java, where I very rarely came across such stories. Interlocutors emphasized that they did not just want to sneak into the country to work but that doing the pilgrimage did really matter to them. Pragmatic economic reasons did not contradict their spiritual aims. However, due to long waiting lists for the hajj, it was more attractive to use an umrah visa, stay in the country to work, study with famous sheikhs, and wait for the hajj season to arrive. Thus this form of mixed migration is a method to jump waiting lists or get around bureaucratic procedures (Lücking 2017, 257).

The umrah sandal jepit can be arranged through informal networks, known as the Madurese mafia (see chapter 2).[3] The large number of Madurese residents in Saudi Arabia has resulted in the establishment of organizational structures to assist newcomers. These networks play a significant role in the arrangement of labor migration, pilgrimage, and education.

Members of this so-called mafia recounted that many people who end up staying and working in Saudi Arabia actually work in the pilgrimage sector. Next to official recruitment for jobs in pilgrimage management, there are numerous unofficial working opportunities. Selling *saté*, a known Madurese culinary specialty, to Indonesian pilgrims was for instance presented as a lucrative business. Other unofficial jobs include the rather ambiguous business of leading other pilgrims to touch or kiss the black stone (*al-ḥağar al-aswad*) at the eastern corner of the Ka'aba. When I asked why it was mainly the Madurese who helped people get closer to the stone, I was informed that they were brave enough and strong enough to push their way through the crowds. There were often taller and bigger people, from Africa or Arabia for example, but the Madurese were not afraid and could assert themselves, I was told.

Besides business opportunities in the context of the pilgrimage, the so-called mafia recruits women for domestic work and men as drivers. People from Madura are also recruited as couples, which is more favored than letting women migrate alone. Madurese research participants criticized the official agencies for rarely helping couples to migrate together. Furthermore, I was informed that people who migrate with the mafia would not have to cohabitate with their employers, but could stay in houses that were rented by Madurese permanent residents in Saudi Arabia, which was seen as another advantage. These Madurese residents, ascribed with the Arabic term *mukimin*, are described as intermediaries between Indonesian newcomers who are looking for work and Saudi Arabians searching for domestic workers or drivers. They take care of the mediation and ensure the Madurese migrants' security. One of the members of an informal network proudly explained that they have connections to Indonesian and Saudi Arabian government officials and to the Saudi Arabian police. If there were a problem, they would solve it. Since the Indonesian government issued a moratorium on labor migration to Saudi Arabia, the informal networks have become more influential as many Indonesians are still interested in working in Saudi Arabia and the demand for Indonesian labor in Saudi Arabia remains high, especially for domestic workers.

Apart from labor migration, Madurese residing in Saudi Arabia and other countries in the Gulf maintain ties to Indonesia and use their networks not only to arrange the mobility of people willing to work but also the exchange of money and goods. As some labor migrants from rural areas do not have bank accounts, money is frequently sent via family members or friends who have a bank account and who subtly become part of the network structure. Sometimes pilgrims are included in the networks when they carry presents, letters, or money for Madurese migrants residing in Saudi Arabia. Furthermore, the Madurese are influential actors in the pilgrimage business.

The booming pilgrimage business has made Madurese connections to the Middle East more valuable. While the mafia is especially active in migration brokerage and apparently more related to the gangster world of the *blatér* (cf. Rozaki 2004), pilgrimage affairs are handled by a network of influential religious elites and the pesantren Qur'anic school networks. However, these two spheres are not completely separate, even though the kyai I met stress that they are not involved in the undocumented labor migration business, there still seem to be some kyai who are indeed involved. As an example, in order to go on an umrah sandal jepit, the candidates are dependent on certain documents from religious authorities in order to obtain a pilgrimage visa. Thus there also seems to be some kind of cooperation between informal labor migrant recruiters and religious authorities. The pilgrimage appears to be an arena in which the two spheres and networks overlap.

While in Central Java the pilgrimage business is mainly run by actors who have experience in the tourism and travel business and extended their offer to pilgrimage journeys, in Madura it is dominated by the religious elite, as many travel agencies are attached to Qur'anic schools run by kyai families. The representatives of the KBIH, the government division for hajj guidance, in Central Java are dominated by religious scholars who are affiliated with the Ministry of Religious Affairs, while in Madura these divisions are controlled by the kyai.

PESANTREN NETWORKS

Apart from the pilgrimage business, the religious elite in Madura maintains educational networks with famous sheikhs in Saudi Arabia and Yemen. These sheikhs are quite often of Hadhrami origin and run schools in which they mostly teach students from Indonesia. In almost every house that I visited in Madura, I found pictures of Sheikh Omar and Sheikh Muhammad on the walls, next to pictures of the holy mosque in Mecca. The studying circles of Sheikh Omar and Sheikh Muhammad in Mecca are famous among the Madurese. I was told that many Madurese pilgrims try to visit them when they go on hajj and the sheikhs visit pesantren in Madura annually. One of the pesantren that actively cooperates with sheikhs in Saudi Arabia and Yemen is the famous Pesantren Shaikhona Kholil in Bangkalan, which is led by the offspring of the famous Kyai Shaikhona Kholil, whose lineage is traced to one of the nine wali (cf. chapter 1). Members of the Shaikhona Kholil family showed me pictures of the sheikhs' visits and recounted that every year their best students and the children of kyai are sent to Mecca and Yemen to study with the sheikhs. A leading member of the Shaikhona Kholil family recounted that he had studied for ten years with one of the sheikhs in Saudi Arabia and explained that the knowledge that one could obtain in the Holy Land was of a higher quality. It was not necessarily new knowledge, in the sense of information that they would receive but a spiritual transformation of this knowledge, deepening it. Moreover, he stressed that Wahhabism was the leading scholarly opinion in state-run educational institutions and public universities in Saudi Arabia, but not in the sheikhs' schools. He argued that the connection to Mecca was crucial and that by studying there, the Madurese would eventually find a way out of the mode of *ǧāhilīya*.

The transnational education networks of the pesantren Qur'anic schools also encompass schools in Yemen. The daughters of the Shaikhona Kholil family informed me that they would go to Yemen for short-term study trips. This appears to go along with a new interest in going on ziarah to Yemen, as discussed by Alatas (2016). Apart from these educational networks, the Shaikhona Kholil family, like many other kyai families, runs a pilgrimage travel agency and exhibits evidence of the pilgrimages that people complete through their agency by making return and departure performative events and documenting the journeys on social media, especially the annual hajj departures but also umrah travel.

Thus, the Hadhrami Arabness, which has been present for centuries in Madura, is also prominent in new connections to the Middle East. Hadhrami reside in large numbers in the Arab compounds (*kampung Arab*) in Pamekasan and Sumenep, where they run so-called Arab shops that are much frequented during the Ramadan and hajj seasons. Furthermore, Hadhrami cultural traditions are in vogue in musical performances.

These two examples, the mafia networks and the pesantren networks, indicate that in Madura, the government has serious competitors in the guidance of mobility to the Middle East. In fact, it seems that in Madura the religious elite is more influential than the government. For this reason, it is argued that the guidance of religious elites is a parallel structure to government guidance, and not only in the context of mobility to the Middle East. The kyai's scope of influence appears to be one reason why Madurese people do not follow the national mainstream discourses.

Meanwhile, Madurese networks in the Middle East are represented as a Madurese characteristic. The Madurese speak with pride about their influential networks. There is a high level of self-confidence, indicating that the Saudis are dependent on undocumented labor migration as well as support in managing Indonesian pilgrims, and the Indonesian travel agencies are dependent on brokers who know how to negotiate with Saudi Arabian officials.

People in Java vouch for the Madurese's ability to "handle" the Arabs. This ability was explained with reference to the bravery and crudeness of the Madurese. The stereotypes about the Madurese (see introduction) were evoked in these discourses and sometimes Javanese people concluded that the Madurese are good at handling Arabs because they *are* a bit like the Arabs, harsh and direct, violent and proud. The economic and spiritual importance of networks to the Middle East in Madura, and the social acknowledgement of this prestigious connection, makes Arabness the outstanding symbolic capital on the island. In contrast to Central Java, there is little prospect of switching to another sphere of cultural symbolism. Madurese people try to access the symbolic capital of Arabness that is much associated with the religious authorities. Apparently, showing one's interest in religious issues and adopting an Arab style as a symbol of one's piety is a way to prove enlightenment and thereby boost one's social status. Persons who are enlightened are considered as having a say in society. Knowledge, access to holy sites, and authority in society are interconnected here. Thus the connection to Mecca is not only related to economic and social capital, but also to political capital and power. To follow the kyai's paths means to open up the chance to take part in public affairs. The reason why mobility toward the Middle East is valued highly is related to the enlightenment that persons are believed to experience in Mecca and the access to various forms of capital. As the above-quoted member of the Shaikhona Kholil family argued, enlightenment does not depend on the content of knowledge, but its spiritual quality. This quality is related to the power of blessings, which is highly determining for leadership claims in Madura.

Blessings from Abroad

The following sequence provides an idea of the power of blessings and Madurese peoples' attraction to it. The situation took place during an annual celebration at Pesantren Shaikhona Kholil, during which I observed how students of the Qur'anic school and participants from the surroundings honored the *nyai*, which is a title of honor for a female leader of a Qur'anic boarding school, equivalent to kyai for male leaders.

> It's a hot evening in May in Bangkalan City. The area near the Qur'anic boarding school Pesantren Shaikhona Kholil is crowded and the air

> is filled with noise from car horns and whistles of the men who try to channel the immense traffic flow, waving luminous signaling discs. My friend Mala and I make our way through the crowds and the minibuses and cars parked at the side of the main road. Students from the pesantren who welcome visitors direct us to the house of the nyai, the female leader of the school, who invited us to join its annual anniversary.
>
> Approaching the nyai's house, we see hundreds of women and girls standing in line, waiting to shake hands with the nyai, who is sitting on a throne-like chair in front of her house. The women bow as they approach the nyai, looking downward, grasping and kissing her hand, avoiding direct eye contact. While shaking and kissing the nyai's hand, the women let rupiah notes pass into her hand. A woman sitting behind the chair is collecting the money into a plastic bag.
>
> Later that evening an older nyai from an allied pesantren in Java prepares to leave. As she heads toward the door, the same practice of grasping or kissing her hand happens. Some people even hug her and put banknotes into her hand. Furthermore, many women approach her with water bottles. They open the water bottles, holding them in front of the nyai while bowing down. She dips her *tasbīḥ*,[4] a chain of prayer beads, into the water, mumbling what sounds like a prayer or short recitation of a Qur'anic verse. "This is to transfer barokah," is Mala's comment in answer to my puzzled expression. (field notes, June 28, 2014)

The shaking and kissing of hands as well as the water bottle phenomenon during the anniversary at Pesantren Shaikhona Kholil in Bangkalan are meant to transfer blessings, or as it is called in Muslim contexts in Indonesia, *barokah* or *berkah*, derived from the Arabic term for blessing, *baraka*. Barokah or berkah, as it transpired during the research, is essential in many Madurese peoples' lives. In similar practices to that describe above, the transferal of blessings was often connected to journeys to the Middle East, as the region is regarded as the Holy Land and thus a powerful source of barokah. Possessing barokah is prestigious and related to ideas of leadership and social status. People seek to gain barokah from Mecca returnees or from religious leaders. Occasions where barokah was transferred include a reciprocal element, like giving money or labor in return. Many people believe that the money they give to the mosque or the pesantren and its leaders will somehow return to them as blessings. Moreover, it is regarded as an honor to serve religious leaders, and if one is given rice or other things in return, this is considered to be extremely valuable and a vessel for blessings. Thus, religious leaders, their property (house and school), and their gifts are attributed the special quality of being filled with barokah.

The idea of barokah reveals the connection of the concepts of knowledge, journeying, and power. The acquisition of knowledge and barokah is an essential element of and reason for spiritual journeys, and it is an attribute associated with leadership. Being blessed and having increased one's knowledge may indicate an increase in power and, subsequently, responsibility. Besides honoring Mecca returnees, there is a tendency to expect them to share their barokah and newly gained wisdom as well as to seek to help with societal issues.

BLESSINGS, KNOWLEDGE, AND POWER

The concept of blessings in Islam is especially prevalent in the mystic Sufi tradition of Islam. The *Encyclopaedia of Islam* defines barokah as a "magic means of obtaining all sorts of good fortune, in particular the healing of diseases and infirmities, not only from God but also from holy men and objects which are supposed to possess the power of conferring blessings. . . . The relics of saints, the clothes which they wore in their lifetime and of course also holy men who are still alive and everything connected with them, are particularly powerful" (EI1).[5] This definition describes the popular belief that human beings as well as objects have the capacity to hold barokah, which can be transferred through physical contact like touching, kissing, or stroking the holy objects. According to three Qur'anic verses mentioning barokah, its sole source is God. Yet the Qur'an describes certain individuals and groups as being especially endowed with God's barokah, including the prophets, important holy places like the Ka'aba in Mecca and the al-Aqṣā mosque in Jerusalem, and the Qur'an itself (EI/Karimi and Negahban 2008).

In daily practice, barokah is attributed to religious authorities and saints. Annemarie Schimmel (1995) describes barokah as the power of blessings, which underlines the element of power attributed to barokah, its enabling, activating, and influential qualities. A person who holds barokah is regarded as particularly righteous and suitable to guide others. Moreover, this power is connoted with special skills, being able to heal or convey happiness, success, and well-being.

In her comprehensive oeuvre on the mystical dimension of Islam, Annemarie Schimmel hints at the conjunction between barokah and knowledge when she explains that in the Sufi tradition, the relationship between teacher and student is the relationship of master and disciple. Only when the disciple has proven his or her worthiness and gained the trust of his or her master or mistress, for instance, by serving the religious authority for many years, will the disciple be initiated into the secrets of Sufism. This includes the physical presence and friendship between master/mistress and disciple, the knowledge of prayer phrases as well as ritual practices and use of certain paraphernalia (Schimmel 1995, 153). Thus the intertwinement of leadership, power relations (master and subordinate), and the gaining of knowledge is prevalent in the concept of barokah.

This resembles the concept of learning in Indonesia's pesantren. The student-teacher relationship is regarded as essential for the successful transmission of knowledge and the most trusted students often become personal servants or assistants of a kyai or nyai—the male and female religious authorities, both of whom are influential in Indonesia. In Madura, religious leadership is accessible not only through devout apprenticeship but even more through inheritance, as many established kyai families have the status of local nobility. Nevertheless, the children of the religious elite have to prove their subordination as students and are therefore sent to affiliated pesantren where they follow and serve another kyai/nyai.

Willingness to serve (*mengabdi*) is an essential condition for the transferal of knowledge and blessings. The relationship between a kyai/nyai and his/her protégé is quite a personal one and it continues after the official graduation from the pesantren. The student keeps honoring his/her teacher even after becoming a teacher him/herself, and this attitude of honor extends to their students, as the behavior toward the older nyai mentioned above indicates.[6] Religious authorities' possession of blessings is related to their connection to holy places. This connection can be spiritual as well as physical, and at the time of inquiry, it seemed that the physical connection in the form of pilgrimage and educational networks among the sheikhs in Yemen and Saudi Arabia was extremely important. In public events, religious authorities emphasize this connection using Arabic-Islamic clothing, Arabic language and music as well as the staging of visits by the befriended sheikhs. Moreover, members of the religious elite document their own journeys to Mecca on Facebook, Twitter, in newspapers, and on TV.

One can obtain barokah through physical contact or ritual practices. Holding barokah means being potentially enlightened and more knowledgeable. Accordingly, knowledge (*ilmu*) is in the first place related to practices rather than to understanding. It is based on experiences and physical and spiritual connections to holy persons, places, or objects. The purpose of knowledge is not restricted to understanding but encompasses performing and acting. Knowledge is applied in order to attain more barokah, which is essential in order to lead a prosperous life.[7] Many Madurese seek spiritual experiences to gain *ilmu* and barokah. Therefore, the ritual transfer of blessings and knowledge is an important event for Madurese Muslims and an opportunity for the religious elite to accumulate financial capital from donations, as I described above in the case of donations to the nyai during the transferal of blessings.

RITUAL GENERATION AND TRANSFER OF BAROKAH

Barokah can be obtained by transferal from people, places, and objects that are filled with barokah, but it can also be obtained through spiritual proximity to God in rituals in the tradition of Sufi Islam, such as recitation of the Qur'an (*pengajian*), community prayers, and meditative *dhikr* rituals that aim at increasing proximity to God.[8] In Madura as well as in other regions in Indonesia, in particular in East Java, some of these rituals take place on a weekly basis in the local pesantren, mosque, or private houses and are led by persons who are regarded as religiously educated, such as a kyai, a *guru ngaji* (worship teacher) or hajj returnees.

Apart from these smaller meetings, there are special events that are regarded as hotspots for barokah. The pesantren in Madura organize various events that provide opportunities for the transferal and ritual generation of barokah. Arabic cultural elements, such as music and clothing styles, are prominent in these events. Among the most important events are the *imtihān*,[9] an annual feast after exams at a pesantren, the *khaol* death commemoration gatherings,[10] and the musical *sholawatan* events.[11] All three events are related to the generation and transferal of barokah and are themed in an Arabic style.

A large *khaol* celebration hosting eight hundred participants took place during the research period in remembrance of Shaikhona Kholil. It started in the afternoon with speeches by the religious authorities and guests from other pesantren; they spoke about the achievements of Shaikhona Kholil, about concerns of daily life, politics, and spirituality. Many participants had visited the tomb of Shaikhona Kholil earlier, thus combining the event with local ziarah pilgrimage. For the religious authorities, the event was an opportunity to engage with the community, to transfer blessings, and to receive money in return. The organizers provided free food for everyone, and there were performances of traditional music, labeled as Arab music. The ritual generation of blessings took place in a *dhikr* ritual and sholawatan singing.

Given the fact that in the remoteness of Madura there is rarely public entertainment, the event was an opportunity to get together, meet friends and neighbors, eat together, enjoy the music, and share the sensory experience of the religious rituals. The visitors were dressed up and days after the event there was still talk about it. The women sitting next to me considered it appropriate to donate money, as they would receive food, blessings, and entertainment in return. The reciprocal element appears to be important here. While I have no data on the balance of costs and income of these events, the few people who criticized them claimed that this was a strategy to accumulate financial capital and exploit the people. In fact, donations seem to be the main income for religious authorities in Madura, as education in the Qur'anic schools is often free of charge or very cheap. Thus, in the provision of guidance and blessings, religious authorities are probably also dependent on the money they receive in return.

Besides obtaining barokah through physical proximity to religious leaders and ritual practice, it is also possible to acquire it at the graves and shrines of holy persons in ziarah visits (Schimmel 1995, 339). However, because the Madurese research participants saw the pilgrimage to Mecca as being more powerful than ziarah, the pilgrimage was thought of as ultimate way to gain barokah.

BAROKAH AND PILGRIMAGES

Unlike the hajj and umrah, local ziarah is not mentioned in the Qur'an, yet the practice of traveling in pilgrimage to the tombs and shrines of holy persons has been common among Muslims since the time of the Prophet Muhammad, as it is said that the Prophet himself advised his followers to accomplish these ritual journeys (Quinn 2008, 64).[12] Among Madurese people, ziarah is especially popular, with the most important pilgrimage sites being the graves of the Wali Songo throughout Java, the tomb of Shaikhona Kholil and the mosque attached to it in Bangkalan, as well as the Asta Tinggi cemetery in Sumenep. Numerous smaller grave sites of deceased kyai are frequented as well, and travel agencies advertise ziarah destinations throughout Madura as *pariwisata religi* (religious tourism). In the context of the pilgrimage to Mecca, the ziarah to the grave site of the Prophet Muhammad is essential for Indonesian pilgrims. The Madurese vociferously protested against the Saudi Arabian authorities' plan to close the grave site.[13]

Essentially, access to barokah through pilgrimages is related to the prospect of economic and political gain. Ubaidillah (2014, 83) uncovered how Abah Anton, the Chinese Muslim mayor of Malang, East Java, used the ziarah to the wali graves to publicly represent his Islamic religiosity. As Madurese migrants who reside in Malang are a significant voting force in Malang, Abah Anton tried to ease the reservations that Madurese voters had about him because of his Chinese heritage by financing their ziarah trips to the five wali graves that are located in East Java. The ziarah wali was very popular, especially among women, and had a significant effect on their sympathy for Abah Anton (Ubaidillah 2014, 82). Similarly, politicians sponsor umrah trips for their most loyal supporters. That those with leadership aspirations complete the pilgrimage to Mecca themselves is inevitable, and politicians and celebrities intentionally draw public attention to their journeys. For persons who have already inherited a reputable position in society, like teachers or public servants, and who have not yet accomplished the pilgrimage, there is social pressure to do so. This indicates that the Madurese are not only inspired by God's *hidāyah* to do the pilgrimage but also by their social environment.

The pilgrimage to Mecca and Medina is thought to provide the ultimate access to blessings among the Madurese people. As completion of the pilgrimage marks an increase in barokah, the returnees are consequently regarded as more enlightened and more capable of taking up leadership positions. It is the returnees themselves, as well as the things they bring home from the journey, that are regarded as filled with barokah and their houses become pilgrimage sites for the *asajère* practice that I described in chapter 2. Evidently, the prospect of accessing barokah through pilgrimage fosters the local as well as the international pilgrimage businesses.

Thus the religious capital of possessing barokah can be exchanged with economic capital. Believers invest in accessing barokah, for instance by making the pilgrimage to Mecca, but can eventually transform their acquired religious capital, in the form of barokah, into symbolic capital that legitimizes leadership claims. Once in a leading position, they can transform this capital into economic capital. Thus the central role of barokah in Madura boosts the pilgrimage business and strengthens hierarchies and local rituals. However, there are significant class differences in the methods of gaining barokah. While persons from lower classes are attracted to ziarah, people with aspirations of leadership focus on the pilgrimage to Mecca. The performative character of the pilgrimage to Mecca makes it a promising undertaking for those who want to boost their leadership qualities.

Following the Kyai

Juxtaposing the Madurese case with Central Java, it seems that many Madurese migrants and pilgrims do not follow the main roads of government administration, national normative discourses, like the Islam Nusantara discourse, and popular media representations. While the Madurese way appears to be an alternative route to the national context, from a Madurese perspective it seems to be almost the only way. There are not many side roads available to Madurese people other than those offered by the kyai. Besides the back road of the mafia networks and blatér networks, the dominant guidance in Madura is that of the religious elite. Being much honored as religious teachers, legal authorities and bearers of barokah, obedience to the religious authorities is widespread, especially among the adult generation who were the focus of my research activities. There is evidence that some parts of the younger generation are more rebellious, wearing jeans, playing guitar, and probing the boundaries of rules in a pesantren. A comprehensive study on relatively widespread same-sex relationships in Qur'anic schools in Madura indicates that not all students follow the rules of the religious authorities (see Dzulkarnain 2012). Students also circumvent the regulations in Qur'anic schools when they meet secretly to smoke or, as the drug tests at Pesantren Shaikhona Kholil indicate, consume prohibited drugs. However, the biographies of pesantren alumni reveal that these rebellious acts are limited to a period of youth rebellion, as most of them return to the guidance of the kyai later on.

The supernatural power that Madurese people associate with barokah is a reason for loyalty to those who can access and generate barokah through their spiritual—and in the context of migration and pilgrimage—physical proximity to God and the holy sites. The prospect of accessing barokah and thereby increasing one's own influence in society is a trigger for mobility toward the Middle East. The symbolic capital related to the possession of barokah and proximity to the Holy Land is related to Arab cultural markers. Rather than Pop Arabness, the demonstration of Madurese Arabness is prevalent. This localization of Arabness is not so much influenced by Wahhabi or Salafi styles as it is by Hadhrami traditions.

The following examples of Madurese Arabness reveal further that most of the practices that are themed with Arab symbolism conflict with Islamic practice in Saudi Arabia. Thus, while labeled as Arab, they are certainly not much in favor of Hanbali and Wahhabi interpretations and traditions of Islam. The examples that I have mentioned above, female religious leadership, Sufi traditions like *dzikr* mediations and ziarah, the transfer of blessings and the potentially magic power of the Arabic language, women frequenting mosques for daily prayers, and female singing are denounced as heretical from a Wahhabi perspective. Nevertheless, in Madura and even more so from the outside perspective of Javanese people, these practices are associated with an affinity for Arabness or even Arabization; again, an indication of the ambivalent use of the term *Arab* in Indonesia. Since there are virtually no other guiding normative discourses and no side roads toward spatial, social, and cultural mobility like K-Pop and East Asian modernities, piety becomes the all-encompassing guiding feature in Madurese society and is of great importance for the translatability of experiences of migration and pilgrimage and for the prospect of accessing different forms of capital. This leads to a situation where "performing" Arabness becomes competitive and creative. Tendencies of outperforming others and claiming to be better Muslims lead to an increase in Arab symbolism in public life. In art and music, this can also entail creative and experimental expressions of Arabness.

Performing Arabness and Madureseness

Engaging with Arabness in a performative manner is a competitive field in Madura. For persons in public positions, the possession of barokah is important for legitimizing their (charismatic) leadership. Thus they are eager to demonstrate their connection to the Arab world. In this regard, spatial mobility toward the Middle East includes cultural mobility, as returnees symbolize their new status through Arab cultural features. However, I argue that this change or mobility of cultural fashions is a homemade Madurese Arabization. The enthusiastic public engagement with Arabic culture in Madura is a vivid example of the circular movement of cultural symbols and vibrant modifications. The cultural styles and practices that are prevalent in public performances originate from longstanding interaction between Madura and the Middle East. Some of these features are the product of intercultural exchange over centuries and enjoy new popularity as the symbolic capital of Arabness becomes a much-desired commodity. The major competitors in the demonstration of Arabness are the religious elites, especially the Qur'anic schools and representatives of all political parties, religious as well as secular. The kyai, the leaders of the Qur'anic schools, compete with one another and with the political establishment, especially because some kyai participate in politics. While religious and political spheres remained separated during the Suharto era, recently the kyai have entered the political arena and have become quite dominant (Azizah 2013; Rozaki 2004, 15; Wiyata 2013, 194). In three of the four *kabupaten* (regencies) the *bupati* (regent) was a kyai at the time of research. In Bangkalan, the political leadership is dominated by one camp of the Shaikhona Kholil family, that of Kyai Fuad Amin who was succeeded as regent by his son Makmun Ibnu Fuad. Both of them are subject to allegations of corruption, polygamy, and drug abuse. Among this dynasty's competitors are their own relatives, the side of the Shaikhona Kholil clan that runs the Pesantren Shaikhona Kholil. The pesantren faction of the Shaikhona Kholil clan denounce kyai participation in politics and assert influence in society through alternative channels. Their criticism of the bupati's involvement in drug trafficking led to the introduction of urine drug tests in their own school.

Besides Pesantren Shaikhona Kholil, the most important Qur'anic schools in Madura are Pesantren Al-Amien Prenduan on the south coast of Sumenep regency and Pesantren An-Nuqoyah in Guluk-Guluk, a village in the interior of Sumenep regency. Al-Amien is classified as a modernist pesantren with strong ties to formal educational institutions in Saudi Arabia and Cairo, while An-Nuqoyah is labeled as a traditionalist pesantren. During visits to both schools, I learned how they try to differentiate from one another in their interpretation of Islamic practices and compete in displays of piety. The representatives of Al-Amien claimed to teach a purer version of Islam, which they relate to elements of Arabness like mastering Arabic language, which is obligatory in everyday interaction among students on two days each week. In An-Nuqoyah the emphasis on local ritual traditions was more distinctive. Both schools display their own version of Arabness and maintain connections to the Middle East. Regarding legal thought, they differ slightly, with Al-Amien showing some sympathy for conservative, modernist, and Salafist traditions. Yet for both schools, Cairo and not Saudi Arabia was the main destination for education abroad. Interestingly, the leaders of both schools also proudly spoke about their travels to Europe.

The Fusion of Madurese and Arabic Culture

Compared to Central Java, the omnipresence of Arabic-Islamic symbolism in Madura is striking. Just after having crossed the Suramadu Bridge from Surabaya to Madura, entering the outskirts of Bangkalan city, there are signs with Arabic calligraphy at the side of the street, displaying the ninety-nine names of God.[14] Shops, not necessarily religious ones but also normal grocery shops, have Islamic names like Toko Medina (Medina Shop) or Toko Al-Huda (Al-Huda Store). Arabic writing, or imitation of it, is used in advertisements and on signboards, especially those concerning religious issues like requests for *zakāt* (alms). Zakāt is also collected on busy traffic routes by volunteers who appeal for funds in Madurese and Arabic.

Arabic language seems to come more naturally to the Madurese than other foreign languages. Madurese people are familiar with the sound and pronunciation of Arabic, integrate some Arabic vocabulary in Indonesian or Madurese conversation, and elderly people are often more familiar with Arabic script than Latin script, as I witnessed when my hosts took notes in Madurese language using Arabic letters, not only for religious issues but very mundane matters like shopping lists, market orders, or harvest calculations. They recounted that they had only completed elementary school and that beyond that they studied in religious contexts, in pesantren or during prayer gatherings in the mosque.

The pesantren and mosques have long been important education institutions in Madura. Apart from fulltime enrollment in pesantren boarding schools, so called *madrasah* schools offer religious education in the afternoons. An encyclopedia by the local government of Pamekasan declares that in 2010, 115,424 children in Pamekasan regency studied in pesantren, while 207,381 were inscribed in schools that applied the national curriculum, some of which were also religious schools, and 84,497 of these students additionally attended a *madrasah* for religious education in the afternoon (Pemerintah Kabupaten Pamekasan et al. 2010, 26). This means that almost two-thirds of students in Pamekasan undertake religious education and are thus engaged with Arabic language on a daily basis. A study from 1990 indicates that at that time there were more religious schools (2,271 pesantren) than public ones (731) in Madura, arguing that pesantren are much more appreciated because they provide welfare services for the broader society (Effendy 1990, 64).

Arabic is also common in kinship terminology. Children address their parents with the Arabic terms *abah* (father) and *ummi* (mother), especially when the parents have completed the hajj. The terms are also common in the pesantren context. Students address religious teachers with the Arabic term for mother or father if they have a special personal relation to them. Thus the terms *abah* and *ummi* are sometimes substituted for the titles kyai and nyai or *ustadz* and *ustadzah*. Similarly, siblings and peers that have the status of mentors or close friends are addressed with the Arabic terms for brother (*akhi*) and sister (*ukhti*) rather than the Indonesian, Javanese, or Madurese terms for older siblings.[15] The Arabic kinship terms evidently carry an elevated sense of respect in the context of hierarchies of religious study. In addition to these titles, Arabic names are favored in Madura and persons who do not have Arabic-Islamic names usually change their name after completing the pilgrimage to Mecca and Medina.

Besides Arabic language and names, clothing and accessories symbolize a pious lifestyle and connections to Mecca in Madura. Persons who have completed the hajj show this through distinctive clothing. Quite often, they dress in white. Men wear a white jubbah or *gamis*, while women wear an abaya. However, as shown above, these Arab clothing items are combined with Madurese ones. Pilgrims put on this special outfit after the completion of the pilgrimage and on special occasions such as the annual feasts *idul fitri* and *idul adha* or the weekly Friday prayer. Arab-style clothing is especially common among religious leaders and hajj returnees but is not reserved to them.

As argued above, Islamic dress is generally common in Madura and happens to be a mixture of localizations of Arab style and Indonesian-Madurese clothing. Almost all women in Madura wear headscarves, even though there are different variants of headscarves. Women in rural areas, from lower classes, frequently tie the headscarf at the nape of the neck, which leaves their neck uncovered. This is apparently regarded as more practical by women working in the market or in the fields. Richer women, women in urban areas, and in the pesantren wear bigger veils that cover not only their heads and necks but also the upper part of the body. Thus, the respective headscarf style is also a means of symbolizing class affiliation.

Most women wear skirts, trousers are very uncommon for women in Madura and even for men, who wear the traditional sarong, especially in religious contexts. The sarong is probably the most important garment in Madura and is strongly associated with Islam. Men and women wear the skirtlike cloth, which is wrapped around the waist, in daily life as well as during special occasions and religious rituals. Women usually wear sarongs made from colorful Madurese batik, while men nowadays tend to wear checkered sarongs in various colors.

Wearing trousers is regarded as extremely inappropriate, with jeans considered haram by some kyai. Wearing them can be a rebellious act.

The most common headdress for men is called *kopiah* in Madura. The round textile cap covering the upper half of the scalp can be found throughout the Islamic world in local variations as a prayer cap but also as an accessory in daily life. The Javanese variant of the kopiah is also called *songkok* or *peci*. The black peci has become a symbol of Muslim identity as well as national Indonesian identity (van Dijk 2002, 64). Politicians usually wear it in official photographs and election campaign posters. The historical pictures of President Sukarno wearing the black peci contribute to the image of the peci as a symbol of Indonesian independence and nationalism (van Dijk 2002, 63). Mecca returnees in Madura tend to wear a white kopiah or peci rather than a black one, marking their status as hajji. Some hajjis and religious public figures wear a white turban or the characteristic black-white or red-white checkered *kufiah* cloth. If a man is not wearing a headdress and meets a religious authority, he covers his forehead with his hand as a sign of humility.

Another element of Arabic style is cosmetics. For marriage, Madurese women put henna paint on their hands and legs. Moreover, Arabic or Indian perfume is quite popular, as is dark eyeliner. The eyeliner is also used for newborns and by young men who study in the pesantren and who consider this as being in

FIG. 12. So-called Arab cosmetics at a market street leading to the tomb of Sunan Ampel, Surabaya, July 2014. Photo by the author.

line with the sunna. This is a practice that is also common among the Bedouin people of Jordan and the Arabian Peninsula. Cosmetics, as well as clothing and paraphernalia such as prayer chains, can be found in the aforementioned Arab shops (Toko Arab), which are mostly run by persons of Hadhrami descent, as for instance in the image of so-called Arab cosmetics that can be found in the market street near the grave of the Sunan Ampel, one of the Wali Songo, in Surabaya.

Another local cultural marker associated with Islam and with the journey to Mecca are rings with akik stones. The philosophy related to akik stones comes from the Islamic tradition from Turkey and Persia. In Indonesia, akik rings are popular among all religious groups, including Christians, Hindus, and Buddhists. The Madurese are particularly famous for trading akik rings. Usually a healer (*dukun*) or kyai recommends to customers what kind of akik stone to put on depending on their needs and interests, with different stones relating to love life, career concerns, or economic aspirations. Moreover, as I mentioned in chapter 2, the Madurese are famous for selling these stones at the holy sites in Mecca and Medina. Rings that are brought home from the Holy Land are deemed to be particularly powerful, even though they might have originated from Indonesia in the first place. One of the reasons for this is the proximity to the holy sites that potentially radiate barokah.

Madurese research participants explained that these outfit preferences are in the tradition (sunna) of the Prophet Muhammad. Apart from language, clothing, and accessories, music and performance are related to the creation or transfer of blessings during rituals and they are exploited with regard to the demonstration of Arabness.

The denouncement of Arab style in the context of the Islam Nusantara discourse annoyed Madurese research participants who have a liking for this style and who consider it not an outward influence but their own Madurese style. Even though Madura is a stronghold of NU, Madurese NU adherents do not feel well represented by this recent public discourse. They argue that living in the tradition of the Prophet is a recommended practice in Islam and should not be stigmatized as Arabization.

Musical Performances of Arabness

In addition to personal lifestyle features, the demonstration and celebration of Arabness is prominent in musical performances. In this context, art and music are not only a matter of aesthetics and entertainment but carry a political subtext (cf. Rancière 2011, 10). In Madura, the promotion of a certain style of music and denouncement of others is related to claims of authority for a certain interpretation of appropriate Islamic lifestyle. In this regard, music can be a sphere that divides people. There is a correlation between ideas of what is aesthetic and what is Islamic: It is music labeled as "Arab" or "Islamic" that is widely acknowledged as aesthetic and unobjectionable in Madura.[16]

A favored musical instrument in Madura is the *gambus* (Arabic: *qanbūs*), a lute with twelve strings, which originated from Yemen and was established in Malaysia and Indonesia with the arrival of Yemeni traders in the nineteenth century.[17] In Madura, the instrument itself as well as the music genre related to it are called gambus. In the Middle East the *oud* (Arabic: *'ūd*) replaced the gambus, yet in Indonesia and Malaysia it continues to be popular and a whole genre of Islamic music has developed around the instrument, which in other areas of the Muslim world is considered haram. This historical journey of the instrument alone shows that even though such instruments are labeled as "Arab," they are also Malay-Indonesian cultural heritage and result from mutual cultural inspiration.

While in Malaysia it is claimed that the gambus *Melayu* is originally from Malaysia (Hilarian 2004, 16), in Madura the gambus is regarded as *khas Arab*, as typically Arabic (Bouvier 2002, 77). This assumption is probably related to the central role that persons of Arabic descent play in this music genre in Madura. As Hélène Bouvier (2002) points out in her comprehensive book on arts in Madura, the Hadhrami manufacture the instrument and are thus called *pengrajin keturunan Arab* (Arabic descent craftsmen). Bouvier observed that it is hard for rural gambus orchestras to obtain a gambus unless they have links to the Hadhrami people in Sumenep or Surabaya (Bouvier 2002, 76). Moreover, she points out that besides manufacturing them, persons of Hadhrami descent also maintain the cultivation of gambus music in all four kabupaten (regencies) in Madura as well as in Surabaya (ibid., 78), showing a high resemblance with gambus events in the Hadhramaut (ibid., 79). Bouvier argues that the use of Arabic language in gambus orchestras is prestigious because of its connection to Islam (ibid., 80). A group of musicians who use a gambus is also referred to as "*Orkes Islam*" (ibid., 77), which underlines that many Madurese regard Arabic as equivalent with Islamic.

The popularity of the gambus illustrates how some cultural markers are labeled as Arab even though they are actually a product of cultural exchange between various regions. When the term *Arab* is used as equivalent with "Islamic" in this context it also implies that the instrument is halal and that the music made with it is considered as aesthetic. During one of our discussions about musical traditions in Madura, Ubed pointed out that some popular gambus songs played in Madura were actually by a Lebanese Christian, but that people in Madura would not be aware of that, as they just regarded everything Arabic as Islamic.

Another type of music widely labeled as Arabic music is the sholawatan tradition. Gambus and drums often accompany sholawatan singing, which is performed during *imtihān* and *khaol* events as well as in separate cultural performances. Sholawatan events are public events somewhere between entertainment and spirituality. Sholawatan performers mostly express praise of the Prophet Muhammad, to whom the performances are dedicated as *sholawat nabi* (*sholawat* for the prophet), asking God to give blessings to the Prophet. A charismatic singer is accompanied by a choir and by Middle Eastern and North African instruments such as the gambus, tambourine, *darbūka* drums, flutes and lutes. It is mainly men who join sholawatan groups, yet I also observed women singing in these groups, which is quite striking as in many Islamic schools of thought female singing is regarded as haram.[18] Apart from the question of whether women's singing is haram, the controversy also relates to women preaching and speaking in public. However, in Indonesia there are some famous female sholawatan singers who are very popular in Madura. Everyone knows the songs of sholawatan celebrities like Sulis or Wafiq Azizah. Thus, interestingly, sholawatan singing is labeled as Arabic and thus halal, even though female singing would be rather unusual in religious contexts in many parts of the Arab world.[19] The texts in sholawatan recitations are in Arabic, Indonesian, Javanese, or Madurese language. It is a free-time activity for layman and semi-professionals as well as for professionals and the commercial music industry, one of the most famous singers being Habib Sheikh Abdul Qadir, a celebrity of Hadhrami, and even Prophetic, descent, as the title *habib* indicates.

Another part of performance arts that is labeled as Arab in Madura is *haddrah*. Bouvier defines haddrah as male singing and choreography (Bouvier 2002, 214) and juxtaposes it with *samroh/qasidah* which is female singing about morality without choreography (Bouvier 2002, 80, 211). During my research, I could not observe this distinction, as my informants referred to both male and female singing and choreography as haddrah. Haddrah is rhythmical singing to give praise, accompanied by so called *rébanah* drums and choreography and is frequently performed for hajj returnees, as was the case at the return celebration for Ibu and Pak Sukis. Some texts for haddrah are said to be composed by famous ulama from Mecca and Medina (ibid., 214).

Besides gambus, sholawatan, and haddrah, Bouvier addresses *dangdut* music in the Islamic music section of her book (Bouvier 2002, 211). Yet there have been changes in this field of music since Bouvier did her research in 1986/87, as today in Madura dangdut music is widely regarded as haram. While in 1982, Frederick (1982) argued that dangdut had given Indonesian Islam a new kind of public identity (ibid., 102), recently there have been controversies about the virtue of dangdut. Dangdut, which developed during the colonial period and is inspired by musical influence from Portugal, Persia, India, and Arab countries, is very diverse nowadays. The "father of dangdut," Rhoma Irama, represents the virtuous version of dangdut, trying to harmonize it with Islam. In contrast, Inul Daratista's work is labeled as haram, prohibited for Muslims through a fatwa by MUI (Majelis Ulama Indonesia), the council of Indonesian ulama. Her performances represent the dirty, tainted, and supposedly pornographic dangdut *koplo* (see Weintraub 2010). Research participants in Madura joked about dangdut, stating for instance that one would have to decide between dangdut and Islamic music for a wedding, because a kyai would not attend the event if there were a dangdut performance. Thus dangdut was contrasted with Arabic music and labeled as inappropriate.

Bouvier concludes that what is labeled as "Islamic art" in Madura is not regarded as part of Madurese folklore in the national context. At that time there had been an Indonesianization in the Indonesian art scene, emphasizing the importance of Indonesian language in fine arts and cinema and subsuming local arts as folklore. In the case of Madura, it was gamelan, an ensemble of percussive instruments, theater, and dance as well as trumpets (*seronen*), which were popular in the feudal *Kraton* tradition in Sumenep, that were promoted as Madurese folklore through government policies, while Madura's rich Islamic art (*seni Islam*), which is much more relevant to the rural population, was not taken seriously (Bouvier 2002, 434).

It is probably this national policy that contributed to the perception that performances of gambus, sholawatan, and haddrah are Arabic, as something from outside, especially from an outward perspective, rather than acknowledging that the local characteristics of these musical forms are uniquely Madurese. Promoting Arabic music might thus also represent opposition against aristocratic rulers and the central government's policies. When Bouvier did her research in the late 1980s, the public policy of the Suharto government aimed at the promotion and marketing of local culture, suppressing Islamic movements. However, after the downfall of the Suharto regime, Islamic parties and organizations could express their opinions more freely.

Today, the musical traditions of gambus, sholawatan, and haddrah are the prevailing styles in Madura. While Arabic music was treated as an artistic influence from outside in the 1980s, it now appears to be regarded as mainstream Madurese culture even if it is still labeled as "Arab." The popularity of this music style mirrors the growing influence of Islamic actors in public life. The religious elite invests heavily in big sholawatan music events, inviting celebrities like Sheikh Habib Abdul Qadir to Madura. The events are welcome entertainment in the remoteness of Madura and the religious authorities convey the message that this is the only appropriate form of music in contrast to dangdut and Western or East Asian pop music. Their investment in art and music is concomitant with competition between religious and worldly rulers in Madura. What is labeled as an increasing Islamization or Arabization of public life is a political issue as well, triggered from within society and elite competition, in which leading actors outperform one another with Arabic-Islamic symbolism.

Remarkably, some Madurese musicians further developed sholawatan, haddrah, and gambus music, engaging with ideological controversies. In spite of being labeled as Arab music and putting on a display of Arabness, some celebrities of the Madurese Islamic music branch actually mock Arabic-Islamic traditions, especially Wahhabist ideology. The music of Khoirul Anwar (alias Anwar Al Abror) aptly portrays the ambivalence of Arab affinity in Madura. The singing imitates the intonation of religious songs and is accompanied by gambus and haddrah choreography, but also by a synthesizer.

In self-mockery, Al Abror performs Arabness creatively, as for instance in his song, *Coca Cola*, where he jokes about the lack of knowledge of English among the Madurese. Juxtaposing Arabic and English language, he sings, among others:

Ca inggris ce' repotdheh	Speaking English is troublesome
Ape-tampe hurufbheh	Piles and piles of letters
Terro faseh je ngajeh	Wanting to be fluent, but it's hard
Akursus ce' abitdheh	Wanting to take a course, but it takes time
Beca'an ben tolesan	Reading each letter
Lanjeng pandhe' tak padeh	Short and long is not the same
Mun ca' Arab tak sulit	Speaking Arabic is not difficult
Ngangghui elmu tajuwid	Using *tajwīd* knowledge[20]
Macah gempang rosloros	Reading it is easy, on and on
Duli lancer tak abid	Fast and fluent, doesn't take long

(Al Abror 2012, translation with Khotim Udaidillah)

In other songs, Al Abror brings engagement with Arabness and piety onto the stage, in combination with harsh criticism of Saudi Arabia. He dedicated a whole album to his criticism of Wahhabist ideology. In this album, called *Toreh De' Martajasah—Makam Nabi e Bhungkarah,* meaning "Let's go to Martajasah—They want to tear down the Prophet's grave site," he broaches the issue of Saudi Arabia's plans to move or tear down the grave site of the Prophet Muhammad. As the title of the album indicates, he not only protests against the destruction of the Prophet's grave site but also promotes the worship of local saints when he suggests going to Martajasah, which is the grave site of Shaikhona Kholil in Bangkalan. An extract of the lyrics gives an example of this mockery:

Bede berita e TV	There is news on TV
E Arab e Saudi	About Saudi Arabia
Wahabi e Madinah	The Wahhabis in Medina
Gentak beres ta genna	They aren't right in the head but crazy
Wahabi la nahdutullah	Wahhabis have risen
Nangin na nabi Allah	Insulting God's Prophet
Presis ben penjahat	Same as villains

(Al Abror 2014, translation with Khotim Udaidillah)

Ironically, in the video for the song, Anwar Al Abror performs in front of an Arabic alphabet artwork on Bangkalan's main road. He is dressed in Islamic-style clothing, with a white peci and a cloth hanging loosely over his shoulder. Provokingly, while mocking Saudi Arabia, he relates to Arabic-Islamic symbolism. The cover image of the album dedicated to the mockery of Wahhabism show Al Abror sitting on a horse that is decorated with the red-white checkered *kufiah* cloth in combination with pictures of camels and imitation Arabic writing. Al Abror has made Arab-Islamic symbolism his own, which makes his criticism of Wahhabism even harsher. The type of music that Al Abror performs would most likely be regarded as haram in Saudi Arabia because of the instruments he uses and because of female singing in the songs.

In this regard, the display of Arabness, the way people dress, the instruments they use and the persons they include in their performances are also a political statement and an endeavor to guide through entertainment and lifestyle. This can either mean promoting music that strengthens one's position, as the religious elite do, or, as in the case of Al Abror, making a certain cultural feature one's own and using it as humoristic critique.

The display of Arabness in clothing styles, music, and arts, as well as ritual practice, are linked to Sufi traditions of Islam and the role of the Prophet plays a particularly crucial role here. Veneration of the Prophet Muhammad is widespread, especially in the context of ziarah and *sholawat* music, but also for the other spheres of performative engagement with Arabness. The common argument that this happens in the tradition of the Prophet's words and deeds (the *sunna*) contradicts claims of Arabization. As regards content, this corresponds with Cak Nun's argument that following the Prophet's path implies opposing Wahhabism and Saudi policies. It is thus not surprising that in August 2014 thousands of Madurese *santri* protested in Pamekasan against the visit of a Wahhabi scholar.[21] While from an outside perspective, like that of the Javanese, Arabization in Madura seems to be prevalent, the Madurese make this Arab style their own and thereby challenge the demonization of Arabness in the Islam Nusantara discourse (Lücking 2016, 21). "Bersama Nabi menantang Arab"—"Challenging Arabs, together with the Prophet"—is how one of my interlocutors put it. However, in the competition over public influence, the appearance of some Arab features increases and changes, as competing elites seek to outperform one another.

Contemporary Politicization of Arabness

Arabness has become a Madurese characteristic, a *ciri khas* Madura. Using Arab symbolism for political purposes is not only prevalent with regard to music. Considering that piety has become the most important frame of reference in Madura, competing with bandit and mafia culture (cf. Rozaki 2004), it is not surprising that Madurese politicians of all political parties try to access the symbolic capital of Arabness and seek to transform it into political capital.

An example of this is the issuance of local regulations (*PerDa*, short for *peraturan daerah*) on sharia law in Pamekasan. This introduction of *PerDa Sharia* (or *Gerbang Salam*, an abbreviation of *Gerakan Pembangunan Masyarakat Islami*/the Movement of Fostering Islamic Society) exemplifies how elites seek to outperform one another in their attempts to use the symbolic capital of Arabness and pious public performance. Like in other Indonesian regencies where local regulations on sharia law have been introduced, the initiators of PerDa Sharia were representatives of secular parties.[22] Buehler has shown that the increase of local sharia regulation in Indonesia happened alongside a simultaneous decline of Islamist parties who had demanded such regulations. In fact, the majority of local government heads adopting sharia regulations were old elites of Suharto's New Order regime and had no ties to Islamist parties, and the majority of seats in the relevant local parliaments were held by secular parties (Buehler 2016, 187). Buehler sees increased competition in Indonesia's political sphere as the reason for the issuance of local sharia regulations. The old elites compete with new political actors, including representatives of nonmainstream brands of Islam who influence public opinion making. In attempting to win the masses' votes, secular parties play with the support of Muslim actors outside institutionalized party politics who are able to influence voters (Buehler 2016, 190–94).

Buehler's conclusions are applicable to the Madurese case as well. Ubaidillah (2010) has suggested that in Pamekasan, the issuing of PerDa Sharia was a political strategy by secular politicians, as the religious ones would risk losing credibility if they opposed their opponents' initiatives. Ultimately, local sharia regulations in Pamekasan became an elitist project in which competing authorities played out their animosities by arguing about the right interpretation of

Islamic law. In election campaigns the image of Madura as *serambi Madinah* (terrace of Medina) was exploited, and since the kyai had become highly influential, non-kyai politicians sought to access the capital of religious symbolism as well. Ubaidillah (2010) argues that sharia regulations in Pamekasan have little impact on ordinary peoples' daily lives. The regulations concern the prohibition of alcoholic beverages, recommendations on Muslim clothing, and a general demand to fulfil Islamic duties such as giving alms (*zakat*) and reading the Qur'an. In contrast to sharia law in Aceh, the regulations are rather loose, and there is no institutionalized sharia law enforcement. Yet despite Ubaidillah's argument about the populations' pragmatic engagement with the regulations, or their ignorance of them, this example indicates how Islamization and what is perceived as Arabization can be triggered from inside society, which is why I argue that the increase in Islamization of the public sphere in Madura is a homemade Arabization, this being especially visible in the increase of mobility toward the Middle East but not primarily inspired by those who become mobile.

Side Roads

Coming back to the questions of what makes people follow, the examples from Madura and Central Java show that migrants and pilgrims seek to extract various forms of capital from their mobile experiences. If the mainstream guidance does not promise upward mobility, deviations from guidance and personal interpretative labor are more likely. Deviation from guidance evidently also happened among other research participants, yet the examples presented here make the nuances of negotiation in a demand-supply relationship of guidance especially obvious.

Prospects for personal gain by following a certain offered guidance are central in determining the level of adherence to it. Migrants and pilgrims aren't blindly following dominant guidance nor are they passive receivers of outward influences. It is the translatability of experiences of mobility into various forms of capital that is crucial here.

The nonaccessibility of the symbolic capital of Arabness for migrant women in Gunungembun, who are labeled as laborers and not as hajjas, reveals the limiting repercussions of leading discourses. However, due to interpretative labor, the women in Gunungembun do not passively submit to these discourses and the social immobility resulting from them. They challenge the stigma of being perceived as lower-class migrant workers. Through their personal reflections and cosmopolitan interests, they do not fit into the role attributed to them. They overcome their exclusion from a pious middle-class lifestyle by moving on the side road of an alternative normative discourse surrounding Asian values and East Asian modernity.

Concerning Indonesians' relationship with the Arab world more generally, I have argued that the center-periphery constellation triggers demarcations against Arab Others to overcome the stigma of being labeled as the periphery of the Muslim world. A similar argument applies to demarcation against middle-class Pop Arabness in Gunungembun. In their reaction to the stigma of being perceived as actors on the margins of society, the women in Gunungembun display a counterimage and claim moral superiority.

Interestingly, in Madura the reaction to marginalization is different. Countering prevailing stereotypes about the "backwardness" of the island and the Madurese people being harsh and stubbornly pious does not involve contradicting this image, but rather attempting to take a stronger lead themselves by promoting alternative routes to the Arab world. Madurese research participants made self-effacing arguments that this corresponds with the stereotype that Madurese occupy positions and commodities that others do not want to take over. Their pride in acting as influential intermediaries in the relationship between Indonesia and the Middle East fosters their proud displays of Arabness.

This leads to the situation in which the Madurese's lively adaptation of Arab symbolism challenges the exclusive Middle Eastern ownership of Arabness as well as the guidance NU seeks to provide with the Islam Nusantara discourse. Moreover, it contradicts claims of Arabization as being outwardly inspired. The examples show that the "homemade" Madurese Arabization is the result of aspirations to gain the power of blessings and power in society. It is the product of fruitful exchange of Madurese, Malay-Indonesian, and Hadhrami cultural heritage. The result of this is Madurese conservatism, not Middle Eastern or Wahhabi-Saudi conservatism.

The endeavor to "become better Muslims" and increase personal morality and piety corresponds with Kloos's (2017) findings for Aceh, where similar dynamics are at stake. This means that inner-Acehnese and inner-Madurese tensions inspire personal motivations for changes in religious practice, including a possible rise of conservatism. Thus, in order to understand the conservative turn in Indonesia, the analysis must focus on internal and local dynamics rather than an outward influence. Where the political sphere is characterized by elite contestation and competition to access religious symbolism (cf. Buehler 2016), people on the ground are left to make their choices between competing guiding representations. In the case of Arabness in Madura, public actors outperform one another in this regard.

Thus, most obviously, Islamization of public life in Madura is not the result of outward ideological influence, as the Madurese are among the most outspoken critics of Wahhabism. The features that are labeled as Arab mostly stem from Malay-Sufi traditions, Hadhrami culture, and NU orthodoxy, all of which contrast with the culture and customs of the Gulf region.

On a national level, the Madurese engagement with Arabness could equally be described as interpretative labor. In order to take over intermediary roles in the pilgrimage business, the Madurese must establish interpretative skills. Their pride in being able to "handle" counterparts in Indonesia and the Middle East is exemplified in the rumors about the legendary mafia. Belief that the Madurese mafia is influential appears to be more crucial than its actual scope of influence, which is hard to determine. Madurese self-confidence in an interpretative surplus apparently makes them less susceptible to Arab-phobic discourses and national guidance.

Madurese research participants proudly describe the Madurese way as unparalleled, but some of them also indicated that it is without alternative. At first sight, it seems as if Madurese migrants do not have to cope with social exclusion like migrant women in Gunungembun. However, the description of Madurese lifeworlds indicates that even though the Madurese appear to move on alternative routes in spatial, social, and cultural mobility in the context of pilgrimage and migration, within Madurese society there is little opportunity to follow paths other than those of the kyai. Madurese migrants and pilgrims who aspire to transform their mobility toward the Middle East into various forms of capital must stick to the overall societal atmosphere of Islamic orthodoxy. Their path might be an exception nationally, but within Madura it remains the mainstream. In the endeavor to appear more pious than Arab people and more pious than one's neighbor or competitor, orthodox and conservative Islamic lifestyles intensify.

Last, the prospect of transforming travel experiences into capital appears to be the crucial factor for adherence to guidance or deviation from it. Furthermore, personal educational background and family background significantly influence the choice of guiding reference points. In Madura, where mosques and Qur'anic schools are the most important suppliers of education, religion is the major frame of orientation, while in Gunungembun, where migrant women grow up in a culturally and religiously heterogeneous environment, alternatives appear to come more naturally to them.

In conclusion, this is another example of how the outcome of experiences of mobility depends on the home context and the guidance to which mobile actors most likely adhere. Additionally to structural guidance in the accessibility of different destinations for labor migration, the plurality of guiding discourses apparently leads to individual reflection and can create resilience, interpretative labor, and self-determined agency. The singularity of one dominant guiding discourse, like in Madura, can equip followers with a strong self-confidence, which may come to the fore in creativity and self-determination, like in the self-mockery and creative criticism of Wahhabism by the musician Al Abror, or to a certain extent even in more self-determined migration. However, the lack of alternatives can also trigger more radical interpretations of the dominant guidance and a jostling for influence whose result is competition to exceed propagated values.

Conclusion

CONTINUITY THROUGH GUIDED MOBILITY

Changing Muslim traditions and lifestyles in contemporary Indonesia might come in the form of Arab garb, but this does not always reveal a specific ideological orientation, nor does it provide evidence of influence from the Middle East. In fact, such an Arab garb can be a medium to communicate specifically Indonesian customs, class affiliations, and local differentiations. Labor migrants' and Mecca pilgrims' experiences in Arab countries and their processing thereof offer vivid examples of how local guidance ultimately informs Indonesian representations of the Arab world—even among those who can draw on firsthand experiences in Arab countries.

Research with Indonesian Mecca pilgrims and labor migrants has shown that experiences in the Middle East are processed in accordance with individuals' respective lifeworlds. For a Mecca pilgrim, the hajj to Mecca can be an overwhelmingly spiritual experience, with a feeling of reaching inner peace and returning to everyday life with strengthened faith. The transformative character of the journey can be fully Indonesian, Javanese, or Madurese, even if the participant's choice of dress or language might change after having traveled to an Arab country. The journey might be a trigger for change; its content however is mostly inspired by local trends and controversies. The juxtaposition with the experiences of female labor migrants brings this insight to the forefront. Sharing the same physical destination with pilgrims, their guidance differs, and the cultural outcomes of their journeys depend on how they can make their mobility meaningful.

Culture, including Arab culture, is not a static entity that physically moves from one region to another. Cultural mobility—like spatial mobility and social mobility—is a process characterized by mutual exchange, complex negotiations, adaptations, and translations. The guidance of this process emerged as a key feature in labor migration and Mecca pilgrimages. As this guidance mostly comes from migrants' and pilgrims' home contexts, through guiding narratives and images as well as personal intermediaries and government control, the result of their spatial mobility is sociocultural continuity rather than change. The prevalence of cultural continuity and the complex and often ambivalent negotiations relate to the third sphere of the triad of mobility that I have examined: social mobility. It seems that cultural continuity and adherence to sociocultural guidance is crucial for upward mobility in postmigration and postpilgrimage lifeworlds. Thus guidance and embeddedness in the local context informs cultural representations and customs.

In order to understand attractions to certain styles, political movements, and ideologies, it is crucial to trace how such interests come into existence. The analysis of how Indonesians experience, perceive, adopt, own, reject, and adjust elements of an (imagined) Arab world, making it *their* Arab world, indicates that the formation of social identities in transnational South-South exchanges contradicts conceptions of homogenous and oppositional national or cultural territories. Furthermore, it shows that conservatism in Indonesia is (1) not monolithic, but rather is regionally diverse and related to class affiliation, and (2) a product of internal competition rather than outward influence.

Indonesian Representations of the Arab World

When Indonesians move toward the Arab world for religious reasons, in actual physical movement and in "mobility imaginaries" (Salazar 2010b), during daily prayers, Sufi rituals, and ziarah visits, they consider this mobility a movement toward God. The Qur'an and the conveyed words and deeds of the Prophet Muhammad are considered the ultimate "guidebooks" for this movement. For Indonesians who look at the Arab world as the Holy Land, the region represents eternal longing. In this longing, Indonesian Muslims feel that this Holy Land belongs to them and to other Muslims around the world alike. Some Indonesian Muslims even demand that they should act as international examples in their authentic ownership of Islam. They feel united with the Prophet Muhammad in the quest to oppose *ǧāhilīya*, ignorance, which they identify not only in pre-Islamic times, but also in contemporary contexts—especially in the land of the two holy mosques, which some denounce as becoming like Las Vegas (cf. Kusuma 2014), a destination for hedonist activities. In humoristic evaluations the perceived tendency of Arab people to be stuck in *ǧāhilīya* is taken as the reason for the historical presence of prophets in the Middle East. The implication is that Indonesians, together with the prophets, stand against *ǧāhilīya* in the Holy Land and in the world. The slogan of NU's annual assembly in 2015, "Strengthening Islam Nusantara for Civilization in Indonesia and the World," echoes this aspiration and self-understanding. However, the apparent Arabization of Indonesian Muslim traditions would seem to contradict the demonization of Arabness and the romanticization of a superior Indonesian ownership of selected parts of Arab culture. The examples presented in this book show that as on the political stage, ordinary Indonesians direct their anti-Arab or pro-Arab sentiments toward a domestic audience. Labor migrants speak about their own moral integrity, distancing themselves from Arab employers, while Mecca pilgrims perform Arabness as a symbol of piety and simultaneously criticize Arab culture and customs. Indonesians' representations and partial ownership of Arabness communicate social affiliations in the return context and are not so much expressions of changed ideologies or—as claims of an Arabization suggest—an Islamic radicalization.

Arabization Revisited

The most recent terrorist attacks in Indonesia happened on May 13, 2018, in Surabaya and Sidoarjo. A family affiliated with Jamaah Ansharud Daulah (JAD), a local branch of ISIS, attacked three churches and a police headquarters, killing twenty-eight people, including themselves. Discussions again arose about an "Arabization" in the sense of Islamic radicalization in Indonesia. In the condemnation of the attack, the fact that the family had been trained in Syria was a widely discussed issue, leading to arguments about the alleged "infiltration" of Middle Eastern violence and the spread of ISIS in Southeast Asia. The "subject of Arab violence," widely seen as the root of terrorism, especially after the Bali Bombings in 2002 (see Gilsenan 2003), was back. What does it mean when a society characterizes violent acts with an ethnic or racial label like "Arab?" And what is actually "Arab" about this violence, or is it in fact also Asian, Indonesian, and Javanese?

The multifarious engagements with Arabness among labor migrants and Mecca returnees indicate that the condemnation of Arabness as potentially violent is a stereotype that falls short of explaining the popularity of certain styles and ideologies. The various adaptations of Arabness challenge the Islam Nusantara discourse, in which Arabness is a counterimage to a pluralist Indonesian Islam and a label for ideologies of violence. For those who are anxious about the increasing Islamization of public life in Indonesia and radicalization of some

Indonesian Muslims, the popularity of Arab cultural markers appears to affirm their perception of an Arabization, giving new fuel to their fears. Islamophobia becomes an Arab-phobia in this context. Through the imagination of Middle Eastern influence in Indonesia, the reasons for Islamic conservatism or even violence are outsourced.

However, outsourcing the reasons for this phenomena is a simplification that ultimately glosses over inter-Indonesian social and ideological frictions. By unraveling the undercurrents of Indonesian engagement with Arabness among ordinary people, I have shown that the diverse Islamization trends are rooted in internal Indonesian social dynamics and domestic religious interpretations. To a significant degree these internal dynamics appear to be related to competition over the access to financial, social, and political capital. The examples of Mecca returnees and labor migrants show this in the microcosms of people in Central Java and Madura.

The Madurese example of the politicization of religion in local politics as well as the most recent political power gambling on the national level mirror identity negotiations on the ground. Muslim middle-class Pop Islam had been assumed to be apolitical (cf. chapter 1, Heryanto 2014a, 143). Parallel to this apolitical post-Islamism, increasing conservatism and Islamists' demands found their way into politics. However, conservative Arab-Islamic markers often appear to be a symbolic commodity in power gambling rather than an expression of an ideology shift. The adoption of Arabness is a trend on which some political actors capitalize and a strategy to gain or appease voters, like in the case of local sharia laws (see Buehler 2016). This can even include Arab ethnicity. That the Hadhrami politician Anies Baswedan won the governor elections in Jakarta while Ahok, his Chinese non-Muslim predecessor in office, is imprisoned because of blasphemy accusations, reflects the relevance of ethnic and religious markers in contemporary public life in Indonesia. However, labor migration and pilgrimage show how relative this commodity is and how quickly it can evaporate. For instance, the case of labor migrants in Gunungembun shows that the prestige of Arab cultural markers is not equally accessible to everybody. The political symbolism of religious markers can be interchangeable. Another example of this is the rising and falling popularity of the FPI leader Habib Rizieq, who is also a Hadhrami and who supports the Aksi Bela Islam and #GantiPresident campaigns (see chapter 1). Meanwhile, the popularity of Habib Rizieq has crumbled since he fled to Saudi Arabia after being charged in a pornography case in Indonesia. This case shows that attributions of Arabness can change quickly from a form of praise—as being closer to the origin of the Prophet Muhammad, in the case of Baswedan—or a condemnation when it comes to controversial issues like Habib Rizieq's involvement with pornography or accusations of radicalism and terrorism. Such examples from public life are similar to negotiation processes on the ground, where migrants and pilgrims refer to the Arab world and Arab cultural markers in ambivalent ways.

Furthermore, the analysis of migrants' and pilgrims' experiences shows how people make sense of these national and international controversies in the context of their own connections to the Middle East. Migrants' and pilgrims' engagement with leading narratives about Arabness shows that the scope of Indonesian orientation toward the Middle East is subject to national controversies and local embeddedness, selective filtering, and overlapping with other cultural markers, like Madurese language and customs of East Asian styles in Central Java. Thus certain lifestyle trends are too quickly evaluated as symptomatic of "ideological Arabization" when in fact little can be concluded from these lifestyle trends about peoples' ideologies. Generalizing labels like "Arab" cover more than they reveal, and the terminological inconsistencies in everyday use are of little help.

In addition to my own findings, there is further evidence from which it can be concluded that Indonesian interests in Middle Eastern ways of life are actually not so far-reaching. Fealy points out that only a minority of Indonesians of an Islamist orientation consume news about the Middle East and feel aligned with their fellow believers in the region (Fealy 2014, 235). He argues that in former times, for instance after the revolution in Iran in 1979, Indonesian interest was more sincere (ibid., 237). Moreover, the pragmatic approaches to Saudi Arabian funding for education and mosque buildings that I observed as well as the demonization of the term *Arab* in the Islam Nusantara discourse indicate that idealizing, demonizing, and pragmatic approaches are present in Indonesia.

Cultural markers of being Asian, Indonesian, Javanese, and Madurese are likewise of high importance, especially when it comes to questions of morality, ideas of success, and cultural traits like politeness. This is expressed to the extent that people consider cultural proximity as more crucial than religious commonality, as I have shown for labor migrants in Central Java. This is not only reflected in the personal life stories of migrants and pilgrims but also in regional politics. Politically ASEAN is much more important for Indonesia than bilateral cooperation with Middle Eastern countries (Fealy 2014, 235). On top of this, regionalism in the ASEAN region is very state centered (Rüland and Bechle 2014), which means that the local home context remains the most important point of orientation. Thus even though at first sight it seems as though religion has become the major reference point in alignments and dealignments in Indonesian society, experiences of mobility to the Middle East foster the awareness of Indonesian customs, values, and habits as being quite distinct from Arab ones.

Indonesian Ways to the Arab World

Despite the widespread stereotypes of Arab Others, many research participants were careful to relativize their generalizations, emphasizing the difference between religion and culture and conceding that there were righteous Muslims among the Arabs as well. "In every country there are good and bad people," is how Pak Raharjo diplomatically put it. This means that in fact, ordinary people appear to have more nuanced views on cultural Others than the guiding actors and narratives who direct them.

However, despite their nuanced reflection, many Indonesian migrants and pilgrims consider themselves to be a little bit better than these other good people. This is obvious in forms of guidance, which refer to local ethics and values, such as patience, politeness, and gender roles. Their own superiority is constructed against images of several cultural Others: the Middle Eastern Arab Others, pilgrims from other countries, the Arab Others in their own society, including Salafi Muslims, Indonesians of Hadhrami descent, the Pop Arab middle-class, and orthodox Madurese Muslims, but also lower-class migrants. Who is identified as the Other and what is labeled as Arab is a matter of perspective. The historiography of Indonesian encounters with the Arab world indicates that the region west of the Indian Ocean has for long been an ambivalent reference point as a place of longing and spiritual experiences, as well as a counterimage from which Indonesians differentiate themselves. In the context of contemporary mobility to the Middle East, images of the Arab world are imagined multifariously, serving different purposes. The perspectives of what Arabness and the Arab world encompass vary between different groups of people and quite often even within individual evaluations. Boundaries between in- and out-groups are drawn, withdrawn, and redrawn. The analysis of different levels of communitas among Indonesians who travel to the Arab world indicates that migrants and pilgrims exhibit feelings of belonging to a larger ummah during their stays abroad, while back home they draw narrative boundaries from those whom they considered as brothers and sisters during their time abroad. Migrants' solidarity with migrant women from other countries as "sisters of the same fate" (see chapter 2) is similarly relativized in postmigration narratives. These boundaries are drawn according to imagined cultural differences and become guiding reference points in self-positioning upon return.

Despite various levels of communitas, including inter-Indonesian boundary making, contemporary mobility from Indonesia to the Middle East especially fosters identification as Indonesian Muslims. Even though a broader understanding of Asianness is also remarkably relevant, identification as Muslim and as Indonesian national citizens is most significant. Claims about migrants and pilgrims as initiators of an Arabization of Indonesian culture are proved wrong by the fact that both forms of mobility are characterized by encounters with the nation-state and the high significance of local customs and values as guiding features. This does not mean that there is no influence from the Gulf in Indonesia at all—but it is to say that migrants and pilgrims are not the vessels of this influence and that many changes in Islamic lifestyles and increasing conservatism result from competition within Indonesia. As I stated above, despite outward Arab cultural markers, the journeys to the Middle East sharpen the differentiation from Arab culture and a distinction between culture and religion. Indonesians make the pilgrimage their own. It becomes an Indonesian, Javanese, and Madurese event. The essential ritual experiences not only include the official, obligatory hajj and umrah rituals, but also a range of practices that are unique to the Indonesian context. These practices happen during the pilgrimage and even more so during preparation and upon return, involving religious as well as mundane spheres, which are in fact often intertwined. The examples I have given concern shopping activities, ziarah pilgrimages to the Prophet's grave site in Medina and to local shrines in Indonesia, the changing of names, reciprocal exchange of souvenirs, communal pre- and postpilgrimage celebrations, meetings with Indonesian officials and sheikhs, and social media documentation of pilgrimage, for instance with a Mecca selfie. These activities are also part of spatial mobility and physical sensation, guiding pilgrims' steps along the beaten tracks of the collective events that are considered part of a full Indonesian pilgrimage experience. Furthermore, I suggested that even the bureaucratic challenges of becoming a hajj candidate can be considered a ritual process that makes the hajj an Indonesian one. Apart from identifying as Indonesian citizens through administrational obligations, government guidance in the form of uniform travel equipment and clothing, and the organizational structure of travel units makes the pilgrimage distinctively Indonesian. This uniformity is likewise adopted by private travel agencies. Fulfilling Indonesian customers' expectations makes the pilgrimage business an undertaking of profitable navigation. Moreover, Indonesians mostly move in Indonesianized environments in their travel units, in hotels, on airplanes, with Indonesian food and Indonesian guides and Javanese/Madurese ethical values.

Even though the Indonesian character of migrants' environments is less pervasive, especially as they cohabitate with their employers abroad, they maintain Indonesian practices and values in demarcation from the foreign environment to which they often have no rightful access or which they avoid. During preparation they are confronted with similar bureaucratic rituals to those faced by pilgrims and experience encounters with the nations-state in training camps. Furthermore, the overall national discourse about migrant women delineates their position in accordance with Javanese gender ideals like modesty, a feeling of shame, remaining patient, and enduring hardships.

Most obviously, the overall guidance of migrants' and pilgrims' mobility to the Middle East, through communal travel and embodied rituals, institutional procedures and regulations, intermediaries' brokerage, societal expectations, social bonds, the sharing of mobility experiences, and normative discourses determines the outcome of their travels. For migrants and pilgrims, the effect of this guided mobility appears to be cultural continuity rather than change. Continuity in the context of migrants' and pilgrims' sojourns occurs in guided channels, in engagement with and reaffirmation of existing norms and hierarchies, such as the leading role of the kyai in Madura, and relationships with friends and family. This can be seen in the situatedness of the representations of their experiences of mobility, which are led by values and social practices that convey meaning in their home contexts.

In order to make their movement meaningful, migrants and pilgrims maintain a homeward vision in their translations of travel experience. The Arab world seems not only to be a reference point for this self-positioning but also a screen onto which travelers project what they imagine Arab to be and what they expect to experience. This projection is connected to a significant degree with the social context from which the traveler departs. In a way, the travelers find what they are looking for and represent what holds validity back home. Therefore, in these two cases, cultural mobility and the traveling of norms must be understood as circular movement.

Taking the dimension of social mobility in the case study of migration and pilgrimage into account, it is obvious why cultural continuity is so crucial in making the journeys meaningful. Beyond the general tendency of a strengthening of self-awareness as Indonesian Muslims, cultural continuity is related to upward social mobility for many and social immobility for some. The guiding customs and values that are promoted in the context of labor migration and pilgrimage relate to normative discourses that define societies' expectations of virtuous pilgrimage returnees, who take on responsibility in their community, and foreign exchange heroines who care for their families and for the nation. Following the guidance of these expectations is crucial for potential upward social mobility. Thus cultural continuity and stability are conditions for upward mobility here. This leads to the ambivalent simultaneity of engaging with Arab cultural markers as symbols of piety and success, and the discursive demarcation from Arab culture and customs as a reassurance of loyalty to local norms and hierarchies.

Thus the contemporary middle-class Islamization trends in Indonesia might appear to be Arab-inspired but are actually "made in Indonesia." After all, many of the practices and likings that are labeled "Arab" in Indonesia, for example, televangelists, including female ones, or popular religious music trends, contrast with religious teachings from the Gulf. Looking at those who are excluded from Islamic middle-class lifestyles and those who outperform one another in displays of Arabness reveals that the Islamization trends are homemade and carry nuances beyond questions of the authenticity of Islamic lifestyles, namely concerning class affiliation, urban and rural areas, and different generations.

Contemporary Muslim identity formation in Indonesia is accompanied by social tensions, demarcations, anxieties, disappointments, and competition over influence and access to capital. In this context, the representations of Arabness and of the Arab world do not only have religious purposes. Representing the Arab world as the Holy Land and thereby evoking religious sentiments can be a selling point for travel agencies and a commodity for politicians. Religious elites in Madura display their Arabness as a symbol of the power of blessings and of their worldly power. Similarly, for hajj returnees, Arab accessories indicate their increased social status and for middle-class umrah pilgrims Pop Arabness is a marker of modernity. In these competitive environments, among ordinary Indonesians, within and between families, in peoples' neighborhoods but also in the public and political arenas, there is a tendency to seek to outperform others. These practices of outperforming others might be symbolic in nature. However, they lead to flow-on effects, like the establishment of local sharia regulations or the adherence to religious rules among hajj returnees. Thus the symbolic engagement with Arabness does have an impact on changes in society, manifested in changed structures.

The examples presented here have also shown that the symbolic capital of Arabness is not equally accessible for everyone. Migrant women in a remote mountain village in Central Java are excluded from the middle-class lifestyle of Pop Arabness. In Madura, in contrast, every migrant seems to be a pilgrim, but here there is virtually no cultural symbolism other than piety and Arabness that carries the potential of translatability into various forms of capital.

Thus, in conclusion, contemporary Islamization trends in Indonesia that are reflected in migrants' and pilgrims' experiences and representations of their mobility can carry an Arab touch, but they are not primarily inspired by culture and customs in the Middle East. In contrast, travel and migration to the Arabian Peninsula sharpen awareness of being Indonesian national citizens and members of local ethnic communities. Moreover, these travels can inspire more nuanced views about the world as the negotiations and translational moments indicate: in some cases, people leave the paved paths of mainstream guidance and choose side streets. Nevertheless, guiding images are usually essentialist and therefore, in the context of pilgrimage and migration, changing lifestyles, including Islamized lifestyles, must be seen as a product of a circular movement of normative discourses and cultural traits. Through an Arab theming of Islamization trends Indonesians create their own "homemade Arabness," or *their* Arab world.

Effects of Guided Mobility

Looking at Indonesians' mobility to the Arab world through the lens of "guidance" revealed the inner-Indonesian workings. The theoretical leitmotif of guided mobility shifts attention from the phenomenon of globalized mobility to its local embeddedness. While some studies see globalized mobility as a driving force for social change, others emphasize the restrictions and the manifestation of boundaries in the course of globalization (see introduction). The guided mobility concept shows how structures and norms enable physical mobility and make it meaningful in sociocultural terms. Finally, guidance through institutions, intermediaries, and norms keeps mobility and social change in channeled paths, compatible with the social environment in the return context. As a result, the effect of guided mobility is not fundamental social change but rather sociocultural continuity. Mobility itself is an opportunity to demand and offer guidance. This means that for the examples of Indonesians' migration and pilgrimage, spatial mobility is important as there would be no guidance without mobility. But it is not the mobility itself that has a constituting effect but rather its guidance.

Guidance at the Intersection of Structure and Agency

Guidance through institutions but also through images as situated representations directs migrants and pilgrims from their decision to go abroad to their return. It determines the general approach of how, where, and with whom to travel, what to "send" or bring home (financial and ideational remittances), and what to make of the mobile experience back home. Those who provide knowledge are intermediaries, some of whom are institutionally organized and others of whom are informal. The example of the experience of communitas in Mecca and the concept of the ummah indicate how people are led through certain metanarratives into collective experiences, which most famously are transmitted in religious teachings. Thus I defined guidance in the context of guided mobility as the intentional directing of peoples' practices and imaginings, with situated representations as a central guiding element.

Besides varying degrees of assertiveness, guidance is more subtle than authoritative leading. It is suggestive and can be manipulative rather than being coercive. This includes guidance through religious doctrines which, in the case of Indonesia, can be the subject of interpretation and competition. Most important, the hierarchical relationship between the guiding and the guided is not as clear cut as it is in the relationship of sovereign and subject, ruler and subordinate, leader and disciple, or master and apprentice. Guidance occurs in all hierarchical constellations as guidance by a superior actor, guidance in an egalitarian relationship, and as guidance by an inferior actor who offers services. Superiority can result from higher social status, being more knowledgeable or more experienced, or possessing larger financial and material goods, all various forms of capital as defined by Bourdieu (1979).

What differentiates these specific forms of guidance from general social interactions is the intentionality of achieving spatial, social and cultural mobility and some degree of dependency on guidance in the process of becoming mobile. Dependency does not imply that the guided party is only dependent on the guiding counterpart. In contrast, if guidance is offered as a paid service, for instance, the guiding counterpart is also dependent on the satisfaction of the guided customer. The different constellations of guidance can be intertwined: a domestic servant might guide his employer in mundane matters, while the employer gives work instructions. Guidance relationships are relationships of mutual dependence. The guided person is dependent on the knowledge, skills, and social networks of the guide. However, the guide also depends on the loyalty and money of, or exchange with, the guided person, which makes the relationship an interdependent one that is marked by negotiation and contestation. Adherence to the indicated direction is likely but not generally required. There is room for nonadherence, deliberation between different offers of guidance, room for one's own innovation, and last, agency.

Apart from interpersonal guidance relationships, guidance happens through the media, lifestyle trends, consumption, laws, regulations, and public discourses. In this sphere, situated representations, as context-bounded normative images, direct through discursive and embodied cultural displays. Interpersonal guidance makes use of these images in the act of explaining, instructing, indicating, advising, accompanying, and channeling.

Departing from this understanding of guidance, I defined guided mobility as movement in space, social strata and cultural orientation that is enabled and intentionally directed through institutional structures, interpersonal relationships and situated representations. Locating guided mobility at the intersection of structure and agency with an emphasis on intentionality and interdependency, I identified the potential of translational moments as an interpretative practice in experiences of guided mobility.

Supply and Demand in Guided Mobility

The analysis of labor migration and pilgrimage indicates why people become mobile and why they follow the guided paths rather than exploring unknown lands. The productive mobilities turn in social sciences has provided essential insights into the materially and culturally transformative effects of spatial mobility (Cresswell and Merriman 2011b; Cresswell 2006; Greenblatt 2010; Ong 1999; Rapport and Dawson 1998; Sheller and Urry 2006; Urry 2007). Recent studies on the "boundedness of mobilities" (Hackl et al. 2016) have criticized the euphoria of the mobilities turn, indicating that not everything is flowing and not everything is changing. In contrast, in the course of spatial mobility, cultural boundaries and social immobility can arise (Cresswell 2011; Glick-Schiller and Salazar 2013; Gupta and Ferguson 1992; Hannam et al. 2006; Salazar 2010a, 2016a, 2016b).

With the conceptual framework of guided mobility, I added a category for forms of mobility that are neither strictly bounded nor free floating. This means that my conclusions about the conditions for the outcomes of mobile experiences apply for this type of mobility specifically.

The category of guidance is grounded in fieldwork observations, where I first discovered it in the intense administrational and institutional structuring of migration and pilgrimage. Studies on tourism and pilgrimage (e.g., Badone and Roseman 2004; Bauman 1996; Salazar 2010b; Turner 1969; Turner and Turner 1973) directed my attention to the guiding function of situated representations, which I have defined as intentional, context-bounded normative images, which direct through discursive and embodied displays.

I describe these representations as "situated" because they are not only visions of Others but also embodied adoptions of cultural features of what is perceived as Otherness. In the cases presented here, in these situated representations, Othering is only partial.

Concerning this partial Othering, evidence of more positive or ambivalent images of Others that have been identified in tourism and pilgrimage is thought-provoking. Salazar (2010b) has shown that European tourists in Tanzania and Indonesia look for the strange and the exotic in its most authentic form. This corresponds with Bauman's (1996, 29–30) view that "in the tourist's world, the strange is tame, domesticated, and no longer frightens; shocks come in a package deal with safety." For tourists there is the notion of "owning" the places they visit (ibid., 30). This applies to the Indonesians' pilgrimages to Mecca, in which they aspire to take the same pictures as every other Indonesian pilgrim and bring home authentic zamzam water and represent the completion of the pilgrimage through Arab clothing. That pilgrims "own" the place they visit, in an ideational way, as Bauman has identified for tourists, is particularly relevant for Muslim attitudes to Mecca. However, apart from Indonesians' spiritual ownership of the Holy Land, there is in fact a new nuance of "ownership" in material terms because of the increased awareness of being the largest global customer in the pilgrimage business. Regarding the amalgamation of spiritual, economic, and hedonistic activities, the conflation of pilgrimage and tourism is obvious here. Therefore, the situated representations in the context of Indonesians' journeys to the Middle East must also be seen as a feature guiding Indonesians' desires to become mobile in the first place. Travel agencies and brokers make use of imaginations of the Arab world when they provide their services of explaining, instructing, indicating, advising, accompanying, and channeling. Because of this interdependence of guiding and following in the context of pilgrimage and migration, the concept of guided mobility proved to be an apt framework for analysis. The examples reaffirmed the definition of guided mobility as a form of mobility that is not totally independent, self-determined, and free-floating, nor strictly controlled, but in-between. The nuances of guided mobility exemplify the varying degrees from obedient adherence to dominant guidance, to more suggestive guidance, selective following, and deviation from guidance.

In order to find out what makes people demand guidance and what makes them follow, I looked at the cost-benefit evaluations that resemble a supply and demand logic. From my empirical findings, I confirm that anxieties (cf. Lindquist 2009), the fear of failure (cf. Kloos 2017) as well as hopes, dreams (cf. Salazar 2010a, 2010b, 2013), and aspirations to success provoke the demand for guidance. Thereby the social actor who is searching for guidance becomes an active counterpart in the guide-follower relationship. Lindquist and Salazar show that intermediaries are dependent on their customers' search for guidance. In my examples of guided mobility it is evident that guidance is not only a profitable business but also an interdependent undertaking. Asking what makes people guide and what makes others follow, it seems that the potential for access to capital is central. Those who provide guidance want to access economic capital, as shown by the example of profitable navigations in the migration and pilgrimage businesses (cf. chapter 2). Some guiding actors are furthermore interested in social capital, as leading figures, like the religious elite in Madura (cf. chapter 4). Those who follow, on the other hand, are ready to pay for guidance if the guidance leads them where they aspire to go, which is again frequently related to the desire to accumulate various forms of capital. Furthermore, social capital plays a crucial role, as the feeling of helping others, doing someone a favor, and establishing reciprocity indicate.

Apart from capital accumulation, following guidance also eases the mind in times of uncertainty and provides orientation during identity formation. Looking at research participants' biographies and with reference to Bauman (1996), Comaroff and Comaroff (2012), Götz (2016), Lindquist (2009), and Said (1978), I argue that the need for guidance is especially prevalent in times of crisis. As an example, Mas Eko, who experienced an identity crisis and aspired to become a better Muslim, seeks orientation in starting his Islamic business, or the village head of Gunungembun refers to stereotypical images of Arab Others when he wants to defend his own moral superiority in the face of rumors of his dishonest economic conduct. Migrant women who find themselves in vulnerable positions seek guidance from public and private actors and sometimes find informal, personal intermediaries more trustworthy.

On a larger societal scale, the search for appropriate ways of being Muslim can also be seen as a form of crisis and images of orientation are welcome. I have shown that many migrants and pilgrims, and even more so Indonesians who are "Arab-phobic," follow generalizing stereotypes about Arab Others in which the perceived threat of increasing conservatism or radicalization is muted by outsourcing the phenomena as a product of foreign influence and thereby creating the impression that it is controllable (cf. Said 2003, 59).

However, as mentioned above, the Othering relationship between Indonesia and the Arab world is only partial. It seems as if Othering in the form of scapegoating and xenophobia become more generalized and dehumanized when the search for guidance is triggered by anxieties over (perceived) financial and political crises, violent threats, and downward mobility. However, when Othering happens in the context of partial admiration and identification with the Other, which is the case for many persons who long to go to Mecca and see parts of Arab culture and customs as intrinsic elements of Islam, the process becomes more complex.

In conclusion, two dimensions seem to trigger the search for guidance and adherence to it: (1) the need for orientation in times of uncertainties and crisis, and (2) the interest in accumulation and transformation of various forms of capital. This latter aspect includes social capital and the obligations in social relationships. In the context of migrants' and pilgrims' experiences of guided mobility, on an individual basis the sphere of capital accumulation appears to be more significant. However, considering the overall pressure on Muslims to position themselves in the global "crisis of Islam" (Lewis 2004) in a post-9/11 world, the orientation for self-identification as modern Muslims and distancing from radicalism is also relevant. This applies not only for the context of the guided mobility of migrants and pilgrims but for Indonesian society more generally, as I have shown in the examples of Arab-phobia and Othering narratives among related groups of research participants (cf. chapter 3). The examples from the everyday lifeworlds of migrants and pilgrims underline that representations and localizations of the Arab world carry meaning within the local context. Actions and narratives of admiring or rejecting Arabness are not directed at Arab people in the Middle East but at local opponents.

Interrelations of Spatial, Social, and Cultural Mobility

For the example of guided mobility, I conclude that the experience of guidance and the interdependence between guiding and following are of crucial relevance for social and cultural mobility. Social mobility occurs in accordance with the political, economic, cultural, and religious structures in migrants' and pilgrims' home communities. Therefore, it seems that social actors have to adhere to local logic in order to experience upward mobility. Spatial mobility can serve as a medium through which to access capital that can be invested and transformed in the local context. Yet the mobility only becomes meaningful through translations of mobile experiences.

In experiences of guided mobility there is an intertwinement of the spatial, social, and cultural spheres. Social capital, in the form of the possession of material goods and social relationships, like contact with intermediaries, is essential to arranging spatial mobility. The completion of spatial mobility can in turn enhance the accumulation of social capital because of bonding experiences through joint physical movement and physical presence at meaningful places and access to blessings. However, social mobility is dependent on guiding normative discourses and the actors' engagement with these discourses. As a matter of fact, the guiding discourses often concern cultural values. This can mean that adherence to and reproduction of cultural values and customs is crucial to experiencing upward social mobility.

The importance of local rituals in the context of pilgrimages and the discursive distancing from Arab Others indicates that cultural continuity is a widespread result of experiences of guided spatial mobility. Social mobility can in turn effect subtle cultural change, and thus cultural mobility. Once persons experience upward mobility, they are eager to maintain their social status through the continuous demonstration of cultural customs and values, like displays of Arabness. If the social positions are especially contested or if persons fear a decline in their status, this can lead to the tendency to seek to outperform one another, which entails cultural change in the end, as in the example of Madurese Arabization and widespread Pop Arabness. In both cases, the actors appear to fear downward mobility—the new urban middle classes as well as the local elite in Madura.

Thus, in the context of guided mobility, physical movement is an opportunity for guidance. It is the guidance of mobility that enhances the aspired social and cultural effects. Yet the physical mobility of migrants and pilgrims legitimizes the blurring of boundaries, which means that the journey remains crucial in the ritual process and upward mobility. Despite its importance, guidance itself, without the act of becoming mobile, would be pointless. In this sense, the concept of guided mobility shares Turner's (1969) understanding of a ritual process in which a time of antistructure is necessary for restructuring—mobility is necessary for the provision of guidance and its social effects.

Translations at the Margins

In hegemonic mappings of the world, which for instance include Western as well as Saudi Arabian perspectives, Indonesia is located at the margins—as the periphery of the Muslim world and as a country in the Global South. I have argued that the Othering from the periphery is partial, selective, and ambivalent, as the centers remain places of longing and admiration. This research project has shown this for specific groups of people and regions in Indonesia, and thereby corresponds to findings on Indonesians' attitudes toward the West (cf. Schlehe 2013b, Schlehe et al. 2013). The practice of Othering in this constellation is a translational process in which Indonesians relate to hegemonic knowledge as well as their own experiences. This hints at the impact of global and local power structures. The selection of guidance is not arbitrary but underlies these power structures. Agency is possible in these power constellations; however, in the examples at hand, people in peripheral positions do not challenge the existing social order but in contrast seek guidance, which maintains it.

In the case study, the center-periphery divide between Indonesia and the Middle East is not the only hierarchical divide. There is also the center-periphery divide between Central Java, the alleged cultural heart of Indonesia, and Madura, one of the most remote areas, where the kyai are a much more important point of reference than the government in Jakarta. Furthermore, the social divide between migrants and pilgrims represents another example of centrality and marginality.

The center-periphery divides (in plural) exist on various levels and enforce the argument that propagations by national actors are directed at local Others, like actors at the Indonesian peripheries in Aceh or Madura. Similarly, middle-class pilgrims' adoption of Arab style is a medium of demarcation from the rural poor. In response to these notions of providing guidance as well as Othering from those at the center, the actors at the periphery are eager to make sense of the guiding discourses and cope with perceived inferiority. In their precarious position, being dependent on those higher up the social ladders, their dealing with Others is an act of "interpretative labor" (Graeber 2012) in which they establish understanding of those at the top and concomitantly distinguish themselves from them, establishing resilience. Interpretative labor can mark a deviation from the mainstream, from leading discourses, inspiring a diversification of views and reflection. Yet, this deviation from leading actors and elements is subtle and does not always result in a substantial questioning of the existing social order. The interpretative skills, as in the case of labor migrants in Central Java, allow a certain maneuvering between guiding discourses but generally the actors remain obedient to authorities. Because of the element of understanding inherent in interpretative labor, there is also empathy for those in superior positions (Graeber 2012, 199). Thus, even though interpretative labor can inspire deviations from the continuity-enhancing guided mobility, it is also unlikely to lead to substantial change.

At the outset of this research project, I presumed that the insights about how Indonesians imagine the Arab world would support the argument that contemporary cultural orientations are marked by pluralism and multipolarity. The relevance of South-South relationships appeared to be especially crucial in this regard, challenging hegemonic mappings of the world that still conceptualize it in binary oppositions. Even though I am still convinced that this is the case, I would relativize the aspect of *challenged* mappings of the world. The question of whether perspectives from the margins really challenge dominant representations of the world depends on the scope of influence of these perspectives from the margins. Research participants often impressed me with their self-confidence and claims that Indonesian Muslims are emerging as an international model for the realization of a modern, harmonious, pluralist and enlightened Islamic tradition, their ideas of an Indonesianization of the Middle East, and their interpretations of history, which foreground the Islamic roots of Western civilization. These very self-confident appraisals were remarkably widespread among migrants and pilgrims of different sociocultural backgrounds. However, the local and global power structures do have an impact on the scope of agency that can result from interpretative labor. Indonesians do not currently occupy leading positions in international committees like the Organization of Islamic Cooperation (OIC), nor in the Council of Senior Scholars at Al-Azhar University or preacher positions in the holy mosque in Mecca. Similarly, on the local level, labor migrants are not in the financial or structural position to become trend-setters in Islamic lifestyles, and nor are the Madurese people. Their moving on side roads remains marginal, yet not without impact.

Most studies, in a sense including my own, look at influence from centers to the peripheries. I have tried to overcome this tendency by showing that Indonesians' engagement with an imagined Arab world is not so much about influence from outside but about home-inspired circulations that cover a transnational spatial distance.

These insights on inner-Indonesian dynamics enhancing a change of Islamic lifestyles—both on the local level among ordinary people and in relation to public evolvements—is a first step in tackling the wider workings of these changes, be they increasingly conservative, traditional, modern, or liberal. The examples in this book show that increasing conservatism grows from within Indonesia and largely works within the established hierarchies. Change emerges especially in the endeavor to access capital, both among pilgrims and migrants on the ground and within politics. Tendencies to outperform others can lead to the normalization and institutionalization of conservative values while simultaneously maintaining sociocultural continuity.

A second step would be the evaluation of the impact of changing Indonesian Islamic lifestyles—both conservative and pluralist or liberal ones—beyond Indonesia. As I have shown, most discourses are directed at opponents and competitors within Indonesia. However, it would be worth investigating their transregional impact. Evidence from Abaza (2011), Fealy (2014), and Mandal (2014) indicates that apart from being a new tourist destination, Southeast Asia appears to be of minor relevance for decision makers in the Middle East. Whether there is another perception among other segments of Middle Eastern societies would be an interesting case to unravel. From my own findings, I can suggest that apart from speculations about Middle Eastern consideration of Indonesian solutions, the official Indonesian public discourses are not directed at the Middle East. Therefore I argue that the potential of concepts like Islam Nusantara as pioneering models, among other things, depends on (1) their intended direction and (2) transregional power structures and alliances. The research findings in this project indicate that propagations of Islam Nusantara on a national level, as well as migrants' and pilgrims' mockery of Arab Others, are directed at domestic opponents and serve as a coping strategy in the face of perceived inferiority or affirmation of one's own status, rather than speaking to an international audience—with the exception of speaking to me, the Western researcher. The multifarious and in some cases nuanced Indonesian representations of Arabness and of the Arab world contradict hegemonic conceptions of centers and peripheries, but do not challenge them radically. In some regards, the Indonesian mappings of the world actually reproduce hegemonic discourses, for example concerning racial stereotypes about "harsh Arabs," "uncivilized Africans," and "exotic Indonesians," all of which are images that are similar to Said's uncovering of orientalist images (e.g., Said 2003, 48). Furthermore, the evidence of this multipolarity does not mean that in the course of increased South-South engagement greater cultural cosmopolitanism and curiosity or counterestablishment ideas emerge. It is because of the demand for guidance that the outcome of guided mobility is cultural continuity and only gradual change. What applies to Indonesians' interpretative labor in dealing with the Middle East as the center of the Muslim world and with the West as a hegemonic global player applies to interpretative labor from the margins of Indonesian society as well.

Interestingly, the outcomes of interpretative labor differ here. Javanese migrant women establish an understanding and empathy for those who exclude them from belonging (the Indonesian middle class, their employers' families) and diplomatically move on a side road. In Madura, Madurese brokers are engaged in interpretative labor as intermediary actors, taking a leading role themselves. Yet the Madurese case is not marked by abrupt change either, since the guidance that people seek to undercut is replaced by another form of guidance that leaves little room for alternative interpretations. Madura remains a very guidance-oriented society, with significant influence of the kyai as leaders of society. These examples highlight that Indonesian attitudes to the Middle East and to Arabness cannot be generalized, and nor does interpretative labor function the same way everywhere. The specific circumstances are relevant.

Interpretative labor and translations from the margins, which describe actions that maneuver gradually and do not radically challenge the status quo in society, are useful concepts for understanding more about peoples' scope of agency and their worldviews. The potential changes in the course of these interpretations might be subtle. As an example, Indonesians' self-understanding as international pioneers for Islamic lifestyle may not be recognized in official international forums in the near future, but their subtle influence might include the soft power of Asian favorites in souvenir shops in Mecca, Indonesian headscarf fashions in Dubai's shopping malls, or halal certification in tourism. Yet, in the same manner, the politicization of religion can look like a mere change of cultural markers for strategic reasons but ultimately leads to the normalization of certain ideologies—even if they were initially only adopted for the purpose of outperforming opponents. Even if these ideologies are only a matter of political gambling and are symbolic rather than filled with content, coming in tweet length, as one of my research participants put it, they have structural effects, manifesting in laws and accepted practices.

Whether or not contemporary guidance in Indonesia will serve blind obedience or nuanced reflection also depends on the guiding actors' ability to provide room for different interpretations of Islamic lifestyles without excluding minorities and those at the margins of society. Furthermore, it depends on whether leading actors provide real perspectives for the access to material and social capital for those who follow them, or resort to spread essentialist guiding images that promise the quick support of voters and clients.

Coming back to the case study, even though Indonesian migrants and pilgrims move on guided paths, the constellation of guiding and following leaves room for personal interpretation when people feel secure and have access to social and financial capital. Subtle traces of interpretative labor and reflexivity surfaced especially in research participants' humor, including self-mockery. The statement at the beginning of this book about prophets' presence in the Middle East indicates that Indonesian evaluations can be playful, humorous, and self-aware. For some people, this self-confidence mitigates the need for guided mobility.

Glossary of Terms and Abbreviations

'alim **(pl.:** ***ulama*****)** religious scholar(s)

abangan Indonesian Muslims whose practices are described as traditionalist and syncretic

abaya long robes, commonly worn by women in the Middle East

'adat/adat local and oral traditions, customary law

AH Anno Hijria, Islamic calculation of times

akik stones with alleged supernatural powers

al-haramayn the two sanctuaries (Mecca and Medina)

ALKACO abbreviation standing for *Aliran Kathok Congklang*, literally, the "short trousers faction," referring to the *salafi* style of wearing trousers that go just to the top of the ankles

Asrama Haji government-run transit centers for Indonesian pilgrims

'aura Islamic theological concept of intimate bodily features that should not be exposed in public or in front of the other sex

Bapak Indonesian equivalent for Mr., literally, "father"; common formulae for addressing male adults

bid'a Islamic theological concept concerning heretical innovations

BNP2TKI Badan Nasional Penempatan dan Perlindungan Tenaga Kerja Indonesia, National Body of the Placement and Protection of Indonesian Labor Migrants, ministerial branches for the placement and protection of Indonesian labor migrants at the national level

BP3TKI Balai Pelayanan Penempatan dan Perlindungan Tenaga Kerja Indonesia, Service Unit for the Placement and Protection of Indonesian Labor Migrants, a ministerial branch for the placement and protection of Indonesian labor migrants at the provincial level

da'wa invitation to Islam/religious missions in Islam

dangdut popular Indonesian music

DepAg Departemen Agama, Department of Religion, subdivision of the Indonesian Ministry of Religious Affairs

dhikr Sufi ritual, meditative recitation of mystic formulas that aim at increasing proximity to God

Dinas Tenaga Kerja dan Transmigrasi Service Unit for Manpower and Transmigration, local subdepartment of the Ministry of Manpower and Transmigration

fiqh Islamic jurisprudence

ǧāhilīya pre-Islamic time of ignorance

gambus a lute with twelve strings, which originated from Yemen and was established in Malaysia and Indonesia

gamelan Javanese percussion orchestra

GOLKAR abbreviation for Partai Golongan Karya (Party of Functional Groups)

guru ngaji worship teacher, a person who is held religiously educated

habib **(pl.:** ***habaib*****)** synonym for *sa'īd* (plural *sādah*) as a title of honor for descent from the Prophet Muhammad, literally meaning "darling" in Arabic

haddrah rhythmical singing in Islamic worship, accompanied by so called *rébanah* drums and choreography

Hadhrami Indonesians of descent from the Hadhramaut (Yemen)
haji mabrur theological concept of the hajj being accepted by God
haji Indonesian synonym for hajj
hajiphobia anxieties in the Dutch colonial administration about subversive powers being strengthened by returning pilgrims
hajj major pilgrimage in Islam, one of the five pillars of Islam and obligatory for every Muslim who is physically, financially, and spiritually able to accomplish it
hajja title of honor for female hajj returnees
hajji title of honor for male hajj returnees
halal permissible, allowed, or preferred in reference to Islamic values
haram forbidden or unmoral in reference to Islamic values
haramayn see *al-haramayn*
Hejaz region on the western coast of the Arabian Peninsula, territory of the holy sites in Mecca and Medina
hidāyah Arabic for "guidance," a theological concept of having experienced being guided by God (Indonesian: *hidayah*)
hijrah exodus from un-Islamic regions to Islamic ones, historically the exodus of the Prophet Muhammad from Mecca to Medina
hijriah Islamic calculation of time, beginning with the *hijrah* from Mecca to Medina in 622 CE (or the year 1 AH)
HTI Hizb-ut Tahrir Indonesia, Indonesian branch of the international fundamentalist Sunni organization Ḥizb at-Taḥrīr (Party of Liberation)
Ibu Indonesian for Mrs., literally meaning "mother," common formulae for addressing female adults
idul adha Islamic feast of sacrifice
iḥrām state of ritual purity in the hajj and umrah
imtihan annual feast at *pesantren,* derived from Arabic *imtīḥān* (examination)
Islam Jawa Javanese Islam, label for a distinctive local tradition of Islam on Java
Islam Nusantara Islam of the Archipelago, concept on Indonesian Islamic thought and practice, promoted by NU
Islam Pesisir Islamic tradition in coastal regions in Indonesia
Islam Pribumi Islam of the Natives, concept on indigenous Islamic customs, propagated by NU
istiġfār Islamic prayer for forgiveness and repentance
jawi/jawi people label under which Southeast Asians residing in the Middle East between the seventeenth and nineteenth centuries were subsumed
Ka'aba cubic building in the Masjid al-Haram in Mecca considered as House of God, destination of the pilgrimage and direction for prayers
KBIH *Kelompok Bimbingan Ibadah Haji,* Cluster for Hajj Guidance
Kejawen Javanese religion/worldview
khaol commemoration of deceased people, more than a thousand days after their death
kitab derived from Arabic, literally meaning book, in Indonesian referring to religious books
kloter abbreviation for *kelompok terbang,* flying groups, cluster of Mecca pilgrims by the Indonesian government consisting of approximately four hundred persons
Kraton palace of the sultan in Yogyakarta
KTKLN *Kartu Tenaga Kerja Luarnegri,* Overseas Workers Card
kufiah red-white or black-white checkered cloth, common headdress on the Arabian Peninsula and throughout the Middle East, symbol of Palestinian nationalism and solidarity with Palestine

kyai meaning teacher or master, Javanese title of honor that is mainly but not exclusively used in Islamic contexts

LP3TKI Loka Pelayanan Penempatan dan Perlindungan Tenaga Kerja Indonesia, Workshop for the Placement and Protection of Indonesian Labor Migrants, a ministerial branch for the placement and protection of Indonesian labor migrants at the regional level

madhab **(pl.:** ***maḏāhib*****)** schools of Islamic thought, the four biggest and most widely acknowledged schools in Sunni Islam are the Hanafi, Maliki, Shafi'i and Hanbali schools

malu feeling of shame

manasik preparation courses for the pilgrimage

Masjid al-Haram holy mosque in Mecca

Masjid an-Nabawi the Prophet's mosque in Medina, second holiest place in Islam after Masjid al-Haram

Mbak Javanese form of address for unmarried women, literally meaning "older sister"

merantau (domestic) migration, describing the act of leaving one's home region

Muhammadiyah second largest Muslim organization in Indonesia, reformist/modernist

MUI Majelis Ulama Indonesia, the council of Indonesian *ulama* or religious scholars

mukimin permanent foreign residents in Saudi Arabia

mutawwif assistants who guide the *tawaf*

Nahdlatul Ulama (NU) Indonesia's largest Muslim organization, traditionalist

nasib fate

nyai female religious authority, title of a female leader of a Qur'anic boarding school

P4TKI Pos Pelayanan Penempatan dan Perlindungan Tenaga Kerja Indonesia, Post for the Placement and Protection of Indonesian Labor Migrants, ministerial branch for the placement and protection of Indonesian labor migrants at regional level

Pak see *Bapak*

pengajian recitation of the Qur'an, prayer gathering

pesantren Qur'anic school(s), Islamic boarding school(s)

PKS Partai Keadilan Sejahtera, Prosperous Justice Party

pribumi indigenous people

qibla/kiblat direction of prayer in Islam

rantau the destination of *merantau*, a place away from home where migrants reside

rébanah drums that accompany *haddrah* to give praise to God

riba Islamic theological concept of the (forbidden) application of interest

sa'īd **(pl.:** ***sādah*****)** title of honor for descendants of the Prophet Muhammad

sa'i **ritual** constituent element of the umrah and hajj rituals, running or walking between the hillocks of Safa and Marwa

santri Islam a branch of Indonesian Islamic traditions that is described as orthodox, scriptural and scholarly Islam, also referred to as *Islam pesisir* or *Islam Arab*

santri (a) students in pesantren or (b) orthodox Muslims

sholawatan popular Islamic singing, derived from Arabic, *ṣalawāt*, meaning a prayer giving praise and asking for blessings

sholawat nabi worship singing, asking God to give blessings to the Prophet

SPPH *Surat Pendaftaran Pergi Haji*, Letter of Hajj Registration

sunna words and deeds of the Prophet Muhammad, also referred to as "tradition," reference of orientation for recommended practices in Islam, conveyed through hadith compilations

talbiyah ritual phrase being used numerous times during hajj and umrah to assert the pilgrims' intention to worship God alone, transmitted through a Hadith (no. 621) by Bukhari

tasbīḥ chain of prayer beads
tawaf circumambulation of the Ka'aba, which is done anticlockwise, starting from the Eastern corner of the Ka'aba
tawḥīd Islamic theological concept of the singularity of God
Tionghoa Chinese Indonesians
ulama see *'alim*
ummah Islamic theological concept of a Muslim community
umrah sandal jepit literally: "umrah in flip flops," describing the strategy of using an umrah visa to enter Saudi Arabia and then staying there to work and/or to wait until the hajj season begins
umrah minor pilgrimage in Islam (also *umroh*)
ustadz derived from Arabic, meaning male (religious) teacher
ustadzah derived from Arabic, meaning female (religious) teacher
Wahhabism orthodox branch of Sunni thought and interpretation of Islam, widespread in Saudi Arabia
Wali Songo nine saints, who are believed to have spread Islam in Indonesia
wayang Javanese shadow puppet play
wuquf literally, "standing," stay in Muzdalifah near the mountain Arafat during the hajj, commemorating the last sermon of the Prophet Muhammad
zakāt obligatory alms, third pillar in Islam
zamzam holy well in Mecca
ziarah local pilgrimage, e.g., to the gravesites of *Wali Songo*

Notes

INTRODUCTION

1. The term *lifeworld*, or *Lebenswelt*, a sociological concept by Alfred Schütz, means everyday conceptions of the world, subjectively constructed, yet perceived as evident by social actors exhibiting an unspoken common agreement on their views of the world that therefore must be understood as intersubjectivity (see Schütz and Luckmann 1988).

2. An insightful overview of the cultural diversity of North Africa and the Middle East is provided by Dale Eickelman (2001).

3. The League of Arab States includes countries from different geographically defined regions like North Africa, the Nile Valley, the Levant, and the Arabian Peninsula, and it excludes countries within these regions or at their borders, such as the Western Sahara and Iran. Today, the League of Arab States consists of twenty-two member states.

4. Examples of such bipolar mappings of the world are Lerner's (1967) theory on modernization and Huntington's (1996) thesis on a "clash of civilizations." Other scholars have shown that globalization is marked by localizations of global phenomena (Robertson 1998), increasing cultural hybridity (Hannerz 1996), "multiple modernities" (Eisenstadt 2000) and "entangled modernities" (Randeria 2006), and the global flows of people, goods and ideas (Appadurai 1996).

5. Stuart Hall's (1992) considerations of diaspora identities in which one finds part of the Other in the self, as he himself experienced through simultaneously identifying as British and as Caribbean, were an important inspiration for the reflection about nonbipolar imaginings of selves and Others. For further theorizations of identity constructions in multicultural societies see also Baumann 1999.

6. The concept of transnationalism has been defined by Glick-Schiller et al. (1992, 11) for the study of migration as "the process by which immigrants build social fields that link together their country of origin and their country of settlement."

7. Max Weber, Alfred Schütz, Talcott Parsons, Pierre Bourdieu, and James Coleman coined sociological action theory. For an overview see Gabriel 2004.

8. Graeber applies these insights with reference to feminist standpoint theory and critical race studies, to other situations where power structures define relationships. He cites bell hooks, who described black domestic servants' psychoanalytic readings of the white Other, their employers, as a strategy for survival in a white supremacist society (hooks 1992, 165, in Graeber 2012, 118).

9. For insights about the Javanese worldview kejawen, see among others, Magnis-Suseno 1989; Schlehe 1998; and Woodward 1989.

10. The province of Central Java consists of twenty-nine regencies (*kabupaten*) and six cities (*kota*) with a total population of 33,753,023 people. The regencies and cities are further divided into districts (*kecamatan*) and subdistricts or villages (*kelurahan/desa*). The province's administrative capital is Semarang. The province of Yogyakarta consists of four regencies and one city, with a total of 3,452,390 inhabitants. While these are the administrative units that are defined by the Indonesian government, and their numbers are increasing as a result of decentralization and the splitting of administrative units, there are local terminologies referring to territorial and social entities that are not always congruent with the official administrative units. In Central Java, the most important of

these local territorial concepts is the *kampong*, the traditional neighborhood compound. The city of Yogyakarta is a multiethnic hub where people from all over Indonesia come together. The surrounding rural areas of Central Java are ethnically rather homogenous, with approximately 97 percent of the population being ethnic Javanese, but religiously slightly more heterogeneous, with about 90 percent official adherents of Islam and about 10 percent Christians, as well as Buddhist and Hindu minorities. Figures from the official government census give only a relative idea of religious affiliation. Many people claim (officially) to be Muslim, although their daily practice combines Islamic religious practice with the Javanese religion of *kejawen*.

11. This pseudonym is a merger of the Indonesian words *gunung*, meaning "mountain," and *embun*, meaning "dew."

12. For the sake of the anonymity of my research participants, I do not give information about the names of the exact places where I conducted the research, referring to the regencies but not the actual villages.

13. TKW is the abbreviation for *Tenaga Kerja Wanita*, meaning female labor migrant.

14. For an analysis of stereotypes about the Madurese, see de Jonge 1995; Rifai 2007.

15. *Kyai* is a Javanese title of honor that is not solely used in Islamic contexts and not only to refer to people, for example the Javanese *gamelan* is sometimes also called kyai.

16. Today, the clan of Shaikhona Kholil's offspring is divided into two competing camps. On one side there is the former *bupati* (regent) of Bangkalan, Kyai Fuad Amin, and his son, Makmun Ibnu Fuad, the *bupati* of Bangkalan at the time of research. During the research period, both of them have been in the news, as Fuad Amin was arrested by the Corruption Eradication Commission (Komisi Pemberantasan Korupsi, KPK) and his son was accused of drug abuse. The Fuad Amin family administrates the grave site of Shaikhona Kholil. The other side of the clan is headed by Fuad Amin's nephew, Kyai Fakhrillah, who runs the famous Pesantren Shaikhona Kholil and owns a pilgrimage travel agency.

17. *PerDa* is an abbreviation for *peraturan daerah*, which means "local regulation" or "local law."

18. The regulations initially emphasized the prohibition of alcoholic beverages, provided suggestions on Muslim clothing, and generally demanded the fulfilment of Islamic duties such as giving alms (*zakat*) and reading the Qur'an. Yet the regulations are, in contrast to the local regulations on sharia law in Aceh, rather loose, and there is no institutionalized sharia law enforcement.

19. This fictional village name is made up of the words *ladang* (field) and *tembakau* (tobacco).

1. INDONESIA AND THE ARAB WORLD, THEN AND NOW

1. However, the pilgrimage to Jerusalem is not obligatory but recommended, like the umrah, which is also referred to as a minor pilgrimage or as a "small hajj."

2. The hijrah, or exodus of the prophet Muhammad from Mecca and his refuge in Medina in 622 CE (the year 1 AH) marks the beginning of the Islamic calculation of time. In the declaration of the "Constitution of Medina" the Prophet Muhammad defined the *ummah* as a community of equals, blurring the boundaries between clans and tribes that had previously structured the social order, equating people of previously competing clans, Arabs and non-Arabs, Jews, Muslims and pagans, revolutionizing the existing social order (Netton 1993, 8).

3. It must be noted that these are scholarly centers of Sunni Islam. The four biggest and most widely acknowledged Sunni schools of Islamic thought, or *fiqh* (jurisprudence), the so called *maḏāhib*, namely the Hanafi, Maliki, Shafi'i, and Hanbali *maḏāhib*, are united in a council of *ulama* (Islamic scholars) in Al-Azhar University in Cairo. The orthodox Saudi

based Wahhabi school of thought is not represented in this council. The schism between Sunni and Shi'a Islam goes back to the conflict about the rightful successor of the prophet Muhammad. The Sunni faction put forward a new leader who practiced the religion in the tradition (the *sunna*) of the words and deeds of the Prophet Muhammad, while the party (Arabic: *shi'at*) of Ali ibn Abi Talib, the cousin and son-in-law of the Prophet Muhammad, identified family descent as the crucial feature of succession of the Prophet. Important centers of Shi'a Islam are mainly in Iran, in Qom, Isfahan, and Teheran, and in Karbala, Iraq.

4. This differentiation is rather problematic though, especially since emic and etic labels were mixed up in Clifford Geertz's (1976) classifications of Islam in Java.

5. For comprehensive overviews of Indonesian history see for example Bowen 2003; Ricklefs 2001, 2010; and Vickers 2005.

6. Yet this Indian filtering apparently took various forms, as there is evidence that traders who traveled during the lifetime of the Prophet via Kerala, on the south coast of the Indian subcontinent, continued to practice Islam in the Arabic tradition and had little contact with other Muslim communities in India, while Muslims of an Indo-Persian Sufi tradition from Deccan, northern India, spread Islam in the interior of the island of Java from the sixteenth century onward (Woodward 1989, 54).

7. Among some Indonesians, especially among the Tionghoa (Chinese Indonesians), Zheng He is an important figure, and along with temples and mosques built in honor of Zheng He in Jakarta, Cirebon, Surabaya, and Semarang (Tan 2009, 220), Chinese-style mosques have become increasingly popular in Indonesia (see Hew 2013).

8. "For Husayn, there were two fundamentally different civilisations: that which derived from Greek philosophy and art, Roman law, and the morals of Christianity, and that which derived from India. Egypt, according to Husayn, belonged to Greek-Roman civilization" (Abaza 2011, 1).

9. For a collection of historical hajj accounts see Chambert-Loir 2013.

10. Vivid examples of this intertwinement include the alliance with Ottoman Muslims against the Portuguese in the sixteenth century (von der Mehden 1993, 2), the Japanese occupation in World War II, which sought to orient Islam toward Asia (ibid.: 86), as well as Pan-Islamic independence movements in postcolonial times (Laffan 2003, 27).

11. The Dutch East India Company (*Vereenigde Oost-Indische Compagnie*; VOC, 1602–1799) was nationalized in 1800, which marks the beginning of official Dutch colonial rule in the Indonesian archipelago. Indonesian independence was recognized by the Dutch in 1949, three years after Sukarno and Hatta had proclaimed independence in 1945.

12. *Hajji* and *hajja* are titles of honor for male/female hajj returnees, the Indonesian wording *haji* can mean both hajj (pilgrimage) and hajji (returnees).

13. Bowen argues that the importance of the journey to Mecca was a transformative process and contributor to improved social status over time. Apparently, only by studying in the Holy Land are religious leaders considered to have achieved "the highest level of religious knowledge and find work as an *'alim* [religious scholar] 'back home'" (Bowen 2008, 35).

14. Besides people of Arab descent, the category of "Foreign Orientals" included people of Chinese and Indian origin. They enjoyed certain privileges and were separated from the indigenous, or *pribumi* people, by the Dutch, residing in designated areas and, along with the indigenous nobility, were encouraged to collaborate with the colonial government. This separated them from the pribumi and enhanced the sense of belonging among their community (Mandal 2014, 302). The division between indigenous (pribumi) and non-indigenous (nonpribumi) people continued to be emphasized in postcolonial Indonesia.

15. Southeast Asians were concerned about the future of the Ottoman caliphate, refusing to accept the end of the caliphate, which had been a symbol of Pan-Islamic unity.

However, after the revolution in Turkey, there was remarkable interest in the establishment of a secular Turkish nation state under Kemal Atatürk and the possibility of a Muslim society with a secular state (von der Mehden 1993, 8–10).

16. Snouck Hurgronje's reports and photographs are the most complete historical sources about Indonesians in Mecca in the nineteenth century. Yet the question of how his representation of Indonesians in the Arab world should be interpreted is still controversial today, as it is not known whether he was loyal to the Dutch colonial administration, disguising himself as a Muslim and investigating as a spy, or if he actually converted to Islam, undermining colonial rule to support fellow Muslims, as the changing of his name to Abdel Ghaffar and his so-called "Islamic policy" imply. His six-month residence in Mecca and later life in Indonesia, which is said to have followed a Muslim lifestyle, remain legendary and with many open questions (Abaza 2007, 423; Laffan 2003, 62).

17. Even though Snouck Hurgronje demystified the danger of hajj returnees, the Dutch government continued to control hajj travel and kept an eye on returning hajjis, fearing that they were returning with ideas of political rebellion (Abaza 2007, 423; Bianchi 2004, 42; Tagliacozzo 2013, 157). Snouck Hurgronje legitimized his "Islamic strategy" by arguing that too-strict surveillance and regulation could have a negative effect on the Dutch colonial rule (Bianchi 2004, 43).

18. Laffan (2003) argues that "the foundations of the jawi ecumene rested in part on the experience of alterity grounded against both foreign Muslims and European colonizers" (ibid., 233, emphasis in original).

19. Apparently, they perceived their homeland as being in a state of *ǧāhilīya*, which means a pre-Islamic time of ignorance, while Arabs were perceived as being enlightened.

20. The development of diverging streams of Islam in the Indonesian archipelago must be seen against the backdrop of world-political events at the time. While anticolonial thinking became more widespread, the Ottoman Empire's power was shrinking and after the post–World War I turbulences, the Wahhabis conquered Mecca under the Al Saud family (van Bruinessen 2015).

21. However, the modernists eventually abandoned the idea of using Arabic language for international communication in the global *ummah*, the worldwide Muslim community, and Arabic script for local languages in the Indonesian archipelago, which is known as jawi script, in favor of Latin script (Laffan 2003, 237).

22. In the declaration of independence, it was not their proposed "Jakarta Charter" that became the preamble of the constitution but the "Pancasila," which based national unity not in Allah but in monotheism more generally (Laffan 2003, 238; see also Bowen 2008, 45), recognizing Islam, Protestantism, Catholicism, Hinduism, and Buddhism as official religions.

23. "NAS" standing for "nationalism," "A" for "*agama*" (religion), and "KOM" for "communism."

24. The IOM report gives evidence that 68 percent of households spend part of the additional income from labor migration on food consumed in the home and 55 percent say they spend it on other utilities for daily needs like fuel and electricity. A similarly large number claim to send remittances for education but these investments are comparably low. Only 14 percent of migrants invest in farmland, and expenditures include the repayment of debts, deposit of savings, transportation, communication, and house maintenance (IOM 2010). There appears to be no statistical evidence for any positive effect of remittances on economic development.

25. Concerning religious remittances, Johnson and Werbner (2010) consider the significance of religion during experiences of living in a diaspora and for the potentials of norm transfer. They see sociocultural remittances as being related to the social relationships within the diaspora and the community of origin.

26. As an example, Filipino migrants who had a stronger interest in politics predominantly migrated to more democratic countries like Hong Kong, where they demanded proper labor rights and from where they were active in sending home democratic political remittances, whereas the political influence of migrants who reside in more autocratic countries like Saudi Arabia is rather minimal or even undemocratic (Kessler and Rother 2016). Another observation shows that Indonesian migrant workers are, compared to Filipino migrant workers, less active in sending home sociopolitical remittances and in being politically active in destination countries (Silvey 2004).

27. This development of commercialization and popularization concerns not only Islamic culture but religion and ethnicity in general (see Ramstedt et al. 2012; Schlehe 2012, 2014; Schlehe and Sandkühler 2014; Slama 2012; van Klinken 2003).

28. Sumit Mandal (2011, 2012, 2014) has argued that the rediscovery of "Arabness" among the Hadhrami must be seen in the context of the end of the Cold War, which led to the dissolution of the Marxist state in South Yemen and a strengthening of the connection between the Hadhrami diaspora in Southeast Asia and the region of their origin. Mobility between Yemen and Southeast Asia has further intensified after 9/11.

29. According to Machmudi's analysis, the Arabic-language newspaper *Sharq al-Awsad* reports very negatively about Indonesians while the English-language newspaper *Saudi Today* reports more objectively (Machmudi 2011, 244).

2. THE BEATEN TRACKS AND EMBEDDED RETURNS OF MIGRANTS AND PILGRIMS

1. The story is further complemented in other chapters of the Qur'an in which Ibrahim is mentioned, among others surah 14, the surah of Ibrahim. A different version of the story can be found in the Torah and the Bible, in Genesis, chapters 21–22.

2. Nevertheless, in this area turmoil and stampedes are common and caused casualties of more than two thousand persons in 2015.

3. *Mbak* is the Javanese form of address for unmarried women, literally meaning "older sister." Throughout this book, I use pseudonyms for the names of hosts and research participants, with the exception of the names of my research partners, who gave their consent to being mentioned personally, and of the names of public figures and academic experts.

4. The name "Tawhid Community" is a pseudonym. The original name of the group includes Arabic and English terms as well.

5. The Indonesian terms *Ibu* and *Pak*, or *Bapak*, literally mean "mother" and "father" and are the common formulae for addressing married adults, more generally meaning Mrs. and Mr.

6. In Indonesia, the Arabic term *ustadz* means a religious teacher. However, it has also become a popular title for televangelist.

7. The Arabic term *ikhlāṣ*, literally meaning faithfulness/loyalty/sincerity, describes a state of inner peace and devotion. It is also the name of the 112th surah of the Qur'an, al-ikhlāṣ, which concerns the concept of *tawḥīd*, the singularity of God (Gibb and Bearman 1960, EI-1).

8. *Abaya* is a traditional long robe or cloak, commonly worn in the Middle East.

9. This was also true for pilgrims, who received a pilgrimage passport, which was, however, changed in 2015, with pilgrims now being granted a normal passport.

10. The ministerial branches for the placement and protection of Indonesian labor migrants have subunits at the national, provincial, and regional levels which are BNP2TKI = Badan Nasional Penempatan dan Perlindungan Tenaga Kerja Indonesia (National Body of the Placement and Protection of Indonesian Labor Migrants), BP3TKI = Balai Pelayanan Penempatan dan Perlindungan Tenaga Kerja Indonesia (Service

Unit for the Placement and Protection of Indonesian Labor Migrants), LP3TKI = Loka Pelayanan Penempatan dan Perlindungan Tenaga Kerja Indonesia (Workshop for the Placement and Protection of Indonesian Labor Migrants), P4TKI = Pos Pelayanan Penempatan dan Perlindungan Tenaga Kerja Indonesia (Post for the Placement and Protection of Indonesian Labor Migrants).

11. The organizational matters are further described by Hooker (2008, 205–43) and Bianchi (2004, 175–210).

12. The waiting periods vary between different regions. In Yogyakarta province, a person that registered for the hajj in 2016 will receive a departure date in 2038, in Central Java the estimated departure would be 2037 and in East Java 2039.

13. The overview of the costs and payment procedures for umrah and hajj are based on online research using the data that is provided by the Ministry of Religious Affairs, visits to travel agencies, reviews of travel magazines and advertisements, and informal conversations with travel guides, as well as participation in umrah and hajj preparation courses in Central Java and Madura. The conversion to US dollars is based on exchange rates at the time of research.

14. The exact costs for the hajj vary slightly between the different provinces and are announced for the twelve Indonesian embarkation centers which are Aceh, Medan, Batam, Padang, Palembang, Jakarta, Solo, Surabaya, Banjarmasin, Balikpapan, Makassar, and Lombok. In 2015, the price for embarkation from Solo, where pilgrims from Central Java depart, was US $2,769 and for Surabaya, the gateway for pilgrims from Madura, was US $2,801 (Ministry of Religious Affairs 2016b).

15. The campaign 5 Pasti Umroh is meant to achieve more transparency and accountability of travel agencies. The term *pasti* is an abbreviation of *pastikan* (to make sure) and refers to five aspects that umrah travelers should check before registration. These are (1) the license of the travel agency, (2) a secure itinerary with a return ticket, (3) the prices and tour package components (carefully investigating what services the packages include and that they are complete), (4) making sure the accommodation is convenient and close to the ritual sites, and (5) ensuring that visas have been acquired (Ministry of Religious Affairs 2016a).

3. ARAB OTHERS ABROAD AND AT HOME

1. Schlehe shows that there is little interest in the neighboring Southeast Asian countries and only limited identification with Asia (Schlehe 2013b, 497, 512). Morality and values are what make identification as Asian significant (ibid., 512).

2. Hew (2012) has shown that recently there has been a general interest in Chinese Muslim Indonesians' harmonization of Chineseness and Islam.

3. R.T. is an abbreviation for *rukun tetangga* and entitles the neighborhood chief, the lowest administrational entity in the political hierarchy in Indonesia. Usually, the post of R.T. is a voluntary side activity, without payment or only minor allowances. The R.T. provides his signature for administrative issues, especially regarding population administration like issuing a *surat domisili* (a letter of residence), one of the documents that is needed to acquire an ID card as well as marriage certificates, passports, and so on. The R.T. reports to the R.W. (*rukun warga*), who administers several neighborhoods, and to the *lurah* (headman) or *kepala desa* (village head) of the village.

4. The examples from Indonesian cinema that I give in the following section are the result of joint analysis with Evi Eliyanah, in which we focused on gendered moral visions of Arab Others on- and offscreen (see Eliyanah and Lücking 2017).

5. Besides *kampong* romanticism, the series features religious topics and was initially produced as a Ramadan special. During Ramadan 2008, the second season of *Upin and*

Ipin was watched by 1.5 million viewers on TV9 in Malaysia, making it the second most watched animated series behind *SpongeBob*. Since then, eight seasons have been released, and the series enjoys vast popularity in Indonesia and Malaysia (Saputro 2011).

6. In his pivotal work on Chinese Muslim identities in Malaysia and Indonesia, Hew Wai Weng (2012) notes that the commercialized and popularized features of "lifestyle Islam" and "lifestyle Chineseness" are sometimes detached from theological content and the different doctrines' interpretations of Islam. He argues: "The commodification of identities has paradoxical outcomes—the diversity of appearances does not always mean a plurality of discourses" (Hew 2012, 179).

7. An example is Ustadz Ahmad Al-Habsyi, one of the so called habib, who trace their descent back to the Prophet Muhammad's bloodline, many of whom are popular and influential public figures.

8. On the role of the Indian (Sindhi) ethnic minority in Indonesian television productions see Myutel 2016.

9. This recent trend of internet-based religious activities has been investigated by Slama, Parvanova, Husein, and Eva Nisa. Among other things, Slama and his colleagues reveal the dialogic aspect of internet-based religious activities (Slama 2017).

10. Most Indonesians appear to access Facebook with their mobile phones, as the percentage of Facebook users accessing the site on their phone was higher in Indonesia than in any other country under study (eMarketer 2015).

11. The Infaq Dakwah Center is a conservative Muslim organization that collects alms.

12. This is an example of how the term *Arab* is used in reference to different streams of Islam, as the Arabs from Yemen are quite different from the Arabic culture adopted by the female graduates of the Infaq Dakwah Center's training program.

13. This goes hand in hand with a recent controversy over Islamic fashion in Malaysia, where the collection of *Jubbah Pahlawan* (Warrior's Jubbah) caused some controversy. The Arabic jubbah was redesigned in bright colors, adjusted to an "Asian" taste. The pictures of "muscular male models wearing the form-fitting robes went viral and drew scorn on social media. Syubaili Aziz, founder of Farbel Exclusive, said he was unfazed by comments that called the male models gay or compared the brightly colored robes—in lime green and pink, among other colors—to women's clothing" (Su-Lyn 2016).

4. ALTERNATIVE ROUTES IN MADURA AND TRANSLATIONAL MOMENTS IN JAVA

1. K-Pop is an abbreviation for Korean Pop and refers to the genre of popular music from South Korea. The globalization of the popularity of Korean pop music and the fashion accompanying this music is called *hallyu* or the Korean Wave (see Choi and Maliangkay 2015). In Indonesia hallyu has been popular since 2002, especially with regard to music, movies, TV series, games, and fashion (Nugroho 2014, 19).

2. Killias shows that the intimacy of cohabitation and the Indonesian nannies' closeness to the Malaysian children represents a threat to Malaysian employers and to the Malaysian nation-state, which seeks to draw boundaries and emphasize Malaysian identity in contrast to Indonesian culture in both private and public rhetoric; this marks a friction between two countries that were formerly labeled "kin states" (Killias 2014, 885). "Working-class 'Indon-maids' are constructed as culturally distinct through a rhetoric of othering, and the proximity to the Malaysian children they look after is being constructed as a threat to the children's belonging to the Malaysian nation-state" (Killias 2014, 886).

3. Madura is generally compared with Sicily because of influential family networks and their informal rule.

4. The *tasbīḥ* is a chain of prayer beads. It usually consists of thirty-three or ninety-nine prayer beads that are used to mark repetitions in prayer, like the repetition of the ninety-nine sacred names of Allah (Schimmel 1995, 241; Schimmel 2008, 20).The tasbīḥ is particularly popular in Sufi Islam and in pilgrimage rituals. It is used throughout the Islamic world by nearly all Muslim groups except the Wahhabis in Saudi Arabia "who disapprove of it as a *bid'a* [heretical innovation] and who count the repetition of the sacred names on their hands" (Wensinck 2012, emphasis added).

5. Arabic: *baraka/barakāt*; Indonesian: *barokah/berkah/berkat*

6. Tracing the line of master-servant/teacher-student relationships is regarded as important in Indonesia. Standing in the line of a famous kyai is, for instance, prestigious and in the pesantren world in Indonesia people count the generation of students as having studied under famous kyai. One of these famous kyai is Shaikhona Kholil, the founder of the Pesantren Shaikhona Kholil in Bangkalan. My Madurese research participants argued that almost all influential religious leaders in Indonesia, for instance, the leading figures of NU and Muhammadiyah, had been educated in the line of Shaikhona Kholil.

7. The idea of knowledge in Islam is connected to belief. The pre-Islamic time is regarded as *ğāhilīya*, as the period of ignorance. Knowledge, consequently, refers to the conversion to Islam, which is the first essential step in gaining knowledge (Wan Daud 1989, 13). The word *islām* literally means submission, which is taken as an argument for the relation between knowledge and hierarchies. Yet there is a hierarchy of different forms of knowledge, especially in Sufism. Every male and female Muslim is obliged to obtain *'ilm* (knowledge), which means the knowledge that is necessary to perform religious duties (Schimmel 2008, 35f). This corresponds with the Indonesian differentiation between *ilmu* and *pengetahuan*. Both terms literally mean "knowledge," yet ilmu carries the connotation of experience and is used in reference to religion, mysticism, and wisdom, whereas pengetahuan refers to sciences and information. Moreover, it is believed that it is not books or teachers that provide true insight; not intellectual knowledge but existential experience (Schimmel 2008, 9). It is said that some Sufi threw away all their books after they experienced the presence of God (ibid., 35). Qur'an recitation is probably the most central method of experiential learning. Since the text is regarded as sacred, its memorization itself is regarded as a spiritual experience. The prophet Muhammad, who was presumably illiterate, is seen as the purest vessel for God's word (ibid., 13).

8. *Dhikr* is a Sufi ritual focused on remembering God (Schimmel 1995, 238), trying to get closer to ultimate truth (ibid., 241). The ritual is a collective recitation of the ninety-nine names of Allah (ibid., 252f), the first part of the *shahada*, the Islamic creed "lā ilāha illā 'Llāh" ("There is no god but God") and sometimes an endless repetition of the word *Allāh*, which becomes a rhythmical breathing, until eventually only the last letter of the word, the *h*, is pronounced by the participants in hushed rhythmical breathing (Schimmel 2008, 19).

9. The Arabic term *imtīhān* literally means examination, test, or trial. The Indonesianized version *imtihān* refers to the end-of-the-year feast or anniversary of a pesantren. Many pesantren organize a big celebration at least once a year, a festivity of reunion for all alumni and a gathering of the community near the pesantren, the *santri* (pupils) and the *santri's* parents.

10. *Khaol* celebrations sometimes take place at the graves of saints. People pray at the grave and replace the cloth that covers the tomb (van Doorn-Harder 2012, EI2). The Madurese khaol celebrations are similar to the Javanese practice of *tahlilan*, which is a prayer for the deceased, held 7, 40, 100, and 1,000 days after death. After the remembrance of the thousandth day after death, rich and influential people hold a khaol once a year, usually on the anniversary of the death, or, as I observed in Madura, during Ramadan.

11. Sholawatan refers to popular Islamic singing, and was established in the Middle East, Andalusia, North Africa and later on in Southeast Asia. It derives from Arabic, *ṡalawāt*, meaning a prayer giving praise and asking for blessings.

12. As *safar ilā ziyārat al-ḳubūr*, the "journeying to visit graves," ziarah exemplifies a specific form of travel in Islam (Meri 2012, EI2). While initially ziarah might have been explicitly connected to grave sites, it is now also used for the visitation of other holy places like caves, mountains, wells, mosques, or even the prophet Muhammad's sandal, as well as visiting living holy and learned individuals in search of "piety, learning, spiritual insight and *baraka*" (Meri 2012, EI2). The idea of gaining new knowledge, new wisdom, and blessings by journeying is inherent in Islamic conceptions of travel in general (Eickelman and Piscatori 1990) and in the specific form of ziarah even more. In Indonesia, there are various ziarah customs with a varying degree of attachment to Islam. In particular, pilgrimages in the *kejawén* tradition draw on Islamic as well as Javanese belief systems. The pilgrimage to the local pilgrimage sites is usually determined by a complex system of coinciding weekly cycles based on the Muslim and Javanese calendars. The nights prior to Fridays (*jumat*), when the first day of the five-day Javanese week (*kliwon*) coincides with the Muslim week of seven days (*Jumaat Kliwon*), are believed to be times when the power of tombs is especially potent (van Doorn-Harder 2012, EI2).

13. In the *ḥanbalī* school of jurisprudence as well as in Wahhabism, which are the leading schools of Islamic thought in Saudi Arabia, ziarah is considered to be a heretical innovation (*bid'a*), as idolatry and polytheism. While the Shafi'i school, the leading school of Islamic law in Southeast Asia, classifies visiting saints' graves as *mandub* (recommended), the Wahhabis in Saudi Arabia denounce this practice as *makrūh* (disapproved). During the early twentieth century, Wahhabi Muslims destroyed the monuments that stood over the tombs of the companions of the prophet throughout the Hejaz to prevent them from being worshipped (Meri 2012, EI2).

14. As an example, *Ar-Rahman* (The All-Compassionate), *Ar-Rahim* (The All-Merciful), *Al-Malik* (The Absolute Ruler), *Al-Quddus* (The Holy One), *As-Salam* (The Source of Peace).

15. The local terms for addressing siblings are *kakak* (Indonesian: older sibling), *mbak/nduk* (Javanese: older sister) and *mas/tole* (Javanese: older brother), or *cebbing* (Madurese: older sister) and *kacong* (Madurese: older brother). These Indonesian, Javanese, and Madurese kinship terms apply when a young peer, not necessarily a family member, of same or higher status is addressed.

16. The question of the admissibility of music is controversially discussed throughout the Muslim world (Salhi 2014, 5). Even though music and performance have been important in the history of Islam from its beginning, there is no general consensus on the role of music. Kamal Salhi elaborates on the distinction between *musiqa* (Arabic for music) and *handasat al-sawt* (the art of sound) in the Arab Muslim world. The latter is a term used by "Arab Muslims to separate the Muslim conception of music from that held in the Western and non-Muslim world," that is regarded as questionable or disreputable (Salhi 2014, 2). While some Muslims fear the "paranormal intoxicating power of music and prohibit it as a tool of the devil," others "find music inspiring and entirely spiritual" (ibid., 5).

17. Building on the findings of Sachs (1940), Kunst (1968), and Picken (1975), ethnomusicologist Larry Hilarian (2004) points out that while the arrival of the gambus in Muslim Southeast Asia is typically connected to the spread of Islam, there were many Malays, especially in Sabah, Sarawak, Brunei, and Kalimantan, who strongly believe that the gambus *Melayu* was of Malay origin, as opposed to gambus *Hadhramaut* (Hilarian 2004, 15). He maintains that there is no exact proof of how the gambus arrived in *alam Melayu*, but since the instrument was already highly developed when introduced into the Malay Archipelago, it most probably originated from outside the region. Hilarian

regards evidence pointing toward the contribution of Muslims from Persia and Arabia in the transmission of the gambus to the Malay Archipelago as substantial and conclusive (Hilarian 2004, 16). The adoption and modification of gambus music was particularly popular in the triangle of Aceh-Johor-Riau. In this vital axis of trade, commerce, and intermarriage, musical styles were shared and developed further (Hilarian 2004, 10).

18. Female singing, and the raising of female voice in general, is a controversially discussed issue in Islamic schools of thought. The female voice is considered part of the female *'aura*, meaning something intimate, and should therefore not be exposed in public. After al-Qardawi, one of the leading and quite controversial Islamic scholars and TV preachers whose TV shows are broadcast on al-Jazeera, issued a fatwa (religious ruling) that permits female singing, there was once again a debate within Islamic religious circles "where playing music and singing were perceived for long as forbidden by the Shariah law" (al-Shibeeb 2010). Other leading Islamic scholars, for instance from al-Azhar University, have divided opinions about female singing, some of them condemning it completely while others allow it when it serves religious purposes (ibid., 2010). It also matters if the audience is male, female or mixed.

19. Female singing is common in many regions and traditions in Indonesia. In the Javanese *wayang* shadow puppet play there are famous female *dalang* (puppeteers/storytellers) and also in cultural traditions that have Islamic themes, like the *saman* dance of the Gayo people in Aceh.

20. The Arabic term *tajwīd* refers to rules for the pronunciation of Arabic in Qur'an recitation.

21. In spite of the decline of Wahhabism in Madura, Saudi Arabia tries to exert influence through financial aid for mosque and mushollah buildings and scholarships for education. The Saudi's counterparts in Madura are factions who favor Wahhabi thought or those who have a pragmatic approach and take the money while ignoring the ideology of the donors. My research participant Pak Malik explained that many people happily take the donations from the Gulf in a pragmatic way. As an example, he mentioned books that are distributed by the Saudi Arabian government during the pilgrimage. Indonesians, he argued, were more interested in the colorful book cover, rather than the content of this literature (personal communication October 15, 2014). This was also the case with the Saudi financed mushollah on the family compound in Ladangtembakau, where I resided.

22. As an example, up to 2010, in seven of the thirteen Indonesian regencies that had introduced sharia regulations, the secular party GOLKAR was the driving force behind the regulations (Ubaidillah 2010, 31–34).

References

Abaza, Mona. 1991. "Some Research Notes on Living Conditions and Perceptions Among Indonesian Students in Cairo." *Journal of Southeast Asian Studies* 22 (2): 347–60. https://doi.org/10.1017/S0022463400003921.

Abaza, Mona. 1993. *Changing Images of Three Generation of Azharites in Indonesia*. Pasir Panjang: Institute of Southeast Asian Studies.

Abaza, Mona. 1994. *Islamic Education, Perception and Changes: Indonesian Students in Cairo*. Paris: Cahiers d'Archipel 23.

Abaza, Mona. 2003. "Indonesian Azharites, Fifteen Years Later." *Sojourn: Journal of Social Issues in Southeast Asia* 18 (1): 139–53.

Abaza, Mona. 2004. "Markets of Faith: Jakartan Da'wa and Islamic Gentrification." *Archipel* 67 (1): 173–202.

Abaza, Mona. 2007. "More on the Shifting Worlds of Islam. The Middle East and Southeast Asia: A Troubled Relationship?" *Muslim World* 97 (3): 419–36.

Abaza, Mona. 2011. "Asia Imagined by the Arabs." In *Islamic Studies and Islamic Education in Contemporary Southeast Asia*, edited by Kamaruzzaman Bustamam-Ahmad and Patrick Jory, 1–28. Kuala Lumpur: Yayasan Ilmuwan.

Acharya, Amitav. 2004. "How Ideas Spread: Whose Norms Matter? Norm Localization and Institutional Change in Asian Regionalism." *International Organization* 58 (2): 239-275. https://doi.org/10.1017/S0020818304582024.

Adams, Richard H., and Alfredo Cuechecha. 2010. "The Economic Impact of International Remittances on Poverty and Household Consumption and Investment in Indonesia." The World Bank, Development Prospects Group, Policy Research Working Paper No. 5433. New York. http://dlc.dlib.indiana.edu/dlc/handle/10535/6716.

Al Abror, Anwar. 2012. "Coca Cola." https://www.youtube.com/watch?v=c5UiOfPkjAg.

Al Abror, Anwar 2014. *Toreh De' Martajasah—Makam Nabi E Bhungkarah*. Sampang: APPRI, DVD.

Alatas, Ismail Fajrie. 2016. "The Poetics of Pilgrimage: Assembling Contemporary Indonesian Pilgrimage to Ḥaḍramawt, Yemen." *Comparative Study of Society and History* 58 (3): 607–35. https://doi.org/10.1017/S0010417516000293.

Alff, Henryk, Andreas Benz, and Matthias Schmidt. 2014. "Mobilities in Asian Contexts." *Internationales Asienforum. International Quarterly for Asian Studies* (1–2): 7–24.

Ali, Abdullah Yussuf. 1999. *The Meaning of the Holy Qur'an*. 10th ed. Beltsville, MD: Amana Publications.

Al-Shibeeb, Dina. 2010. "New Islamic Ruling on Singing Stirs Debate." *Al Arabiya News*, September 18. http://www.alarabiya.net/articles/2010/09/18/119639.html.

Amira, Lola. 2010. *Minggu Pagi Di Victoria Park:* Pic[k]lock Production.

Ananta, Aris, and Evi Nurvidya Arifin, eds. 2004. *International Migration in Southeast Asia*. Singapore: Institute of Southeast Asian Studies.

Ananta, Aris, and Evi Nurvidya Arifin. 2014. "Emerging Patterns of Indonesia's International Migration." *Malaysian Journal of Economic Studies* 51 (1): 29–41.

Appadurai, Arjun. 1996. *Modernity at Large: Cultural Dimensions of Globalization.* Minneapolis: University of Minnesota Press.

Arab News. 2019. "Saudi Arabia Issues More Than 4.1 Million Umrah Visas." February 25. http://www.arabnews.com/node/1457471/saudi-arabia.

Arenz, Cathrin, Michaela Haug, Stefan Seitz, and Oliver Venz, eds. 2017. *Continuity Under Change in Dayak Societies.* Edition Centaurus—sozioökonomische Prozesse in Asien, Afrika und Lateinamerika. Wiesbaden, Germany: Springer VS.

Assad, Muhammad. 2011. *Notes from Qatar 1: Positive, Persistence, Pray.* Jakarta: Elex Media Komputindo.

Assad, Muhammad. 2012. *Notes from Qatar 2: Honest, Humble, Helpful.* Jakarta: Elex Media Komputindo.

Assad, Muhammad. 2014. *Notes from Qatar 3: Dream, Do, Deliver.* Jakarta: Elex Media Komputindo.

Atkinson, Jane Monnig, and Shelly Errington, eds. 1990. *Power and Difference: Gender in Island Southeast Asia.* Stanford, CA: Stanford University Press. http://www.loc.gov/catdir/description/cam024/89078330.html.

Augé, Marc. 1992. *Non-lieux, introduction à une anthropologie de la surmodernité.* Paris: Éd. du Seuil.

Azizah, Nurul. 2013. *Artikulasi Politik Santri: Dari Kyai Menjadi Bupati.* Jember: STAIN Jember Press.

Azra, Azyumardi. 2001. "Networks of the Ulama in the Haramayn: Connections in the Indian Ocean Region." *Studia Islamika* 8 (2): 83–120.

Azra, Azyumardi. 2004. *The Origins of Islamic Reformism in Southeast Asia: Networks of Malay-Indonesian and Middle Eastern 'Ulama' in the Seventeenth and Eighteenth Centuries.* Honolulu: Allen & Unwin and University of Hawai'i Press.

Badone, Ellen, and Sharon R. Roseman. 2004a. "Approaches to the Anthropology of Pilgrimage and Tourism." In *Intersecting Journeys: The Anthropology of Pilgrimage and Tourism,* edited by Ellen Badone and Sharon R. Roseman, 1–23. Urbana: University of Illinois Press.

Badone, Ellen, and Sharon R. Roseman, eds. 2004b. *Intersecting Journeys: The Anthropology of Pilgrimage and Tourism.* Urbana: University of Illinois Press.

Barendregt, Bart. 2010. "'Dangdut Daerah': Going Local in Post-Suharto Indonesia." In *Dangdut Stories: A Social and Musical History of Indonesia's Most Popular Music,* edited by Andrew N. Weintraub, 201–24. New York: Oxford University Press.

Bauman, Zygmunt. 1996. "From Pilgrim to Tourist—or a Short History of Identity." In *Questions of Cultural Identity,* edited by Paul Du Gay and Stuart Hall, 18–36. Los Angeles, CA: Sage.

Baumann, Gerd. 1999. *The Multicultural Riddle: Rethinking National, Ethnic, and Religious Identities.* New York: Routledge.

Bayat, Asef. 2007. *Making Islam Democratic: Social Movements and the Post-Islamist Turn.* Stanford, CA: Stanford University Press.

Bearman, Peri, Thierry Bianquis, Clifford Edmund Bosworth, Emeri J. van Donzel, and Wolfhart P. Heinrichs, eds. 2012. *Encyclopedia of Islam.* EI-2. Leiden: Brill.

Beck, Ulrich, ed. 1998. *Perspektiven der Weltgesellschaft.* Frankfurt am Main: Suhrkamp.

Berg, Birgit. 2011. "Musical Modernity, Islamic Identity, and Arab Aesthetics in Arab-Indonesian Orkes Gambus." In *Islam and Popular Culture in Indonesia and Malaysia,* edited by Andrew N. Weintraub, 166–84. Abingdon, UK: Routledge.

Bianchi, Robert. 2004. *Guests of God: Pilgrimage and Politics in the Islamic World.* New York: Oxford University Press.

Bianchi, Robert. 2015. "The Hajj and Politics in Contemporary Turkey and Indonesia." In *Hajj: Global Interactions through Pilgrimage*, edited by Luitgard E. M. Mols and Marjo Buitelaar, 65–84. Leiden: Sidestone Press.

Bierschenk, Thomas, Matthias Krings, and Carola Lentz, eds. 2013. *Ethnologie im 21. Jahrhundert*. Ethnologische Paperbacks. Berlin: Reimer.

Bougleux, Elena. 2016. "Im/mobilities in Subjects and Systems." In *Bounded Mobilities: Ethnographic Perspectives on Social Hierarchies and Global Inequalities*, edited by Andreas Hackl, Miriam Gutekunst, Sabina Leoncini, Julia S. Schwarz, and Irene Götz, 13–18. Bielefeld, Germany: Transcript.

Bourdieu, Pierre. 1979. *La Distinction : Critique Sociale du Jugement*. Paris: Les Éditions de Minuit.

Bouvier, Hélène. 2002. *Lèbur! Seni Musik dan Pertunjukan dalam Masyarakat Madura*. Jakarta: Yayasan Obor Indonesia.

Bowen, John R. 2003. *Islam, Law, and Equality in Indonesia: An Anthropology of Public Reasoning*. Cambridge: Cambridge University Press.

Bowen, John R. 2008. "Intellectual Pilgrimages and Local Norms in Fashioning Indonesian Islam." *Revue d'Etudes sur le Monde Musulman et la Méditerranée* (123): 37–54.

Bowen, John R. 2015. "Contours of Sharia in Indonesia." In *Democracy and Islam in Indonesia*, edited by Mirjam Künkler and Alfred Stepan, 149–67. New York: Columbia University Press.

Bramantyo, Hanung. 2008: *Ayat-Ayat Cinta*. Jakarta: MD Pictures.

Bubandt, Nils. 2013. *Democracy, Corruption, and the Politics of Spirits in Contemporary Indonesia*. London: Routledge.

Buehler, Michael. 2016. *The Politics of Shari'a Law: Islamist Activists and the State in Democratizing Indonesia*. Cambridge: Cambridge University Press.

Buitelaar, Marjo. 2015. "The Hajj and the Anthropological Study of Pilgrimage." In *Hajj: Global Interactions through Pilgrimage*, edited by Luitgard E. M. Mols and Marjo Buitelaar, 9–26. Leiden: Sidestone Press.

Bukhari. n.d. "Hadith 621, Narrated by 'Abdullah Bin 'Umar., Available at: Book 2, Volume 26." Qur'an Explorer. Accessed August 27, 2016. http://www.quranexplorer.com/Hadith/English/Index.html.

Burhani, Ahmad Najib. 2010. "Westernization vs Arabization." *Jakarta Post*, February 15. http://www.thejakartapost.com/news/2010/02/15/westernization-vs-arabization.html

Burhani, Ahmad Najib. 2013. "Liberal and Conservative Discourses in the Muhammadiyah: The Liberal and Conservative Discourses in the Muhammadiyah, Struggle for the Face of Reformist Islam in Indonesia." In *Contemporary Developments in Indonesian Islam: Explaining the "Conservative Turn,"* edited by Martin van Bruinessen, 105–44. Singapore: Institute of Southeast Asian Studies.

Bustamam-Ahmad, Kamaruzzaman, and Patrick Jory, eds. 2011. *Islamic Studies and Islamic Education in Contemporary Southeast Asia*. 1st ed. Kuala Lumpur: Yayasan Ilmuwan.

Carrier, James. 1992. "Occidentalism: The World Turned Upside-down." *American Ethnologist* 19 (2): 195–212. https://doi.org/10.1525/ae.1992.19.2.02a00010.

Chambert-Loir, Henri, ed. 2013. *Naik Haji Di Masa Silam: Kisah-Kisah Orang Indonesia Naik Haji (1482–1964)*. 3 vols. Jakarta: Perpustakaan Nasional Republik Indonesia.

Chan, Carol. 2014. "Gendered Morality and Development Narratives: The Case of Female Labor Migration from Indonesia." *Sustainability* 6 (10): 6949–72. https://doi.org/10.3390/su6106949.

Chan, Carol. 2015. "In Sickness and in Wealth." *Inside Indonesia* 123. http://www.insideindonesia.org/in-sickness-and-in-wealth.
Chaplin, Chris. 2014. "Imagining the Land of the Two Holy Mosques: The Social and Doctrinal Importance of Saudi Arabia in Indonesian Salafi Discourse." *ASEAS—Österreichische Zeitschrift für Südostasienwissenschaften* 7 (2): 217–35.
Chaudhuri, K. N. 2007. "Indonesia in the Early Seaborne Trade of the Indian Ocean." *Indonesia Circle: Newsletter of the School of Oriental and African Studies* 12 (33): 3–13.
Choi, JungBong, and Roald Maliangkay. 2015. *K-Pop: The International Rise of the Korean Music Industry*. New York: Routledge.
Comaroff, Jean, and John L. Comaroff. 2012. *Theory from the South: Or, How Euro-America Is Evolving toward Africa*. London: Paradigm Publishers.
Corbin, Juliet M., and Anselm L. Strauss. 1990. *Basics of Qualitative Research: Techniques and Procedures for Developing Grounded Theory*. Los Angeles: Sage.
Coronil, Fernando. 1996. "Beyond Occidentalism: Toward Nonimperial Geohistorical Categories." *Cultural Anthropology* 11 (1): 51–87.
Cresswell, Tim. 2006. *On the Move: Mobility in the Modern Western World*. New York: Routledge.
Cresswell, Tim. 2011. "Mobilities I: Catching Up." *Progress in Human Geography* 35 (4): 550–58.
Cresswell, Tim, and Peter Merriman, eds. 2011a. *Geographies of Mobilities. Practices, Spaces, Subjects*. Farnham, UK: Ashgate.
Cresswell, Tim, and Peter Merriman. 2011b. "Introduction: Geographies of Mobilities—Practices, Spaces, Subjects." In *Geographies of Mobilities. Practices, Spaces, Subjects.*, edited by Tim Cresswell and Peter Merriman, 1–18. Farnham, UK: Ashgate.
Danarto. 1984. *Orang Jawa Naik Haji. Catatan Perjalanan*. Jakarta: Grafiti Pers.
Danarto, and Harry Aveling. 1989. *A Javanese Pilgrim in Mecca*. Monash University, Centre of Southeast Asian Studies, Working Paper 58. Clayton, Australia: Centre of Southeast Asian Studies.
de Jonge, Huub 1995. "Stereotypes of the Madurese." In *Across Madura Strait: The Dynamics of an Insular Society*, edited by Kees van Dijk, Huub de Jonge, Elly Touwen-Bouwsma, and C. van Dijk, 7–24. Leiden: KITLV Press.
Dinkelaker, Samia, and Kristina Grossmann. 2010. "Weibliche Arbeitsmigration, Islamisierung und die Rückwirkung auf Geschlechter- und Familienverhältnisse in Tulung Agung, Java, Indonesien." In *Das Echo der Migration: Wie Auslandsmigration die Gesellschaften im Globalen Süden verändert*, edited by Niklas Reese, 179–85. Bad Honnef: Horlemann.
Du Gay, Paul, and Stuart Hall, eds. 1996. *Questions of Cultural Identity*. Los Angeles, CA: Sage.
Dzulkarnain, Iskandar. 2012. *Dekonstruksi Sosial Budaya Alaq Dalaq Di Madura*. Yogyakarta: Peraton.
Effendy, Bisri. 1990. *An Nuqayah: Gerak Transformasi Sosial Di Madura*. Jakarta: Perhimpunan Pengembangan Pesantren dan Masyarakat (P3M).
Eickelman, Dale F. 2001. *The Middle East and Central Asia: An Anthropological Approach*. Upper Saddle River, NJ: Prentice Hall.
Eickelman, Dale F., and James P. Piscatori, eds. 1990. *Muslim Travellers: Pilgrimage, Migration, and the Religious Imagination*. Berkeley: University of California Press.
Eisenstadt, Shmuel N. 2000. "Multiple Modernities." *Daedalus* 129 (1): 1–29.
Eliyanah, Evi, and Mirjam Lücking. 2017. "Images of Authentic Muslim Selves: Gendered Moralities and Constructions of Arab Others in Contemporary Indonesia." *Social Sciences* 6 (3): 103. https://doi.org/10.3390/socsci6030103.

El Shirazy, Habiburrahman. 2004. *Ayat-Ayat Cinta*. Semarang: Basmala.

El Shirazy, Habiburrahman. 2005. *Pudarnya Pesona Cleopatra*. Semarang: Basmala.

El Shirazy, Habiburrahman. 2007a. *Ketika Cinta Bertasbih*. Semarang: Basmala.

El Shirazy, Habiburrahman. 2007b. *Ketika Cinta Bertasbih 2*. Semarang: Basmala.

El Shirazy, Habiburrahman. 2011. *Langit Makkah Berwarna Merah*. Semarang: Basmala.

El Shirazy, Habiburrahman. 2012. *Bulan Madu Di Yerussalem*. Semarang: Basmala.

eMarketer. 2015. "Facebook Users in Indonesia Have Highest Mobile Usage Rate Worldwide: Indonesia Is Home to the Third-Largest Facebook Mobile Phone Audience." *eMarketer*, January 22. Accessed April 12, 2016. http://www.emarketer.com/Article/Facebook-Users-Indonesia-Have-Highest-Mobile-Usage-Rate-Worldwide/1011896.

Evers, Hans-Dieter. 1987. "The Bureaucratization of Southeast Asia." *Comparative Studies in Society and History* 29 (4): 666–85.

Fealy, Greg. 2004. "Islamic Radicalism in Indonesia: The Faltering Revival?" *Southeast Asian Affairs* (1): 104–21.

Fealy, Greg. 2008. "Consuming Islam: Commodified Religion and Aspirational Pietism in Contemporary Indonesia." In *Expressing Islam: Religious Life and Politics in Indonesia*, edited by Greg Fealy and Sally White, 15–39. Singapore: Institute of Southeast Asian Studies.

Fealy, Greg. 2014. "'Look Over Here!': Indonesian Responses to the Arab Spring." In *Democracy and Reform in the Middle East and Asia: Social Protest and Authoritarian Rule after the Arab Spring*, edited by Amin Saikal and Amitav Acharya, 233–47. London: Tauris.

Fealy, Greg. 2016. "The Politics of Religious Intolerance in Indonesia: Mainstream-Ism Trumps Extremism?" In *Religion, Law, and Intolerance in Indonesia*, edited by Tim Lindsey and Helen Pausacker, 115–31. London: Routledge.

Fealy, Greg. 2019. "Indonesia's Growing Islamic Divide. The Polarisation as Seen in Latest Election Will Affect Interfaith and Intra-Faith Relations in Years to Come." *Straits Times*, May 3. https://www.straitstimes.com/opinion/indonesias-growing-islamic-divide.

Fealy, Greg, and Sally White, eds. 2008a. *Expressing Islam: Religious Life and Politics in Indonesia*. Singapore: Institute of Southeast Asian Studies.

Fealy, Greg, and Sally White. 2008b. "Introduction." In *Expressing Islam: Religious Life and Politics in Indonesia*, edited by Greg Fealy and Sally White, 1–14. Singapore: Institute of Southeast Asian Studies.

Feener, R. Michael, ed. 2004. *Islam in World Cultures: Comparative Perspectives*. Santa Barbara, Calif. ABC-CLIO.

Formichi, Chiara, ed. 2013. *Religious Pluralism, State and Society in Asia*. London: Routledge.

Frederick, William H. 1982. "Rhoma Irama and the Dangdut Style: Aspects of Contemporary Indonesian Popular Culture." *Indonesia* (34): 103–30.

Frey, Nancy. 2004. "Stories of the Return: Pilgrimage and Its Aftermaths." In *Intersecting Journeys: The Anthropology of Pilgrimage and Tourism*, edited by Ellen Badone and Sharon R. Roseman, 89–109. Urbana: University of Illinois Press.

Frishkopf, Michael Aaron. 2010a. "Introduction. Music and Media in the Arab World: A Metadiscourse." In *Music and Media in the Arab World*, edited by Michael A. Frishkopf, 1–66. Cairo: American University in Cairo Press.

Frishkopf, Michael Aaron, ed. 2010b. *Music and Media in the Arab World*. Cairo: American University in Cairo Press.

Fuchs, Martin, Antje Linkenbach, and Shalini Randeria. 2004. "Konfigurationen der Moderne. Zur Einleitung." In *Konfigurationen der Moderne: Diskurse zu Indien*, edited by Shalini Randeria and Ewald Gramlich, 9–34. Soziale Welt Sonderband 15. Baden-Baden: Nomos-Verl.-Ges.

Gabriel, Manfred, ed. 2004. *Paradigmen der akteurszentrierten Soziologie*. 1. Aufl. Wiesbaden: VS Verl. für Sozialwiss.

Geertz, Clifford. 1960. "The Javanese Kijaji: The Changing Role of a Cultural Broker." *Comparative Studies in Society and History* 2 (2): 228–49.

Geertz, Clifford. 1968. *Islam Observed: Religious Development in Morocco and Indonesia*. Chicago: University of Chicago Press.

Geertz, Clifford. 1976. *The Religion of Java*. Chicago: University of Chicago Press.

Geertz, Clifford. 2001. "The Near East in the Far East. On Islam in Indonesia: Unpublished Occasional Paper." https://www.sss.ias.edu/files/papers/papertwelve.pdf.

Gibb, Hamilton Alexander Rosskeen, and Peri Bearman, eds. 1960. *Encyclopaedia of Islam*. EI-1. Leiden: Brill.

Gilsenan, Michael. 2003. "Out of the Hadhramaut: The Arab Diaspora in South-East Asia." *London Review of Books* 25 (6): 7–11.

Glaser, Barney G., and Anselm L. Strauss. 1967. *The Discovery of Grounded Theory: Strategies for Qualitative Research*. Chicago: Aldine.

Glick-Schiller, Nina, Linda G. Basch, and Cristina Blanc-Szanton, eds. 1992. *Towards a Transnational Perspective on Migration: Race, Class, Ethnicity, and Nationalism Reconsidered*. New York: New York Academy of Sciences.

Glick Schiller, Nina, and Noel B. Salazar. 2013. "Regimes of Mobility Across the Globe." *Journal of Ethnic and Migration Studies* 39 (2): 183–200.

Glidden, Harold W. 1972. "The Arab World." *American Journal of Psychiatry* 128 (8): 984–88.

Gottowik, Volker, ed. 2014. *Dynamics of Religion in Southeast Asia: Magic and Modernity*. Amsterdam: Amsterdam University Press.

Götz, Irene. 2016. "Mobility and Immobility: Background of the Project." In *Bounded Mobilities: Ethnographic Perspectives on Social Hierarchies and Global Inequalities*, edited by Andreas Hackl, Miriam Gutekunst, Sabina Leoncini, Julia S. Schwarz, and Irene Götz, 9–12. Bielefeld, Germany: Transcript.

Graeber, David. 2012. "Dead Zones of the Imagination: On Violence, Bureaucracy, and Interpretive Labor. The 2006 Malinowski Memorial Lecture." *HAU: Journal of Ethnographic Theory* 2 (2): 105–28.

Greenblatt, Stephen. 2010. *Cultural Mobility: A Manifesto*. Cambridge: Cambridge University Press.

Gupta, Akhil, and James Ferguson. 1992. "Beyond "Culture": Space, Identity, and the Politics of Difference." *Cultural Anthropology* 7 (1): 6–23.

Hackl, Andreas, Miriam Gutekunst, Sabina Leoncini, Julia Sophia Schwarz, and Irene Götz, eds. 2016. *Bounded Mobilities: Ethnographic Perspectives on Social Hierarchies and Global Inequalities*. Bielefeld, Germany: Transcript.

Hadiz, Vedi R. 2016. *Islamic Populism in Indonesia and the Middle East*. Cambridge: Cambridge University Press.

Hall, Stuart. 1992. "The Question of Cultural Identity." In *Modernity and Its Futures: Understanding Modern Societies*, edited by Stuart Hall, David Held, and Tony McGrew, 274–316 4. Cambridge: Polity Press.

Hall, Stuart, David Held, and Tony McGrew, eds. 1992. *Modernity and Its Futures: Understanding Modern Societies*. Vol. 4. Cambridge: Polity Press.

Hannam, Kevin, Mimi Sheller, and John Urry. 2006. "Editorial: Mobilities, Immobilities, and Moorings." *Mobilities* 1 (1): 1–22.

Hannerz, Ulf. 1996. *Transnational Connections: Culture, People, Places*. London: Routledge.

Harian Pelita. 2014. "Peserta Umrah Meningkat Satu Juta Jamaah. Harian Pelita." Accessed May 22, 2014. http://kliping.kemenag.go.id/download.php?file=17278.

Heryanto, Ariel. 2008a. "Pop Culture and Competing Identities." In *Popular Culture in Indonesia: Fluid Identities in Post-Authoritarian Politics*, edited by Ariel Heryanto, 1–36. London: Routledge.

Heryanto, Ariel, ed. 2008b. *Popular Culture in Indonesia: Fluid Identities in Post-Authoritarian Politics*. London: Routledge.

Heryanto, Ariel. 2011. "Upgraded Piety and Pleasure: The New Middle Class and Islam in Indonesian Popular Culture." In *Islam and Popular Culture in Indonesia and Malaysia*, edited by Andrew N. Weintraub, 60–82. New York: Routledge.

Heryanto, Ariel. 2014a. "The Cinematic Contest of Popular Post-Islamism." In *Religion, Tradition, and the Popular: Transcultural Views from Asia and Europe*, edited by Judith Schlehe and Evamaria Sandkühler, 139–56. Historische Lebenswelten in populären Wissenskulturen. Bielefeld, Germany: Transcript.

Heryanto, Ariel. 2014b. *Identity and Pleasure: The Politics of Indonesian Screen Culture*. Singapore: NUS Press.

Hess, Sabine, and Vassilis Tsianos. 2010. "Ethnographische Grenzregimeanalyse. Eine Methodologie der Autonomie der Migration." In *Diskurse, Praktiken, Institutionen in Europa*, edited by Bernd Kasparek and Sabine Hess, 243–264. Berlin: Assoziation A.

Hew, Wai Weng. 2012. "Expressing Chineseness, Marketing Islam: Hybrid Performance of Chinese Muslim Preachers." In *Chinese Indonesians Reassessed: History, Religion, and Belonging*, edited by Siew-Min Sai and Chang-Yau Hoon, 178–99. London: Routledge.

Hew, Wai Weng. 2013. "Cosmopolitan Islam and Inclusive Chineseness: Chinese-Style Mosques in Indonesia." In *Religious Pluralism, State, and Society in Asia*, edited by Chiara Formichi, 175–97. London: Routledge.

Hilarian, Larry. 2004. "The Gambus (Lutes) of the Malay World: Its Origins and Significance in Zapin Music." Paper presented at the UNESCO Regional Expert Symposium on Arts Education in Asia, Hong Kong. http://portal.unesco.org/culture/en/files/21757/10891257253hilarian.pdf/hilarian.pdf.

Hitchcock, Michael, and Victor T. King, eds. 1997. *Images of Malay-Indonesian Identity*. Kuala Lumpur: Oxford University Press.

Hoesterey, James B. 2008. "Marketing Morality: The Rise, Fall, and Rebranding of AA Gym." In *Expressing Islam: Religious Life and Politics in Indonesia*, edited by Greg Fealy and Sally White, 95–112. Singapore: Institute of Southeast Asian Studies.

Hooker, Michael Barry. 2008. *Indonesian Syariah: Defining a National School of Islamic Law*. Singapore: Institute of Southeast Asian Studies.

Howell, Julia Day. 2001. "Sufism and the Indonesian Islamic Revival." *Journal of Asian Studies* 60 (3): 701–29. https://doi.org/10.2307/2700107.

Howell, Julia Day. 2010. "Indonesia's Salafist Sufis." *Modern Asian Studies* 44 (5): 1029–51. https://doi.org/10.1017/S0026749X09990278.

Huntington, Samuel P. 1996. *The Clash of Civilizations and the Remaking of World Order*. Charlesbourg, Quebec: Braille Jymico.

Huotari, Mikko, Jürgen Rüland, and Judith Schlehe, eds. 2014. *Methodology and Research Practice in Southeast Asian Studies*. Basingstoke: Palgrave Macmillan.

Husson, Laurence. 1977. "Eight Centuries of Madurese Migration to East Java." *Asia and Pacific Migration Journal* 6 (1): 77–102.

Husson, Laurence. 1995. *La migration maduraise vers l'est de Java: Manger le vent ou gratter la terre?* Paris: Editions l'Harmattan.
Ichwan, Moch Nur. 2013. "Towards a Puritanical Moderate Islam: The Majelis Ulama Indonesia and the Politics of Religious Orthodoxy." In *Contemporary Developments in Indonesian Islam: Explaining the "Conservative Turn,"* edited by Martin van Bruinessen, 60–104. Singapore: Institute of Southeast Asian Studies.
Indonesian Ministry of Religious Affairs/Kementerian Agama Republik Indonesia. 2013. "Laporan Evaluasi Penyelenggaraaan Ibadah Haji Tahun 1434H/2013M." https://vdocuments.site/laporanevaluasipenyelenggaraanibadahhaji1434hfinal.html.
Indonesian Ministry of Religious Affairs/Kementerian Agama Republik Indonesia. 2015. "Hajj Waiting List." http://haji.kemenag.go.id/v2/basisdata/waiting-list.
Indonesian Ministry of Religious Affairs/Kementerian Agama Republik Indonesia. 2016a. "5 Umrah Pasti." http://haji.kemenag.go.id/v2/content/video-grafik-motion-vgr-5-pasti-umrah-0.
Indonesian Ministry of Religious Affairs/Kementerian Agama Republik Indonesia. 2016b. "Embarkasi." www.daftarhajiumroh.com/besaran-bpih-2014-embarkasi/.
Indonesian Ministry of Religious Affairs/Kementerian Agama Republik Indonesia. 2016c. "Haji Pintar." http://haji.kemenag.go.id/v2/content/haji-pintar-pendaftaran-haji-reguler.
Indonesian Ministry of Religious Affairs/Kementerian Agama Republik Indonesia. 2016d. "Hajj Quota." http://haji.kemenag.go.id/v2/content/pelunasan-hari-keduabelas-87-persen-jemaah-lunas.
Indonesian Ministry of Religious Affairs/Kementerian Agama Republik Indonesia. 2016e. "Waiting List." http://haji.kemenag.go.id/v2/basisdata/waiting-list.
Indonesian Ministry of Tourism/Kementerian Pariwisata dan Ekonomi Kreatif Republik Indonesia. 2018. "Indonesia Dominates World Halal Tourism Awards 2016. Winning 12 Top Categories." https://www.indonesia.travel/kr/en/news/indonesia-dominates-world-halal-tourism-awards-2016-winning-12-top-categories.
Institute for Policy Analysis (IPAC). 2018. "After Ahok: The Islamist Agenda in Indonesia." IPAC Report No. 44. Jakarta: Institute for Policy Analysis. http://file.understandingconflict.org/file/2018/04/Report_44_ok.pdf.
International Organization for Migration (IOM). 2010. *Labour Migration from Indonesia. An Overview of Indonesian Migration to Selected Destinations in Asia and the Middle East.* Geneva, Switzerland: International Organization for Migration.
Jakarta Post. 2017. "Indonesians Love of Mecca Boosts Lucrative 'Umrah' Business." February 21. https://www.thejakartapost.com/news/2017/01/21/indonesians-love-of-mecca-boosts-lucrative-umrah-business.html.
Jayaram, Kiran. 2016. "Capital." In *Keywords of Mobility: Critical Engagements*, edited by Noel B. Salazar and Kiran Jayaram, 13–32. Vol 1. New York: Berghahn Books.
Johnson, Mark, and Pnina Werbner. 2010. "Diasporic Encounters, Sacred Journeys: Ritual, Normativity, and the Religious Imagination Among International Asian Migrant Women." *Asia Pacific Journal of Anthropology* 11 (3–4): 205–18.
Jones, Carla. 2010. "Materializing Piety: Gendered Anxieties about Faithful Consumption in Contemporary Urban Indonesia." *American Ethnologist* 37 (4): 617–37.
Kahn, Joel S. 2015. "Foundational Islams. Implications for Dialogue." *Arena Magazine* 134: 22–26.
Karimi, Mahmoud, and Farzin Negahban. 2008. "Baraka." In *Encyclopaedia Islamica: An Abridged Translation of the Dā'irat Al-Ma'ārif-I Buzurg-I Islāmī*, edited by Wilferd Madelung. Leiden: Brill.

Kasparek, Bernd, and Sabine Hess, eds. 2010. *Diskurse, Praktiken, Institutionen in Europa*. Berlin: Assoziation A.

Keeler, Ward. 1990. "Speaking of Gender in Java." In *Power and Difference: Gender in Island Southeast Asia*, edited by Jane M. Atkinson and Shelly Errington, 127–52. Stanford, CA: Stanford University Press.

Kessler, Christl, and Stefan Rother. 2016. *Democratization through Migration? Political Remittances and Participation of Philippine Return Migrants*. New York: Lexington Books.

Khafid, Supriyantho. 2015. "Indonesia Wins Three Awards in World Halal Travel Award." *TEMPO*, October 21. http://en.tempo.co/read/news/2015/10/21/055711606/Indonesia-Wins-Three-Awards-in-World-Halal-Travel-Award.

Killias, Olivia. 2014. "Intimate Encounters: The Ambiguities of Belonging in the Transnational Migration of Indonesian Domestic Workers to Malaysia." *Citizenship Studies* 18 (8): 885–99.

Killias, Olivia. 2015. "Distant Friends and Intimate Strangers: On the Perils of Friendship in the Context of Iranian Migration to Malaysia." Paper Presentation at the Conference *Dynamic Alignments and Dealignments in Global Southeast Asia*, Freiburg Institute for Advanced Studies (FRIAS). Freiburg im Breisgau, June 25.

Killias, Olivia. 2017. *Follow the Maid: Domestic Worker Migration in and from Indonesia*. Gendering Asia 13. Copenhagen: NIAS Press.

Kloos, David. 2017. *Becoming Better Muslims: Religious Authority and Ethical Improvement in Aceh, Indonesia*. Princeton, NJ: Princeton University Press.

Kovacs, Amanda. 2014. "Saudi Arabia Exporting Salafi Education and Radicalizing Indonesia´s Muslims." *GIGA Focus International Edition English* 7. Accessed April 6, 2020. https://www.giga-hamburg.de/en/publication/saudi-arabia-exporting-salafi-education-and-radicalizing-indonesia%E2%80%99s-muslims.

Kronholm, Tryggve. 1993. "Arab Culture: Reality or Fiction?" In *the Middle East—Unity and Diversity*, edited by Heikki Palva and Knut S. Vikør, 12–25. Copenhagen: NIAS Books.

Künkler, Mirjam, and Alfred Stepan, eds. 2015. *Democracy and Islam in Indonesia*. New York: Columbia University Press.

Kunst, Jaap. 1968. *Hindu-Javanese Musical Instruments*. Dordrecht: Springer Netherlands.

Kusuma, Mirza Tirta, ed. 2014. *Ketika Makkah Menjadi Seperti Las Vegas. Agama, Politik, Dan Ideologi*. Jakarta: PT Gramedia Pustaka Utama.

Laffan, Michael Francis. 2003. *Islamic Nationhood and Colonial Indonesia: The Umma Below the Winds*. London: Routledge Curzon.

Laffan, Michael. 2004. "An Indonesian Community in Cairo: Continuity and Change in a Cosmopolitan Islamic Milieu." *Indonesia* 77: 1–26.

Laffan, Michael Francis. 2011. *The Makings of Indonesian Islam: Orientalism and the Narration of a Sufi Past*. Princeton, NJ: Princeton University Press.

Lerner, Daniel. 1967. *Passing of Traditional Society: Modernizing the Middle East*. New York: Free Press.

Levitt, Peggy. 1998. "Social Remittances: Migration Driven Local-Level Forms of Cultural Diffusion." *International Migration Review* 32 (4): 926. https://doi.org/10.2307/2547666.

Lewis, Bernard. 2004. *The Crisis of Islam: Holy War and Unholy Terror*. Paperback ed. New York: Random House.

Lindquist, Johan. 2009. *The Anxieties of Mobility: Migration and Tourism in the Indonesian Borderlands*. Honolulu: University of Hawai'i Press.

Lindquist, Johan. 2012. "The Elementary School Teacher, the Thug and His Grandmother: Informal Brokers and Transnational Migration from Indonesia." *Pacific Affairs* 85 (1): 69–89. https://doi.org/10.5509/201285169.

Lindsey, Tim, and Helen Pausacker, eds. 2016. *Religion, Law, and Intolerance in Indonesia*. London: Taylor and Francis.

Lucas, Robert E. B., and Oded Stark. 1985. "Motivations to Remit: Evidence from Botswana." *Journal of Political Economy* 93 (5): 901–18.

Lücking, Mirjam. 2014. "Making 'Arab' One's Own. Muslim Pilgrimage Experiences in Central Java, Indonesia." *Internationales Asienforum: International Quarterly for Asian Studies* 45 (1–2): 129–52.

Lücking, Mirjam. 2016. "Beyond Islam Nusantara and "Arabization": Capitalizing "Arabness" in Madura, East Java." *ASIEN: The German Journal on Contemporary Asia* 137 (April): 5–24.

Lücking, Mirjam. 2017. "Working in Mecca: How Informal Pilgrimage-Migration from Madura, Indonesia, to Saudi Arabia Challenges State Sovereignty." *European Journal of East Asian Studies* 16 (2): 248–74. https://doi.org/10.1163/15700615-01602007.

Lücking, Mirjam. 2019. "Travelling with the Idea of Taking Sides: Indonesian Pilgrimages to Jerusalem." *Bijdragen tot de taal-, land- en volkenkunde/Journal of the Humanities and Social Sciences of Southeast Asia* 175 (2-3): 196–224. https://doi.org/10.1163/22134379-17502020.

Luqman, A. 2000. *Komik Haji: Cara Mabrur Naik Haji & Umroh*. Jakarta: Nirmana.

Ma'arif, Samsul. 2015. *The History of Madura. Sejarah Panjang Madura Dari Kerajaan, Kolonialisme Sampai Kemerdekaan*. Yogyakarta: Araska.

Machmudi, Yon. 2011. "Muslim Intellectuals or Housemaids? The Saudi Perceptions of the Indonesian Domestic Workers." *Journal of Indonesian Islam* 5 (2): 225–46.

Mackerras, Colin, ed. 2003. *Ethnicity in Asia*. London, New York: RoutledgeCurzon.

Madelung, Wilferd, ed. 2008. *Encyclopaedia Islamica: An Abridged Translation of the Dā'irat Al-Ma'ārif-I Buzurg-I Islāmī*. Leiden: Brill.

Magnis-Suseno, Franz. 1989. *Neue Schwingen Für Garuda: Indonesien zwischen Tradition und Moderne*. München: Kindt.

Mandal, Sumit K. 2009. "Challenging Inequality in a Modern Islamic Idiom: Social Ferment Amongst Arabs in Early 20th-Century Java." In *Southeast Asia and the Middle East: Islam, Movement, and the Longue Durée*, edited by Eric Tagliacozzo, 156–75. Stanford, CA: Stanford University Press.

Mandal, Sumit K. 2011. "The Significance of the Rediscovery of Arabs in the Malay World." *Comparative Studies of South Asia, Africa, and the Middle East* 31 (2): 296–311.

Mandal, Sumit K. 2012. "Creole Hadramis in the Malay World in the 1800s: Fragments of Biographies and Connected Histories." *Cultural Dynamics* 24 (2-3): 175–87. https://doi.org/10.1177/0921374013487269.

Mandal, Sumit K. 2014. "Arabs in the Urban Social Landscapes of Malaysia: Historical Connections and Belonging." *Citizenship Studies* 18 (8): 807–22.

Mansurnoor, Iik Arifin. 1990. *Islam in an Indonesian World: Ulama of Madura*. Yogyakarta: Gadjah Mada University Press.

Marinescu, Valentina, ed. 2016. *Global Impact of South Korean Popular Culture—Hallyu Unbound:* Lexington Books.

Mas'ud, Abdurahman. 2006. "The Religion of the Pesantren." In *Religious Harmony: Problems, Practice, and Education*, edited by Michael Pye, Edith Franke, Alef Theria Wasim, and Mas'ud Abdurahman, 221–30. Berlin: Walter de Gruyter.

Mayasari, Nuki. 2014. "Recharging Faith: The Practice of Multiple Umrah Trips among the Middle Class in Yogyakarta." M.A. Thesis, Gadjah Mada University.
Meri, Josef W. 2012. "Ziyara." In *Encyclopedia of Islam*, edited by Peri Bearman, Thierry Bianquis, Clifford E. Bosworth, Emeri J. van Donzel, and Wolfhart P. Heinrichs. EI-2. Leiden: Brill. https://referenceworks.brillonline.com/entries/encyclopaedia-of-islam-2/ziyara-COM_1390?s.num=0&s.f.s2_parent=s.f.book.encyclopaedia-of-islam-2&s.q=Ziarah
Metcalf, Barbara. 1990. "The Pilgrimage Remembered: South Asian Accounts of the Hajj." In *Muslim Travellers: Pilgrimage, Migration, and the Religious Imagination*, edited by Dale F. Eickelman and James P. Piscatori, 85–107. Berkeley: University of California Press.
Meuleman, Johan H., ed. 2002. *Islam in the Era of Globalization: Muslim Attitudes towards Modernity and Identity*. London: Routledge.
Meutia, Sari. 2009. *Catatan Perjalanan Haji Seorang Muslimah*. Jakarta: PT Lingkar Pena Kreativa.
Migdal, Joel S. 2001. *State in Society: Studying How States and Societies Transform and Constitute One Another*. Cambridge: Cambridge University Press.
Miichi, Ken, and Omar Farouk, eds. 2015. *Southeast Asian Muslims in the Era of Globalization*. New York: Palgrave Macmillan.
Missbach, Antje. 2015. *Troubled Transit: Asylum Seekers Stuck in Indonesia*. Singapore: ISEAS—Yusof Ishak Institute.
Mols, Luitgard E. M., and Marjo Buitelaar, eds. 2015. *Hajj: Global Interactions through Pilgrimage*. Leiden: Sidestone Press.
Muhammadiyah. 2019. "Tentang Muhammadiyah." http://www.muhammadiyah.or.id/id/content-44-cam-tentang-muhammadiyah.html.
Mulder, Niels. 1997. "Images of Javanese Gender." In *Images of Malay-Indonesian Identity*, edited by Michael Hitchcock and Victor T. King, 138–47. Kuala Lumpur: Oxford University Press.
Muzakki, Akh. 2012. "Islamic Televangelism in Changing Indonesia: Transmission, Authority, and the Politics of Ideas." In *Global and Local Televangelism*, edited by Pradip Thomas and Philip Lee, 45–63. Houndmills, Basingstoke, UK: Palgrave Macmillan.
Myutel, Maria. 2016. "Indians and National Television in Indonesia: Behind the Seen." Ph.D. diss., Australian National University. https://openresearch-repository.anu.edu.au/handle/1885/113156.
Nahdlatul Ulama. 2019. "Basis Pendukung." https://www.nu.or.id/static/9/basis-pendukung.
Netton, Ian Richard, ed. 1993. *Golden Roads: Migration, Pilgrimage, and Travel in Mediaeval and Modern Islam*. Richmond: Curzon Press.
Nooteboom, Gerben. 2015. *Forgotten People: Poverty, Risk, and Social Security in Indonesia: The Case of the Madurese*. Leiden: KITLV Press.
Nugroho, Suray Agung. 2016. "Hallyu in Indonesia." In *Global Impact of South Korean Popular Culture—Hallyu Unbound*, edited by Valentina Marinescu, 19–32: New York: Lexington Books.
Oesterheld, Christian. 2017. "Genealogies of Anti-Madurese Violence in Kalimantan." In *Continuity under Change in Dayak Societies*, edited by Cathrin Arenz, Michaela Haug, Stefan Seitz, and Oliver Venz, 163–88. Wiesbaden, Germany: Springer VS.
Ong, Aihwa. 1999. "Graduated Sovereignty in South-East Asia." *Theory, Culture, and Society* 17 (4): 55–75.
Ong, Aihwa. 2007. "Neoliberalism as a Mobile Technology." *Transactions of the Institute of British Geographers* 32 (1): 3–8.

Palva, Heikki, and Knut S. Vikør, eds. 1993. *The Middle East—Unity and Diversity*. Copenhagen: NIAS Books.
Parreñas, Rhacel Salazar. 2001. *Servants of Globalization: Women, Migration, and Domestic Work*. Stanford, CA: Stanford University Press.
Pemerintah Kabupaten Pamekasan and Fakultas Ilmu Budaya Universitas Gadjah Mada, ed. 2010. *Ensiklopedi Pamekasan: Alam, Masyarakat, Dan Budaya*. Klaten: PT Intan Sejati.
Picken, Laurence. 1975. *Folk Musical Instruments of Turkey*. London: Oxford University Press.
Pribadi, Yanwar. 2018. *Islam, State, and Society in Indonesia: Local Politics in Madura*. London: Routledge.
Pye, Michael, Edith Franke, Alef Theria Wasim, and Mas'ud Abdurahman, eds. 2006. *Religious Harmony: Problems, Practice, and Education*. Berlin: Walter de Gruyter.
Quinn, George. 2004. "Local Pilgrimage in Java and Madura. Why Is It Booming?" *IIAS Newsletter* (35): 16.
Quinn, George. 2008. "Throwing Money at the Holy Door: Commercial Aspects of Popular Pilgrimage in Java." In *Expressing Islam: Religious Life and Politics in Indonesia*, edited by Greg Fealy and Sally White, 63–79. Singapore: Institute of Southeast Asian Studies.
Quinn, George. 2019. *Bandit Saints of Java*. Burrough on the Hill, Leicestershire, UK: Monsoon Books.
Ramstedt, Martin, Martin Slama, and Christian Warta. 2012. "Ethnizität und Religion als Kapital: Prozesse der Kapitalisierung von Kultur im Indonesien nach Suharto." *ASIEN: Journal of Contemporary Asia* (123): 7–11.
Rancière, Jacques. 2011. *Dissensus: On Politics and Aesthetics*. London: Continuum.
Randeria, Shalini. 2006. "Civil Society and Legal Pluralism in the Shadow of Caste: Entangled Modernities in Post-Colonial India." In *Hybridising East and West: Tales Beyond Westernisation; Empirical Contributions to the Debates on Hybridity*, edited by Dominique Schirmer, 97–124. Berlin: Lit.
Randeria, Shalini, and Ewald Gramlich, eds. 2004. *Konfigurationen der Moderne: Diskurse zu Indien*. Baden-Baden: Nomos-Verl.-Ges.
Rapport, Nigel, and Andrew Dawson. 1998. *Migrants of Identity: Perceptions of Home in a World of Movement*. Oxford: Berg.
Reese, Niklas, ed. 2010. *Das Echo der Migration: Wie Auslandsmigration die Gesellschaften im Globalen Süden verändert*. Bad Honnef: Horlemann.
Reid, Anthony. 1988. *Southeast Asia in the Age of Commerce, 1450–1680: The Lands below the Winds*. New Haven: Yale University Press.
Reid, Anthony, ed. 2012. *Indonesia Rising: The Repositioning of Asia's Third Giant*. Singapore: Institute of Southeast Asian Studies.
Ricklefs, Merle C. 2001. *A History of Modern Indonesia Since ca. 1200*. 3d ed. Basingstoke, UK: Palgrave.
Ricklefs, Merle C. 2008. "Religion, Politics, and Social Dynamics in Java: Historical and Contemporary Rhymes." In *Expressing Islam: Religious Life and Politics in Indonesia*, edited by Greg Fealy and Sally White. Singapore: Institute of Southeast Asian Studies.
Ricklefs, Merle C. 2010. *A New History of Southeast Asia*. Houndmills, Basingstoke, UK: Palgrave Macmillan.
Rifai, Mien Ahmad. 2007. *Manusia Madura: Pembawaan, Perilaku, Etos Kerja, Penampilan, Dan Pandangan Hidupnya Seperti Dicitrakan Peribahasanya*. Yogyakarta: Pilar Media.

Rifai, A. Mien, Umi Purwandari, Mutmainnah, Syaiful Arif, and Iskandar Dzulkarnain, eds. 2013. *Seserpih Garam Madura: Bunga Rampai Tulisan Tentang Masalah Masyarakat Madura Beserta Kiat-Kiat Pendidikan Buat Mengatasinya*. Bangkalan: UTM Press.

Rifki, Daniel. 2014. *Haji Backpacker:* Falcon Picture.

Robertson, Roland. 1998. "Glokalisierung, Homogenität und Heterogenität in Raum und Zeit." In *Perspektiven Der Weltgesellschaft*, edited by Ulrich Beck, 192–221. Frankfurt am Main: Suhrkamp.

Robinson, Kathryn. 2007. *Asian and Pacific Cosmopolitans: Self and Subject in Motion*. Basingstoke: Palgrave Macmillan.

Rodemeier, Susanne. 2009. "Zartes Signal einer Wende. Aktueller Arabischer Einfluss auf Java." *Südostasien. Zeitschrift für Politik, Kultur, Dialog* (4): 52–55.

Roff, William R. 1970. "Indonesian and Malay Students in Cairo in the 1920s." *Indonesia* (9): 73–87.

Rother, Stefan. 2009. "Changed in Migration? Philippine Return Migrants and (Un) Democratic Remittances." *European Journal of East Asian Studies* 8 (2): 245–74. https://doi.org/10.1163/156805809X12553326569713.

Rozaki, Abdur. 2004. *Menabur Kharisma Menuai Kuasa. Kiprah Kiai Dan Blater Sebagai Rezim Kembar Di Madura*. Yogyakarta: Pustaka Marwa.

Rudnyckyj, Daromir. 2009. "Market Islam in Indonesia." *Journal of the Royal Anthropological Institute* 15: 183-S201.

Rudnyckyj, Daromir. 2010. *Spiritual Economies: Islam, Globalization, and the Afterlife of Development Expertise*. Ithaca, NY: Cornell University Press.

Rüland, Jürgen, and Karsten Bechle. 2014. "Defending State-Centric Regionalism Through Mimicry and Localisation: Regional Parliamentary Bodies in the Association of Southeast Asian Nations (ASEAN) and Mercosur." *Journal of International Relations and Development* 17 (1): 61–88. https://doi.org/10.1057/jird.2013.3.

Sachs, Curt. 1940. *The History of Musical Instruments*. New York: W. W. Norton.

Sahal, Ahkmad, and Munawir Aziz. 2015. *Islam Nusantara: Dari Ushul Fiqhi Hingga Sejarah*. Bandung: Mizan Pustaka.

Sai, Siew-Min, and Chang-Yau Hoon, eds. 2012. *Chinese Indonesians Reassessed: History, Religion, and Belonging*. London: Routledge.

Said, Edward W. 1978. *Orientalism*. 1st ed. New York: Pantheon Books.

Said, Edward W. 2003. *Orientalism*. London: Penguin.

Saikal, Amin, and Amitav Acharya, eds. 2014. *Democracy and Reform in the Middle East and Asia: Social Protest and Authoritarian Rule After the Arab Spring*. London: Tauris.

Salazar, Noel B. 2010a. "Towards an Anthropology of Cultural Mobilities." *Crossings: Journal of Migration and Culture* 1 (1): 53–68.

Salazar, Noel B. 2010b. *Envisioning Eden: Mobilizing Imaginaries in Tourism and Beyond*. New York: Berghahn Books.

Salazar, Noel B. 2011. "The Power of Imagination in Transnational Mobilities." *Identities* 18 (6): 576–98.

Salazar, Noel B. 2013. "Imagining Mobility at the 'End of the World.'" *History and Anthropology* 24 (2): 233–52.

Salazar, Noel B. 2016a. "Conceptual Notes on the Freedom of Movement and Bounded Mobilities." In *Bounded Mobilities: Ethnographic Perspectives on Social Hierarchies and Global Inequalities*, edited by Andreas Hackl, Miriam Gutekunst, Sabina Leoncini, Julia S. Schwarz, and Irene Götz, 283–90. Bielefeld, Germany: Transcript.

Salazar, Noel B. 2016b. "Keywords of Mobility: A Critical Introduction." In *Keywords of Mobility: Critical Engagements*, edited by Noel B. Salazar and Kiran Jayaram, 1–12. New York: Berghahn Books.

Salazar, Noel B., and Nina Glick-Schiller, eds. 2014. *Regimes of Mobility: Imaginaries and Relationalities of Power*. London: Routledge.

Salazar, Noel B., and Kiran Jayaram, eds. 2016. *Keywords of Mobility: Critical Engagements*. New York: Berghahn Books.

Salhi, Kamal, ed. 2014. *Music, Culture and Identity in the Muslim World: Performance, Politics, and Piety*. Oxford, New York: Routledge.

Saputro, M. Endy. 2011. "Upin & Ipin: Melayu Islam, Politik Kultur, Dan Dekomodifikasi New Media." *Kontekstualita* 26 (1): 39–69.

Saudi Gazette. 2017. "A Million Indonesians to Perform Umrah This Season." November 18. http://saudigazette.com.sa/article/522168/SAUDI-ARABIA/A-million-Indonesians-to-perform-Umrah-this-season.

Saudi Gazette. 2018. "1.2m Indonesians Coming for Haj, Umrah This Year." June 11. http://saudigazette.com.sa/article/536789.

Schimmel, Annemarie. 1995. *Mystische Dimensionen des Islam: Die Geschichte des Sufismus*. 3d ed. München: Diederichs.

Schimmel, Annemarie. 2008. *Sufismus: Eine Einführung in die Islamische Mystik*. München: Beck.

Schirmer, Dominique, ed. 2006. *Hybridising East and West: Tales Beyond Westernisation; Empirical Contributions to the Debates on Hybridity*. Berlin: Lit.

Schlehe, Judith. 1998. *Die Meereskönigin des Südens, Ratu Kidul: Geisterpolitik im Javanischen Alltag*. Berlin: D. Reimer.

Schlehe, Judith. 2001. "Zum Bedeutungswandel einer Straße: Die Jalan Malioboro." *Kita: Das Magazin der deutsch-indonesischen Gesellschaft* 1: 17–23.

Schlehe, Judith. 2012. "Moderne Paranormale als spirituelle UnternehmerInnen in Indonesien?" *ASIEN: Journal of Contemporary Asia* 123: 95–111.

Schlehe, Judith. 2013a. "Wechselseitige Übersetzungen." In *Ethnologie im 21. Jahrhundert*, edited by Thomas Bierschenk, Matthias Krings, and Carola Lentz, 97–110. Berlin: Reimer.

Schlehe, Judith. 2013b. "Concepts of Asia, the West and the Self in Contemporary Indonesia: An Anthropological Account." *South East Asia Research* 21 (3): 497–515.

Schlehe, Judith. 2014. "Popularised Religiosity and the Paranormal Practitioners' Position in Indonesia." In *Religion, Tradition and the Popular: Transcultural Views from Asia and Europe*, edited by Judith Schlehe and Evamaria Sandkühler, 185–204. Historische Lebenswelten in populären Wissenskulturen. Bielefeld, Germany: Transcript.

Schlehe, Judith, and Sita Hidayah. 2014. "Transcultural Ethnography: Reciprocity in Indonesian-German Tandem Research." In *Methodology and Research Practice in Southeast Asian Studies*, edited by Mikko Huotari, Jürgen Rüland, and Judith Schlehe, 253–72. Basingstoke, UK: Palgrave Macmillan.

Schlehe, Judith, Melanie V. Nertz, and Yulianto Vissia Ita. 2013. "Re-Imagining 'The West' and Performing 'Indonesian Modernities': Muslims, Christians and Paranormal Practitioners." *Zeitschrift für Ethnologie* 138: 3–22.

Schlehe, Judith, and Eva F. Nisa. 2016. "The Meanings of Moderate Islam in Indonesia: Alignments and Dealignments of Azharites." Southeast Asian Studies at the University of Freiburg. Occasional Paper Series Number 31. http://www.southeastasianstudies.uni-freiburg.de/publications/op-series.

Schlehe, Judith, and Evamaria Sandkühler, eds. 2014a. *Religion, Tradition and the Popular: Transcultural Views from Asia and Europe*. Historische Lebenswelten in populären Wissenskulturen. Bielefeld, Germany: Transcript.

Schlehe, Judith, and Evamaria Sandkühler. 2014b. "Religion, Tradition, and the Popular in Asia and Europe." In *Religion, Tradition and the Popular: Transcultural Views from Asia and Europe*, edited by Judith Schlehe and Evamaria Sandkühler, 7–28. Historische Lebenswelten in populären Wissenskulturen. Bielefeld, Germany: Transcript.

Schütz, Alfred, and Thomas Luckmann. 1988. *Strukturen der Lebenswelt*. Neuwied und Darmstadt: Luchterhand.

Sheller, Mimi, and John Urry. 2006. "The New Mobilities Paradigm." *Environment and Planning A* 38 (2): 207–26.

Sidel, John. 2008. "The Islamist Threat in Southeast Asia: Much Ado about Nothing?" *Asian Affairs* 39 (3): 339–51. https://doi.org/10.1080/03068370802341032.

Silvey, Rachel M. 2004. "Transnational Domestication: State Power and Indonesian Migrant Women in Saudi Arabia." *Political Geography* 23 (3): 245–64.

Silvey, Rachel M. 2006. "Consuming the Transnational Family: Indonesian Migrant Domestic Workers to Saudi Arabia." *Global Networks* 6 (1): 23–40. https://doi.org/10.1111/j.1471-0374.2006.00131.x.

Silvey, Rachel M. 2007. "Mobilizing Piety: Gendered Morality and Indonesian-Saudi Transnational Migration." *Mobilities* 2 (2): 219–29. https://doi.org/10.1080/17450100701381565.

Skinner, W., ed. 1959. *Local Ethnic and National Loyalties in Village Indonesia: A Symposium*. New Haven: Yale University Press.

Slama, Martin. 2008. "Islam Pribumi. Der Islam der Einheimischen, seine "Arabisierung" und arabische Diasporagemeinschaften in Indonesien." *ASEAS—Österreichische Zeitschrift für Südostasienwissenschaften* 1 (1): 4–17.

Slama, Martin. 2012. "'Coming Down to the Shop': Trajectories of Hadhrami Women into Indonesian Public Realms." *The Asia Pacific Journal of Anthropology* 13 (4): 313–33.

Slama, Martin. 2014. "Hadhrami Moderns. Recurrent Dynamics as Historical Rhymes of Indonesia's Reformist Islamic Organization Al-Irsyad." In *Dynamics of Religion in Southeast Asia: Magic and Modernity*, edited by Volker Gottowik, 113–32. Amsterdam: Amsterdam University Press.

Slama, Martin. 2017. "A Subtle Economy of Time: Social Media and the Transformation of Indonesia's Islamic Preacher Economy." *Economic Anthropology* 4 (1): 94–106. https://doi.org/10.1002/sea2.12075.

Soegianto. 2003. *Kepercayaan, Magi Dan Tradisi Dalam Masyarakat Madura*. Jember: Tapal Kuda.

Soeharjanto, Guntur. 2013. *99 Cahaya Di Langit Eropa 1*. Jakarta: Maxima Pictures.

Soeharjanto, Guntur. 2014. *99 Cahaya Di Langit Eropa 2*. Jakarta: Maxima Pictures.

Stahlhut, Marco. 2015. "Die schleichende Islamisierung." *FAZ*, July 8. http://www.faz.net/aktuell/feuilleton/debatten/die-schleichende-islamisierung-in-indonesien-13688333.html.

Statista 2014. "Leading Countries Based on Number of Facebook Users as of May 2014 (in Millions)." *Statista*. http://www.statista.com/statistics/268136/top-15-countries-based-on-number-of-facebook-users/.

Sutton, Anderson R. 2011. "Music, Islam, and the Commercial Media in Contemporary Indonesia." In *Islam and Popular Culture in Indonesia and Malaysia*, edited by Andrew N. Weintraub, 85–100. Abingdon, UK: Routledge.

Su-Lyn, Boo. 2016. "Designer Claims Made RM2m from 'Jubah Pahlawan' after Online Ridicule." *The Malay Mail*, February 29. https://www.malaymail.com/news/malaysia/2016/02/29/designer-claims-sold-2m-jubah-pahlawan-after-online-ridicule/1070113

Syarifah, Umaiyah. 2009. *Motif Sosial Melakukan Ibadah Hajj Pada Masyarakat Desa Umbulmartani Di Kecamatan Ngemplak*. Yogyakarta: Universitas Islam Negri Sunan Kalijaga. http://digilib.uin-suka.ac.id/3642/1/BAB%20I,V.pdf.

Tagliacozzo, Eric, ed. 2009. *Southeast Asia and the Middle East: Islam, Movement, and the Longue Durée*. Stanford, CA: Stanford University Press.

Tagliacozzo, Eric. 2013. *The Longest Journey: Southeast Asians and the Pilgrimage to Mecca*. Oxford: Oxford University Press.

Tan, Ta Sen. 2009. *Cheng Ho and Islam in Southeast Asia*. Singapore: Institute of Southeast Asian Studies.

Thimm, Viola. 2018. "Embodying and Consuming Modernity on Muslim Pilgrimage: Gendered Shopping and Clothing Practices by Malaysian Women on 'Umrah and Ziarah Dubai.'" *Asian Anthropology* 17 (3): 185–203. https://doi.org/10.1080/1683478X.2018.1483477.

Thomas, Pradip, and Philip Lee, eds. 2012. *Global and Local Televangelism*. Houndmills, Basingstoke, UK: Palgrave Macmillan.

tho Seeth, Amanda. 2016. ""Pure, Like Plain White Rice": A Saudi Higher Educational Microcosm in Jakarta: The "Institute of Islamic Science and Arabic" (LIPIA)." Paper presented at the Conference: Religious Education and Islamic Popular Culture—Trans-l Encounters, University of Marburg, May 27.

tho Seeth, Amanda. 2019. "Contesting the Centre-Periphery Divide in the Muslim World: Indonesia´s Islamic Soft Power Diplomacy." Paper presented at the EuroSEAS Conference 2019, Berlin, September 12.

Triana, Neli. 2016. "Negeri Timur Tengah Di Puncak Raya." *Kompas* (January 12, 2016). http://print.kompas.com/baca/2016/01/12/Negeri-Timur-Tengah-di-Puncak-Raya.

Turner, Victor. 1969. *The Ritual Process: Structure and Anti-Structure*. 1st ed. Lewis Henry Morgan Lectures. Somerset: Taylor and Francis.

Turner, Victor. 2005. *Das Ritual: Struktur und Anti-Struktur*. Frankfurt am Main: Campus.

Turner, Victor, and Edith L. B. Turner. 1973. *Image and Pilgrimage in Christian Culture: Anthropological Perspectives*. New York: Columbia University Press.

Ubaidillah, Khotim. 2010. *Sejarah Upaya Penerapan Syariat Islam Di Kabupaten Pamekasan Tahun 1998–2002*. B.A. thesis, Universitas Negeri Malang.

Ubaidillah, Khotim. 2014. *Dinamika Perantau Madura Dalam Politik Kota Malang. Suatu Kajian Antropologi Politik*. M.A. thesis, Universitas Gadjah Mada Yogyakarta.

Umam, Chaerul. 2009. *Ketika Cinta Bertasbih*. Jakarta: SinemArt.

Urry, John. 2007. *Mobilities*. Cambridge: Polity.

van Bruinessen, Martin. 1987. "Bukankah Orang Kurdi Yang MengIslamkan Indonesia?" *Pesantren* 4 (4): 43–53.

van Bruinessen, Martin. 1990. "The Origins and Development of Ṣūfi Orders (Tarekat) in Southeast Asia." *Studia Islamika* (67): 150–79.

van Bruinessen, Martin. 2012. "Indonesian Muslims and Their Place in the Larger World of Islam." In *Indonesia Rising: The Repositioning of Asia's Third Giant*, edited by Anthony Reid, 117–40. Singapore: Institute of Southeast Asian Studies.

van Bruinessen, Martin, ed. 2013a. *Contemporary Developments in Indonesian Islam: Explaining the "Conservative Turn."* Singapore: Institute of Southeast Asian Studies.
van Bruinessen, Martin. 2013b. "Introduction: Contemporary Developments in Indonesian Islam and the "Convervative Turn" of the Early Twenty-First Century." In *Contemporary Developments in Indonesian Islam: Explaining the "Conservative Turn,"* edited by Martin van Bruinessen, 1–20. Singapore: Institute of Southeast Asian Studies.
van Bruinessen, Martin. 2013c. "Overview of Muslim Organizations, Associations, and Movements in Indonesia." In *Contemporary Developments in Indonesian Islam: Explaining the "Conservative Turn,"* edited by Martin van Bruinessen, 21–50. Singapore: Institute of Southeast Asian Studies.
van Bruinessen, Martin. 2013d. "Postscript: The Survival of Liberal and Progressive Muslim Thought in Indonesia." In *Contemporary Developments in Indonesian Islam: Explaining the "Conservative Turn,"* edited by Martin van Bruinessen, 224–32. Singapore: Institute of Southeast Asian Studies.
van Bruinessen, Martin. 2015. "Ghazwul Fikri or Arabization? Indonesian Muslim Responses to Globalization." In *Southeast Asian Muslims in the Era of Globalization*, edited by Ken Miichi and Omar Farouk, 61–85. New York: Palgrave Macmillan.
van Dijk, Kees. 2002. "The Indonesian Archipelago from 1913 to 2013: Celebrations and Dress Codes Between International, Local, and Islamic Culture." In *Islam in the Era of Globalization: Muslim Attitudes Toward Modernity and Identity*, edited by Johan H. Meuleman, 37–50. London: Routledge.
van Dijk, Kees, Huub de Jonge, Elly Touwen-Bouwsma, and C. van Dijk, eds. 1995. *Across Madura Strait: The Dynamics of an Insular Society*. Leiden: KITLV Press.
van Doorn-Harder, Nelly. 2012. "Ziyāra in Indonesia." In *Encyclopedia of Islam*, edited by Peri Bearman, Thierry Bianquis, Clifford E. Bosworth, Emeri J. van Donzel, and Wolfhart P. Heinrichs. EI-2. Leiden: Brill.
van Klinken, Gerry. 2003. "Ethnicity in Indonesia." In *Ethnicity in Asia*, edited by Colin Mackerras, 64–97. London: RoutledgeCurzon.
van Klinken, Gerry, and Joshua Barker. 2009a. "Introduction: State in Society in Indonesia." In *State of Authority: The State in Society in Indonesia*, edited by Gerry van Klinken and Joshua Barker, 1–16. Ithaca, NY: Southeast Asia Program Publications.
van Klinken, Gerry, and Joshua Barker, eds. 2009b. *State of Authority: The State in Society in Indonesia*. Ithaca, NY: Southeast Asia Program Publications.
Vickers, Adrian. 2005. *A History of Modern Indonesia*. Cambridge: Cambridge University Press.
von der Mehden, Fred R. 1993. *Two Worlds of Islam: Interaction between Southeast Asia and the Middle East*. Gainesville: University Press of Florida.
Wajidi, Ahmad. 2015. "Mengenal Istilah Haji Mabrur. Pengertian Dan Kiat Dalam Meraihnya." In *Wisata Khalifa*. http://www.wisatakhalifa.com/haji-dan-umroh/haji-mabrur/.
Wan Daud, and Wan Mohd Nor. 1989. *The Concept of Knowledge in Islam and Its Implications for Education in a Developing Country*. London: Mansell.
Wee, Vivienne, and Amy Sim. 2004. "Transnational Networks in Female Labour Migration." In *International Migration in Southeast Asia*, edited by Aris Ananta and Evi N. Arifin, 166–98. Singapore: Institute of Southeast Asian Studies.

Weintraub, Andrew N. 2010. *Dangdut Stories: A Social and Musical History of Indonesia's Most Popular Music*. New York: Oxford University Press.

Weintraub, Andrew N., ed. 2011a. *Islam and Popular Culture in Indonesia and Malaysia*. Abingdon, UK: Routledge.

Weintraub, Andrew N. 2011b. "The Study of Islam and Popular Culture in Indonesia and Malaysia." In *Islam and Popular Culture in Indonesia and Malaysia*, edited by Andrew N. Weintraub, 1–18. Abingdon, UK: Routledge.

Wensinck, A. J. 2012. "Niyya." In *Encyclopedia of Islam*, edited by Peri Bearman, Thierry Bianquis, Clifford E. Bosworth, Emeri J. van Donzel, and Wolfhart P. Heinrichs. EI-2. Leiden: Brill. http://referenceworks.brillonline.com/entries/encyclopaedia-of-islam-2/niyya-SIM_5935.

Werbner, Pnina. 1999. "Global Pathways. Working Class Cosmopolitans and the Creation of Transnational Ethnic Worlds." *Social Anthropology* 7 (1): 17–35.

Wibowo, Efendi. 2014. "Budaya Turis Arab Di Puncak Lahirkan Generasi Tanpa Harga Diri." *Merdeka*, September 14. http://www.merdeka.com/peristiwa/budaya-turis-arab-di-puncak-lahirkan-generasi-tanpa-harga-diri.html.

Wildan, Muhammad. 2013. "Mapping Radical Islam: A Study of the Proliferation of Radical Islam in Solo, Central Java." In *Contemporary Developments in Indonesian Islam: Explaining the "Conservative Turn,"* edited by Martin van Bruinessen, 190–223. Singapore: Institute of Southeast Asian Studies.

Wiyata, A. Latief. 2002. *Carok: Konflik Kekerasan Dan Harga Diri Orang Madura*. Yogyakarta: LKiS Yogyakarta.

Wiyata, A. Latief. 2013. *Mencari Madura*. Jakarta: Bidik-Phronesis.

Woodward, Mark R. 1989. *Islam in Java: Normative Piety and Mysticism in the Sultanate of Yogyakarta*. Tucson: University of Arizona Press.

Woodward, Mark. 2011. *Java, Indonesia, and Islam*. Dordrecht, New York: Springer.

World Bank. 2014. "GDP Per Capita (Current US$)." http://data.worldbank.org/indicator/NY.GDP.PCAP.CD/countries/ID?display=default.

Xiang, Biao, and Johan Lindquist. 2014. "Migration Infrastructure." *International Migration Review* 48 (1): 122–48. https://doi.org/10.1111/imre.12141.

Ziemek, Manfred. 1983. *Pesantren. Traditionelle islamische Bildung und gemeindeorientierte ländliche Entwicklung in Indonesien. Ein Beitrag zur politisch-orientierten Pädagogik in der Dritten Welt*. Frankfurt am Main: Universität.

Index

Page numbers followed by letters *f* and *m* refer to figures and maps, respectively.

CPSIA information can be obtained
at www.ICGtesting.com
Printed in the USA
LVHW041048250322
714381LV00015B/584